AF342653

LEONARDO DA VINCI
The Daedalian Mythmaker

Also by Giancarlo Maiorino
The Portrait of Eccentricity: Arcimboldo and the Mannerist Grotesque
The Cornucopian Mind and the Baroque Unity of the Arts
Adam "New Born and Perfect": The Renaissance Promise of Eternity

Giancarlo Maiorino

LEONARDO DA VINCI

The Daedalian Mythmaker

The Pennsylvania State University Press
University Park, Pennsylvania

Library of Congress Cataloging-in-Publication Data

Maiorino, Giancarlo, 1943–
    Leonardo da Vinci: the Daedalian mythmaker / Giancarlo Maiorino.
        p.   cm.
    Includes bibliographical references and index.
    ISBN 0-271-00817-2 (alk. paper)
    1. Leonardo, da Vinci, 1452–1519—Criticism and interpretation.
2. Art and mythology.   I. Title.
N6923.L33M34   1992
709′.2—dc20   91–20274
                                                                          CIP

It is the policy of The Pennsylvania State University Press to use
acid-free paper for the first printing of all clothbound books.
Publications on uncoated stock satisfy the minimum requirements of
American National Standard for Information Sciences—Permanence of
Paper for Printed Library Materials, ANSI Z39.48–1984.

*For
my daughter
Lisa,
the smile of my life*

Contents

List of Illustrations

Acknowledgments

As always, I want to acknowledge Eugene Eoyang for help and insight on matters of titology. Because of challenges and inquiries beyond my initial leads, I am grateful to the students of my seminars on Leonardo da Vinci and Michelangelo (fall 1988)—Patricia Burns, Laura Clergen, Cynthia Dillard, Dana Johns, Velda Kaune, Devin Last, Kathy Meacham, Joyce Owens, Steven Patti, Martha Robertson, Anne Sampson, Mingfei Shi—and on Leonardo da Vinci (fall 1990)—Paul Dever, Anthony Guneratne, Edward Newell, Francesca Parmeggiani, Tracey Rollison, Laura Salsini, Jody Shiffman, Megan Soske, Julie Talatinian, and Susan Udry. I "tried" the initial and final versions of this manuscript on them, and I got in return at least as much as I put into my teaching.

For plates and permissions, I thank the following: Biblioteca Ambrosiana (Milan), Art Resource (New York), Royal Library (Windsor Castle), National Gallery of Art (Washington, D.C.), Library of Christ Church College (Oxford), Réunion des Musées Nationaux (Paris), Photographie Bulloz (Paris), Photographie Giraudon (Paris), the Metropolitan Museum of Art (New York), Sächsische Landesbibliothek (Dresden), and the Pierpont Morgan Library (New York).

Introduction

> *Of all the men who have ever lived those most powerful to excite the imagination are the figures looming out of the twilight world where history and legend meet. They are spoken of now as gods, now as men: they weave an ambiguous path between heaven and earth, myth and fact. They merge with the everlasting archetypes at the depths of the human mind. . . . Daedalus was such a figure, perhaps the most interesting of them all, for he is said to have been the first artist who ever lived, if not in the flesh at least in the minds of men.*
>
> —*Vincent Cronin*

While writing notes and digressions on the "method" of Leonardo da Vinci, Paul Valéry must have become ever more convinced that mythmaking is a permanent activity of the human mind.[1] From Gide to Joyce, modernity has tested and traded myths, whose resilience has not failed to play a central role in Western culture.[2]

Yet the testing and trading of myths took on a defiant posture at the time of Leonardo. Pagan gods were revived, but they could not retain all their splendor amid mythmaking triumphs of Renaissance excellence. In a panegyrical mode, Pico della Mirandola bestowed godlike dignity on man, who became a "divine" creator, an artist, a discoverer, and an inventor.[3] As in ancient Greece, poets and artists shaped the sacred into the aesthetic. After the Greeks, they did not relinquish legendary quests. Even if progress has exposed much of their metaphorical content, the psychological effectiveness of myths has endured. Nietzsche's words still call for reflection: "Every culture that has lost myth has lost, by the same token, its natural, healthy creativity. Only a horizon ringed about with myths can unify a culture" (*The Birth of Tragedy,* xxiii). Amid the flux of life and against the futility of historical vicissitudes, Leonardo never wavered in his belief that mythology was source and cradle of human ingenuity.

Among myths of human power, Prometheus, Hermes, and Daedalus would have shared in any synthesis of man's archetypal creativity, which Paul Valéry identified with Leonardo da Vinci: "I felt that this ruler of his own resources, this master of design, of symbols, and of calculations, had found the central attitude from which all the enterprises of learning or science and all the operations of art are equally possible, and a successful co-operation between analysis and action is singularly probable."[4] Had Leonardo not existed, we would have created him out of fundamental yearnings rooted in legendary memories, primeval longings, and the symbol-making process of Jungian archetypes.[5]

2

But Leonardo did exist; like everybody else, he fed on myth. Any study of his creative frame of mind, therefore, must confront the Daedalian range of his mythmaking mode of activity, which affected art and technology alike.

In myth, Daedalus was inventor and artist. At the beginning of the Renaissance, Petrarch renewed his fame in Latin verses:

GALLUS: Tell me, Who was the genius, who with a craft so artful
Fashioned its snow-white ivory and to it attached the speaking
Cords and the musical numbers? Disclose who it was, Tyrrhenus;
Daedalus? Or a disciple like him in his art and his talent?

TYRRHENUS: Daedalus, even he. Your guess is the right one, Gallus.
Craftsman supreme of all time, whose manhood amazes Nature,
Mighty and wise though she be. From that most excellent master
I have received the bow and the pick and the notes of my music.[6]

The poetic markers of "craft," "master," and "craftsman" do not focus on inspiration, which is Apollo's prerogative, but on what criticism has called the ability to actualize it.[7] The creator had to be a maker as well.

Amid Renaissance makers, Leonardo became a universal man, perhaps the most universal of them all. His "opening" performance in Milan, where he was expected to be first and foremost a "maker," was as a musician. We do not know what he played, but we do know that he constructed a bizarre lyre for his debut. It was made from a horse's skull, with ram's horns, a snout that resembled a bird's head, and strings stretched across the roof of the mouth. However extravagant, his exploit placed artistic talent and technological ingenuity within a tradition that edged on archetypal forms of beauty and power.

Among forms of myth, the Homeric *Hymn to Hermes* (32–33) presents the deity as a schemer, robber, and maker of dreams; he was bound

> to show forth glorious deeds among the immortal gods. One of
> those deeds was the invention of the lyre, which he made out of a
> tortoise shell. On it, he
> stretched seven harmonious strings of sheep-gut.
> And when it was finished, he held up the lovely toy
> and with the plectron struck it tunefully, and under his hand
> the lyre rang awesome. The god sang to it beautifully. (51–54)

By tradition, the "chorded shell" (*testudo*) was a synecdoche for lyres and flutes.[8] In Florentine art, a lyre fashioned from a stag's skull appears in Filippino Lippi's *Allegory of Music* (c. 1500). Its source—however indirect—was Lucian's *Dialogues of the Sea-Gods,* in which Polyphemus's lyre was made of "a stag's head deprived of its flesh, with the antlers for handles." By the time Ronsard wrote his *Hymne de Mercure,* Hermes had added his invention of metals and chemicals to that of the lyre: "*Cet fut toy qui premier effoudras la tortue.*" Hence it would be quite difficult to take Leonardo's gesture as mere coincidence.

Because he saved Zeus from the monster Typhon, Hermes became a protector of heroes. Likewise, Leonardo's military ingenuity was meant to save Borgias and Moors. Hermes reassembled Zeus's mutilated body, and Leonardo's anatomical studies courted similar undertakings. By so doing, one rescued the discourse of mythology, which the other kept alive after the medieval Christianization of pagan gods.

3

In a spirit of aphoristic incantation, Goethe wrote toward the end of his life that "no man, however rich in attainment, can live on without longing; true longing cannot but look for the unattainable." If one were to pick an artist whose life best embodied quests that could be neither abandoned nor fulfilled, Leonardo da Vinci would readily stand out. Often, his efforts reached a point where success spawned either confinement or distraction. Because he insisted that man "must cling to his faith that the unknowable is comprehensible,"[9] Goethe shared with Leonardo a kinship that was less a matter of influence than of elective affinities.

On the eve of the Age of Discovery, Leonardo did not sever reason from experience; instead, he took notice of geometric perspectives and mythic points of view.[10] His blend of empiricism and abstraction brought to the fore salient aspects of what I shall call Leonardo's antihumanist posture vis-à-vis the predominant tradition of humanists who worshiped the "known clarity" of theoretical knowledge.

Rather than a term of denial, the prefix *anti* centers on interactions between rule and experience. Although critical of "normative sources," Leonardo recognized that "no human investigation can be termed true science if it is not capable of mathematical demonstration" (McMahon, 3). On pictorial matters, "perspective is a rational demonstration, confirmed by experience" (52), and "those who are in love with practice without knowledge are like the sailor who gets into a ship without rudder or compass and who never can be certain whether he is going. Practice must always be founded on sound theory, and to this perspective is the guide and gateway" (19). Empirical adjustments would correct the geometric abstraction of linear perspective, which, "as bearing on drawing, is divided into three principal sections; of which the . . . second treats of the diminution in colours in these objects. The third [deals with] the diminished distinctness of the forms and outlines displayed by the objects at various distances" (16). Exemplary as he was of Florentine Humanism at its best, Piero della Francesca thought of mathematical perspective as a "science necessary to painting" (*De prospectiva pingendi*), and Leonardo demanded that "no man who is not a Mathematician" should approach the art of painting; otherwise, "with the crowds of the sophists, you deceive yourselves and others, despising the mathematical sciences, in which truth dwells and the knowledge of the things included in them" (3, 1210). On the subject of unity in multiplicity, Leonardo—like Leon Battista Alberti—accepted classical recommendations that artists should "take the best parts of many beautiful faces" (587) in order to represent the image of Helen. However, while the humanists chose a selective ideal of beauty, the antihumanist wrote that "beauty and ugliness seem more effective through one another" (McMahon, 277).[11] Ugliness gained recognition, and lyres were shaped into grotesque forms.

By now critics agree that Renaissance artists pursued rule and antirule in excess of selective labels such as *Antirinascimento* and Counter-Renaissance, which center either on fantasy and abnormality or on cultural and religious primitivism.[12] Actually, even as paradigmatic a humanist as Alberti could be critical of his own outlook: "It seems to me that we only like all that which nature denies us, and we find pleasure in that which is burdensome and in many ways against nature."[13] From a Renaissance standpoint, therefore, antihumanist pursuits would not uphold recent claims that the Age of Man is coming to a close. Modern echoings of the Sartre-Foucault debates would not have hindered the provocative diversity of fifteenth-century culture.[14]

By the same token, my endeavor does not draw from structures of knowledge based on polarity; in this study, *anti* is more relational than antagonistic. Even scholarship on Alberti has turned toward reconciliation. Accordingly, irony has been highlighted to tone down clashes between "optimistic" readings centered on *De iciarchia* and *Della famiglia* and more cautious judgments drawn from *Momus* and the *Intercoenales*.[15] Since they favor coexistence, such interactive approaches to Renaissance texts are in order more often than one might suspect, and I think that the Platonic *pharmacia* would easily accommodate humanist-antihumanist dialogues.[16]

In terms of pharmaceutical nomenclature, Alberti linked his praise of the healing power of patience to disease: "By the gods, what great and diverse maladies completely fill the lives of men! You will find no man so happy that he is not also most unhappy in many respects. . . . And man's lot and condition seem to me worse than ever, now that in treating his diseases I have begun to know him more truly than before. . . . And to this that no place is free of problems, and that no moment of time fails to yield to a completely different one. One thing opposes and harms another." His discussion of happiness submits that "all human judgment concerning happiness and unhappiness is shaped solely by opinion."[17] Since conceptual diversity produced a variety of artistic forms, criticism is bound to develop suitable modes of evaluation.

4

Leonardo's Anti-Humanism could be neither measured nor defined apart from Albertian Humanism; nor could the concept of Renaissance dispense with either term.[18] I would suggest that a double focus was at the core of fifteenth-century culture. Leonardo therefore operated in the midst of what Mikhail Bakhtin would call a condition of *heteroglossia,* which highlights the primacy of context over text. From *renaissance* to *anti*humanism, contextuality affected the semantic markers of the age. Recovery of ancient texts stirred concerns with matters of origin and originality, much as empirical preferences and technological progress turned toward postclassical sources. In spite of outspoken leanings meant to favor one side over the other, eclecticism survived. To maintain a critical focus, I have anchored Anti-Humanism to Leonardo da Vinci, even though its context exceeds my treatment of it. Borrowing from Bakhtinian terminology, the fifteenth century was the "locus where centripetal and centrifugal forces" collided.[19] Suspicious as he was of excessive book learning, Leonardo led the charge by rallying "anti-intellectuals" and "empiricists" who could deny neither observation nor progress. His *furor* did not call for religious fervor in the tradition of Botticelli, Ficino, or Savonarola, but for ardor of experiment and fever of research.[20] Because it often stemmed from the very texts that sanctioned humanist and antihumanist preferences on both sides of *anti,* dialogism remained central to fifteenth-century culture, whose diversity fostered neither gratuitous polarities nor anticonventionalism for its own sake. What some call dialogism, others define as "intertextuality," the difference being a rather elusive shift from "an embarassing multiplicity of meanings" to a "more inclusive meaning." It seems to me that "dialogic" carries a more synchronic sense of the interactive unity of text and context, whereas "intertextuality" is a better qualifier for the diachronic recovery and emulation of classical texts.[21] This study gives a horizontal thrust to the operative range of dialogism.

5

In the fields of art, science, and technology Leonardo stood at the forge of human nature, where he vindicated *sperienza* as the cornerstone of knowledge. *Studioli* were safe islands of "learned" knowledge, but existence had to go on outside. And it did, to the advantage of both.

Chapter 1 traces the roots of Leonardo's Anti-Humanism back to those very texts that we consider humanist masterworks. Although it came to fruition with Leonardo, Anti-Humanism could be traced back to Petrarch and Alberti, who had been lured—though not seduced—by Mistress Experience. A twin birth therefore led culture to depend on the gilded wealth of the *homo oeconomicus* as much as on the golden forms of the artist-scholar.

Chapter 2 moves to the higher grounds of Leonardo's visual images. Tensions between theory and experience emerged the moment he linked the growth of body and soul to testing processes of decay and regeneration. Saint Jerome's willful struggle against age and heritage is the subject of his earliest painting, which set a style and an ideology that took on humanist standards.

Chapter 3 takes strife back to the beginning of Christianity. Its birth was staged against the death of paganism in the Uffizi *Adoration*. Both traditions raised problems for Leonardo, who saw history as a carrier of struggle, betrayal, and doom. At the beginning, he explored the earth's source in the *Virgin of the Rocks,* which also sheltered the primeval enclave of Christianity (chapter 4). At the end of human life, Saint John the Baptist would point toward supernal unity through the androgynous forms of Oneness (chapter 5). For Leonardo, archetypal beauty had to be traced back to its source, where every form of temporal dividedness could recover its primeval unity.

Between the birth of a human fetus and the Deluge's universal demise, myth alone could redeem the disheartening procession of human vicissitudes. Leonardesque mythmaking steered art and science toward the untapped potential of technology. In the Daedalian mode, Michael Ayrton recommends, man must "complete a pattern" to become a myth.[22] Leonardo's mythological plan ranged from birth to death, and his creative output challenged Daedalus's talents as artist, inventor, and technologist. Chapter 6 centers on the ambiguity of the inventor's rhetoric of power, while chapter 7 takes up the imaginative synthesis of myth, experience, and prophecy that stands at the core of Leonardo's Daedalian talents.

If we accept the idea that man is made in the image of God, then we might wonder why God is so often symbolized through geometric figures. Dante's final revelation was not a face, but the brightest point within the circle of perfection. Archetypes of beauty and power, in fact, fall back on symbols that could be either anthropomorphic or geometric.

One is individual and emphasizes resemblance, while the other is functional and underlines constructiveness. It is Adam versus Prometheus, and I believe that they are intertwined in the *Vitruvian Man*. Its humanist circumference of order, in fact, is pinned to the umbilical cord of the body's antihumanist navel (chapter 8).

Visual metaphors of that kind are at once "mixed" and contradictory. Yet they are indicative of holy as well as unholy alliances that science and technology have imposed on organic growth and mechanical construction. Perhaps Daedalus only lived in the minds of men. Leonardo, instead, lived in the flesh, and Benvenuto Cellini called him *"un angelo in carne"*;[23] an angel indeed, but with Faustian wings. After Daedalus, Leonardo stopped at a crossroad where human ingenuity could produce biological inventions that would have steered progress toward the "forbidden" (chapter 9). To that extent, Leonardo was a forger of experience insofar as he altered empiricism to suit mythic pursuits he shared with the predominant ideology of Humanism.

Chapter 10 undertakes a "dialogic" reading of Raphael's *School of Athens,* whose synthesis of Platonic idealism and Aristotelian humanness pivoted on the concept of the "mean." At the dead center of the fresco, the old philosophers are but dialogic mentors to Leonardo and Alberti, founders of a new Athenian School whose leadership rested with the artist's mythmaking.[24]

Chapter 11 sets the dialogic of Humanism and Anti-Humanism within the larger context of the Renaissance.

At the center of dialogic stillness, *Mona Lisa* stands as a figure of ultimate unity. Dialogism reached a point of fullfillment when Leonardo created La Gioconda by an act of will that dissolved facts and ideas into hope's legendary smile. At last, Adamic remembrances and Faustian challenges bonded creator and creature into the human form of Leonardo's myth of myths (chapter 12).

6

On matters of method, my interdisciplinary approach is meant to draw Leonardo's manifold experiences into an interpretative synthesis.

Whatever the iconographic depth and iconological breadth of Leonardesque ingenuity, it is the aesthetic form of individual artworks that delimits my critical commentary. Because they serve that method, references to history, science, culture, and philosophy are instrumental. They would prove unsatisfactory for specialists whose research I rather build on than make a test of. On principle, I acknowledge areas of competence and distribution of work. Above all, I cherish commitments to treat interrelationships. In Leonardo's case, my interdisciplinary methodology is not a choice, but a matter of course.

My essay is for unrepentant worshipers of the beauty of form, whose multifaceted potential supports theses that can draw from diverse fields of human knowledge. Ultimately, I would like to think, steadfast concerns with the study of artistic forms ought to enhance our growth in the appreciation of the aesthetic sense of life. "We pass our lives," Octavio Paz writes, "between living history and interpreting it. In interpreting it, we live it."[25] I believe that there are times when critical acts of interpretation can lead scholarship to yield epiphanies.

With an eye to life in our own days, we can take pride in having survived Minotaurs and atomic bombs, even though our universe might be dangerously tangled into labyrinthine discontinuities. Yet I choose to introduce this study in a hopeful mode. In the late 1940s there were thoughtful minds who still believed that only a new synthesis could make the future beautiful, as it had been during times of "synthetic knowledge" that had given birth to Phidias and Leonardo. To build that future, scientists, philosophers, and historians would join talents on the assumption that an age of synthesis is always an age of art. And any age of art could not but bring forth a "new humanism."[26]

At a time when the very concept of synthesis has been challenged at its very core, my endeavor to unearth values whose continuity has sustained the weight and direction of our Western experience may amount to no more than a critical gesture. Our historical belatedness, however, is no excuse for downgrading interpretation "from feast to fast." The only theses that count, Geoffrey Hartman insists, are those "which may seem fantastic."[27] Inasmuch as it may foster an excess of interpretative cohesiveness, my own thesis could appear to be somewhat imaginative. Yet could I have approached such a glorious age of "synthetic knowledge" any other way?

References to Leonardo's writings are (1) *The Notebooks of Leonardo da Vinci,* 2 vols., ed. J. P. Richter (New York, 1970), with entry number indicated in the text; (2) *Treatise on Painting,* 2 vols., ed. P. McMahon (Princeton, 1955), with last name (McMahon) and entry number indicated in the text (only vol. 1 is used); (3) *The Notebooks of Leonardo da Vinci,* 2 vols., ed. E. McCurdy (New York, 1968), with last name (McCurdy) and page number indicated in the text (only vol. 1 is used).

Translations of Alberti's treatises are: *On Painting,* trans. John Spencer (New Haven, 1976), with page number indicated in the text (*O.P.*); *On the Family,* translated as *The Family in Renaissance Florence,* trans. Renée Watkins (Columbia, 1969), with page number indicated in the text (*O.F.*). For Castiglione, references are to *The Book of the Courtier,* trans, Charles Singleton (New York, 1959), with page number indicated in the text (*Courtier*).

At the Forge of Human Nature

1

Leonardo's Antihumanist Roots

No man ever peered more penetratingly into nature than Leonardo, and yet even he was "seeking a symbolic language for something within him that already existed." What gives such disturbing power to his drawings is that the "something within him," call it rhythmic organization or what one will, was analogous to an objective truth in nature, the continuum of energy and growth. . . . His moments of vision are not only emotionally true . . . but scientifically true as well.

—*Kenneth Clark*

In Leonardo's mind, experience, causality, and necessity brought to light a natural order almost as closely knit as geometric forms. At least hypothetically, the idea of keeping reason and experience in balance intrigued even Leon Battista Alberti, who wrote that "many things in this world are better understood by experience than by speculation and theory. We who are schooled in books become erudite through time" (*O.F.,* 294). Even authoritative voices agreed that the wisdom of age could stand on equal footing with theoretical knowledge.

If only as rhetorical gestures, alliances between norm and experience were part of the humanist project. However outspoken about the superiority of Mistress Experience, Leonardo fostered a "holier" cooperation between fact and thought. In the humanist mode of virtual accomplishments, there were times when he linked empiricism to "the inception" rather than "the result" (McCurdy, 88).

2

It is indeed significant that the humanists sought forms in nature whose organic function and geometric structure seem to have reconciled plan with growth. The societal mechanism of ants and bees, in fact, revealed to Alberti a model of behavior almost as flawless as the one he legislated upon in *On the Family*. Such a paradigmatic treatise charged the ideal family leader "with a heavy task: managing one's possessions, ruling and moderating the affections of the spirit, curbing and restraining the appetites of the body, adapting oneself and making good use of time, watching over and governing the family." To discharge his duties, he would act like the spider, who sits at the center of his web: "He remains in that place once his work is spun and arranged, but keeps so alert and watchful that if there is a touch on the finest and most distant thread he feels it instantly, instantly appears, and instantly takes care of the situation. Let the father of a family do likewise" (O.F., 206). The comparison is visually effective, for it sets action on a perspectival ground plan where human endeavors can be carried out in man-made environments.

External "touches" amount to innocuous threats whose function is not so much to test as to flaunt the spider's superiority. While presiding over an autonomous world of its own making, the zoomorphic simile seems to have led to a disclosure of individual motivations and social conduct. Read Cicero and look at spiders! One could bet on that winning combination. Beneath that rhetoric of enticement, however, we sense an authorial search for concrete images that were meant to make abstract arguments at least more accessible, if not more forceful. Given the intellectual restrictions that he imposed on his "plans," Alberti did the best he could, but it was not enough. He forged a metaphysical spider in the literal as well as in the metaphorical sense of the word.

Traditionally, spiders and their cobwebs have stood as signposts of peaceful inactivity from Euripides and Sophocles to Plutarch and Tibullus. They gave visual texture, so to speak, to the state of idleness in which weapons of war had been kept. Since they are found in places where atmospheric and biological activity is minimal, spiders are symbolic of undisturbed space and dust-settled time. Even Jules Michelet noted that the animal's control over functional environments is limited. "The insect braves with impunity the strongest odors and mephitic miasmas. The spider cannot endure them. Instantly affected by them, it falls into convulsions, struggles, and expires."[1] Moreover, cobwebs are spun in empty air. It is quite understandable, therefore, that the spider would entice the hypothetical bent of the humanist frame of mind, which thrived at the periphery of living processes. However beautiful their geometric patterns, cobwebs are made of thin threads. Their transparent filaments must be pinned to something over which the insect has no control. In much the same way as artists created the perspectival grids of fifteenth-century art, Alberti set the spider at the center of a construct it had woven and over which it had control.

Leonardo, instead, plunged the spider into an environment whose phenomenal unpredictability would make it at once predator and prey. Since he was neither as idealistic nor as systematic as his humanist counterparts, Leonardo let destiny take its course: "The spider, being among the grapes, caught the flies which were feeding on those grapes. Then came the vintage, and the spider was cut down with the grapes" (1314). Because they have to be pinned to the instability of the outside world, spiders are tiny creatures at the mercy of nature's whim. The men of dogma, Bacon would agree later on, "resemble spiders, who make cobwebs out of their own substance" (*Novum Organum*, aphorism 95). And so did humanist theoreticians whose dogmatism proved to be deficient in both humanism and humanness. Utopian plans of reasonable men were doomed, and one may wonder whether reasonable men could last at all. Self-sufficiency bestowed privileges, but it also entailed a price. In the critical vocabulary of Ernesto Grassi, "any humanism that attempts to transcend formal thinking by taking into account the problems of life, of man in his real context, is excluded. . . . Rationality becomes the terror of the human."[2] Leonardo took on life's problems without giving up formal thinking. Especially as an inventor and a technician, his antihumanist posture was an antidote, if not a panacea, against intellectual rigor.

3

Although some of his most daring intuitions were to remain unknown for centuries, Leonardo's critique of Humanism was timely indeed. Throughout the quattrocento, humanist intellectualism set standards, but could not mute the popularity of artworks in which chivalrous deeds yielded to mock-heroic behavior, as in Luigi Pulci's *Morgante*. Leonardo echoed its irreverent style in his own prose: "If Petrarch was so fond of bay (*lauro*), it was because it is of a good taste in sausages and with tunny; I cannot put any value on their foolery" (1332). Visually, parody inspires the sketch of an old man crowned with a laurel wreath and

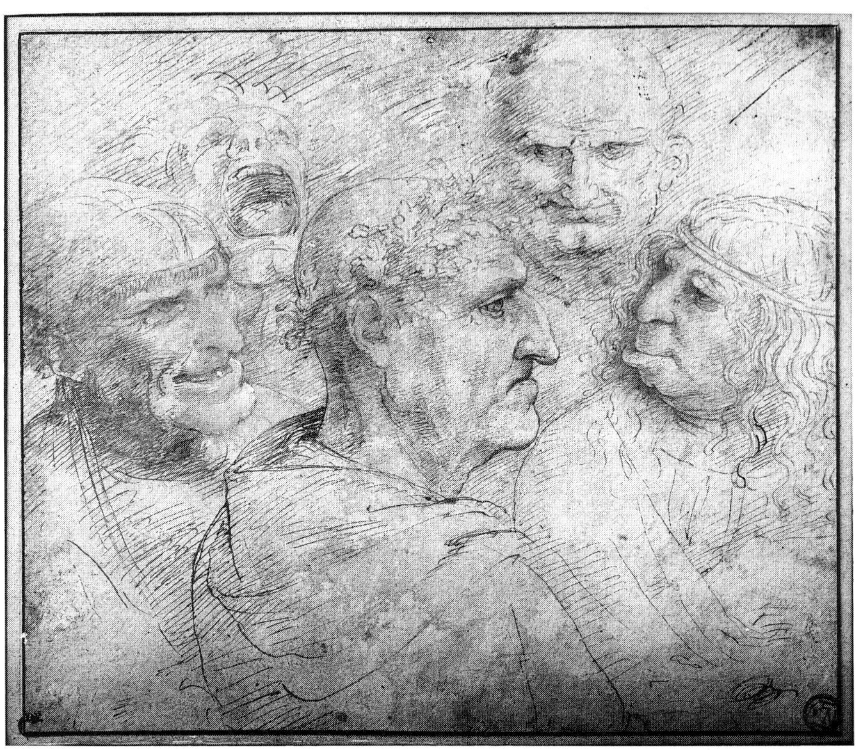

FIG. 1.   Leonardo da Vinci, *Five Grotesque Heads* (c. 1494)
Royal Library, Windsor Castle

surrounded by four "grotesque" heads (Fig. 1). Parenthetically, scholarship supports Leonardo's acquaintance with both writers as well as his
affiliation with Florentine anti-Petrarchism.[3] Whether exotic, grotesque,
or fantastic, unconventional artforms flourished amid an eclectic culture
familiar with antinormative "constants."[4] Their marginal status set confrontational attitudes toward the "other side" and "other voices." Such
an opposition was conducive to a range of undertakings clustered
around a competitive, if not confrontational, core.

However proud of the laurel wreath that had crowned him poet
laureate in Rome (April 8, 1341), Petrarch looked on laurel twigs as
nothing but empty "tokens," since any "knowledge of literature is
useful only when it is translated into action."[5] With an eye to the

nomenclature of vegetal kinship, Alberti turned to the ivy in one of his dinner pieces:

> When a pear-tree saw some priests adorn their temple with ivy, thus giving this weed a place of considerable honor amid ornaments of gold, she exclaimed: "How can this be? Will they dedicate to religion and holy rites this wanton and barren weed, which, born for no good purpose, has often dragged temple walls down to ruin and never ceases daily to cause various damage to the buildings of the gods? I harm no one, yield swift fruit, feed the poor, and am the delight of rich men's desserts. Yet any boy can strike me with sticks and rocks." As the pear-tree complained of her unjust fate and of the priests' wickedness, the ivy replied: "Weren't you aware that this breed of men has always revered and loved the wicked, and those who can harm them most? Come, then, be hard and bitter."[6]

The critical tone of this passage is indeed reminiscent of Leonardo's fables. Both of them reversed humanist perspectives in order to expose the way man used nature to his own disadvantage. Humanist learning and humane maturity coexisted at a time when classical rebirths and Platonic flights were set against the expansion of economy, science, and geography.

Eclectic pursuits of intellectual *curiositas* tested medieval practices. Pilgrims continued to take trips in the name of faith, but grew ever more fond of human encounters along the way. Richard de Bury's *Philobiblon* set forth journeys in the world of books, while Petrarch, Salutati, and their cohorts sought out ancient manuscripts throughout Europe.[7] Often, humanist *virtù* and antihumanist *sperienza* enhanced each other, and Machiavelli finally sanctioned the dialogism between ideal and empirical truth—*verità ideale* and *verità effettuale*.

Any articulate notion of *humanitas* had to call for versatility. Alberti wanted people to act like Alcibiades, "who could imitate the chameleon" (*O.F.,* 311). Unlike those who "chose to excel in one thing," Lorenzo de' Medici's "versatile and superior mind" could "be equally excellent in many."[8] Coluccio Salutati insisted that knowledge (*scientia*) stems from the activity of all nine muses (*De laboribus Herculis,* 1.9.11). And Machiavelli justified his own eclecticism by calling on "nature, who is variable; and he who imitates her cannot be blamed."[9] Since he made it imperative that the painter be "universal" (*essere universale*), Leonardo insisted that "he is not versatile who does not love equally all things that are contained in painting" (McMahon, 93). Writing on the symbolism of Proteus, A. Bartlett Giamatti concludes that "man is not Protean because he is civilized; he is civilized because he is Protean, and the role of civic Proteus is central to the Renaissance's view of man in society."[10]

Often, eclecticism stemmed from common sources that spurred dialogic interactions between Humanism and Anti-Humanism. Petrarch took on humanist pride when he scaled down the authority of the classics, since experience had taught him that Aristotle was "a very great man," but "he was human. I know that much can be learned from his books, but I am convinced that outside of them much can be learned also." A similar criticism was leveled against Virgil's semimythic view of Aeneas as "the strong and perfect man."[11] Models of humanist perfection were set next to the process of human perfectibility, which would transform individuals "from human creatures into 'men.' " Often enough, Petrarch favored that which "suddenly" sprang from his mind over learning. Since "it is impossible for everybody to follow the same method of living," experience would invalidate definitions of any kind. Cicero was right in saying that we "can only express opinions that are probable" amid a reality in which talent can give us only a fighting chance against the unknown.[12] Concerns of that sort probably led Petrarch to believe that the first duty of a human being is to be human.[13]

4

The humanist consensus was that culture had to be sheltered in *studioli* and *accademie,* which became places where knowledge remained largely past-oriented. Petrarch, however, did not wander across Europe only to recover ancient manuscripts. Travel was necessary to well-rounded men whom Homer and Virgil would describe as world-wanderers, "everywhere learning something new."[14] Back home, Alberti insisted that men of letters "can rarely find a moment of rest. Loneliness, hard work, and continuous tensions" fill their lives with "labors and torments."[15] Earthly and heavenly barriers of all sorts were torn down, since knowledge was to be pursued with unprecedented intensity inside and outside places of scholarship.

Whereas many humanists rediscovered geography in ancient books, Petrarch wrote that Venetian ships sailed "for the river Don, for that is the limit of navigation in the Black Sea; but some of its passengers will there disembark and will not halt until they have crossed the Ganges, and the Caucasus, and have come to the farthest Indies and have reached the Eastern Ocean. Whence comes this fierce, insatiable thirst for possessions that rides the minds of men? . . . When I could no longer follow the ships through the darkness, I picked up my pen again, moved and stirred."[16] It was a learned act, but it was not too long before Christopher Columbus set out on his eventful journey. Poetic longings were about to yield to historical records. Human experience was stretching its spatial and temporal range to lengths undreamed of. Antihumanist probings into science were crucial in breaking open cultural boundaries. Man still was the measure of all things, but things were being discovered that defied measurement. A rather straight path therefore spurred antihumanist restlessness toward the Copernican "breaking of the circle."

Attitudes of that kind were familiar to Leonardo, whose approach to geography pierced the earth's surface. Above ground level, he could draw rather accurate maps from a bird's-eye point of view, much as his sight could outline mountain ranges (Fig. 2) whose boundlessness would be matched only by romantic longings of later times.

Below visual surfaces, Leonardo could explore primeval landscapes through layers of geological changes. At the bottom of Alpine bedrocks,

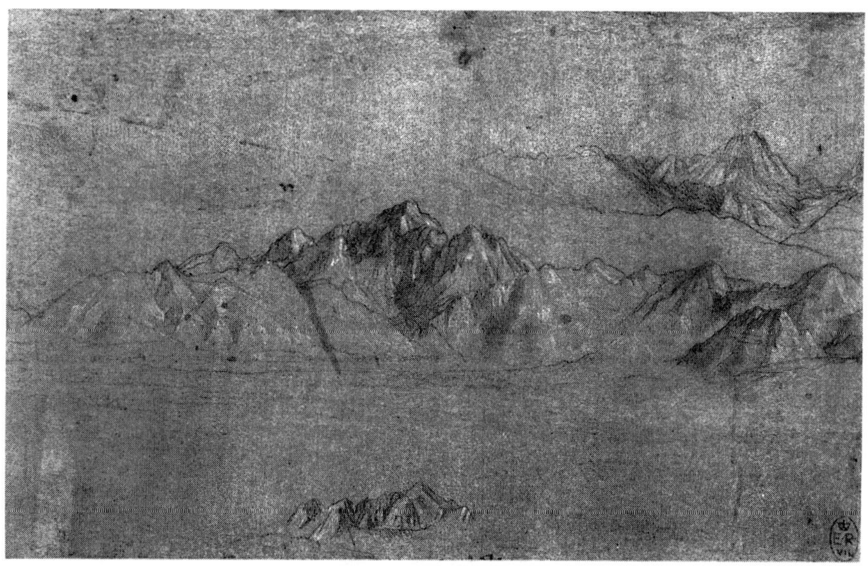

Fig. 2.   Leonardo da Vinci, *Mountain Range*
Royal Library, Windsor Castle

he found the bones of a fish that had become "an armour and support to the mountain which lies above it" (McCurdy, 1128). He was indeed among the most avid readers of nature's book, whose authorship Ralph Waldo Emerson later attributed to fate. As we turn its gigantic pages, we are led to a mental journey as outreaching as the human imagination has ever been able to utter. The modern text reads: "One leaf she lays down, a floor of granite; then a thousand ages, and a bed of slate; a thousand ages, and a measure of coal; a thousand ages, and a layer of marl and mud; vegetable forms appear . . . the face of the planet cools and dries, the races meliorate, and man is born" (*The Conduct of Life,* Fate). In Leonardo's encompassing nomenclature, the sight of shellfish, the drawing of an embryo, and the pictorial landscape of the *Virgin of the Rocks* (see Fig. 13) were bookmarkers for every thousand ages. It no longer was a matter of *naissance* and *renaissance* of kindred cultures, but of necessity, freedom, and growth before culture and beyond race. Compared to the humanist calendar, Leonardo's chart of past and future was one that could pinpoint eons of time.

5

It was a humanist belief that "fortune has in her hand only the man who submits to her . . . in political affairs and in human life generally reason is more powerful than fortune, planning more important than any chance event." At least theoretically, the Albertian *virtù* was all-powerful: "Nobility of soul, we cannot but recognize, is itself sufficient to ascend and to possess the highest peaks" (*O.F.,* 28–30). Because the treatise was meant to set flawless standards, the ideal family leader remained as hypothetical as the clan and the state that he would build around himself. However abstract, that form carried the day and became a model for the prince and the courtier. Amid the flux of antihumanist experiences, Alberti conceded that *fortuna* "sends the gods to heaven, and then throws them out, whenever it so decides." Instead of trying "to achieve knowledge beyond what man should know," people ought to realize that *prudenza* and *industria* "illuminate and influence" human events.[17]

Yet those priorities were reversed later on. Virtue pleaded with Mercury that Fortune had brought her Olympian state of grace to an end. While Plato began to discourse on the duty of the gods, she uttered: "Be off, wordy fellow! Slaves have no business pleading the gods' cause." The orator Cicero had also begun to urge his counsels, but the "powerful

Mark Antony burst out of the armed mob, flaunting his gladiator's chest, and struck Cicero in the face with his heavy fist. At this, my other friends took flight in panic. No one—not Polycletus with his brush, Phidias with his chisel, Archimedes with his sun-dial, or the others, who were unharmed—was able to defend himself against these armed bullies, who were used to plunder, murder, and war. Deserted by all the gods and men present, I was severely battered by blows and kicks."[18] Metaphor pitched art against nature and beauty against power; the latter was clearly the victor. It was a classical and humanist belief that the sheer beauty of grand structures would stop barbarians from destroying them. More often than not, however, the test of history has proved that beauty is rather powerless against any latter-day Marc Antony. Actually, artists had grown accustomed to the idea that beauty and virtue were subordinated to might. Leonardo knew as a matter of fact that cannons were more important to the warring Moor than any equestrian statue.

Granted that it plays only the minor role of counterpoint, experience shares in the dialogic form of the Albertian treatise, which legislated over a field of demonstrative certainties. For the humanists, nature had no form and experience would help the artist to learn ways for molding the shapeless into the shaped.[19] Because it was pinned to a "known vision" free of circumstance, reality was limited to theoretical designs. And we might agree that Alberti's versatility was more verbal than factual. He produced instructions rather than works, prone as he was to say what should be done rather than to act himself.[20] In the antihumanist mode, search overrode demonstration. While some never doubted their convictions, Lorenzo Valla referred to Daedalian wings as a means of "research" that his probing mind would never let go idle.[21]

Faith in experience shouldered Leonardo's criticism of humanist erudition in the *Libro della pittura:*

> I am fully conscious that, not being a literary man, certain presumptuous persons will think that they may reasonably blame me, alleging that I am not a man of letters. . . . They will say that I, having no literary skill, cannot properly express that which I desire to treat of; but they do not know that my subjects are to be dealt with by experience rather than by words; and (experience) has been the mistress of those who wrote well (10).

The external world remained the true battlefield of knowledge. Leonardo's critical stand earmarked Heraclitean statements: "Whatever comes from sight, hearing, learning from experience: this I prefer" (Frag.

14). Criticism of humanist ideology also found a source in the solitary pre-Socratic: "Much learning does not teach understanding. For it would have taught Hesiod and Pythagoras, and also Xenophanes and Hecataeus" (Frag. 18). For the humanists, visual images foregrounded patterns of the mind. Leonardo, instead, discovered similar networks in the depths of a reality where "necessity is the mistress and guide of nature" (1135). We find here another echo of the Heraclitean worldview: "There is a certain order and fixed time for the change of the cosmos in accordance with some fated necessity" (Frag. 93a). Order is dynamic, and stability itself is transformational. This is but the first reference to a pattern of shared attitudes. Leonardo's note on flowing water ("the water you touch in a river is the last which has passed, and the first of that which is coming," 1174) recalls the classical fragment: "One cannot step twice into the same river, nor can one grasp any mortal substance in a stable condition, but it scatters and again gathers; it forms and dissolves, and approaches and departs" (Frag. 51). We thus come to the core of Leonardo's art and thought: "Painting is proved to be philosophy because it treats of the motion of bodies and the rapidity of their actions, and philosophy also includes motion" (McMahon, 7). The humanists looked on empirical knowledge as a first step toward abstraction. Leonardo, instead, placed experience next to science. Actually, *sperienza* meant experiment, that is, a scientific inquiry into causes and effects. Yet Leonardo's experimentalism was not scientific in a modern—or even in a Galilean—sense. Like Agostino Nifo and earlier Paduan writers, he replaced casual observation with stronger empirical evidence.[22]

Commitments to verification aside, the wider context of *sperienza* implied a suprascientific, if not poetic, knowledge of the archetypal principles that govern the world of phenomena. Actually, science was part of human knowledge, and experience included man's faith and destiny. Much like *virtù* (Alberti, Machiavelli) and *sprezzatura* (Castiglione), *sperienza* was a polysemous compound; it edged on a kind of epiphanic reliability that Leonardo anchored to visual knowledge. Art and science found a common source in the eye.

6

Since he equated clarity of sight with certainty of knowledge, Piero della Francesca focused objects across the pictorial field regardless of their distance from the ground plane. That choice allowed the system of linear perspective to keep form and color free of perceptual instability. Intuitive forms of knowledge were to be avoided on principle. As long as it did not exceed the limits of our visual range, reality could be measured, known, and therefore mastered. Only darkness and infinity would disturb visions of plenitude, which rested on linearity, uniform lighting, geometric space, and narrative control. In art, reality could be clearer than reality itself.

By contrast, Leonardo could not separate light from darkness; their mutual dependence was crucial to perceptual observation. Actually, "brightness and darkness, that is, light and shadow, have an intermediary (*mezzo*) which can neither be called bright nor dark, but participates equally in the bright and the dark; it is sometimes equally removed from both the bright and the dark, and is sometimes nearer one than the other." Since "light and shadow together with foreshortening constitute the ultimate excellence in the art of painting" (McMahon, 842, 840), representation ranged from pure light to total obscurity. Its symbolism linked matter to spirit.[23] The forms of art thus thrived in the flux of existence: "The boundaries of these bodies are the least of all things . . . the lateral boundaries of these bodies is the line forming the boundary of the surface, which line is of invisible thickness. Wherefore O painter! do not surround your bodies with lines, and above all when representing objects smaller than nature; for not only will their external outlines become indistinct, but their parts will be invisible from distance" (49). It was Leonardo's call for *sfumato*. "In a nutshell, *sfumato* is a word used to describe the subtle blending of formal outlines to produce the illusion of atmospheric thickening. The edges appear hazy and indefinite. By destroying the boundaries of forms the three-dimensional illusion can be enhanced under certain conditions of the use of subdued tone and colour."[24] Emphasis is placed on depth, volume, indistinctness, and perceptual conditions. To set up a contrast that is historically relevant, we are reminded that the classical ideal of aesthetic beauty fell back on the Greek standard of clearness, which denies shadows any power of plastic illusion. Likewise, Greek intellectualism imagined its concepts as linear forms. Only their *seen appearance* was essential.[25]

Since it affects experiences that are more problematic than explanatory, *sfumato* tests clarity and narration. "Closed" and "finished" forms yielded to a poetics replete with the vitality of becoming itself. Because it thrives on indeterminacy, *sfumato* heightens the tentative nature of knowledge, teaching us that all forms become vulnerable the moment they enter the flux of existence.

The technique of *chiaroscuro* brought to the surface interactions between light and shadow. Students of Rembrandt speak of it as a method of composition and an artistic device that exploited visual contrasts and psychological complexity.[26] *Sfumato,* in turn, made it possible to blend volume with depth to such an extent that space was injected, so to speak, into physical forms. Atmospheric complexity became psychological as well, and Leonardo's figures took on a "phenomenal" identity unknown before. By affecting a reality beyond the control of light, and therefore of reason, *sfumato* forced mimesis to confront realms of experience in which knowledge could not brush aside the mind's own contradictions.[27]

Leonardo anticipated that pictorial technique in his writings. On literary grounds, in fact, philosophic indeterminacy and rhetorical foreshadowing turned out to be *sfumato*'s equivalents. Suggestive at heart, his aphorisms paved the way for Machiavellian ambiguity: "This by experience is proved, that he who never puts his trust in any man will never be deceived" (McCurdy, 89). Human nature calls for caution. Much as Machiavelli told us that people do not forget their fathers' estates as quickly as their deaths, Leonardo wrote that "the memory of benefits is frail as against ingratitude" (McCurdy, 89). If we were to consider, as I think we should, Heinrich Wölfflin's reminder that "every history of vision must lead beyond mere art," we meet a challenge, namely that "the history of art as the doctrine of the modes of vision can claim to be, not only a mere super in the company of historical disciplines, but as necessary as sight itself."[28] Keeping the interdisciplinary symbolism of visual sight in mind, Leonardo exploited that area of fluid interactions midway between the unflawed brightness of perfection and the brewing darkness of experience. There he lodged visual equivalents to contemporary clashes between Machiavellian *verità effettuale* and *verità ideale,* or dichotomies between Castiglione's *grazia* and *invidia.* And it is on grounds midway between Pico della Mirandola's orations on human dignity and Erasmian praises of folly that we can sharpen the cohesiveness and contextuality of antihumanist postures.

Recent studies on Renaissance naturalism and the rise of aesthetics have pointed out that Leonardo's invention of *chiaroscuro* owed to the Aristotelian recognition of intermediate colors between the extremes of brightness and darkness. As a result, painting had to confront the rhetoric of the visual. A new epistemological density emerged, and Leonardo exploited the complementarity of painting as both "value contrast" and "visual contrast."[29] Complexity also lies at the heart of Leonardo's approach to color. He did not make uncompromising divisions between dark and bright, whose interactions flashed out "accidental colors."

Such imponderables spawned a visual indeterminacy akin to the role that chance (*fortuna*) played in life. Much as antihumanist *sfumato* blurred humanist clarity, so did Machiavelli and Guicciardini test the unbridled freedom of Albertian *virtù* against the travails of existence.

Humanist idealism still shed theoretical clarity across the broader horizons of history. The errors of the past could be corrected, since effects and causes were presumed to be linked. Machiavelli let analogies between antiquity and modernity spawn forms of complete knowledge that gave him godlike powers he could share with the Adam-God painted on the Sistine ceiling. At least theoretically, there were no uncertain transitions; neither gains nor losses could have altered the overarching—or recurrent— "sameness" of Western culture. By contrast, history taught Guicciardini that man's inability to correct past mistakes stems from his failure to trace effects back to their causes. He foregrounded variables, reversals, and deviations. In terms of historical images, it suffices to refer to his portrait of Lorenzo de' Medici: "In important matters his words would be few and vague." He was highly suspicious and he exploited the "appearance of external forms" (*The History of Florence,* ix). Utopian clarity was set against empirical *chiaroscuro.*[30]

From a visual standpoint, Leonardo had already written that "the same action will appear to be infinitely different because it can be seen from an infinite number of positions" (McMahon, 361). Even his approach to architecture took into account the shadowy nature of loyalty and betrayal at court:

> The lord of the manor must be able to go through the entire fortress, including the upper, the middle and the lower parts, using tunnels and underground passages, which shall be disposed in such a way that none of them could be sued to reach the dwelling of the lord, without his agreement. And through these ways using portcullis and other devices he must be able to imprison in their residence all those of his retinue, who may plot against him, and may close or open the door of the main entrance and the relief route. And this danger is even greater than the enemy itself because those on the inside have greater opportunity to do harm than the enemy who is shut out. (Madrid manuscript ii 89v)

Subterfuge, control, and mistrust double up in Leonardo's mind, which could look at friends and foes with dispassionate aloofness.

To complete the symbolism of *sfumato* by the seat of power, Castiglione turned to those antithetical forces that make up *sprezzatura.* In an earlier version of his book, he took up the troublesome art and discipline of "court service—*professione di questa Cortigiania.*"[31] Leonardo also linked art to discipline in his "science of painting," and his antihumanist concerns with the problem of light as knowledge bore on thought and style alike. I would like to submit that Leonardo's "dark manner" in painting emerged at a point in history when Guicciardini and Castiglione made us equally familiar with the darker tones of human nature.[32] Their dim view of history claimed no *Ur*-point on which they could peg analogues of plenitude. It was clear to them that similarities between birth and rebirth could be more apparent than substantial.

Sfumato promoted an art of transition across the whole field of expressive endeavors. It is not by accident, I think, that José Ortega y Gasset linked the "pedagogy of suggestion" to his analysis of Western culture, in which depth is fatally condemned to become a surface if it wants to be visible.[33] And we could insist that *sfumato* became predominant in the arts at a point in history when more probing interactions between visibility and insight were about to foster changes in the very fibers of knowledge.[34]

The medieval unity of inner and outer man was breaking down amid spaces where vicissitude affected both microcosm and macrocosm. In the practice of fifteenth-century art, uniform lighting was typical in the works of Piero della Francesca. Leonardo, instead, took notice of atmospheric variations that included even "smoke and dust" (468). Furthermore, "our true perception of an object diminishes in proportion as its size is diminished by distance. . . . When you represent in your work shadows which you can only discern with difficulty, and of which you cannot distinguish the edges so that you apprehend them confusedly, you must not make them sharp or definite lest your work would have a wooden effect" (233, 236). Statements of this sort shed light on the wooden stiffness of the mannequin-like figures of Piero della Francesca and Paolo Uccello, whose "geometrizing" style emptied human forms of any lifelike vitality.

Leone Ebreo sealed the validity of analogical constructs:

> The infinite beauty of the Creator is depicted and reflected in finite created beauty like a beautiful face in a mirror, and although the image is not commensurate with its divine pattern, none the less it will be its copy, portrait and true likeness. Man, the created world, and more especially the angelic world, can therefore be made in the image and likeness of God without bearing any proportion to His great beauty.[35]

Because it broke down the clarity and contours of linearity, *sfumato* undermined the very concept of a finite beauty that mirrored its infinite counterpart. The blurred mirror had become the surface of a *materia tenebrosa* that had been generated by the *tenebroso chaos* of instinct, matter, and sensuality.

Sfumato therefore tested the spatial concept of similitude, which could be perceived in rather nebulous terms:

> Be not deceived by the meaning of the word "infinite," which signifies an indeterminate and imperfect quantity far removed from divine beauty; for we can only speak of God and incorporeal things in words which in some sense are corporeal, since our tongue and speech are corporeal in themselves. Again, "perfect" is a word inapplicable to the Divinity, because it means entirely made, and there is nothing made in the Divinity. But by "perfect," we mean free from all defect and containing every perfection, and by "infinite," that the perfection, wisdom and beauty of God the Creator cannot be related to or compared with any other created perfection.[36]

Since perfection no longer could be taken as a figurative concept of un-flawed clarity, God began to be perceived as a force rather than as an image. The analogue shifted from sight to vitality. The *tenebrosa materia* was neither deficient nor unholy, but as shaded and brewing as human nature itself. In the train of such a shift, *sfumato* blended the finite with the infinite. Light, color, space, and man himself were thrust into the ever-changing process of life. In Leonardo's botanical drawings, we have been reminded a while ago, plants can be seen striving, living, and growing. Vitruvian exceptions notwithstanding, men likewise live, work, struggle, and change in his drawings.[37] Tonal unity led to a sharing of emotional states of mind whose intensity could defy rhetorical forms. In a fundamental sense, *sfumato* brought to the fore an operative reality in which people could act of their own volition instead of enacting assigned roles. Giorgione and the Venetians lost no time in making that choice their own.

7

Like the humanists, Leonardo did not pursue mere imitations of nature; his landscapes are as unreal as those of Piero della Francesca. At the heart of their conception of art, be it humanist, metaphysical, or naturalistic, there lies a common attempt to represent the ultimate forms of reality.

Because they believed that talent could not master the elusive complexity of nature, the humanists relied on abstraction to shape much of their godlike potential. Yet Alberti himself made fun of humanist intellectualism: "Not to be eaten by the mouse, the book in which the entire science of book-knowledge is contained asked for help. And the mouse laughed about it."[38] The impotence of book learning was magnified to a point of utter futility. Knowledge was reduced to a treasure that even a little mouse could make liable to damage. The obvious lesson is that one had to deal with the facts of life, however irrelevant they could appear to be.

The Leonardesque turn of mind, instead, was Heraclitean at heart. The metamorphic dynamics of the ancient thinker were central to his modern heir, whose inquisitive mode of knowledge fell back on the spirit of the pre-Socratic axiom: "He who does not expect will not find out the unexpected, for it is trackless and unexplored." At a time when Christopher Columbus was discrediting trodden paths, Leonardo set out on one of the most daring adventures in which the human mind has ever been engaged.

2

Saint Jerome
and the Trials of Age

*Human consciousness is in perpetual pursuit of a language
and a style. To assume consciousness is at once to assume
form. Even at levels far below the zone of definition and
clarity, forms, measures, and relationships exist.*
—Henri Focillon

At the earliest antihumanist juncture, Leonardo stated a preference for
forms caught in the process of time, and Leonardesque *forza* generated a
power that set body and spirit ablaze in his *Saint Jerome* (c. 1482, Fig.
3). Once the Church Fathers Christianized the agonistic vocabulary of
Roman culture, hermits and scholars became athletes of God.[1]

The very iconography of sainthood gave credence to historical exploits and popular wisdom alike. After Aristotle and Cicero had qualified virtue as moral fortitude, phrases such as "invincible" and "unconquerable athletes" were common among early Christians. The
symbolism of Jacob wrestling with the angel was ascetic, but Saint John
Chrysostom considered Paul and John the Baptist athletic ideals. Later,
Peter Damian still thought of Cluny as a spiritual gymnasium. Martyrs
were victorious individuals sanctioned by tradition. The prophetic
strain of asceticism somehow offset the decline of pagan oracles.[2] The
rise of the Holy Man, therefore, fostered measures of spiritual superiority that often were couched in the heroic mode. Jerome himself de-

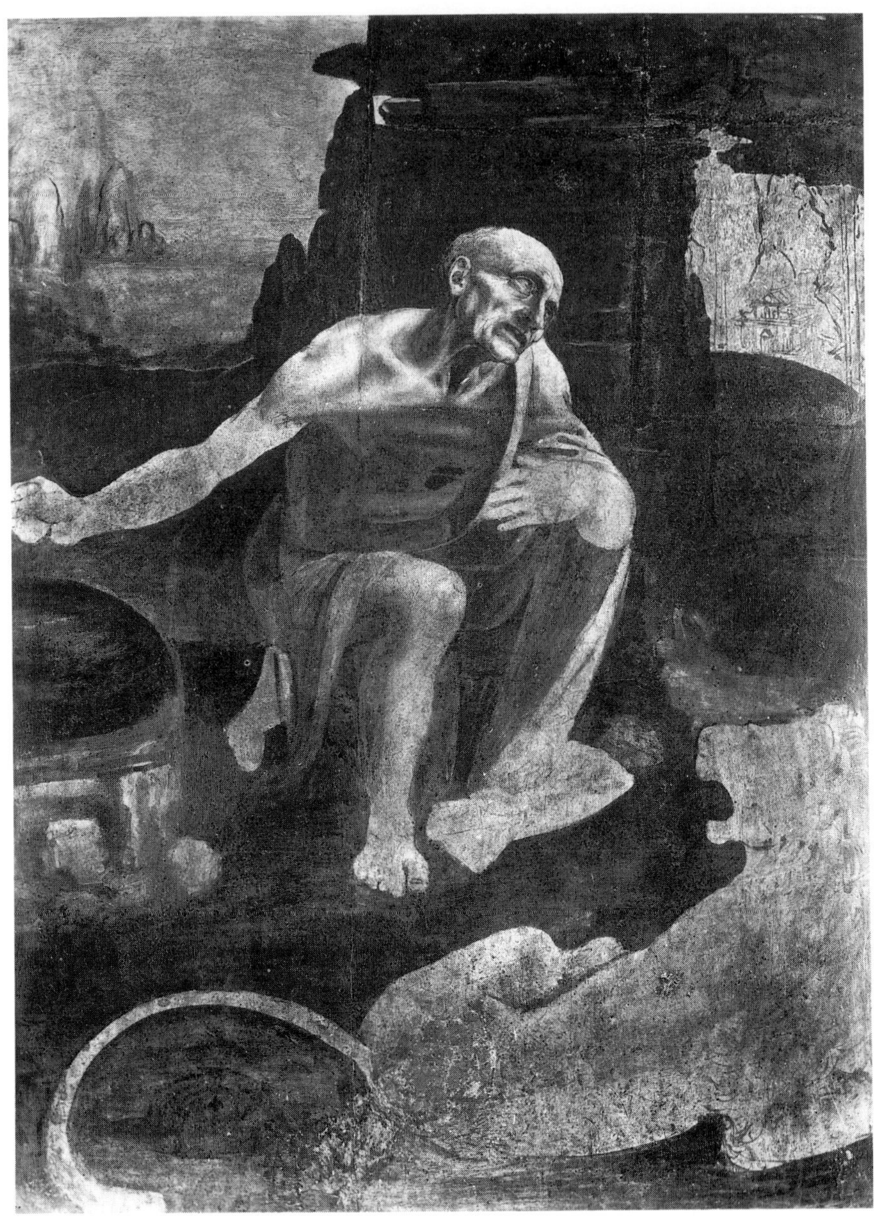

FIG. 3.   Leonardo da Vinci, *Saint Jerome* (c. 1482)
Vatican Museum, Rome

scribed one of his friends' spiritual ascent as a victorious "effort" put forth by a warrior "wearing the Apostle's armor" (Letter iii). In Leonardo's Vatican picture, Jerome holds a rock in his hand, which points to the physical nature of self-punishing humility. Unlike mysticism, asceticism must bear witnesses, and Jerome's outreaching posture displayed bodily performance. Hagiography, in fact, recorded memorable deeds.

With an eye to Renaissance mythology at the turn of the sixteenth century, Michelangelo sculpted David (1501–4, Fig. 4) as an athlete of virtue. Jerome, instead, linked his life to different standards of excellence. A youth about to conquer a fateful victory stood against an older man close to trying revelations. Jerome would survive the desert, and David would defeat Goliath. In spite of formal and psychological contrasts, sculpture and painting illustrate complementary aspects of a culture whose bent toward idealism left a mark on the rhetoric of classical panegyrics and Christian hagiography. Both models tested facts, which were made to fit molds that favored exemplarity over accuracy. Warriors conformed to the deeds of ancient heroes from Alexander to Caesar, and the lives of saints glossed one another. David exuded *terribilità,* and Jerome enacted a sacred pride—*sacra superbia*—that Pico della Mirandola called a holy ambition in his oration on human dignity.[3]

David and *Saint Jerome* fleshed out the emergent poetics of two artists at the beginning of their careers. The Michelangeloesque statue bodied forth the ageless perfection of youth. He is greater and other than life: size is gigantic, nudity is other-than-wordly, and symbolism stands on a pedestal above the gravity of everyday life. By contrast, Jerome's kneeling position shares in the stark landscape that surrounds him. He is just as vulnerable and inspired as any man who has reached the wisdom of a tormented maturity. The commemorative sculpture is set in a civic arena; by contrast, Jerome roams in a place where the soul confronts uncertainty. His experience is one of unfolding crisis instead of panegyrical pride. The rock in David's hand signals victory over others; Jerome, instead, uses it to achieve victory over himself.

The iconography of Jerome in the desert updated the imitation-emulation of Jesus and the Baptist. We thus move toward the very core of Leonardo's figurative world, which arched from *Saint Jerome* and the *Last Supper* to *Saint John the Baptist.* Whether civic or hagiographic, the fifteenth-century rhetoric of encomium turned facts into legends that were meant to be ethically true.[4]

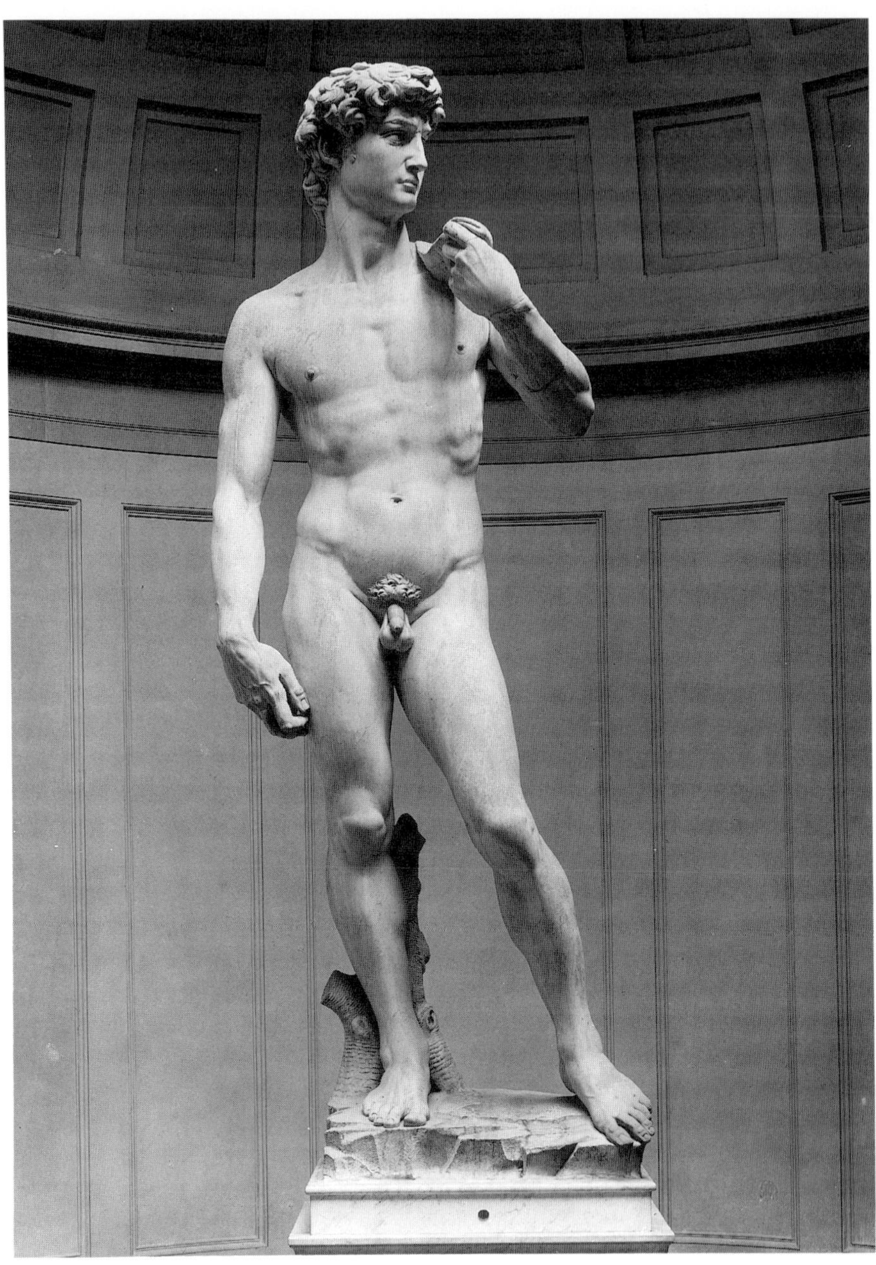

Fig. 4.   Michelangelo, *David* (1501–4)
Accademia, Florence

2

It is a matter of record that Jerome left for the Syrian desert when he was about forty years old and stayed there for two or three years (374–5?) reading, corresponding, and taking several exceptions to the rule of solitude. Whether humanist or antihumanist, the Renaissance turn of mind never thought of saints and scholars as nature seekers. Life was lived in the city, and there had to be special reasons for leaving it.

The visual image of Jerome's skull-like face in the Vatican painting betrays an array of emotional tensions that have consumed the beauty of youth; his aging manhood heightens expressive powers. Like Augustine and Petrarch, Jerome took years to answer an ambiguous question raised by Tertullian in the third century: "What has Athens to do with Jerusalem, the Academy with the Church?" And "what is there in common between the pupil of Hellas and the pupil of Heaven?" Throughout his life, Jerome was torn between reverence for the classical style and loyalty to the languge of biblical truths. The saint's pictorial image foregrounded a most intense moment of spiritual testing; knowledge gained through books was being incarnated into a living experience.

While humanist iconography informs us that a life of Saint Jerome had been published during the 1490s, Antonello da Messina isolated him in a privileged island of learning, the saint-scholar's *studiolo.* And so did Van Eyck and Ghirlandaio (*Saint Jerome,* c. 1480, Church of Ognissanti, Florence), who painted him as a diligent philologist amid the instruments of his labors: candle, spectacles, and scissors. Scholarship so dominated his life that he became the herald of Christian adherence to the scriptural text. During the second quarter of the fifteenth century, however, paintings and drawings—from Bono da Ferrara to Jacopo Bellini—began to place him in the wilderness, where he would meditate, read, or beat his breast with a rock. The iconography of the penitent Jerome dressed in a humble sackcloth thus emerged.[5]

When he left for Jerusalem to become a soldier of Christ, Jerome wrote that he "could not do without the library" he had set up in Rome. It was normal for him "to fast and then read Cicero" (Letter xxii). He read, traded books, and kept copyists busy even in the desert. During the Middle Ages, libraries often amounted to no more than a ubiquitous *armarium,* which meant a wardrobe kept in church or other places that had nothing to do with later *studioli.*[6] Jerome kept books wherever he journeyed, and finally installed them in a library at Bethlehem. As the humanists—with Erasmus at their forefront—well understood, the "Christian Cicero" excelled his predecessors in Latin and

Hebrew. With him, asceticism in the West put monastic learning to the service of culture.[7]

3

Leonardo took the saint to the desert, where naked flesh and humble sackcloth bore out the consuming effects of age amid harsh conditions of life so very familiar to John the Baptist. References are to the iconography of the "saint in the wilderness," which Andrea Castagno established in Florentine art. His *Vision of Saint Jerome* (1454–55) placed the saint outdoors beating his breast with a jagged rock. The image of the penitent Jerome, Eugene F. Rice points out, "was invented in Italy around 1400. It is not to be understood as a medieval image superseded by Renaissance representations of the saint in his study . . . both postdate, though they do not entirely displace, the typical medieval St. Jerome as a doctor of the Church."[8]

The divided iconography of Jerome as either a humanist scholar or a Christian penitent became even more confrontational in the canvases of Giovanni Bellini, who painted several versions of the subject between 1445 and 1505. They present him as a very old man barefooted and wearing a sackcloth out in the desert. In the oldest picture (*Saint Jerome*, 1445–50, Fig. 5), the saint preaches to the lion while reading from a book. His attitude is quietly receptive. Although physical conditions are less than urbanlike, knowledge is pursued in the humanist mode. Reading keeps Jerome in a seated position, while the book underlines scholarly activity, guides gestural action, and sustains meditation. Meaning still thrives on the heritage of canonical models. However stark the image, we look at a figure in a landscape of referential markers.

Between 1471 and 1474, Giovanni Bellini painted the *Coronation of the Virgin* (or *Pala di Pesaro,* Fig. 6) with seven attendant scenes in the predella. One of them is a version of the penitent Jerome, whose representation pointed toward Leonardo's treatment of the subject ten years later. To begin with, the book is gone, and Jerome is poised in a kneeling position of prayer with a rock in his hand. Faith has stirred the emotional intensity of a living experience. The old man looks straight ahead toward a rocky enclosure symbolic of hidden spirituality. It is an image of hopeful humility that weighs man down. As a scholar, his seated position is framed by inorganic rocks. As a penitent soul caught in the act of prayer outdoors, he stands next to the trees around him. Visually,

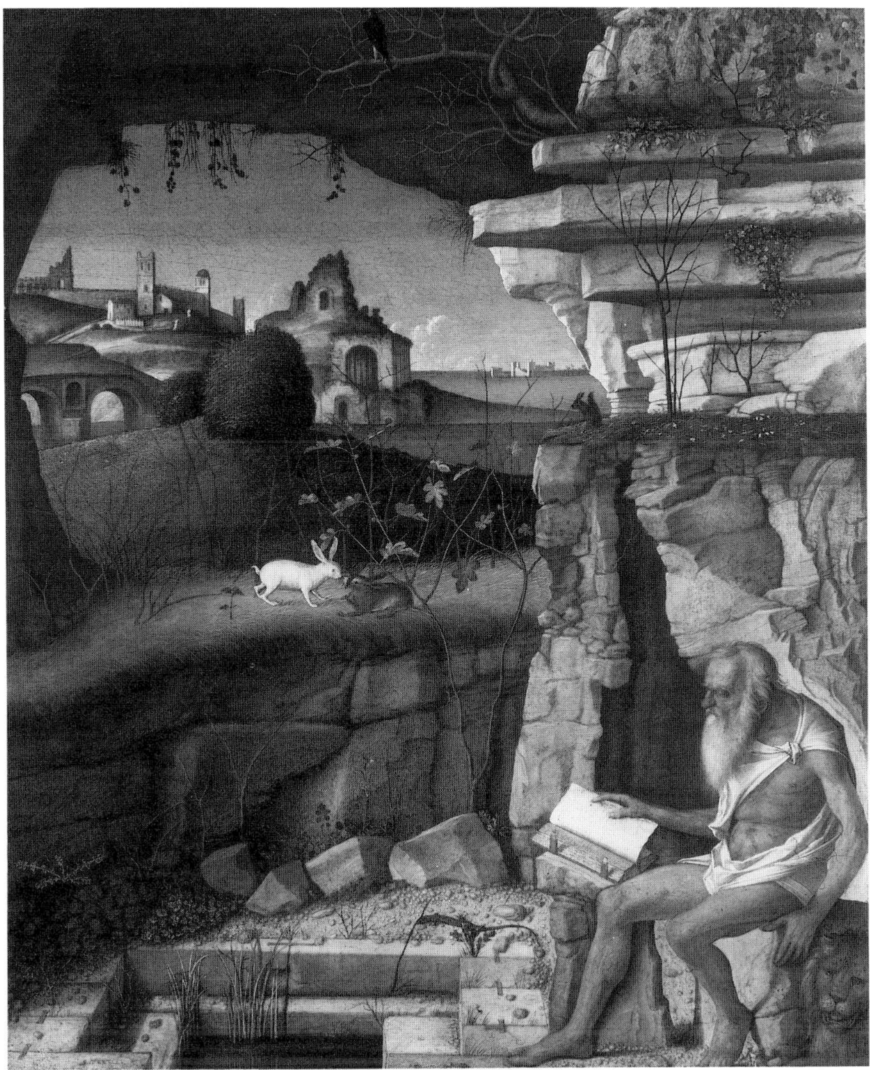

FIG. 5. Giovanni Bellini, *Saint Jerome* (1445–50)
Barber Institute of Fine Art, Birmingham

therefore, Jerome shares in God's works of nature. The expression of faith has shifted from memory to presence. The rock that Jerome holds in his hand points to a disvestiture; bodily punishment chastises the pride of knowledge. Faith enacts, does not recollect, historical deeds.

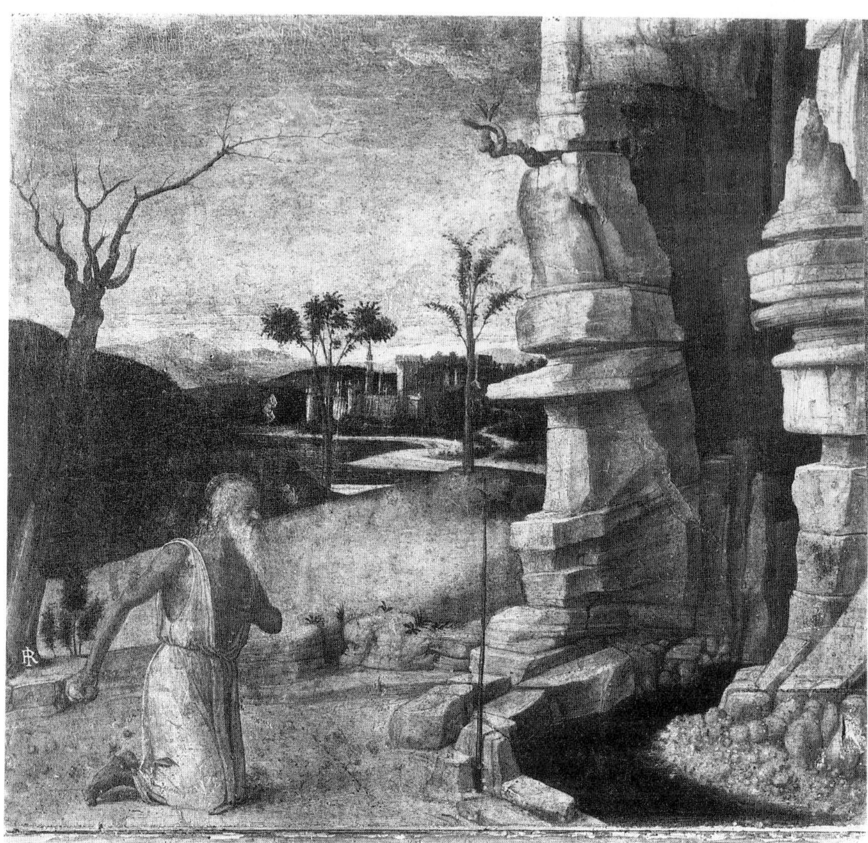

FIG. 6.   Giovanni Bellini, *Saint Jerome* (1471–74), predella, *Coronation of the Virgin*
Museo Civico, Pesaro

Since the desert is one of those enclaves that culture has touched the least, the ascetic is more prone to renew himself into "another"—and better—life. The narrativity of Christian accounts yields to an unfolding experience. Associations with Leonardo's picture are evident; seclusion betrays the futility of written words about the elusiveness of a God whose divinity calls for direct experience. Christianity provided authoritative sources for shifts of that sort. Gregory of Nyssa, one of the Cappadocian Fathers of the Church, wrote in a letter *On Perfection* that imitation cannot adequately bring forth spirituality. Even his rhetoric bore on the difference between book and rock: "And when Christ is called 'a rock,' this word assists us in the firmness and permanence of our virtuous life, that is, in the steadfastness of our endurance of suffering, and in our soul's opposition and inaccessibility to the assaults of sin. Through these and such things, we also will be a rock, imitating, as far as is possible in our changing nature, the unchanging and permanent nature of the Master." Books can be read and misread, whereas rocks translate words into deeds. Through incarnational acts of imitation, our whole being can achieve a kind of archetypal beauty. Because he led a virtuous life, Paul became an "imitator of Christ." Christianity's prime dogmas, in fact, are based on events ranging from crucifixion to resurrection.[9] Book and rock point to what Geoffrey Harpham has called the "hyper-articulated ambivalence" of Christian asceticism, which has always "raised the issue of culture" through simultaneous endorsement and condemnation.[10] Although the so-called Desert Fathers brought books to the wilderness, most of them returned to the *polis*.

Giovanni Bellini painted landscapes with Jerome. By contrast, Leonardo foregrounded Jerome, whose imposing size stood on almost equal footing with nature; we look out toward one, but we are confronted by the other. Although consumed by time, he still retains the vitality of an imposing figure yet to be weighed down by either age or despair. Whereas he kneels in Bellini's panel, Jerome is caught in a posture of transition in the Vatican painting. One knee touches the ground, but the other is raised. It is not clear whether his motion is downward or upward, but there is no doubt that his posture is transitional. The body is torn between the restlessness of upright pride and the stasis of genuflected humility. Because it is turned heavenward, his gaze gives the whole body a sort of uplifting thrust; the spirit guides the flesh. The monochrome darkness is pierced neither by angelic wings nor by supernal beams of light. Yet spiritual intensity seems to have reached a point where one could believe that divinity has sunk into the depths of the human soul. We witness no miraculous epiphany, but man's experience of God at the living core of his own self. A scorched wasteland turned into a place of conflict between penance and redemption. Even biblical history could be interpreted in terms of the wilderness motif, which drew on the fall from a garden devastated by sin as well as from visions of a second Eden.[11]

The faint drawing of the church in the background of *Saint Jerome* heightens the institutional presence of faith on earth. A tension is thus created between the religion of the desert and that of the city. While the rock flaunts anticulturalism, the church reminds us of a place where books are kept and communities gather to remember their heroes through reading and ritual. For Leonardo, virtuous men were rare, and most vulnerable amid urban dwellers. It was safe for them to "take refuge in hermitages and caves or other solitary places." But he never got to fulfill his next wish: "If any such be found pay him reverence, for as these are as gods upon the earth they deserve statues, images and honours" (McCurdy, 85). Since people failed standards of virtue everywhere he went, it was only fitting that he should never finish the equestrian statue in Milan; at heart, it would have been a mock-heroic venture.

Jerome's kneeling leg and outstretched arm flesh out spatial expansion in a place of hardship where the Holy Wild Man sought cleansing rather than primitivism. In the loneliness of the wild, man tested himself, and by so doing he came to discover his real self. Transcendence and self-knowledge stemmed from endeavors typical of Jerome's frame of mind.[12] To that extent, the painting bears on antihumanist pursuits of growth. Symbolically, the prelapsarian Adam fell into existence, struggled as much with sin as with faith, and took the name of Jerome. However aged, he never relented from testing dignity and belief against the process of life. At least for a few, desert trials would redeem Edenic falls.

Landscape in *Saint Jerome* evokes the bareness of a land forever ravaged by heat in the midst of rocky cliffs that sheltered hermits and cave dwellers. We enter a place where Jerome doubted, the Baptist was tempted, and Moses disclosed God's word. From Leonardo to Giovanni Bellini, rocky backgrounds point to unique experiences. The sequential time of the book yields to the "living time" of an event in unison with nature. Spiritual longing foregrounds a mystic atemporality. The very technique of unfinished underpaint adds to the stark unity of form and content. While colors induce "no cause for wonder except their beauty," a subject "can be dressed in ugly colors and still astound those who contemplate it. . . . What is beautiful is not always good" (McMahon, 108, 110), that is to say, conventional. On matters of structure, Leonardo insisted that if "an unfinished composition turns out to be consistent with your invention, it will satisfy all the more." Since the overriding concern was with "movements or other actions" (McMahon, 261), the very concept of beauty was about to make of expression a dynamic attribute at once mental and physical.

Jerome's own words give a fuller measure of Leonardo's visual adherence to the subject: "In that vast solitude which is scorched by the sun's heat and affords a savage habitation for monks . . . whenever I saw some deep valley, some rugged mountain, some precipitous crags, it was this I made my place of prayer, my place of punishment for the wretched flesh . . . my limbs were roughly clad in sackcloth—an unlovely sight.

My neglected skin had taken on the appearance of an Ethiopian body." In terms of the human figure, the *ekphrasis* is striking, especially if one centers on the emotional intensity that the pictorial skull-like face draws out of the saint's own words: "My face was pale from fasting, and my mind was hot with desire in a body cold as ice. Though my flesh, before its tenant, was already as good as dead, the fires of passions kept boiling within me" (Letter xxii). And so they kept haunting him in the desert and throughout his life. Attention is called to a physical condition of motionlessness (ice, dead) that stands in sharp contrast to spiritual unrest. Even a body almost drained of life could mortify human longings. Leonardo translated a portrait of the inner self into an image of arresting power. The earthbound thrust of bent leg and outstretched arm seems to reach a point of resolution in the eyes, where pull yields to thrust. At once weighed down by age and yet uplifted by faith, the body carries out the double vision that seized Jerome in the desert, where he could see himself either in the company "of angels" or amid "the delights of Rome" (Letter xxii).

The scorching brightness of the literary text has yielded to the ominous darkness of the pictorial landscape. The whole Christological underpinning of Western culture from Plotinus to Augustine was centered on the visual concept of divinity as a fountain of light radiating the love of Christ. And so was Grünewald to paint the visual transfiguration of the risen Jesus, who gave the blind man sight so that he could see the light of the world. Once Christ began his retreat from the world, certainty of sight gave way to an impending darkness that stirred belief. He told Thomas: "Blessed are they that have not seen, and yet have believed" (John 20:29). Leonardo shaped faith into human expressions beyond the reach of touch and vision. Rather than light, the sight of the newborn in the *Adoration* (see Fig. 8) disoriented people, whose visual epistemology plunged them into depths hitherto unknown. The painter seems to have made a deliberate attempt to set faith apart from knowledge. At the end of his lifelong experience, Saint John the Baptist (see Fig. 16), whose prophetic spirit had to trust the unseen, barely emerges from a dark background wherein his finger points toward an unseeable source.

The fact is that Jerome lived at a watershed of the Judeo-Christian tradition. While in the Holy Land, he learned that Alaric and his Visigoths had sacked Rome, which had thus become "the mother and the tomb of its people" (*Commentariorum in Ezechielem Liber* III, preface). It was his destiny to mold a sort of Christian classicism out of traditions that were trying to turn Genesis into an epic and the Gospels into Socratic dialogues.[13]

Out in the desert, the scholarly Jerome shared solitude—wilderness as *eremus*—with monks clad in garments made of hair, loaded with heavy chains, and eating herbs. Their eccentric devotion was meant to crush carnal desire. Some lived in caves, huts, and on pillars that were raised in height so as to be closer to heaven.[14] Among them, Saint Anthony of Egypt founded monasticism, and Saint Simeon Stylites spent the last thirty years of his life on a pillar outside Antioch. Ironically, his efforts to live in solitude drew crowds to him.

4

Because it is heavy on the base line, Leonardo's triangular composition weighs the saint down. One knee touches the ground, the other stands parallel to it, and the left arm points toward the rocks behind the figure. Man and nature partake of a sloping curve whereby the human figure makes the transition between near and far. Set as it is at the dead center of the composition, Saint Jerome's bent leg is bone and rock, supporting a skeletal chest as ridged as the mountainous pillars behind him. The emergence of bones under the skin bares the erosion of beauty through layers of human experiences. In old men, Leonardo wrote, the surface of limbs is "wrinkled, rugged, and knotty" (367). The visual image therefore reveals spiritual nakedness at its most intense. The antihumanist integration of art and science beyond geometric bounds showed forth. Whereas the *Vitruvian Man* (see Fig. 41) gave form to abstract theories of human proportions, Jerome foregrounded science as observation rather than as speculation; the form of human life was to be lived, not constructed. And the technique of *non finito* reflected the disintegration of beauty at the hand of life's vicissitudes.

The lion in the foreground of the painting is not mentioned among the "scorpions and wild beasts" (Letter xxii) that surrounded Jerome in the desert. Rather, it refers to the saint's extraction of a thorn from the animal's paw in an apocryphal legend transposed from Saint Gerasimus. The lion also was a reminder of martyrdom in the arena, which then became a desert where mystics would fight the demons of temptation. At the other end of the iconographic spectrum, the lion's friendly presence points to a pre-Adamic harmony between saints and beasts that Saint Francis had turned into legends of tameness. Concerns with all living forms take on a biographical touch if we think of Leonardo's own gesture at the marketplace, where he bought birds to set them free.

Neither should we forget the intimacy with animals that primitive "wild men" have held, and which Leonardo was to claim for his androgynous myth of unity in *Saint John the Baptist.*

In symbolic terms, however, the lion's "active" turn of the head and open mouth betray reactions to unseen powers; nature's organic and inorganic forms complement one another. Instinct, emotion, and uncertainty make the desert pulsate with life. Jerome himself called for meaning: "Our adversary the devil, as a roaring lion, goes about seeking what he may devour" (Letter xxii). Because spiritual powers could tame ferocity, the artwork drew the hierarchies of nature and faith together. Men and animals were antagonists in Homeric epics and Greek art, which portrayed leonine ferocity as uniquely bestial. Christianity turned lions into benevolent symbols of endurance that assisted monastic solitude.[15] Traditionally, animals have been signposts of human excellence vis-à-vis primitivism and sainthood. Much as sin caused Adam to lose control of animals, so did medieval Ywain (*Ywain and Gawain*) relinquish self-mastery when he lost control over the lion. In terms of desert nomenclature, wild and grotesque beasts assailed Saint Anthony in the dreadful visions painted by Hieronymus Bosch. They also lurked amid ruins as pagan symbols out to torment ascetics who sought a life of primeval rectitude in which man and beast could live in peace.[16]

As symbols of strength, constancy, and faithfulness, lions secured God's presence in the wilderness, where John the Baptist would roam in search of spiritual perfection. Jerome himself considered him one of the founders of desert life in *The Life of Saint Paul the First Hermit,* and called on his experience: "John the Baptist lived in the desert, and seeking Christ with his eyes, refused to look at anything else. . . . His rough garb, hid girdle made of skins, his diet of locusts and wild honey were all alike designed to encourage virtue and continence" (Letter lxix). Even the Baptist had rejected priesthood in the Temple for life in the desert. The beginning and the end of Leonardo's mythography were thus lodged in the symbolism of his first landscape. His Christian mythmaking started earlier than one might suspect.

While sharing Jerome's concerns with the conflict between paganism and Christianity, the humanists tried to find arguments in favor of complementary—rather than divided—loyalties. While Petrarch praised Christian texts without rejecting secular ones, Pier Paolo Vergerio found the study of eloquence harmful whenever it exceeded what was necessary for a better reading of Scripture. And Lorenzo Valla argued that the judge in Jerome's dream lashed out against Ciceronian philosophy, not eloquence.

5

The unfinished condition of the Vatican canvas makes it clear that Leonardo's "act of painting" had rejected Albertian notions of polished "finish." Blank areas, strokes of either sketches or afterthoughts, and a pervasive lack of clarity lose definition to process. The saint's mystic wonderment paralleled the artist's own commitment to push his talents to the limit. Even before the *Adoration*, representation was treated as a phenomenon inimical to demands of "detailed" craftsmanship. Restraint claimed priority over completion. The time had come when art could express the intensity and elusiveness of mental forms that tested mimesis.

On matters of the unfinished, the little church facade sketched in the upper right corner of *Saint Jerome* may have been meant as a casual pre- or afterthought that was never finished. Its stylistic linearity sets a tensive relationship with the "painterly" forms around it. Maurizio Calvesi's remarks are valuable: "His is a line that probes and investigates, that delves into things acutely and indefatigably. So subtle and searching is his line that it dissolves into atmosphere, into *sfumato*, and while recording the various gradations and possibilities of knowledge, it elicits (or rather translates into cognitive terms) the limit of the mysterious and ineffable, beyond which human knowledge cannot go."[17] Any form of human construction would have set limits to the ineffability of belief, and the architectural outline could not amount to more than a detail at odds with the rest of the canvas. However tentative its visual value, the church is there, and we have to take it as part of the whole picture, since Leonardo's practice of overlapping drawings did not affect his paintings. Incongruities of scale and distance, however, alert viewers to a representation out of joint with both mimesis and linear perspective. We are looking at a landscape in which memory remains predominant.

In terms of personal memories, the church could evoke Jerome's "secular" experiences at Treves, around Roman basilicas, and amid Antioch's worldly pleasures. The desert experience was therefore liminal vis-à-vis humanist preferences for life in the *polis*. When the *polis* in question was Rome, however, Christian spiritualism implied short pilgrimages toward the outskirts of the city, where Constantine built grand places of worship on imperial grounds. By contrast, the urban center remained crowded with administrative buildings and temples of the old gods. There he built the triumphal arch by the Colosseum, the Janus Quadrifrons at the cattle market, and the baths on the Quirinal. In the heart of Rome, the more powerful core of Roman aristocracy was and remained pagan until the end of the fourth century. Grand church buildings never made it downtown, where the emperor clashed with the Senate in A.D. 326. He left shortly thereafter, never to return. To give a Christian capital to a Christian empire, Constantine had to migrate eastward; in A.D. 330, Constantinople was chosen to head Christendom. That cultural dividedness was part of Jerome's experience.[18]

The architectural drawing also sets humanist constructs against the painterly naturalism of Leonardo's antihumanist frame of mind. Granted that the sketch's linearity plays an ancillary role amid the powerful volumes of nature, it is there nonetheless. And it seems to point back to the dialogic experiences of Jerome's journeys from the city to the desert: "But to me a town is a prison and a solitude, paradise. Why do we long for the bustle of cities, we whose very name (*monachus*) speaks of loneliness?" (Letter lxix). Like the Church itself, man was a pilgrim (*homo viator*). Iconographically, Lorenzo Lotto made the urban reference so explicit that the city in the background of his *San Girolamo* shows the Roman Castel Sant'Angelo. However odd to modern viewers, dislocations of that sort were to be expected at a time when Giovanni Bellini painted Saint Francis in the desert by mixing the Apennine landscape of La Verna with a fauna that included Egyptian herons.[19] From a hagiographical standpoint, desert experiences leaned toward "gradational structures" of spiritual growth.[20] Jerome himself favored a kind of mental geography: "I should see the desert, the most wonderful of cities" (Letter ii). The church took up the ecclesiological meaning of the desert as a special arena for the people of God and Israel.

Spatial incongruity and the flimsy appearance of the church facade could invite us to read *Saint Jerome* as a journey into one's self. Since style bears on substance, I cannot but refer to Jerome's famous dream, in which the judge accused him of being a "Ciceronian, not a Christian. . . . I held my tongue at once. He had ordered that I should be flogged. . . . Lord! If ever I own profane books again, or if I read them, it will mean that I have denied you! . . . Upon this oath, I came back to earth. To everyone's surprise, I opened my eyes. They were bathed in tears" (Letter xxii). The dream was a fashionable literary device among rhetoricians, and Jerome himself used it to utter emotions that ranged from feverish delirium to ecstatic visions and providential warnings. More than once, "in the endless solitude scorched by a pitiless sun, in that horrible habitation of the monks, have I not dreamed I was back amid the delights of Rome!" (Letter xxii). If he knew anything about the life of the saint, Leonardo must have known this passage. And so did Aeneas Sylvius

Piccolomini. As a humanist, however, he took Jerome as a model, "whom all would do well to emulate who want to live a holy life and arrive at eloquence. . . . No page of his could be convicted of being un-Ciceronian in style. . . . I am willing to allow anyone to come to the same decision he did, that is, to renounce secular literature after he has seen, read, and learned all there is to know in this field. . . . I feel that there are appropriate times and circumstances in life for every kind of study." The humanist had been able to reconcile paganism with Christianity to an extent that Jerome could not master. For his part, Leonardo went back to watershed experiences at antiquity's twilight. If painting registers the synecdochal sign of temporal expanse, his painting did not fail to test that restriction.[21]

Writing about an inspired friend, Jerome added that "he beholds the glory of God, which even the apostles beheld only in the wilderness. He does not, indeed, behold towered cities, but he has inscribed himself in the citizenry of a new city. His limbs are a sorry sight in their ugly sackcloth, but thus he will be the better taken up in the clouds to meet Christ. . . . Picture this to yourself, my dear friend, and with all your mind's reflection concentrate upon the scene" (Letter iii). It is a wishful picture in relation to which the church sketch could stand for urban life left behind or urban life transformed by spiritual power. However fragmentary, the temporal expanse is stretched to the edge of transcendence. And the cavelike rock formation through which we peek into the background gave visual form to the spelunking theology of early Christianity. Following the advice of Eusebius (bishop of Caesarea in Palestine), the three great Constantinian basilicas in the Holy Land were equipped with caves or grottoes.

Symbolism and representation are so complex in Leonardo's canvas that we are faced with at least two focal points; that of the artist standing next to us outside the artwork, and the one placed in the saint's mind inside the painting. We stand at the brink of experiences split between past and future. Stylistically, the "unfinished" never tires of turning back on its unsolvable and yet dialogic "dividedness," much as the visual image does not let meaning dwindle down into mere illustration. As a result, we are led to share in the drama of message and mimesis. By a paradoxical twist, age and *sfumato* disintegrate the permanence of matter. Solidity itself seems to become phenomenal, and forms do not cross the threshold of mimetic thoroughness. I would therefore suggest that Leonardo gave us an artistic image that brought out the testing nature of much of his poetics, namely the clash between individual trials and structures of dogma.

6

At the earliest stage of his pictorial career, Leonardo put the humanist preference for ideal maturity to the test of age. Adam's unflawed physiology of transcendental health on the Sistine ceiling stood next to the passionate aging of Saint Jerome. His skeletal body shares in the ageless matter of the petrified landscape. His left forearm and hand stretch out into the ridges of his chest. Life was not set in lapsarian or postlapsarian realms of either bliss or banishment, but in the midst of spiritual longings that come to rest on the saint's bent knee. In the words of a modern poet who confronted old age, the contrast between David and Jerome was but another instance of a standing experience:

> Weaker and weaker, the sunlight falls
> In the afternoon. The proud and the strong
> Have departed.
>
> . . . .
>
> Those that are left are the unaccomplished,
> The finally human,
> Natives of a dwindled sphere
> (Wallace Stevens, *Lebensweisheitspielerei*)

The adverbial "finally" underlines trying processes of growth in a humane—rather than humanist—spirit that tested soul and flesh alike in Leonardo's drawings of aging nudes (Fig. 7). The proud figures that humanist mythographers had shaped in the utopian light of transcendental adulthood—from Piero della Francesca and Uccello to Verrocchio and Michelangelo—surrendered much of their agelessness in the phenomenal world of Leonardo.

To sharpen the formative dynamics of the Leonardesque worldview, Jerome's "test of age" must be set against humanist counterparts. Because they were conceived as newborn and perfect, Adam, the Albertian family leader, and the courtier were models who would be neither repeated nor superseded. Life only needed to offer pretexts for making promises; where life would more likely fail, art would glorify human potential. Often enough, acts of faith overshadowed facts. Accordingly, Leonardo Bruni modeled his *Panegyric to the City of Florence* after Aristides' *Panathenaicus*. In the ancient text, Athens was recognized as the only *polis* which, "when brought to the test," proved "superior to its fame." That standard of value echoed Pericles, who had reserved honor and power not to those "who want them" but to those "who have been tested."[22] Overlooking

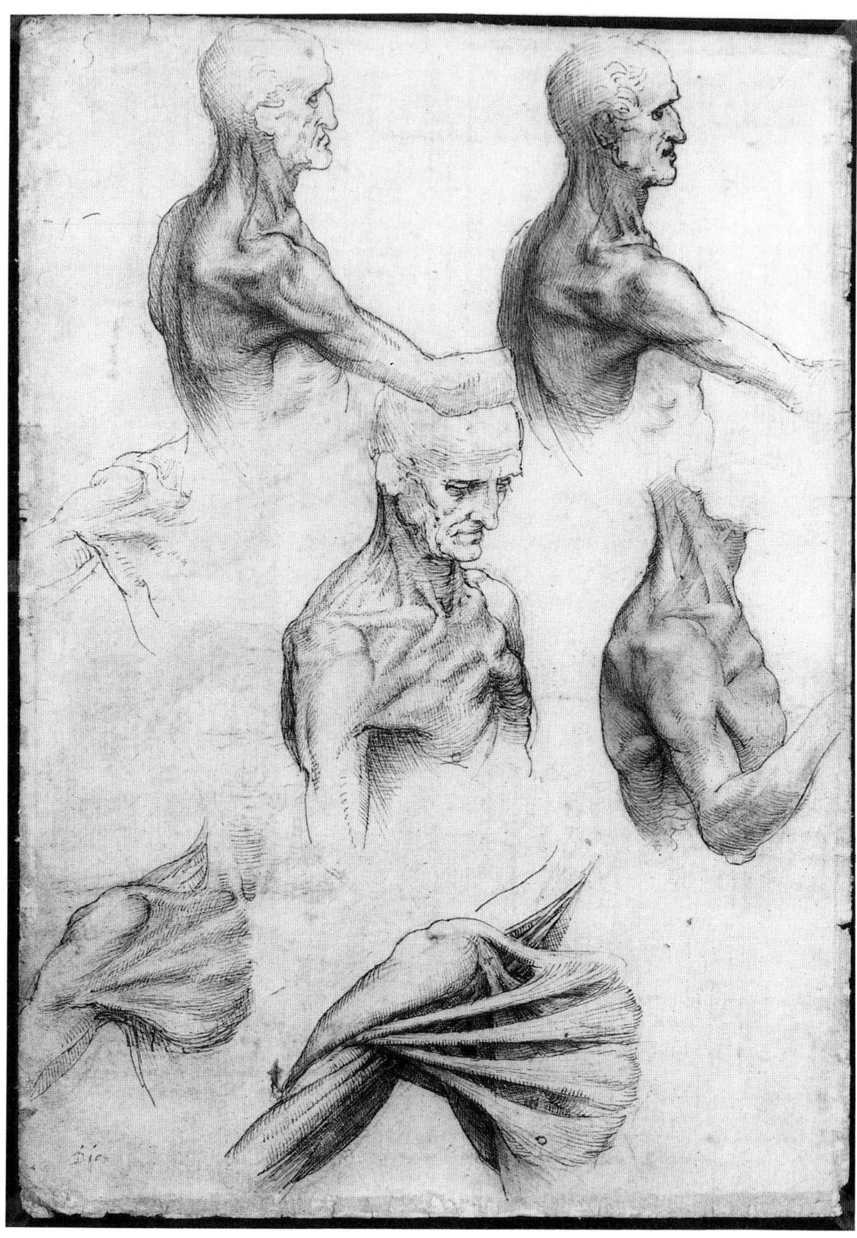

FIG. 7.   Leonardo da Vinci, *Anatomical Drawing*
Royal Library, Windsor Castle

the emphasis that the ancients placed on achievement, Bruni's comparison edged on wishful thinking in 1403, when Florence could only show a bright promise of her future splendor. Tests could have discredited claims of greatness as either premature or unfounded.

In Castiglione's Urbino, "the greatest part of those persons who are introduced in the conversations were already dead." Had those men lived, "they would have attained such eminence that they would have been able to give to all who knew them clear proof of how praiseworthy the Court of Urbino was" (*Courtier*, 2, 286). Again, the conditional mode coated longings with the veneer of oncoming certitude. But the "clear proof" never materialized; it thrived on the promise of a brightest day that would never come. *The Book of the Courtier* thus portrayed an incomparable elite at its cultural peak. Amid historical circumstances, however, it would have declined, had it been allowed to endure "a very long life." While the brave die young, "the passing years take with them many of the good things of life" (*Courtier*, 89). Premature deaths did not allow the test of time to betray promises nurtured in the illusion of inevitable success; in a way, they flourished because growth had been denied. Death did not let the future vilify the present. Hope and remembrance therefore shaped time into the guise of the would-be, to which memory added the aura of the must-have-been. The transformation of time into value turned expectations (*opinioni*) into certainties (*certezze*). At a personal level, Ficino had "no wish to depend on the future, the uncertain, and thus be deceived. No! I stand in the present, the certain. . . . I act because it satisfies me now and in eternity, and not with a view to its satisfying me at some future time, and then but for a while."[23] The humanist worldview was folded onto itself;[24] man could move forward by looking backward, and what he found validated foregone conclusions.[25]

In the antihumanist mode, Jerome brought the wisdom of age to a spiritual quest that his own writings had cherished since childhood: "When I was a child, I talked like a child, I had the intelligence, the thoughts of a child; since I became a man, I have outgrown childish ways." Furthermore, "I had no idea how to write. My hand shook and my fingers trembled. I haven't learned such a very great deal since then, but at least I've absorbed that sentence of Socrates: 'I know that I know nothing' " (Letter iii). Lines of that sort betray an "educational modality" that would qualify as novelistic if we were to think of a literary genre linked to the process of growth. And we ought to remember that Jerome wrote three *vitae,* namely the lives of Paul of Thebes, Malchus, and Hilarion. However fictive, endeavors of that kind stressed duration.

Even the antihumanist bent of Alberti's literary output sustained concerns with growth and age. Having introduced him as a paragon of empirical wisdom in the third book of his treatise on the family, Alberti returned to the old Giannotto in *Profugiorum ab Aerumna,* which presented him as "*buono uomo e umanissimo vecchio*" even though he lacked "*cognizione di lettere.*"[26]

Theogenius, on the other hand, was completely dedicated to an aging figure who looks back on life. And Alberti worded his praise of old age in the same outspoken tone of panegyrical enthusiasm he showered on the family leader: "*E truovo in questa mia vecchiezza non minima utilità, ove molte cose molestissime quali me soleano infestare giovane, ora o sazio o libero nulla meco possono. . . . Ora di me stesso contento a me stesso gratifico*" (And I find in this old age of mine rather significant comforts. Whereas many annoying things used to bother me while I was young, now they are armless against me. . . . Because now I am happy with myself, I relish my self-confidence). This is not the image of a spider weaving its thread outward to extend its power. Rather, the little animal has run out of thread, and quite happily so. His outreaching thrust has reversed itself into thoughts on one's lifetime accomplishments. The active yielded to the contemplative, and the builder turned into a social counselor: "*Truovomi ancora per la età reverito, pregiato, reputato; consigliansi meco, odonmi come padre, ricordanmi in suoi ragionamenti aprovano, seguono i miei ammonimenti*" (Because of my age, I enjoy respect, reputation, and reverence; everybody seeks my counsel, they listen to me as to a parent, they mention me in their discussions, they approve of me, and they follow my suggestions). The Albertian cult of civic humanism turned the archetypal figure of the old man into a gravitational model of knowledge out to dispense wisdom. Language is deliberately relational, and recognition of communal merits is but a measure of excellence. Giannozzo was an older spider whose authoritative knowledge would be parceled out with magnanimity. That attitude came back in *Profugiorum ab Aerumna,* in which the old man dispensed counsels (*consigli*) that would help younger people to become worthy of *virtù.*[27] The rhetoric of praise then proceeded to list older Romans known for their heroic deeds on the battlefields of antiquity.[28] Yet we still read about exemplary cases; everyday processes of growth by means of trial and error were not taken into account.

By way of comparison, it is evident that Leonardo did not consider old age a point of arrival to be enjoyed amid the popularity of collective approval. Age could not slow down lifelong quests, which in fact set ever higher goals. For Alberti, one of the wise man's privileges was that he could replace the company of uninteresting people with an "elected" solitude he would share with Plautus, Apuleius, Terence, Horace and the great writers of the Roman past. To that, Jerome added the future-oriented process of discovering God. Jerome was a scholar and an ascetic saint, not a martyr. We do not remember him for heroic deeds, and Leonardo chose to portray him as an old man toiling in the desert. Although aging, he was about to renew himself into a better self. His posture of unrelenting strife bodied forth Christian longings that Gregory of Nyssa had so worded: "Let no one be grieved if he sees in his nature a penchant for change. Changing in everything for the better, let him exchange 'glory for glory,' becoming greater through daily increase, ever perfecting himself, and never arriving too quickly at the limit of perfection. For this is truly perfection: never to stop growing towards what is better and never placing any limit on perfection" (*On Perfection*). Against the classical and humanist grain, perfection was not an epiphanic given. Leonardo's pictorial image, in fact, is one of endurance and commitment; the virtues, that is, of steadfast continuity that would energize baroque forms.[29] Asceticism itself has been seen as a self-formative activity.[30]

Jerome's spiritual intensity was gained the hard way and stood at variance with the ambiguous smile of Leonardo's typical figures. He was what Baudelaire would call a wise man, whose stoic sobriety could indulge neither in smile nor laughter, for such expressions betray a lack of spiritual balance. In fact, "the sage of all sages, the Incarnate Word, has never laughed. In the eyes of Him who knows and can do all things, the comic does not exist."[31] To follow the poet, therefore, it was Leonardo's forthcoming task to balance the drama and expectation of *Saint Jerome*, the *Adoration*, the *Virgin of the Rocks*, and the *Last Supper* with the strangeness and laughter of his grotesque sketches, literary *facezie*, and prophecies.

7

The humanist iconography of youthful Davids—made familiar to us by Donatello, Verrocchio, and Michelangelo—had to face the antihumanist maturity of souls at war within the depths of their own selves. Expression therefore surged toward a divestiture of the self that Donatello dramatized in the wooden *Magdalen* and Michelangelo was to confront in the rugged volumes of *Saint Matthew;* in both of them, age did not mute spiritual intensity. Dialogic interactions between humanist beauty and antihumanist vitality tested Leonardesque poetics.

In the Vatican picture, Jerome's emaciated face projects a spiritual intensity that prayers could not quite quench. While attainment remains out of reach, efforts triumph, as they would again when Bernini sculpted his *David* in the spirit of baroque commitments to formative efforts. Writing on the "formative" arts, F.W.J. Schelling insisted that "the absolute is by nature an eternal act of producing."[32] From that standpoint, *Saint Jerome* foregrounds a threshold moment; the image partakes of presence and absence. Although it is burdened with lifelong experiences, the old body is about to surge toward a final vision. Projected as it is beyond visual representation, meaning betrays a future-oriented poetics.

In terms of doctrine, the Christian concept of history takes *futurus* to measure time as a continuum in which the present shapes the future. In that sense, continuity does not call for significant changes. From a humanist standpoint, any forward-looking temporality would perpetuate forms of a utopian present. For Petrarch and Castiglione, futurity was a memory of the present-as-immediate-past which subordinated chronicity to the preservation of golden moments. By contrast, *adventus* involves a break from the past. We have been told that the Christian *adventus* derives from the Latin word for "arrival." The Greek equivalent, *parousia,* meaning the "visible presence or appearance of someone," is used with equivalent meaning in the New Testament. Arrival and revelation implied changes, even apocalyptic discontinuities of a kind that we find in the Tiburtine Sibyl (late fourth century), Tyconius (303–90), and Jerome himself. Saint John the Divine twice called Christ "the Lord, which is, and which was, and *which is to come*" (Rev. 1:4,8). He foresaw a moment that would break in upon human consciousness from beyond time.[33]

Once age and consciousness had eroded most of his human time, Jerome strove to capture glimpses of a spiritual soul somehow retrieved from eternity. A cornerstone of Leonardo's poetics was therefore set. *Saint Jerome* introduced the thematics of dramatic changes, which the *Adoration* opened up to mankind's destiny. After the Deluge sketches, *Saint John the Baptist* would announce the Coming of Jesus and point toward the Second Advent of Christ. As a form of radical novelty, *adventus* defies representation as well as foreseeable modes of reception, whether they be visual or literary. Saint John the Divine is downright curt about it: "If any man shall add unto these things, God shall add unto him the plagues that are written in this book" (Rev. 22:18). Language is inadequate, much as Leonardo's *sfumato* utters nonrhetorical forebodings to which the density of shadows lends symbolic depth. At the same time, *non finito* adds to the discontinuity of an earth-shaking advent. Even though the visual metaphor insists that "to see clearly is to know with certainty," clarity of sight is overshadowed by an event at the edge of man's emotional prefiguration.

8

Jerome would suggest that, however late in life, strife is never over. Like him, we are always about to get up or to kneel down. In any case, we have to tear ourselves away from the demeaning stasis of sheer matter, of life wasted by quotidian survival.

Saint Jerome did not rush in the "waning" cloudiness of the Middle Ages, but did confront the solarity of Humanism at the autumn brink of a human experience that fifteenth-century art had to bring to the fore-front of its cultural achievements.

3

Fractures of Faith in the
Adoration of the Magi

*On the whole, moments of vision do not come to us so
frequently when we are within the humanist scale of proportion. Perhaps the great intellectual achievement known as
perspective, by which figures of human size could be related
to each other in some plausible and measurable system,
tended to paralyze the intuitive faculty by which objects are
seen with immediate vividness.*

—*Kenneth Clark*

After the life of a saint who lived pagan and Christian experiences,
Leonardo tested the very concept of history in the *Adoration of the Magi*
(begun 1481, Fig. 8). He abruptly steered that theme away from the
iconographic tradition of courtly tales one finds in the pageantries of
Ghirlandaio and Gentile da Fabriano. Botticelli's own *Adoration of the
Magi* (1470s, Fig. 9) stopped the epiphanic cortege at the center of the
painting, where the Magi worship the Savior amid ancient buildings that
frame the shift from paganism to Christianity.[1] While antiquity is reduced to ruins in the background, the whole composition flaunts the
sartorial luster of modern times.

Leonardo also set his subject at the center of the picture, where the
narrative range of the *istoria* was contracted into a moment of disquieting vitality. But then, what is the subject of the *Adoration,* and how has
it been interpreted? Epiphany traditionally refers to the Magi, the baptism of Christ in the river Jordan, and the wedding at Cana.[2] Because
they imply growth and recognition, such episodes draw people to share
eventful instants with divinity. Whatever its outcome, the event brings

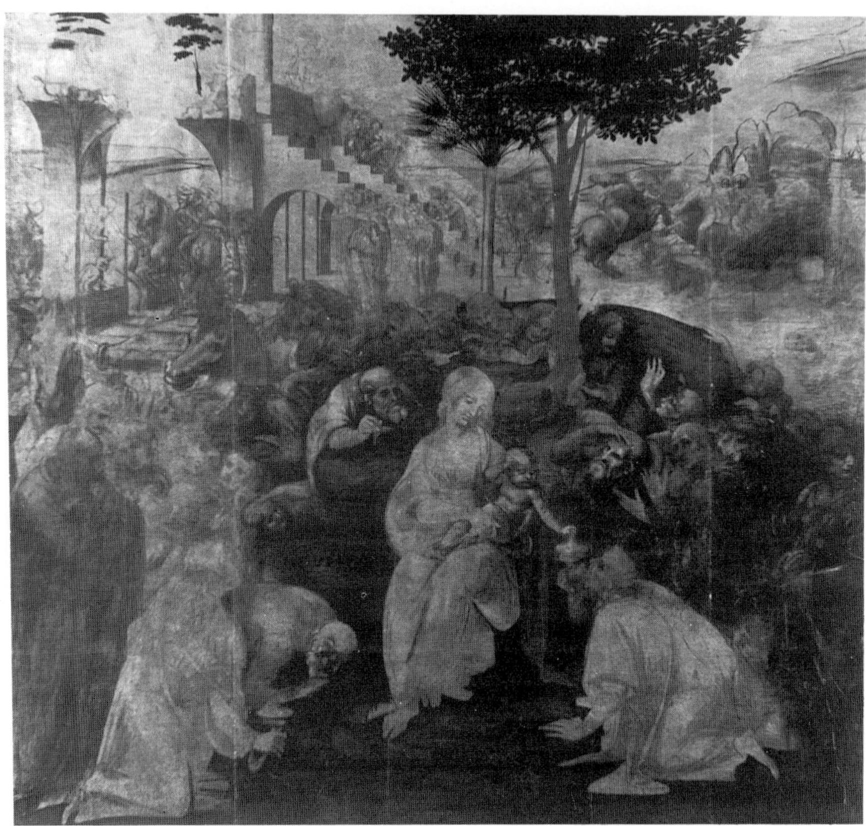

FIG. 8.   Leonardo da Vinci, *Adoration of the Magi* (begun 1481)
Uffizi, Florence

new energy to the communion of inner and outer selves. As phenomenon, the *Adoration* expanded the core of Leonardo's poetics. Life and faith are acts, and value lies in activity. In a kind of explosive moment, divinity is about to touch humankind. Its reactions are unleashed in a setting that tests the geometric laws of linear perspective. The very kernel of creative power—human and natural alike—could be either constructive or destructive; at all times, however, it had to be active.

2

The literary theme is but a starting point in the *Adoration*, which confronts us with a moment of awesome bewilderment. The painting pivots

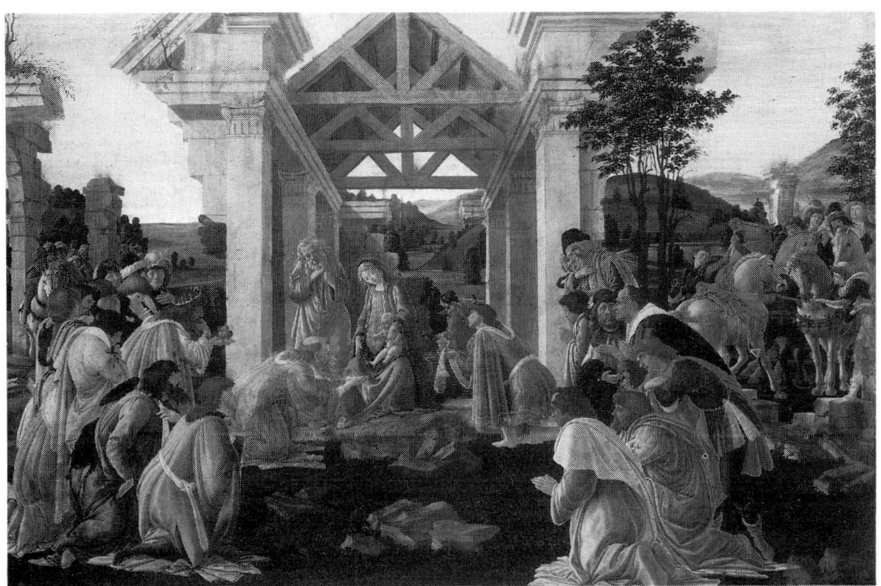

FIG. 9.   Sandro Botticelli, *Adoration of the Magi* (1470s)
National Gallery of Art, Washington D.C.

on the cultural and religious synchretism of Christianity at a time when it was still emerging from Graeco-Roman experiences. Martin Kemp has drawn attention to "the deliberately paganizing quality of the background," wherein "the shadowy inhabitants of the ancient world have plunged themselves into a chaos of self-destructive conflict."[3] Men and animals suggest tensions, while ancient ruins are crowded with horseback riders and people climbing steps. Amid an architecture that seems to be mostly classical, men and animals roam in states of disarray, confusion, and outright warfare.

The horse's head to the left nearest the group around the Virgin steers background violence toward the Magi, whose gifts of faith had to be saved for the future of Christianity. From Pisanello to Gentile da Fabriano, horses enacted courtly *giostre* throughout the fifteenth century. For Leonardo, instead, they became vectors of power that carried forth human violence. And it is by keeping in mind the cartoon for the *Battle of the Stendard* and the background of the *Adoration* that we ought to read his note about animals "furiously carrying men to the destruction of their lives" (1295). Indeed, this is a far cry from the Sforza steed that was to outdo the equestrian statues of Donatello (*Gattamelata*) and Verrocchio (*Colleoni*).

The *Adoration* confronts viewers with states of psychological flux as persistent or ephemeral as each character could make it. Perhaps the youths above Mary are angels; perhaps the people pressing in from the right are shepherds.[4] But what can we make of the group at the far right, where heads without bodies and skulls without flesh barely emerge from darkness? We are looking at areas of human emotions woven through darkening textures that blur the edge between past and present, dream and reality. The dust and cinder of the past seem to flesh out images too evanescent to remind us of individual portraits in the tradition of Botticelli and Ghirlandaio. Rather, the pictorial *sfumato* evokes ghostly presences, as if of lives coming back to witness an event for which humanity—dead and alive—had been waiting.

To the left of the *Adoration,* a faint lighting warms disincarnate figures who expose their weightless shells to the Savior's birth. People are caught in the process of fulfilling a quest that death itself could not deny. We confront mankind's collective response to a fateful event. It is an apocalyptic scene of Christian mythology including old and young (the standing figures at both ends), lost bodies and redeemed souls, which are all set against the "waning" of paganism.

Human presence in the Uffizi painting is woven between and betwixt forewarnings of birth, death, and revelation. We are faced with a gestural language that is neither recitation (*epos*) nor reflection (*logos*); instead, it seems to lean toward the poetic utterances of *mythos*. The matter of history is linked to an array of individual responses that language could never record. Leonardo's images went back to a time before the rule of Christian dogma would order belief.[5] That "pluralized vision" gained strength from its own complexity. Recent analyses of composite views on the subject of romantic art could shed light on the *Adoration*. In fact, Leonardo—and Turner after him—let painting speak its own painterly language, which could exploit complex, antithetical, and incomplete readings. As a result, retrospection led to foresight, recollection produced hope, and memory begot forgetfulness. Reading could be most effective when linked to activities antithetical to reading itself.[6]

3

Light-dark contrasts are symbolic in the *Adoration*. Medieval and postmedieval speculations had linked light and darkness to Platonic and Neoplatonic abstractions on the nature of pure form. Because it carried spirituality rather than realism, light had to illuminate the transcendence of purity. It was form without matter, quality without quantity. Therefore, light could condone shadow neither as symbol nor as phenomenon. In medieval concepts of beauty, the aesthetics of proportion remained quantitative. The experience of light, instead, was *qualitative,* and its coloristic brilliance was not allowed to blur into *sfumato* effects.[7] By contrast, Leonardo's *sfumato* gave light an atmospheric instability consistent with empirical perception; transparency yielded to a painterly opacity.[8]

Human volumes in the *Adoration* confronted Leonardo with the problem of placing figures in space, which in turn became part of the figures themselves; the result was spatial subjects rather than objects contained in space.[9] Individuals took on three-dimensional fullness, and incomplete volumes bodied forth existence. Although the picture is little more than a monochromatic surface awaiting pigment, its *sfumato* effects blend outlines to produce the illusion of atmospheric thickening. Since the edges appear hazy and indefinite, the three-dimensional illusion blurs the boundaries of forms.[10]

We have been told that style is more apt to describe figures in space than a type of existence in time. Such a spatial emphasis underlines the fixity of idealism, which Piero della Francesca put to the humanist test. Yet, style has to make adjustments once forms are plunged into the flow of time.[11] In the Bakhtinian sense of the word, the chronotopic symbolism of Leonardesque *sfumato* linked space, volume, and mass to psychophysiological vicissitudes. The three-dimensional solidity of physical roundness betrayed an equally independent volition of mind. Inevitably, differences between Albertian modeling and Leonardesque *sfumato* touched on content. Because the practice of modeling made figures "lightweight," their volumetric deficiency pointed to a commensurate lack of dramatic gravity.[12] By contrast, Leonardo shaped figures at the peak of their weighty and restless maturity.

4

Stylistically, Leonardo insisted that the most important things that one could find in the analysis of painting are the "movements appropriate to the states of mind of each living creature" (McMahon, 111). To achieve expression, painters were called upon to study models that were naturally antirhetorical. The mute, in fact, make "gestures better than any other sort of men." Even the dumb can teach "better through facts than will all the other masters through words" (McMahon, 248, 250). At issue here is the efficacy of discourse to capture the inner life of emotions in excess of verbal scaffoldings. The realm of unresolved feelings was not inhuman, and it certainly found expression in the *Adoration*,[13] which fell back on the visual rhetoric of body language. Sequential relationships could not be drawn, and reactions to the event became frightfully visual. The *istoria* turned into the reenactment of human responses that never made it into the history books. Even the incarnation was to be taken as an ongoing disclosure of the past into the present; not the progress of history, but the recurrence of myth.[14]

I cannot but turn to William Blake's criticism of historians who remained unable to disarrange self-evident reality. Acts "alone are history," and such acts belong neither to Plutarch nor Voltaire. "Tell me the Acts, O historian. . . . All that is not action is not worth reading." Before Blake, Leonardo pulled the rug from under humanist historians in a class with Leonardo Bruni and Machiavelli, whose studies of history were interpreted and mediated by textual narratives. The *Adoration*, instead, shifted from words to deeds whose significance could not be touched by any "turner and twister of causes and consequences," namely the "reasoning historian" (Blake, *A Descriptive Catalogue*). For Leonardo, actions were unbreakable wholes. They alone could preserve the integrity of historical events whose truth would follow our reenactment of them according to a symbolic memory that would give priority to reconstruction over repetition.[15]

However different in character and intensity, *renovatios* of antiquity were called for throughout our Western experience. The present tended to cherish the past in times of renaissance and renascences; what ensued were images of an antiquity that had never existed. The Florentines invented a new Athens and a new Jerusalem, just as the Athenians had made of their city more than Athens itself. In a classical mode, there was "this" (historical) and "that" (imaginary) Athens, as would be the case with Rome and Florence.[16] In both instances, however, there were fixed models to fit. Leonardo, instead, left the future open. Whichever direction it could be pointed at, historical time had no panacea to offer.

Logical connections between foreground and background are severed in the *Adoration*, just as the empty darkness around the Virgin blocks contacts with the people around her. Yet it is less than a paradox to state that uncertainty lets the phenomenon linger on. *Istorie* have a beginning and an end, and they happen only once. The phenomenon, instead, is rooted in the immediacy of the present, and its resilience is boundless.

Audiences listen to the story, but phenomena force knowledge "to happen." The crowd of figures in the foreground of the picture is caught up in overwhelming emotions. Description yielded to intimation, and the allegorical gap lodged human engagements that Leonardo made all the more compelling.

As such, revelation implies novelty, and therefore a break with the past. That cleavage works at all levels in the *Adoration;* between linear and atmospheric perspective, story and phenomenon, paganism and Christianity.[17] Repeatedly, Leonardo's discussion of narrative art brings home the idea that he "who gives the best resemblance is the worst composer of action painting." To secure the narrative flow, no detail ought to stand out. Whenever talent is limited "to one part of the painting" only, its "power of expansion" trades the universal for the particular, and continuity for discontinuity. Eclecticism would correct those who do "not love equally all things that are contained in the painting." Since "what is beautiful is not always good" (McMahon, 92, 93, 110), details are dependent on a visual action that is phenomenal rather than documentative; the story happens, is not told. The past was as unsettling as the present.

We might guess that Paul Ricouer would see in the *Adoration* a clash between abstract and concrete history. Abstract history rests with the "accumulation of acquirements," namely those classical artifacts Mantegna, Flavio Biondo, and Francesco Colonna made a religion of. Even Leonardo flaunted artifacts of that kind in the *Annunciation* (Fig. 10), whose foreground is decorated with a lectern made from a Roman sepulchral urn with acanthus body and lion feet. There "is no drama" at that

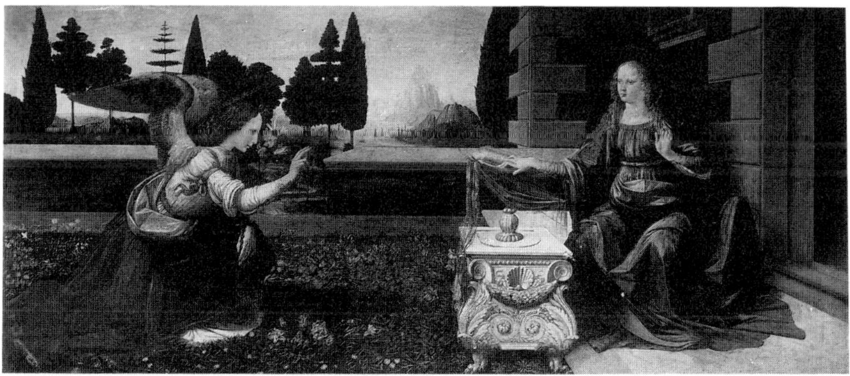

FIG. 10.   Leonardo da Vinci, *Annunciation* (1476?)
Uffizi, Florence

level, since "only the works of man and the accumulation of his vestiges are considered."[18] The humanist emphasis on narrativity forced human actions to fit stylized codes; acquired knowledge was staged while freedom of expression was hindered.

Concrete history, instead, deals with events, which occur simultaneously in the *Adoration.* The art historian would find the painting synoptic, in that it represents different actions, places, and people as one; and synchronous, in that it represents different moments as one. The range of such actions is as pluralistic as could be found in fifteenth-century painting, before Raphael upgraded Leonardo's multifigural composition.[19] Likewise, the historian would point out that Caesar's crossing of the Rubicon was not a one-man act, but a multitude of men crossing the river in different conditions of body and soul. Each human event, therefore, is geared to plurality; it is a cross section of actions and reactions that traditional history has largely ignored.[20]

In the background of the *Adoration,* classical "acquirements" are scattered amid a barren landscape; archaeological evidence and iconographic value fade at the edge of recognition. The downfall of antiquity is played out through acts of pointless violence somehow symbolic of the chaos of ideas that plagued the last days of antiquity. Stoicism, Neoplatonism, Neo-Pythagoreanism, Oriental and Christian Gnosticism, and Mystery religions had fractured the native cults of Greeks and Romans beyond any hope of healing.[21]

On matters of history, differences between Mantegna and Leonardo paved the way for splits between neoclassical and romantic approaches to history. Like Machiavelli, Montesquieu and Hume insisted on the "sameness" of human nature. Its historical unfolding through events that have acted on reality along a pattern of linear clarity stood at the core of Gibbon's *Decline and Fall of the Roman Empire.* By contrast, Carlyle's *French Revolution* opens amid uncertainty, speculation, complexity, and what has been called *chiaroscuro* representations.[22] Carlyle believed that history should confront not only actual deeds but also a range of events that occurred within the same situation. And a lot happened at the breakdown of paganism.

5

Botticelli had exploited the religious symbolism of decayed buildings in both versions of his *Adoration.* In the Old Testament, ruins refer to

Jewish history. We read in Amos's prophecy "In that day will I raise up the tabernacle / of David that is fallen" (9:11). The tabernacle of David foreshadowed the Temple of Solomon, which also fell into ruins. Whether Jewish, Roman, or more generally ancient-looking, much architecture could be imagined in a state of decay at the birth of Christ. The breakdown of perspectival order in the background of Leonardo's *Adoration* could indeed epitomize the loss of a pagan center in the culture of late antiquity. Forms either fading or incomplete convey the visual markings of a world order that is collapsing. Memories of classical rationalism and Diocletian's efforts at restoring some sort of Latin spirituality had become nightmares at last. When he got to the city, Jerome wrote that "the gilded Capitol falls into disrepair; dust and cobwebs cover all Rome's temples. The city shakes on its foundations, and a stream of people hurries, past half-fallen shrines, to the tombs of the martyrs" (Letter cvii). Inevitably, the breakdown of institutions betrayed a loss of faith in the political space of the *polis*.

Images of clashes between paganism and Christianity were rare in fifteenth-century art, which usually kept the two traditions apart. Yet Piero della Francesca's *Flagellation* (1450s, Fig. 11) somehow met that challenge. On the right, three Romans (or moderns) converse in a rather demonstrative mode while Christ is being scourged to the left. The connection between the two halves is obscure. What is clear, however, is that Jesus is the intruder in a setting whose geometric beauty is liable to the disruptiveness of change. Dialogue is past- and present-oriented, while punishment is meant to keep a different future at bay. The artwork bears on inexplicable gaps between knowledge and action.

Christianity's intrusion in the *Adoration* has shattered the architectural armor of the ancient world order. The background lodges disintegration rather than inheritance, and enmity instead of fellowship. Antiquity had ceased to tell triumphant stories and could be judged only on the evidence of a self-destructive will. The pictorial scene brings forth the collapse of a civilization whose people fight blindly without a banner to believe in, while motherhood is spent in women luring exhausted warriors. People exist in the moment of action, which fails to steer human energy toward some sort of constructive purposefulness.

"Where there are gods, there are wars." So uttered Icarus in the modern retelling of Theseus's story. Still, denunciation yielded to hope: "There are no gods, but a God." Yet André Gide had lived long enough to learn that pagan and Christian kingdoms alike have brought war no less than peace.[23]

Faiths changed, but strife endured. Augustine had no doubts as to the

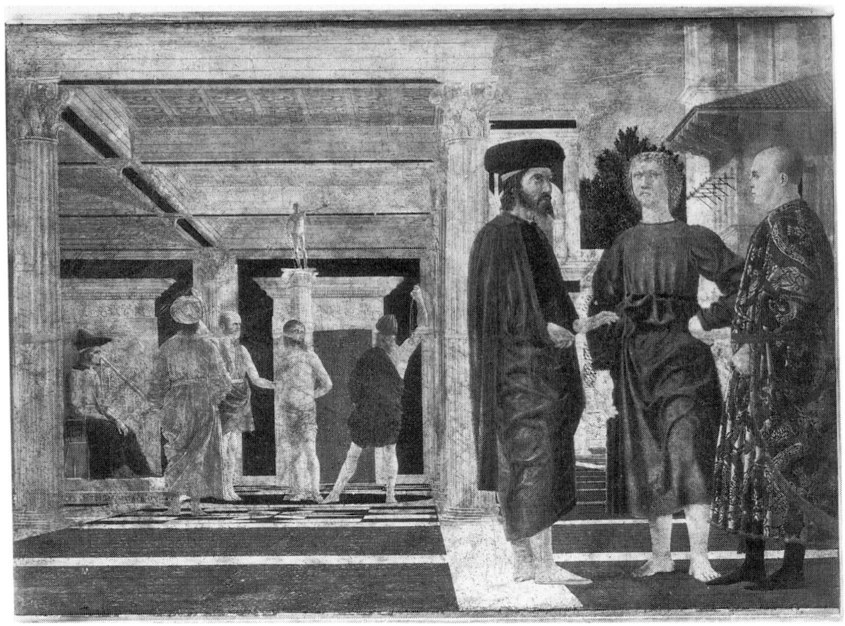

FIG. 11.   Piero della Francesca, *Flagellation* (1450s)
Palazzo Ducale, Urbino

future of Christianity. Pope Leo the Great stopped Attila the Hun with his word, but Jerome wrote from Bethlehem before the city was sacked in A.D. 410: "What is safe if Rome is destroyed?" The Leonardesque *Adoration* confirmed that beginnings are fraught with uncertainty. Antiquity had been reborn to Humanism. Yet Leonardo understood that the ancient past had served its purpose, and it was time to let go of it. The Middle Ages were not the only culture that was "waning" at the turn of the sixteenth century. Rebirths were about to foster their own demise at a time when art had been obsessed with the recurrent theme of a single everlasting Resurrection. The disembodied *epos* of classicism yielded to the incarnated *logos* of Christianity.[24] The adoration of Christ forced history to acknowledge the growth of personality, and the modern painting set the tragedy of decadence next to the lingering futility of unkept promises. Although ignorant of classical historiography, Leonardo got to its spiritual core, where events were judged in their thematic relation to other events, regardless of chronological frames.[25] Against the grain of post-Newtonian time, judgment preceded measurement in antiquity. By the same token, the *Adoration* took on the postclassical B.C./A.D. dating system, which allows us to measure events with a precision no ancient historian could imagine.[26] Incongruence was spatial as well as temporal. Both of them invalidated arbitrary lines drawn between overlapping cultures caught in the midst of flux.

6

Because chronological linearity was yet to emerge, the *Adoration* underlined redemptive history, which centers on events that have made significant changes. Among them, the birth of Christ became a measure of judgment for the pagan disarray that preceded his coming. Before Jesus' birth, Leonardo found disorder in the *Adoration,* mystery amid primeval spaces in the *Virgin of the Rocks,* and prophetic warnings in the piercing gesture of *Saint John the Baptist.*[27]

With an eye to the emergence of Christianity, people build a cumulative longing for an eventful epiphany around the Virgin. Absence of objects in the foreground of the *Adoration* bears on world-denial; "unseen" values emerge against the collapsing structures of the *civitas*-state in the background. In no uncertain terms, the artwork presents the entry of Christianity into the conscience of people who had to weigh the intelligibility of rational "plans" against the mystery of faith. In reading Leonardo's picture, F.W.J. Schelling would remind us that the incarnate God was not an eternal figure, but one that entered the transitoriness of time. By becoming human, Christ also brought to a close the time of antiquity. He was the last god.[28]

By the older side of that fateful divide, Leonardo painted the violent exit of a pagan world whose intellectual excellence was hopelessly out of joint with political wisdom. Almost at the cutoff point between the lower and the upper half of the *Adoration,* two trees stand behind the Virgin. Iconographers tell us that one of them is a carob tree, which recalls the one from which Judas hung himself. The adoration of the infant Christ linked up to his betrayal. Since birth foreshadowed death, bewilderment bore on ominous forewarnings that pointed toward the *Last Supper.* Symbolism weighed on a break of trust at the dead center of the artwork.

The historical appearance of Christianity was bathed in revelation and denial alike. The meaning of scriptural truth was so enigmatic that it spawned relativism of doctrine, Marcion's heretical split between the

God of Justice and that of love, and contradictions between Old and New Testament. Leonardo understood that the expressive potential of that break had to shape form as much as content. By the same token, viewers would be challenged to search for meaning within a gap of untamable energies brewing at the edge of history's "before" and "after." A gulf existed between aims and results on both sides of that watershed. Ancient myths of *pax romana* crumbled, while the birth of Jesus brought no more than hopes of rest under the palm tree. Older promises had failed, and more recent prophecies were yet to come true. Completion of the Uffizi picture would have called for an interpretative conclusion at odds with Leonardo's approach to the open-endedness of phenomena.

As the common denominator of the *Adoration,* tension is at first physical in the background and then psychological in the foreground, where the inner consciousness of Christian souls breaks through. However disquieting, mental reactions to the newborn are by far more valuable than pointless action. It is perhaps a sign of wishful thinking that Leonardo let Jesus come to life in a barren environment symbolic of faith's open and humble future.

7

In humanist terms, ideology was spatially located on a perspectival grid that made contextuality predominant. In the Christian foreground of the *Adoration,* instead, space unfolds around single figures. Neither recession nor planimetry are clearly drawn. As a matter of fact, figures are piled up in a way closer to Gentile da Fabriano than to Masaccio. The volumetric bodies parcel out space and unify it through emotional intensity; the city of man stands behind that of God. Because it is split between faith and rule, space turns into a fit location for the equally divided origins of Christianity. Greek teachers educated the Church Fathers, and Hellenistic thought played a role in the dissemination of the new religion. Hence, the canvas foregrounded Christian concerns—from Paul to Augustine—that tested the relationship between law and faith.[29] In terms of the perspectival metaphor, knowledge as sight yielded to knowledge as belief.

The aimlessness of ancient riders in the *Adoration* breaks up the perspectival order, as if to heighten the fracture between spiritual power and physical vigor. A wedge was drawn between different concepts of spatial unity. We have learned from Erwin Panofsky that the medieval "law of disjunction" separated classical forms from classical subject matter, before Mantegna would join them into "stable compounds." Yet reintegration of form and content did not foster faithful renditions of classical space. In Mantegna's ancient stories, in fact, the centralized focus of linear perspective replaced the multifocal fragmentariness of classical space. The ancients had neither known nor pursued geometric homogeneity. Leonardo probably sensed it and fractured the system of linear perspective also to remind us that fifteenth-century space was a *naissance,* not a *renaissance.*

The perspectival metaphor became a battleground for clashes between mythic and rational concepts of space. The first is a place where live events unfold, where emotions prevail over measurements, and where objects do not have to conform to lines and planes. That break is clear in the division between the pagan front and the Christian rear in the *Adoration.* In the background, spatial and architectural measurements no longer dictate a rational mode of being to men and animals unleashing the powers of instinct. While they seem to be slipping on uncongenial pavements to the left, rearing horses are more at home on natural dirt at the opposite side.

Even architectural stability brings up the dual nature of ruins, which date antiquity after antiquity itself. Displacements of that sort were innate to the very concept of renaissance, which thrived on anachronism. Leonardo acknowledged the "symbolic" relevance of linear perspective the very moment he found it necessary to outgrow it. Perception made claims against intelligibility, and the perspectival fracture in the *Adoration* let random actions disregard the order of construction. The famous perspective drawing for the painting (Fig. 12) shows a centralized plan that was abandoned; stylistic consistency yielded to spiritual truth. Since it demands that any form of activity be visible, how could the geometric space of linear perspective utter faith and despair in moments of bewilderment, contemplation, or uncertainty? Kenneth Clark's epigraph to this chapter nails Leonardo's dilemma between deliberate and intuitive concepts of space at a time when Donatello's relief of the *Miracle of the Irascible Son* (1446–50) set a spatial fracturing appropriate for the theme of Saint Anthony healing the broken leg of a young man.[30] For Mantegna, the abrupt foreshortening of his *Dead Christ* (after 1466) symbolized violence. And so did the break in the perspectival structure of the Leonardesque picture.

The past spends its last energies on the geometric stage of the *Adoration,* where actions elude classical and humanist calls for restraint. Peo-

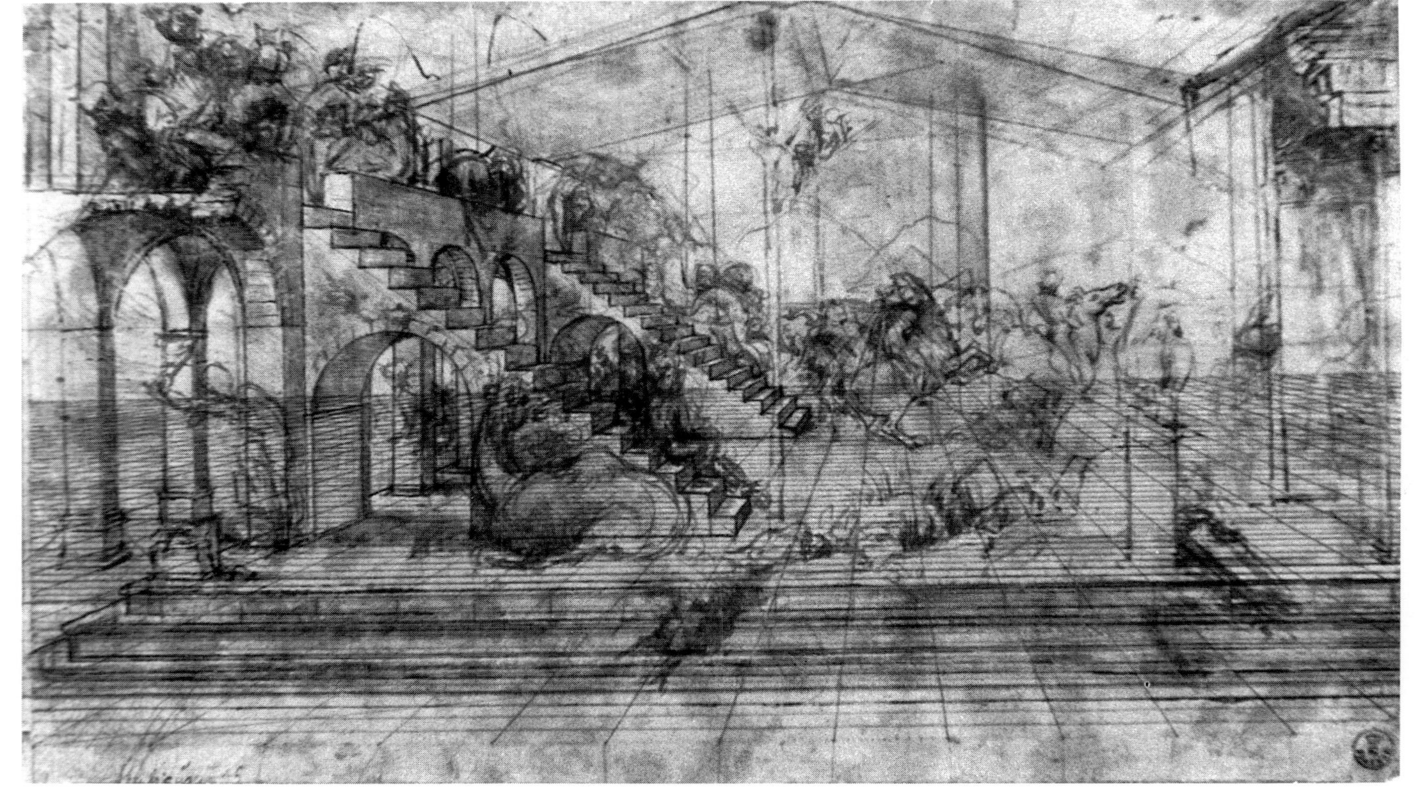

FIG. 12.   Leonardo da Vinci, *Architectural Perspective for the Adoration* (c. 1481) Gabinetto dei Disegni e Stampe, Uffizi, Florence

ple and animals carry out the dismemberment of an age that had lost its measure. While Alberti gave new life to the Pythagorean notion that "man is the measure of all things," Leonardo pointed to the limits of rebirths, renovations, and attempts at setting the geometry of mental constructs at pace with the spirituality of Christian progress.

While Piero della Francesca conditioned time, space, and mankind to intellectual stability, people are emotionally alive in Leonardo's picture. With regard to man and nature, geometry was being replaced by dynamics, the new science that Leonardo applied to the idea of development of bodies and to the mutation that it caused in limbs and proportions.[31] That operative view affected nature and human conduct alike. The artist thus confronted a dilemma: how could geometric planes make existence possible in the *Adoration,* whose spatio-temporal coordinates fell beyond the rhetoric and rationality of humanist painting?

Since it thrives on systematic contrasts, the *Adoration* pits humanist against antihumanist values. The *istoria* is suggested but not developed, and mathematical space takes in the three-dimensional forms of the phenomenal world. While tradition lost validity, novelty remained vague in the mind of a painter who brought to art a vitality no longer compatible with the mathematical basis of perspectival representation.[32]

In varying degrees, clashes between system and perception would linger on throughout Leonardo's career. At issue was the concept of harmony, which could be defined either as quantitative measure and proportion or qualitative color, mood, and character. When faced with the difference between painting and sensory impression, Leonardo could blur the edges of the problem, but he could not make it vanish.[33] The forger could not master his own forging, but to no detriment of the *Adoration*'s form and content. Quickly, much of his dilemma became familiar to Giorgione and the Venetians, who also succeeded in finding glorious solutions for it.[34]

8

Because Leonardo's language was visual, but a language nonetheless, the *Adoration*'s perspectival fracture points to a break between means and ends in the rebirth of antiquity. The painting, in fact, tested the validity of allegorical structures that had served Christian translations of the classical past. Antiquity did not compel the moderns to draw practical lessons from either *aemulatio* or *renovatio*. Instead, juxtapositions, influences, and analogues could be drawn at will; as a result, the Virgin could be Diana, Minerva, or a beautiful nude born from a seashell. Botticelli was not alone in making figures at once ancient and modern. Neoplatonic images, André Chastel and E. H. Gombrich have taught us, often were replete with obscure meanings. Through allegorical means, invention slowly steered toward aesthetic autonomy. And Donatello found it legitimate to put a modern hat on the biblical David, while Gattamelata was clad in ancient armor. At the peak of that trajectory, we find the "Apollonic Christ type."[35]

Because he realized better than most that linear perspective was modern, Leonardo could not be charged with allegorical anachronism. Since there was no ideal antiquity to fall back on, he exposed *imitatio* and exploited *aemulatio*. Antiquity could not be modernized without distorting both past and present.[36] Matters of incongruity, however, could be interactive. Christianity was born in the Middle East, and much of it was Greek-speaking in the early days. From the Graeco-Roman world to Arabic-Spanish experiences, history fed on the migration of ideas. And the *Adoration* gave visual form to a fracture in one of those transitional stages.[37]

While the composition recedes toward a charismatic point of order at the center of the *Adoration,* human actions in the background have broken free of ideological unity; their centrifugal pull seems to draw from the breakdown of narration. Leonardo did not present the past under the triumphant banner of Caesar or Constantine, but at the sunset of its own self-consumption. Mantegna was careful to link the utopian symbolism of perspective to moments when classical grandeur reached its cultural best. Because he saw phenomenal processes rather than "chosen moments," Leonardo could not ignore the life of instinct lurking in the twilight of a culture whose achievements had waned toward Stoic endurance.[38] In the modern fiction of W. H. Auden, Herod wonders why "legislation is helpless against the wild prayers of longing." There is no answer, but Herod knows that reason, law, and the "Poetic Compromise" of mythic tales no longer would hold the world together. The pagan can only resort to prophecy: "Reason will be replaced by Revelation. Instead of Rational Law, objective truths perceptible to any who will undergo the necessary intellectual discipline, and the same for all, Knowledge will degenerate into a riot of subjective visions" (*The Massacre of the Innocents*). Herod's words could indeed stand as a commentary on the ideological fracture that Leonardo painted in the *Adoration.* Beyond analogues of plenitude, history could prove to be a nightmare in which obscure forces presided over progress and survival.

Since the perspectival framework is modern, such a reading would seal
the Leonardesque continuum past-present-future into a common destiny
that was bound to stage humanity's betrayal of any savior.

Leonardo's earlier *Annunciation* (see Fig. 10) turned back toward an
angelic "source" that would order events yet to unfold. The image is
peaceful because it is imbued with the bliss of an epiphany about to affect
a single soul but still far from touching crowds. Although an earth-
shaking event, the nativity of Christ illuminated hearts, but did not ap-
pease baser instincts. The adoration was but a bright moment within the
overarching darkness of foreground and background in the Uffizi picture.
Because it promised to lead mankind out of ungodly shadows, Christianity stirred wonder around the serenity of mother and child. Much against
classical and medieval traditions, Leonardo paved the way for Machiavelli when he pointed out that violence and disorder are natural to the
human condition. Both of them would suggest that any demand for moral
integrity in a chaotic world amounts to self-deception.[39]

Focusing on more theoretical grounds, Raphael's *School of Athens*
(see Fig. 54) gave visual form to the Platonic belief that "the knowledge
at which geometry aims is knowledge of the eternal," since geometry
"will draw the soul toward truth, and create the spirit of philosophy"
(*Republic*, 527). Conversely, Leonardo tested the Platonic and Neoplatonic symbolism of intellectual perfection against human demises that
are scattered throughout history. To confirm his foresight, Borgias and
Sforzas would teach him lessons consistent with opportunistic pursuits.

9

Albertian narration called for knowledge of the past. The very rhythm of
invention had to be set at pace with the recovery of completed events.
Because they demanded conformity and shunned novelty, *istorie* restricted the expressive order of the human mind. As a theorist, Alberti
followed the dictates of *ut rhetorica pictura,* which assumed that the
linear clarity of discourse would set standards adverse to any probing
individualism.

Because it relied so much on *imitatio,* the humanist *istoria* preceded—
and conditioned—artistic choices. Yet it could not be denied that Piero
della Francesca, Castiglione, and Raphael found that structural mode
congenial to their artistic makeup. From rebirth to revival, the Renaissance at large drew strength from looking backwards. To a great extent,

progress was a renaissance of antiquity.[40] And many humanists believed that recovery of the past took precedence over explorations of the future, just as any creative activity had to be kept within the perimeter of a Ptolemaic frame of order.

Once Leonardo appeared on the scene, modes of expression that stemmed from historical learning were set against the uncharted pursuits of an artist who never tired of testing the limits of his own freedom. Notes and sketches brought up forms of an eruptive mind that often found it difficult to cope with its own dynamics. The historian has been compared to the geologist insofar as the facts of history are perceptible only by the vestiges which they have left behind. The modernity of Botticelli's *Adoration* must have struck Leonardo as credible. Its historical authenticity, however, was deficient; neither could it be mitigated through the camels and black Magi that Mantegna added to his own *Adoration of the Magi* (1464). Long before the modern historian, Leonardo realized that reality at its fullest could be expressed neither by speech nor by writing.[41]

Even as demonstrative a painting as the *Adoration* offered insights into the workings of a mind whose investigative bent brushed the very concept of completion aside. We shall never know what it could have been. But we can guess that originality would have clashed with the drawn-out fastidiousness of execution. From the start, Leonardo's art did not body forth ameliorative solutions to a problem; instead, it shaped the very forms of the problem. He did not focus on the purposiveness of humanist narrativity, but on the spatio-temporal interactions of antihumanist probings that are still challenging our understanding. We might as well agree that the *Adoration* could not have been better than it is.

Archetypes of Beauty

4

At the Spring of Memory:

The *Virgin of the Rocks* and the Lure of the Source

Does not every civilization as it approaches or recedes from its full moon seem as it were to shiver into the premonition of some perfection born out of itself, perhaps even of some return to its first Source?

—W. B. Yeats

It was in Milan that Leonardo painted the *Virgin of the Rocks* (Fig. 13), which unlocked an approach to landscape unknown to either Piero della Francesca or Mantegna.

The earlier *Adoration* (see Fig. 8) had set the divine epiphany at the awe-inspiring divide between paganism and Christianity. The *Virgin of the Rocks,* instead, nestled faith in nature. Christ already has a follower, and the Virgin shelters them by means of a gestural act that exudes maternal care. Faith is represented in its infancy, which is about to become doctrine at the threshold of history.

Once again, a sequential recurrence seems to emerge among Leonardo's works.[1] While he has come to rest amid classical artifacts and decorative details in the earlier *Annunciation* (see Fig. 10), the angel stands by the Virgin on less "civilized" grounds in the Louvre picture. By pointing toward the Baptist, his gaze and finger suggest a transcendental "before"; he is the carrier of a beginning before time. While human landmarks are absent, his hand bridges the distance between prophecy and history, a function which the Baptist himself was to carry out in

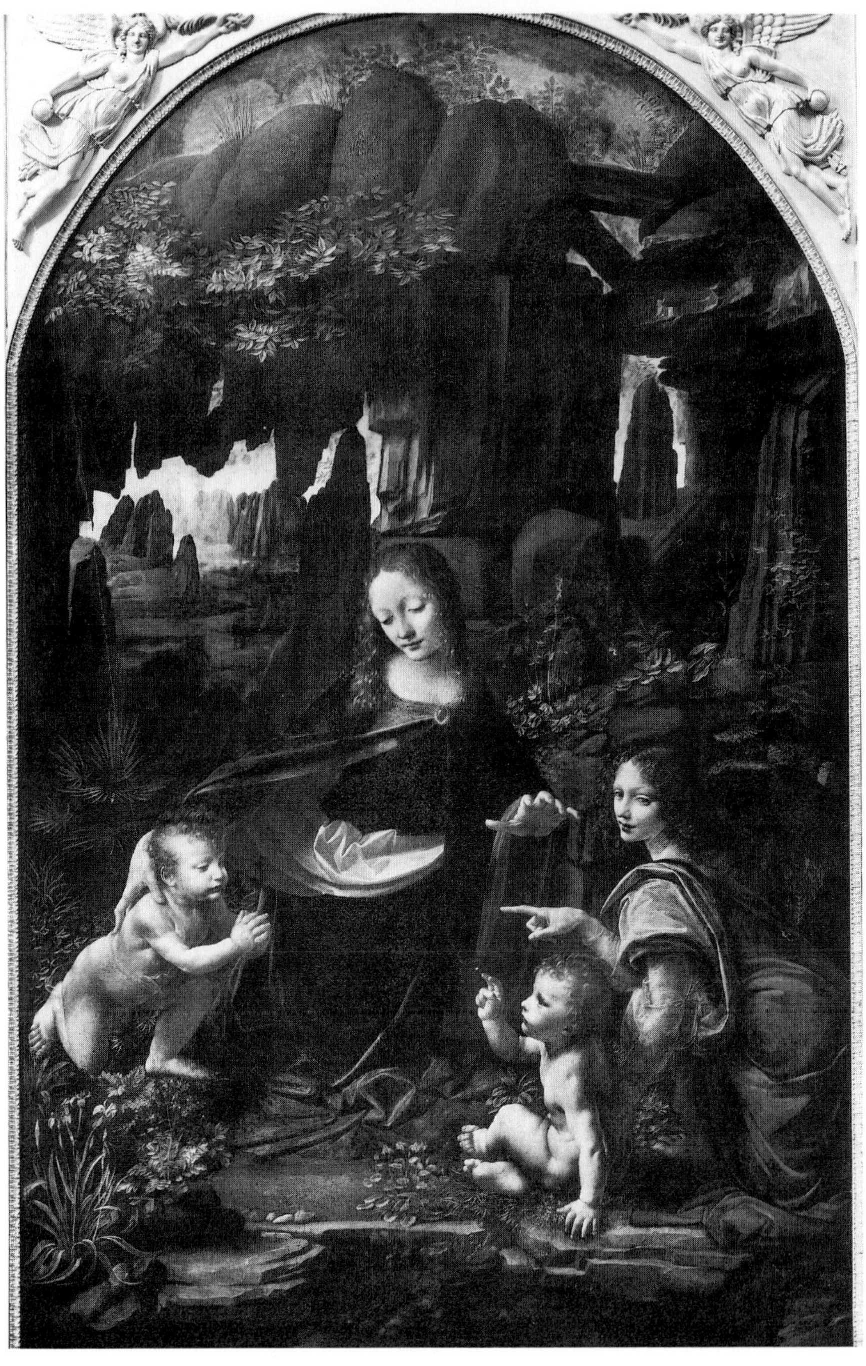

FIG. 13. Leonardo da Vinci, *Virgin of the Rocks* (1483–86)
Louvre, Paris

biblical texts and Leonardesque paintings alike. Having already announced the Savior's birth to the Virgin, the angel points to John in order to lead us toward the herald of spiritual growth.

The *Virgin of the Rocks* links the future of Christianity to the hopes and deeds of two growing children. Their ritual gestures seem to aim toward an appointed destiny. Foreknowledge rests with "agents" of Christian mythology, namely the angel and the Virgin. Life's experiences, instead, are handed out to adolescents who assert an air of hopeful freshness against the "retrospective" mode of humanist priorities. What emerges is an image of origins that lets humankind partake in the Baptist's worship of the infant Christ. Iconography therefore traced contacts between John and Jesus back to childhood. They shared physical traits that set parallels in motion. From the two versions of the *Virgin of the Rocks* to the Burlington House cartoon, John and Jesus would not part company. Like Jesus, John proclaimed the kingdom and threatened opponents with the wrath of Judgment. Like Jesus, he was refused belief, and the cross that he traditionally held in his hand forewarned Christ's own martyrdom. Absence of historical objects behind the human group points to a barren space that John would colonize with a new covenant of disciples.[2] He was the bridge between Judaism and Christianity.[3] Emphasis therefore lies on intuition and relationships, which Leonardo would foreground again in the *Last Supper* and the Louvre *Madonna with Saint Anne*.

The archetypal enclave in the *Virgin of the Rocks* is set in a landscape of primeval beginnings. While her suspended arm is forever ready to shelter every child yet to be born, the Virgin's hand is about to reach out and lead us toward the new kingdom. Placed as she is behind the two infants, the Holy Mother pushes the rise of Christianity toward the foreground, where viewers are to inherit a spiritual future. And we might as well take Dante Gabriel Rossetti's poetic *ekphrasis* as a lead into Leonardo's pictorial image of the source:

> Mother, is this the darkness of the end,
> > The Shadow of Death? and is that outer sea
> > Infinite, imminent Eternity?
> > > (*Madonna of the Rocks*)

2

Leonardo's complex system of space representation no longer could take the vanishing point as a symbol of infinity. Instead, light, color, and matter actually "vanish" in the farthest background of the *Virgin of the Rocks,* whose ageless depths disintegrate Christian stories and geological millennia. Space therefore shapes itself into forms of archetypal memories as layered as man's own sense of "origin." Such a visual nomenclature could describe instants in terms of points, length, quantity, and "the space of time" (916), which we now call geological time. Beyond the reach of human-bound experiences, the background reveals an ever more barren image of the primeval brew of life: light, water, and rocks. They all form a boundless landscape that is plausible but not real.

Leonardo painted layers of rocks that rushed in a new awareness of geology, to which he made scientific contributions. His notes on the presence of marine fossils in the Alps tested the Deluge theory. Long before it became clear to Nicolaus Steno (Nils Stensen), Leonardo understood that fossils were remains of organisms which slow changes in the earth's surface had washed away from their natural habitats. Biblical chronology faltered, and so would later attempts to add floods that made lands sink in excess of what the original two hundred days of rain could warrant.[4] Adjustments of that sort were undertaken to justify the thickness of sediments and the large size of shells.

Rocks emerge from the water like solidified waves in the Louvre painting. They absorb light, crystallize moisture, and offer soft spots for the growth of plants that shed beauty on the birth of Christianity. Conversely, the arch-cave leads us back toward the womb of biological growth. We plunge amid a kind of lunar geology beyond the dawn of human history.[5]

For Leonardo, space lays out images of life through their evolution since primordial times. The *Virgin of the Rocks* created a kind of organic view of depth whereby landscape turned into "timescape."[6] In Goethe's words, the picture could visualize "facts which have a sensuous basis yet are not visibly perceptible, so that imagination, memory, and understanding may be stimulated to fill in what is missing." Actually, "the further one advances in experience, the closer one comes to the unfathomable,"[7] which was archetypal for the artist. Leonardo knew the difference between the past of mankind and that of nature: "Since things are far more ancient than letters, it is not to be wondered at if in our days there exists no record of how the aforesaid seas extended over so many countries."[8] Much of his life was spent in reading a cosmic textbook in which human events could amount to no more than spurious notes. Because of his imaginative approach to science, Leonardo could look back toward the dawn of life. Sight was knowledge, which meant observation.

Around the Arno Valley, in fact, there had been two lakes, "the first of which is where we now see the city of Florence flourish together with Prato and Pistoia." Early in the day of geological creation, "the peaks of the Apennines stood up in this sea in the form of islands surrounded by salt water" (McCurdy, 333, 340). Since landscape was a matter of presence and origin alike, the natural sciences became philological instruments of inquiry just as effective as Valla's method of linguistic investigation.[9] The book of nature offered Leonardo "sources" even more distant and just as authoritative as the classical texts Petrarch had learned to unearth from under the symbolism of medieval incrustations. Knowledge as either *techné* or intuition was at stake. A kind of teleological parallel seems to emerge if we compare the way Leonardo looked at seashells in the Alps and the way Charles Darwin would look at sea turtles on the Galápagos Islands. Both of them could trace geological and biological changes. Both of them responded with a sort of poetic sensibility to the staggering mutations that forms have undergone in order to pay tribute to the resilience of life's own vitality. Yet, while Leonardo settled with a study of the present in relation to the source, Darwin took origin as a step toward evolution. By dint of some kind of anthropological memory, Erwin Panofsky has linked Piero di Cosimo's images of early human history to evolutionist theories. Such a bizarre "world seems fantastic, not because its elements are unreal, but, on the contrary, because the very veracity of his interpretation is convincingly evocative of a time remote from our potential experience. His pictures emanate a pervasive atmosphere of strangeness because they succeed in conjuring up an age older than Christianity, older even than paganism in the historical sense of the word—in fact, older than civilization itself."[10] Whether through memory or intuition, the artistic range of the age contextualized Leonardo's primeval images.

3

Concerns with sequence and simultaneity led Leonardo to draw organic and inorganic temporality into a single view. As our eyes move toward the background of the *Virgin of the Rocks,* spatial recession is hard to measure, much as perspectival means break open into what John Pope-Hennessy has called a mindscape of eternity. The artwork depicts one of those rare moments of synthesis when the time of history and the immortality of myth test each other along the lifeline of generational—and generative—cycles.

Since matters of beginnings are central to the *Virgin of the Rocks,* its symbolism draws from the classical topos of the "source," which stood as a common point of origin at the convergence of the earth's rivers. At that mythic juncture, the Dionysian element of moisture kept the nourishing matter of creation amid primeval waters.[11] The pre-Socratics introduced the idea of a generative fluid that Thales identified with water and Anaximander linked to the boundless. Christian commentators refer to a regenerative abyss that nurtured the Fountain of Life, which gave rise to the four rivers of the world (Gen. 1:10–14). From Spenser to Milton, much Renaissance literature made use of that iconography. Whether they were controlled by divine will or human ingenuity, waters could bestow life-giving powers or burst into biblical floods, and Leonardo himself set the *Deluge* sketches against plans for the drainage of marshes.[12]

In the footsteps of Plato (*Phaedo*) and Virgil (*Fourth Eclogue*), the pastoral world of Sannazaro's *Arcadia* updated the theme of the source in the description of Ergasto's dream, which put into words much of what Leonardo would paint in the *Virgin of the Rocks:*

> At last we came to the cavern whence all that water issued; and from that one then to another whose vaulted walls, as I seemed to apprehend, were all made of rough pumice stones. . . . The Nymph who was guiding me . . . made me pass further on to a place more broad and spacious, where many lakes were visible, many springs, many caves that poured forth water, from which the rivers that run over the earth take their first beginning.

At the source, Ergasto is shown the mysterious wholeness of a hydrologic cycle crucial to the unity of all things:

> O marvellous handiwork of almighty God! The earth, that I thought was solid, encloses in its womb so great a hollowness! Then did I begin to feel no amazement at how the rivers should be possessed of such abundance and how with unfailing current they should keep their courses forever.[13]

The interdisciplinary *ekphrasis* has drawn paganism and Christianity into a place where poets trailed after natural forces, Virgilian voices of reason, and the powers of faith: "All streams run to the sea but the sea is not full; the place where the streams flow, they flow again" (Eccles. 1:7). By the time fifteenth-century art colonized Arcadia, *naissance* and *renais-*

sance could hardly be sorted out in the primordial cavern, whose rocky walls had never been inscribed with either names or pictures.

From literary to philosophical texts, Leone Ebreo's views about generation and the beginning of life also edged on archetypal paraphrase: "The nexus of procreation is clearly exemplified by the offspring of the elements. Observe what things are generated in the regions of air by vapours risen from earth and sea. . . . Plants, grasses and trees so love earth," which, "like a tender mother, not only brings them forth with great affection and love, but is ever careful to nourish them with her own liquors, drawn from her entrails to the surface . . . the seed received by earth from heaven is dew and rain."[14] Images and functions underline a rather Leonardesque integration between man and nature. While the topoi of source and river affect concerns with origin and originality, words and images point to a metaphoric geography replete with cultural symbols.[15] And Coleridge would call the sacred river that ran through caverns measureless to man Alph, which is the first letter of the Greek alphabet (alpha). In *Kubla Khan,* therefore, language itself gave validity to the coexistence of source and river.[16]

Since antiquity, searches for fluvial wellsprings have tested the range of the human mind. To know the river is to know the history of the world, and to know the source is to know the very secret of nature. Creation thrives on the encounter of water and light, which energizes matter. By so doing, the One becomes Many, and generation turns the shapeless into the shapely. To keep at pace with fluvial symbolism, the downstream journey from source to river would take us from the archetypal *Virgin of the Rocks* to the historical artifacts of Giorgione's *Tempest.*[17] Both painters took up the turbulence of air and water in literary and pictorial representations of *fortune* and *tempeste.* Yet thunder and lightning could not strike at the other side of the Leonardesque archcave, which sheltered the undisturbed radiance of a primordial twilight.

At the outer edges of the horizon, Leonardo found a life-giving power that "is infinite together with time" (McCurdy, 381, 506–7). Nature's vitality, therefore, was as immaterial as the spiritual force that had been born to humanity in the foreground of the *Virgin of the Rocks.* Correspondences of that sort can be multiplied once we turn to Leonardo's notes. If force is infinite, "weight is finite together with the weight of the whole globe of the terrestrial machine." Beyond rocks and plants, the new landscape of the spirit could endure time through generations that would be inspired by the Baptist's prophecies and blessed with the Virgin's maternal care. Quickly, primeval waters would serve for baptismal immersions at the start of journeys toward purification. Nature's archetypal source in the background of the painting became spiritual in the foreground, where Christ stood as the second fountain of living waters. At the well, he announced to the Samaritan woman: "but whoever drinks of the water that I shall give him will never thirst, the water that I shall give him will become in him a spring of water welling up to eternal life" (John 4:14). The *Virgin of the Rocks* made room for the chronotopic range of natural growth and human becoming. Leonardo's own infinitives would describe the artwork as a synthesis of *preimaginare* (*e lo imaginare le cose che saranno,* imagining the things that are to be) and *postimaginare* (*e imaginare le cose passate,* imagining the things that are past, 839). Language gave representation power for acting out its own potential; definitions opened up to the unfolding of phenomena.

4

Time stems from eternity in the *Virgin of the Rocks,* whose foreground yields to the gravity of human bodies. The ageless vitality of nature is set behind that of faith. At once, the artwork is an image of concreteness and of spirituality. The angel's pointing finger magnifies the symbolic distance that separates John from Christ, marking yet another measure of *preimaginare* and *postimaginare.* One is incarnated in the Baptist's hands, which are clutched in expectation; the other is beheld in the Child's blessing gesture, which confirms that prophetic hopes have come true. Etymologically, the word *angel* means "messenger" or "runner." The Baptist himself was a messenger of the Lord's coming. He was the athlete of virtue whose running toward Christ came to rest once the Child himself took his first steps toward the future.[18] It is as a runner, in fact, that he appears in Luca Signorelli's *Madonna and Child with Saint John the Baptist* and the Doni *Holy Family* by Michelangelo (see Fig. 24).

Childhood also emphasizes beginning. And so does iconography, since the Church celebrates only three nativities; those of the Virgin, Christ, and the Baptist. Throughout the Middle Ages, symbolic commentaries such as Honorius d'Autun's *Speculum Ecclesiae* (twelfth century) noted that the birth of John diminished the time without Christ, whose own birth started the Christian calendar.[19] Actually, the saint's nativity was set at the summer solstice (June 24), when the day begins to shorten; and that of Christ at the winter solstice (December 25), when daytime again begins to lengthen.[20]

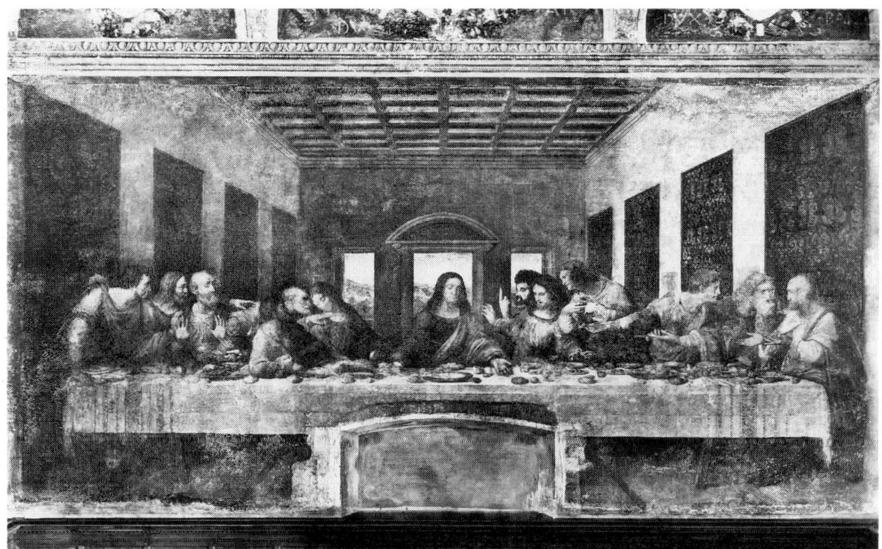

FIG. 14.   Leonardo da Vinci, *Last Supper* (1495–97)
Santa Maria delle Grazie, Milan

In light of Leonardo's pictorial mythology, the symbolism of the angel's pointing hand was to reappear with Thomas in the *Last Supper* (Fig. 14), Saint Anne in the cartoon with the Virgin and Child, and finally *Saint John the Baptist.* Kenneth Clark is unequivocal on the originality of the heavenly creature: "That angel is quite different from the obedient, decorative angels of the fifteenth century." Leonardo did not see angels as "guardians, but intermediaries."[21] In the guise of a willful intermediary, that angel is qualitatively different from its Leonardesque peers; one is obedient in the *Annunciation,* and another is aimlessly inspired in Verrocchio's *Baptism of Christ.*

Leonardo drew inspiration neither from Piero della Francesca's angels (*Baptism of Christ*) nor from the array of musical angels in northern Italian paintings from Mantegna to Giovanni Bellini. Instead, the Louvre angel is a symbol of activity to be sustained after Christ's birth. From a gestural point of view, we near the heartbeat of Leonardo's philosophy, which assumes that "movement is the cause of life" (McCurdy, 72). Because it deals with bodies in motion, painting is philosophy: "Weight and force always desire their death, and each is maintained by violence" (McCurdy, 506). Leonardo made an axiom of Aristotle's statement in his *Ethics:* "Man is worthy of praise and blame solely in respect of such actions as it is within his power to do or to abstain from" (McCurdy, 65–66). It is action that delimits knowledge and assigns responsibility in the *Virgin of the Rocks*. Actions unfold in time, and images of human experience stretch out toward the future. So framed, the angel's pointing finger signals the trajectory of relationships that infancy promises to consume for a long time to come.

At its most intuitive, Leonardo's pictorial language gave plastic form to what F.W.J. Schelling was to consider the overriding principle of Christianity, which "has no perfected symbols but rather only symbolic *acts*. The entire spirit of Christianity is that of action. . . . To the extent that the *church* viewed itself as the visible body of Christ of which all individuals are the members, it constituted itself through acts . . . and its cult a living work of art, a kind of spiritual drama in which each member had a part."[22] The *Virgin of the Rocks* is an image of the Church incarnated into human forms of ritual.

Beyond the ecclesiastical corruption and cultural anachronism denounced from Francis of Assisi and Dante to Savonarola, the Leonardesque array of painterly gestures purged spiritualism of secular rhetoric. Only through a return toward some form of archetypal purity would art lead people back to the source of Christianity, whose incarnated mythology spoke a visual language of faith at its interhuman purest.

To better evaluate the open thrust of the angel's gesture in the Louvre picture vis-à-vis humanist canons, we ought to turn to a detail in Donatello's equestrian statue of Gattamelata (Erasmo di Narni, Fig. 15). The horse is rooted on the pedestal. All lines are checked against each other and within a tightly drawn design under the willful control of the rider, who enforces a configuration of intellectual solidity. Not to disturb that effect, the sculptor has placed a ball under the hoof of the animal's front leg. Criticism tells us that such a detail was an ironic device meant to pay homage to the Medicis, since Gattamelata may have helped the Florentines more than the Venetians. However slightly raised, the horse's leg points to some kind of movement uncalled for in a funerary monument meant to glorify the atemporality of fame. The leg raises fractions of time that had better been left lapsing. Iconographic expediency aside, the sculptor needed to exhaust time and energy into a foreclosed design that would block any lingering act.

For Aristotle (*Physics* 2.2.193b, *Metaphysics* 1.8.989b), mathematics produces abstract figures that can be separated from motion, and nothing that is derived from mathematics moves. Those statements were dear to humanist aesthetics. By contrast, the angel's pointing hand in the *Virgin of the Rocks* holds before and after in the antihumanist flow of

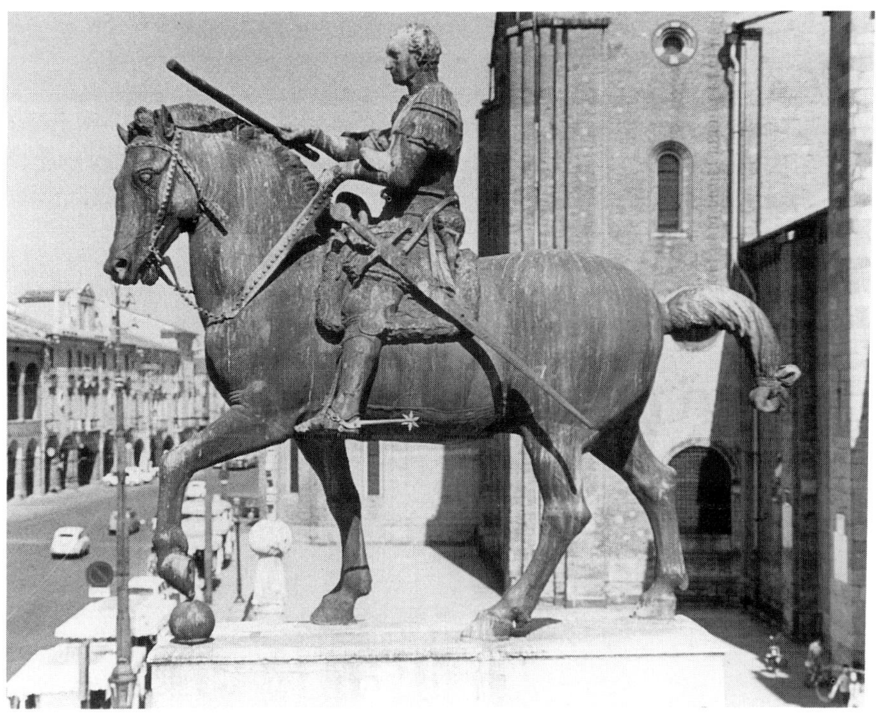

FIG. 15.   Donatello, *Gattamelata* (1443–53)
Piazza del Santo, Padua

human interactions. And Leonardo would let the Baptist himself point toward heaven in his last painting; "before" had been spent, and "after" would soon take leave of time.

5

Consistent with their utopian ideals, the humanists created a metahistorical realm immune to process. Concepts of *imitatio, renovatio,* and *aemulatio* acknowledged history as a field of choices in which matters of spiritual affinities could not make room for change. Their search for certainty yielded theoretical models of universal validity. So framed, reality was narrowed to visual presence, which was presumed to resemble what the ancients themselves saw.

Because his pictorial range extended beyond antiquity, Leonardo could reach back toward what had been visible at the very beginning of time. The early *Annunciation* (see Fig. 10) flaunted cultural layers that foregrounded the ambiguous coexistence of Christian mysteries and pagan markers. The Virgin herself seems to be caught in a rather unsettling pose. Since she sits by a lectern much like a humanist scholar in a strangely "open" *studiolo,* revelation is scaled down to a timid intrusion; space lodges learning more than faith. Ambiguities of that sort are gone in the *Virgin of the Rocks.* The angel points to human divinity as an act, while the divinity of nature springs from some soil we shall never walk on.[23] Beyond history and archaeology, the background opens to unsettling forms that fade into nebulous shapes.

Better than most, Leonardo knew that time is progressive as well as cyclical. Since it thrived on what historians call the coexistence of temporal multiplicity, the *Virgin of the Rocks* made possible the copresence of geological rock formations in the background, biological rhythms of flowers and grass in the foreground, the adolescents' fast-paced growth, the metaphysical sign of a pointing angel, and the Virgin's maternal stand at the edge of spirituality.

In the beginning, nature was different from what it would become, and Leonardo painted his landscape of origins by drawing on geological imagination. Visually, the primeval background of the *Virgin of the Rocks* had to appear other than any space anyone could be familiar with. Yet the artist never relented from trying to bridge the gap between forms of origin and the morphology of existence. He saw lakes where Florence stood and mountains where water had been predominant at earlier times. He therefore brought a scientific frame of mind, if not a fully thought-out method, to the forms of mutation. Yet his daring competence in the field of geology became guarded at the threshold of human history. He was more at ease in finding the master key to changes in the depths of nature than inside the human mind.

6

Postimaginare and *preimaginare* stretched temporality into webs of outreaching exchanges. Since the texture of life is innately polyphonic, each event is a landscape of activities whose diversity the magic of art can somehow hold together. Leonardo's paintings are disquieting also because of their interactive simultaneity. He had to lodge the origin of life within and amid a cluster of unrelenting tensions.

Time and space converge to a vanishing point in the background of the *Virgin of the Rocks,* where the solid world of forms melts into the moisture of creativity. Such a time-defying process fascinated Leonardo: "Between water and stone in equal quantities are an almost infinite number of different grades of weight . . . so there will be pure water, the water with a very small quantity of earth in it, and then this is increased little by little until it forms mud, and then this mud becomes more solid, and at last it becomes solid earth" (McCurdy, 310). Slowly, this passage seems to distill words into the geological formation of stalactites and stalagmites. At an equally primordial level, the arch-cave shelters the inner recesses of nature. By the same token, the imagination becomes a gate through which Leonardo leads us toward as archetypal an image as one could find for the principle of cosmic generation from the One into the Many. At that *Ur*-point, "this earth seeks to lose its life, desiring only continual reproduction" (1219).

What counts is the beginning, where the cycle reverts back to its cause. The old poet wrote that air never

> Ceases to be engendered off of things
> And to return to things, since verily
> In constant flux do all things stream.
>   Likewise,
> The abounding well-spring of the liquid light,
> The ethereal sun, doth flood the heaven o'er
> With constant flux of radiance ever new
>   (Lucretius, *De Rerum Natura* V)

All forms of life, Leonardo echoed, long to return to the "primal chaos" and their "source" (McCurdy, 75); the very concept of life thrives on those dynamics. Criticism has told us that the beginning might have been a cloud; certainly, it was no single point of origin. In the words of the modern poet, nature's beginnings present *"moins des montagnes que des instruments à créer le monde, pures idées au matin de la Création, dans cette eau qui a précédé le matin!"*[24] In light of such precedents, the *Virgin of the Rocks* seems to foreground the ontological emergence of form.

However unaware of the ancient myth, Leonardo's concept of the source was quite analogous to the Demogorgon myth that Leone Ebreo updated at the end of the quattrocento: "Chaos was the eternal companion of God, that it was created by Him from all eternity and that God created all other things freshly out of that Chaos at the beginning of time. . . . It is said that the first issue of Chaos was strife, because what first issued from first matter was the distinction of things, which lay therein indistinct, and were made distinct at birth by the hand and power of their father Demogorgon. This attainment of distinctness is called Strife," which first causes "a disturbance in the womb of Chaos."[25] We are reading about the generative organism of Leonardo's *potenza-forza,* which was pre-Socratic at heart.

Plutarch noted that the etymological meaning of chaos in Hesiod's *Theogony* ("In truth then foremost sprang Chaos") refers to water pouring out in a space where creation unravels. At the farthest point of recession in the *Virgin of the Rocks,* we find water and moisture, that is to say, Leonardo's original indicators of chaos. At the source, therefore, matter exists in the shapelessness of a liquid state. We are looking at the primeval "mist" or "vapor" (*aer*) of atmospheric cycles of condensation and separation. At that juncture, Leonardo echoed the doctrines of philosophers who thought that everything is derived from air and water. At the source, the Milesian cosmology of Thales and Anaximenes found that nature and origin are the same. And so did Plato, speaking of natural philosophers with whom Leonardo would have associated.[26] In the wake of Parmenides and Lucretius, he paid equal attention to natural beginnings and human psychology. Science tied him to the present, but art led him back to myth. He was out to discover the way things had come to be.

Longings of that sort gained strength from Leonardo's concept of *forza* (force), whose anthropomorphic description does not discredit scientific relevance. Force

> constrains all created things to change of form and position, and hastens furiously to its desired death, changing as it goes according to circumstances. When it is slow its strength is increased, and speed enfeebles it. It is born in violence and dies in liberty; and the greater it is the more quickly it is consumed. It drives away in fury whatever opposes its destruction. It desires to conquer and slay the cause of opposition, and in conquering destroys itself. . . . Without force nothing moves. (McCurdy, 520)

At the spring of hope and memory, Leonardo did not place analogues of godlike beauty, but the self-consuming powers of life in the process of staging its own heroics. Life is action, and action is performance. A "life well used brings happy death" (McCurdy, 67) only when human commitment has spent all available strength.

Michelangelo followed tradition when he created Adam as a younger God whose life and destiny are charted out at birth. The beginning itself offers a complete explanation.[27] At the beginning, Leonardo did not find unflawed brightness, but the energy of creativity. The source is not an illumination, but a mystery. We could guess that the absence of pagan deities in his work signaled a rejection of Olympian cosmology as something less than original, if we accept the idea that the Olympians ruled by right of conquest rather than by right of birth. It is more likely that Leonardo would have turned back to the pre-Olympian mythology of chaos, earth, and Eros. Because it thrived on becoming, his source was Orphic at heart.[28]

Even Heraclitus set the uniqueness of the Primal One beyond men and gods: "The ordering, the same for all, no god nor man has made, but it ever was and is and will be: fire everlasting. . . . The death of fire is birth for air, and the death of air is birth for water" (Frags. 37, 91, 92). Since it could not be authored, chaos exceeded the restrictions of the humanist frame of mind. Hence Leonardo's "primal chaos" would be taken as neither the opposite of cosmos nor as a logical construct necessary to establish concepts of order. Chaos does not define matter before Creation, but before division into the plurality of specific forms. For Claude Lévi-Strauss, in fact, myth is lodged between undifferentiation and differentiation, that is to say, between disorder and order. Traditionally, disorder has been linked to disturbance, turbulence, and fluctuation, whose mythic relevance points to the role that the flood has played in mythology.[29]

Leonardo's own *Deluge* sketches (see Fig. 40) refer to the disintegration of reality before chaos would stir renewal. Visually, we edge on the demise of mimesis. Whirlwinds shatter the last remnants of form long before similar fragmentations would occur in oceans closer to modern shores. Visually speaking, a parallel emerges with Turner's vortex at sea in *Snowstorm: Steam-boat off a Harbour's Mouth* and on land in *Snowstorm: Hannibal and His Army Crossing the Alps*. Life and history collapse into swelling curves of force that test their own destructive vitality. The vortex stands as a node of self-regenerative force that twists power from within itself, as it does with equal prominence in Leonardo's water studies. In both artists, the vortex seems to energize the very core of chaos, which identifies the transformational source of birth and death. In one breath, we look at beginning and end, at the creative "betweenness" of archetypal contrariety.[30]

After Lucretius had presented chaos as the brewing matter of potential becoming (*De Rerum Natura* V), Pico della Mirandola insisted that "chaos means nothing other than matter, full of all forms, but confused and imperfect."[31] Later, Milton found womb and grave intertwined without length, breadth, and height. Chaos is where "Time and place are lost" (*Paradise Lost* II, 893–94). On matters of origin, therefore, ancient and modern loyalties to the finite completeness of cosmos were set against the unbounded creativity of chaos.

7

As an artist, Leonardo understood that figures of discursive order failed to do justice to natural forms whose expressive power was other than rhetorical. Their "origin" and character were not anthropomorphic. It is with such concerns in mind that we ought to approach Leonardo's interest in chance images:

> I cannot forebear to mention among these precepts a new device for study which, although it may seem but trivial and almost ludicrous, is nevertheless extremely useful in arousing the mind to various inventions. And this is, when you look at a wall spotted with stains, or with a mixture of stones, if you have to devise some scene, you may discover a resemblance to various landscapes, beautified with mountains, rivers, rocks, trees, plains, wide valleys and hills in varied arrangements; or again you may see battles and figures in action; or strange faces and costumes, and an endless variety of objects, which you could reduce to complete and well drawn forms. And these appear on such walls confusedly, like the sound of bells in whose jangle you may find any name or word you choose to imagine. (508)

The passage begins with "things" but ends with names and "words"; problems of translation and completion trade originality for accessibility.

Leonardo's *machie* paved the way for nineteenth-century interests in the texture of African marble, which ignited Vittorio Imbriani's pictorial idea of the *macchia*. For a critic like Benedetto Croce, *macchie* do "not exist objectively in things,"[32] but are equated with the moment of artistic intuition. Yet such pictorial ideas are drawn neither from myth nor history, but from the very textures of visual matter. Human deeds notwithstanding, nature can prompt imaginative reconstructions of itself.

Gaston Bachelard would suggest that the blot is "the rough sketch of unrestricted dreams."[33] Dreams can produce completed forms, but blots do not; in a way, they are chaotic kernels, from which a range of forms could spring. The pictorial mode of chaos, therefore, is other than the anthropocentric order made in the image of man and measured by man-made standards.

Chaos is not anthropocentric, but biocentric, in that it contains the matter of creation as an energy whose formal potential is not man-measured at all. Long before the Darwinian turn of mind took root, Leonardo refused to lodge the beginning into the human-like simile of a subject at the source (as Michelangelo did with his *Creation of Adam*). Instead, he recognized a force yet to yield to human criteria of selection and arrangement.[34] Hence, beauty and ugliness would be undifferentiated, for the One would in fact be a composite unity apt to generate all forms.

It is on matters of creation and renewal that Leonardo updated Heraclitean concerns with the thirty years' cycle, "when nature returns from human seed-time to seed-time" (Frag. 95). There we find the etiology of life at its nuclear core, where birth and death struggle to overcome one another. The source of life is not a point of beginning, but a stage at which tension does not halt continuity.[35] Leonardo foresaw a point in time when fire would reduce the surface of the earth to ashes (1218). Yet nature would survive, taking pleasure "in creating and making constantly new lives and forms. . . . Because she knows that her terrestrial materials become thereby augmented, is more ready and more swift in her creating, than time in his destruction. . . . This earth therefore seeks to lose its life, desiring only continual reproduction" (1219). The earth's "spirit of growth" (1000) would outlast doomsdays. Likewise, the creational power of seeds is bound to survive even in fable form: "The ant found a grain of millet. The seed feeling itself taken prisoner cried out to her: 'If you will do me the kindness to allow me to accomplish my function of reproduction, I will give you a hundred such as I am.' And so it was" (1270). In terms of expression, that kind of biocentric art tends to be nonverbal. It does not attempt to speak a man-created and human-based language, but one that would do better justice to the natural world as such.

Leonardo himself confronted anthropomorphic and biocentric points of view:

> Painters oftentimes deceive themselves by representing water in which they render visible what is seen by man; whereas the water sees the object from one side and the man sees it from the other;

> and it frequently happens that the painter will see a thing from above and the water sees it from beneath, and so the same body is seen in front and behind, and above and below, for the water reflects the image of the object in one way and the eye sees it in another. (McCurdy, 906)

We only need to add that there are notes in which writing frames and explains a drawing of the same subject matter. As a kind of twofold signature,[36] verbal description and visual image coexist. Leonardo seems to have anticipated a Nietzschean dilemma: "Is the world really beautified by the fact that man thinks it beautiful? He has *humanized* it, that is all. But nothing, absolutely nothing, guarantees that man should be the model of beauty. Who knows what he looks like in the eyes of a higher judge of beauty?" (*Twilight of the Idols*, 19). Biocentric art could indeed claim aesthetic legitimacy for nonanthropomorphic criteria of beauty. Nonverbal forms of expression would favor images over words, so as to do away with metaphorical meanings. For Leonardo, *disegno* brought forth biocentric utterances. The eye's visual language is drawing. Since it is not merely anthropomorphic, design "is not only a science but a deity whose name should be duly commemorated, a deity which repeats all the visible works of God the highest" (McMahon, 102). Because it can be at once anthropomorphic and biocentric, drawing displays a godlike range.

By extension, painting alone could represent "the forms of nature's works with more truth than does the poet. The works of nature are of much more value than are words" (McCurdy, 31). Painting is the only vehicle of expression for representing the source, the boundless, or any archetypal principles of creation. The humanist analogue man-God centered on the deity as a sculptural maker; Leonardo, instead, would have turned to Leone Ebreo: "For Chaos, once more becoming pregnant with the divinity, gives birth to material substances" that undergo "generation and corruption" in the corporeal world.[37] Chaos was the source where the cornucopian creativity of birth forever outnumbered losses to death. That myth had to be artistic as well as scientific. Whether seed or blot, "origin" had to have a form at once real and mythological.

8

Leonardo's antihumanist frame of reference was mythic. Eugenio Garin has called attention to the influence that astrological works such as the

Picatrix—originally known in Arabic and then through Spanish and Latin translations—had on fifteenth-century culture from Pico to Ficino. At one point, Hermes discusses the "hidden secret" of nature: "When I wanted to reveal the science of the mystery and of the processes of creation, I found a dark cave, full of shadows and winds. I could not discern anything because of the darkness."[38] We can easily move to Leonardo's cave:

> For a time I remained stupified, not having been aware of its existence, my back bent to an arch, my left hand clutching my knee, while with the right I made a shade for my lowered and contracted eyebrows; and I was bending continually first one way and then another in order to see whether I could discern anything inside, though this was rendered impossible by the intense darkness within. And after remaining there for a time, suddenly there were awakened within me two emotions, fear and desire, fear of the dark threatening cavern, desire to see whether there might be any marvellous thing therein. (McCurdy, 1127)

Confrontation heightens the fact that man *gives* meaning to the cave. The mystery of nature is not a Lucretian "given"; instead, it depends on human *sperienza,* whose probings make the unknown relevant.[39] For Aristotle, Leonardo's posture would have been at once mythic and philosophical, since it courted the wonder of the unknown: "He who loves myth is sort of a philosopher too; for myth is composed of wonders" (*Metaphysics* 928b). Superior individuals are discoverers and stand as interpreters between mankind and nature, whose mystery is similar to that of art; both of them depend on human ingenuity.

Had Leonardo been able to peek into the distant depths of the cavern, he might have come to face first causes and primal potency. Perhaps he would have discovered that he had already painted the human-bound forms of what Heraclitus has called a "hidden harmony" (Frag. 116) in the *Virgin of the Rocks,* whose landscape nestled art, truth, and myth.

Beyond the last threshold of mimesis, Carl Jung has told us, we find "a boundless expanse full of unprecedented uncertainty, with apparently no inside and no outside, no above and no below, no here and no there, no mine and no thine, no good and no bad. It is the world of water, where all life floats in suspension; where the realm of the sympathetic system, the soul of everything living, begins; where I am indivisibly this *and* that; where I experience the other in myself and the other-than-myself experiences me."[40] It could be the fluid landscape of primeval recesses we look at in the *Virgin of the Rocks*. It also could be the void that surrounds *Saint John the Baptist,* who reconciled otherness within himself at the threshold of an androgynous reunion. At the threshold, Leonardo's archetypes converged toward the source. There, his forms of mythic wholeness were sheltered beyond the divided experiences of human history.

5

Saint John the Baptist:

The Androgynous Watchman of Eternity

*The trouble with humanism is that man as God remains man,
but there is an extension of man, the leaner being, in fiction, a
possibly more than human human, a composite human.*
—*Wallace Stevens*

Having given form to the primeval source in the *Virgin of the Rocks*, it was inevitable that Leonardo would look for an image of human origin as well. Archetypal wholeness, Mircea Eliade has taught us, took a human guise in the prehistory of *coincidentia oppositorum*, which rested on the unity of the One before fragmentation into the life of the Many.[1]

The Saffron-picker in the oldest wall painting of the Knossos palace in Crete is neither man nor woman; only the whole human being could pluck the mythic Herb of Life.[2] Once he inspired a portrait of androgynous sexuality, the symbolism of Leonardo's *Saint John the Baptist* (c. 1515, Fig. 16) touched on primeval experiences of unity and division that paganism shared with Christianity.

2

From an iconographic standpoint, Masaccio brought Jerome and the Baptist together in the left wing of the *Miracolo della neve* triptych,

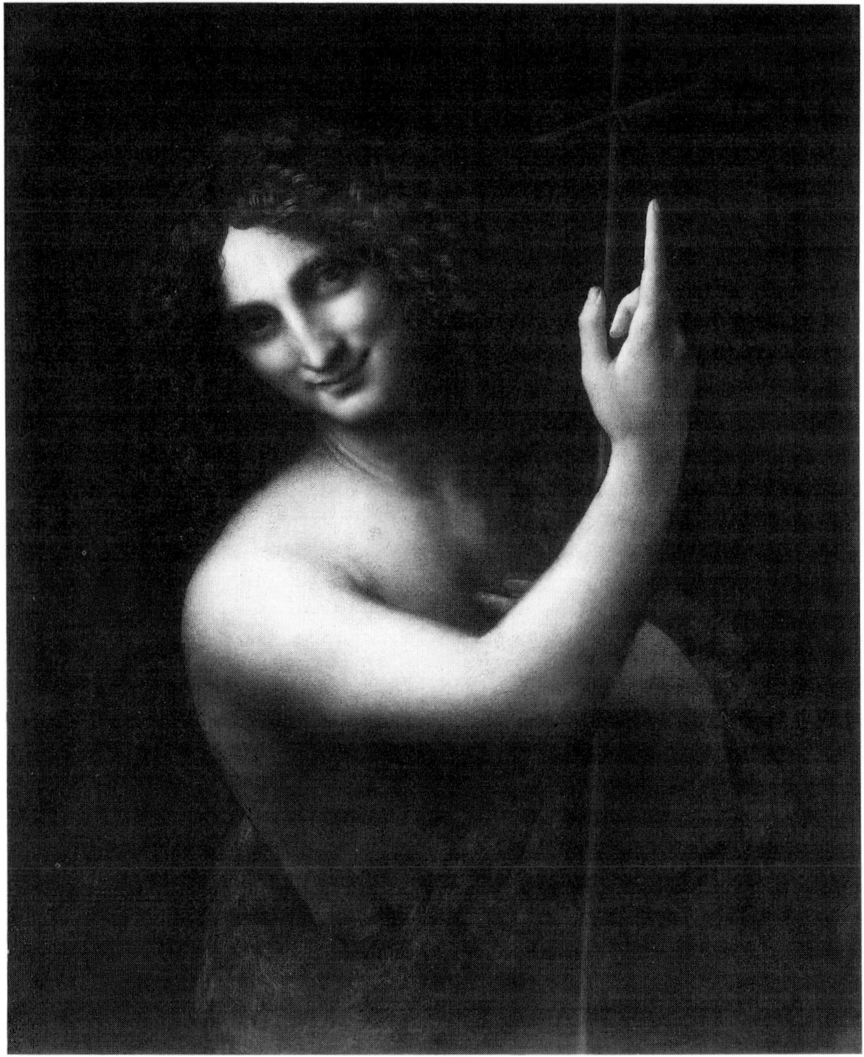

Fig. 16.   Leonardo da Vinci, *Saint John the Baptist* (c. 1515)
Louvre, Paris

whereas Domenico Veneziano painted *Saint John the Baptist in the Wilderness* (predella panel of the Saint Lucy altarpiece) as a rather classical nude. In Leonardo's picture, wiry hair and pelt establish John as saint and wild man. There are no doubts about his familiarity with a medieval tradition that was prominent around the Alps and in Lombardy,[3] where certain footmen were "undressed to try on some costumes of wild men" (1458) for a festivity that Leonardo arranged in honor of Galeazzo San Severino. Even the heir to the throne of France wore a wild man's costume in the tragic "Dance of the Wild Men" held at the French court near the end of the fourteenth century. That vogue was bound to prosper even though one of the flaxen costumes caught on fire, dancers were burned to death, and the prince himself was nearly killed.[4]

Paradoxically, the wild man is at once a figure of synthesis and separation, so much so that medieval writers were split between his humanity and his animalism. Classical and medieval sources, however, emphasize John's solitude, which betrayed a contempt for both agricultural and urban life-styles. As a prophet, he held up the faith of the cross; as a wild man, he abstained from social comforts. At all times, he scorned historical experiences.

Along the final divide of Leonardo's life, the symbolism of the Baptist drew from a tradition that took wildness to tap the more pristine aspects of Christianity. Because he was placed in a pictorial void that denied nature as well as history, the Baptist's stark appearance betrayed a human divestiture. The adolescent's lifelong journey achieved its goal. At the end, he embodied the prophet of spiritual Oneness, who appeared in the guise of androgynous unity.

Michel Foucault would suggest that Leonardo's insistence on the figure of the Baptist takes up concerns with the unique nature of human origins. It is "always against a background of the already begun that man is able to reflect on what may serve for him as origin." He falls back on "the already-begun of labour, life, and language." Matters of origin cannot escape historicity. "Far from indicating the moment of the Same at which the dispersion of the Other has not yet come into play, the original in man is that which articulates him from the very outset upon something other than himself."[5] Dualism is intrinsic to John's physical ambiguity; and it is extrinsic inasmuch as the cross heightens his dialogic relationship with Christ. As a prophet, John identified the goal of his life with the coming of the Savior, who would fulfill aspirations too burdensome for anyone else to carry out. In that sense, his finger does not point toward an "end," but toward reintegration.

3

On matters of man's origin, Michelangelo's *Creation of Adam* on the Sistine ceiling presents a male mythology. Although the first man stands for mankind, his sexual identity is explicit. In the Platonic myth, instead, unity rests with the original coexistence of male and female attributes in a bisexual body: "The sexes were not two as they are now, but originally three in number; there was man, woman, and the union of the two, having a name corresponding to this double nature, which had once a real existence, but is now lost, and the word 'Androgynous' is only preserved as a term of reproach" (*Symposium* 190). That race revolted against Zeus, who split it into male and female; they diminished in strength and increased in number. Yet memories of primordial unity did not vanish, and longings for it lingered on.

Above names and forms, even sexual divisions are bypassed in the Louvre picture.[6] We could therefore face the Cosmic Man, a mythic figure that the Kabbala called Adam Kadmon, the universal Man. The unfallen androgyne is the cosmic inscape of an anthropomorphic unity independent of natural settings. A spatial void, in fact, sustains androgynous symbolism in the Leonardesque painting.

On the Sistine ceiling, Michelangelo painted the Cuman Sybil (Fig. 17), whose breasts are the only sign of femininity in a massive body whose other features are otherwise masculine. Her prophetic power seems to draw from a mixture of male and female attributes. We cannot but think of the mythic Tiresias, whom T. S. Eliot set "Throbbing between two lives / Old man with wrinkled female breasts" (*The Waste Land* iii). Because of his more complete human experience, he could foretell the future. On aesthetic grounds, Johann Winckelmann so assessed antiquity's pervasive concerns with androgynous-like forms: "This ideal consists in the incorporation of the forms of prolonged youth in the female sex with the masculine forms of a beautiful young man, which they consequently made plumper, rounder, and softer. . . . For to some of these the ancients gave both sexes. . . . This commingling is especially peculiar to Apollo and Bacchus." The result was a whole spectrum of "equivocal beauties" strikingly evocative of the Leonardesque Baptist.[7]

At the end of the fifteenth century, Leone Ebreo so worded the original unity of the human being:

> It is indeed true that Man is an image of the whole universe, and therefore the Greeks called him "microcosm," which means "little world." However Man, as indeed all the higher animals, includes male and female, but in the Hebrew tongue, which is the mother and source of all other languages, Adam, which means man, connotes both male and female, and its proper meaning covers both alike.[8]

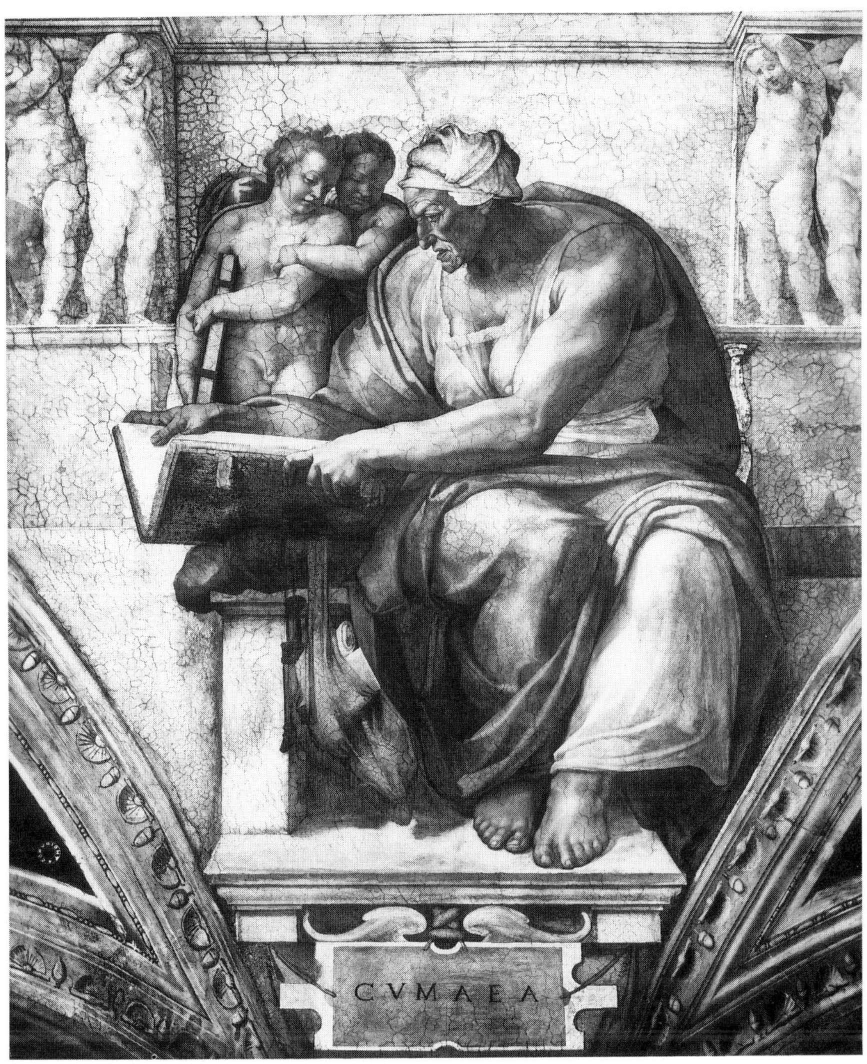

FIG. 17. Michelangelo, *Cuman Sybil* (1508–12)
Sistine Chapel, Vatican, Rome

Allegorical wisdom (*sapienza allegorica*) consists in the ability to see union amid division, and vice versa. Even Castiglione wrote that, "as one sex alone shows imperfection, ancient theologians attribute both sexes to God: hence, Orpheus said that Jove was male and female; and we read in Holy Writ that God created man male and female in His own likeness" (*Courtier*, 216). If one were to choose a face for the androgyne, Leonardo's *Saint John the Baptist* would indeed bear on humanist and classical attempts at "reuniting our original nature, making one of two, and healing the state of man. Each of us when separated, having one side only, like a flat fish, is but the indenture of a man, and he is always looking for his other half" (Plato, *Symposium* 191). The recovery of one's lost half was central to Heroet's *Androgyne,* a sixteenth-century adaptation of Aristophanes' fable in the *Symposium.* Platonic myth and Mosaic tradition were reconciled by means of allegory, which exploited the scriptural ambiguity of Genesis accounts.[9]

Visually, we ought to consider Leonardo's reconciliation of male-female and pain-pleasure in *Allegory of Virtue and Envy* (Fig. 18). In a study for *Madonna and Child with Saint Anne* (Fig. 19), profiles are sexually ambiguous, and the juxtaposition of three heads at the bottom right wavers undecidedly between ages and genders.

Even Pico della Mirandola touched on the creation of man:

> It is not without mystery why God created man male and female. It is, in fact, the prerogative of the celestial souls to undertake simultaneously both the function of contemplating and dominating the bodies. . . . Especially among the ancient people, it was the custom, as we observe in the Orphic hymns, to designate by the terms "male" and "female" these two powers in the same substance, one of which contemplates while the other rules the body (*Heptaplus* II, 6).

Voicing the Kabbala tradition, Jakob Boehme placed the androgyne at the center of his anthropology in *Mysterium Magnum,* a commentary on the book of Genesis. Only a virgin-boy or a man-androgyne could be the image and likeness of God, and Adam was neither man nor woman before the creation of Eve. It goes without saying that Leonardo could hardly resist the challenge of giving a human guise to that mystery.

For some, the androgyne is the sex of prelapsarian purity. For others, he is the Adam from whom Eve has not yet emerged. Better yet, the androgyne is the first complete Adam before human generation started. Hence androgyny was a way out of biological reproduction. It was personality versus sexuality, that is to say, the maturity of a superior love no longer at the service of generation.[10]

If the drawing of the human fetus has become emblematic of unity at the beginning of life (Fig. 20), Leonardo's study of the human coitus

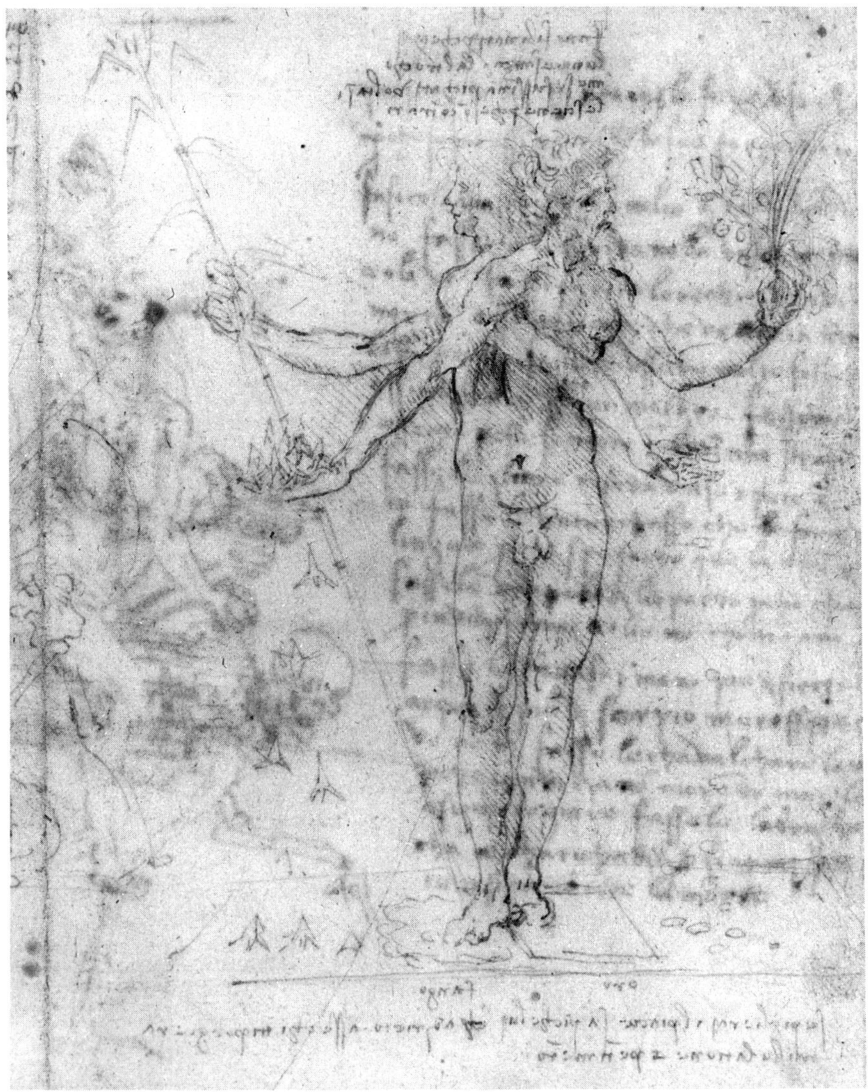

FIG. 18. Leonardo da Vinci, *Allegory of Virtue and Envy*
Library of Christ Church College, Oxford

(Fig. 21) is more than a scientific illustration. Although anatomically detailed, the image is cold and quite lifeless; it denies the vitality that is typical of his drawings of people, plants, and animals. Such a representation of the act that begins life could not claim a humanizing status. Yet it

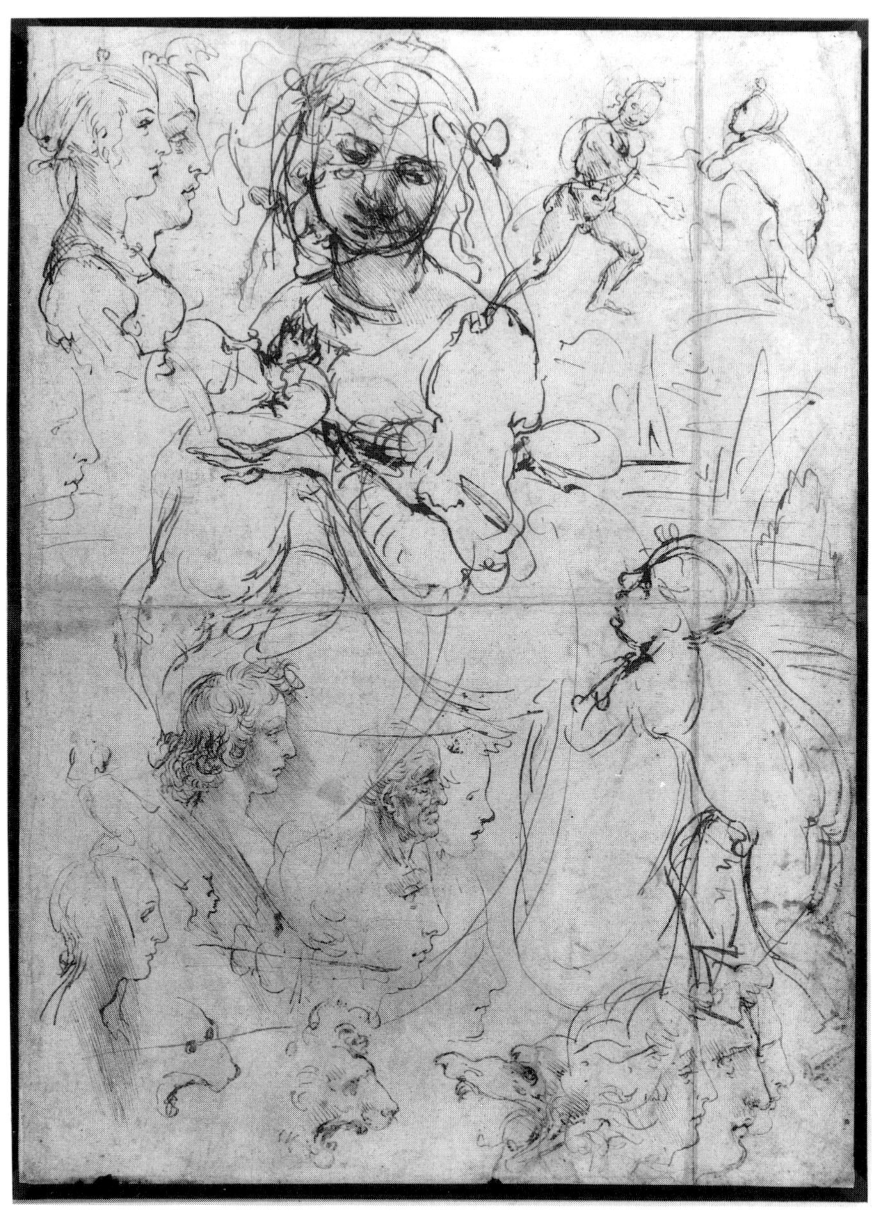

Fig. 19.   Leonardo da Vinci, *Madonna and Child*
Royal Library, Windsor Castle

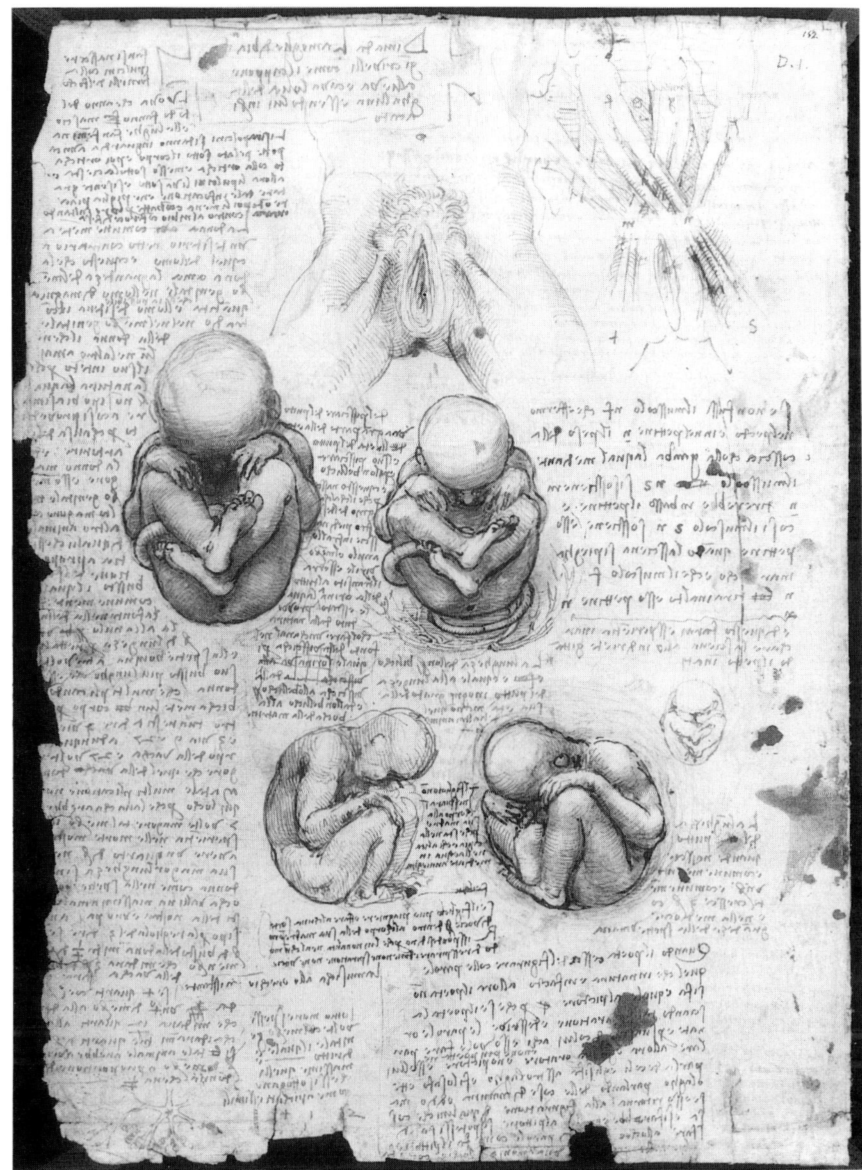

FIG. 20.   Leonardo da Vinci, *Fetus*
Royal Library, Windsor Castle

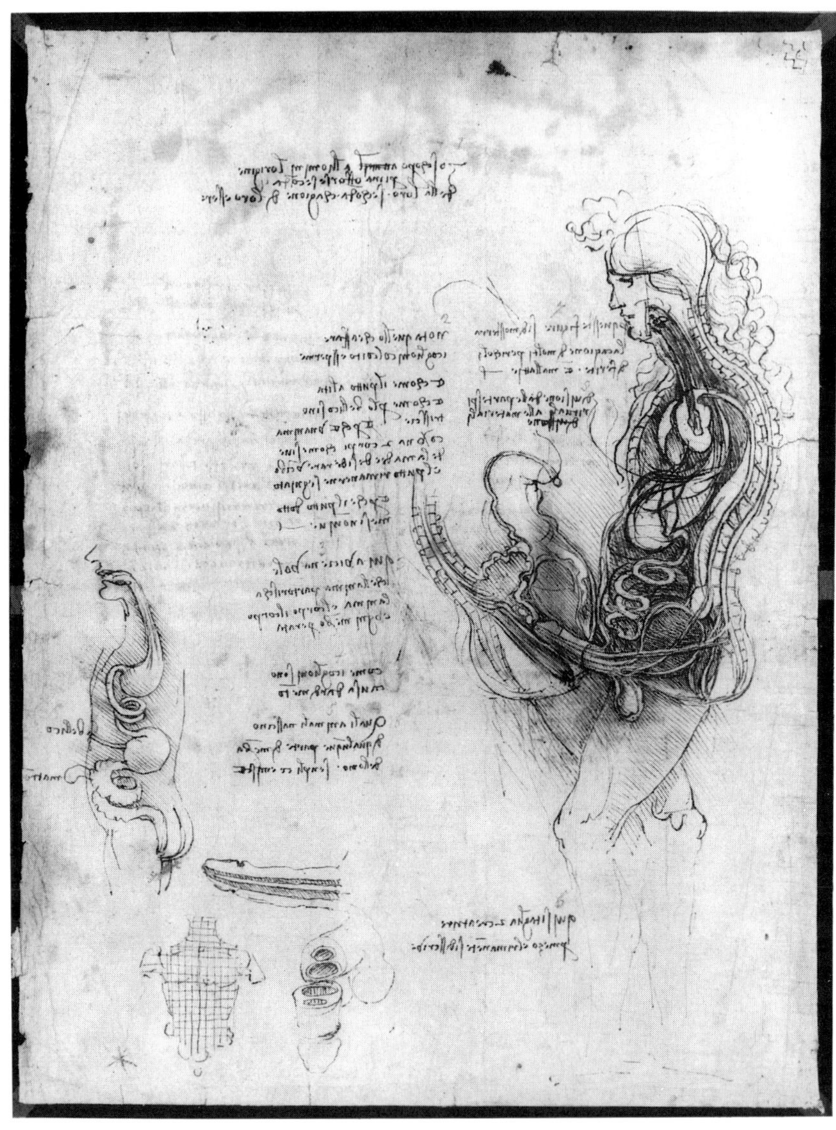

Fig. 21.   Leonardo da Vinci, *Drawing of Coition*
Royal Library, Windsor Castle

is an image of moral restraint, if we compare it to Leonardo's words: "The act of procreation and the members employed therein are so repulsive, that if it were not for the beauty of the faces and the adornments of the actors and the pent-up impulse, nature would lose the human species" (McCurdy, 97). Mechanism and impulse downgrade one another: "Lust is the cause of generation." And whoever fails to curb "lustful desires puts himself on a level with the beasts" (McCurdy, 90). The drawing scales down any sense of human belonging to biological functions. We look at anatomies without personality; the couple seems to share the same "icy" aloofness of the Vitruvian Man. They are creatures who have not been born out of love's wonder.

The philosophical underwriting to such a stand dated back to Aristotle's *Problems,* which were central to one of Castiglione's debates: "Why is it that a woman always naturally loves the man to whom she first gave herself? And why, on the contrary, does a man hate the woman he first enjoyed?" And, in giving the reason, he affirms that this is because in such an act the woman takes on perfection from the man, and the man imperfection from the woman; and that everyone naturally loves that which makes him perfect, and hates that which makes him imperfect" (*Courtier,* 217). Somehow, sexuality turned into a power struggle between the perfection of male form and the imperfection of female matter. Leonardo, instead, took sexuality out of philosophical concerns altogether. On biological matters, Matteo Palmieri would have approved of the coitus drawing inasmuch as it was "a most miserable, vile, and ugly act." It could be compared to nothing less than "a bestial game—*giuoco bestiale*"[11]—whose only justification was the welfare of the human species.

4

To borrow from William Blake, the Baptist stood for "a resurrection to Unity" after man's "fall into Division" (*Four Zoas* I, 4:4). Obviously, sexual difference had to be located in time and space, which Blake found to be male and female. From a Blakean perspective, the void surrounding John would point to Leonardo's final elimination of spatio-temporal differences.[12] As a result, the artwork was removed from the causality of phenomena for reasons that anyone even summarily familiar with the tradition of the *Corpus Hermeticum* would find sound. Its first book pins the androgyne's fall into division to the moment when he fell in love

with nature and was therefore split into sexes. By contrast, the painting
has left nature behind. A journey that had started amid the primeval
landscape of the *Virgin of the Rocks* came to rest by a void ready to take
in a fateful reunion.

It was in the *Virgin of the Rocks* that the angel pointed toward the
infant Baptist as a threshold figure with a mission vital for Christianity;
the hand underlined the earthbound thrust of a human story about to
unravel. The visual rhetoric of the angel *montreur* surged toward spirituality when it became the Baptist's own. A lifetime story thus came to a
resolution. To make such a sense of achievement complete, we ought to
turn to the arm holding the cross, which ended Christ's dividedness
between humanity and divinity. Furthermore, the cross brought forth a
process of divinization that stressed Jesus' passion. The Florentine iconography of the Baptist, in fact, had slowly changed. The early emphasis
on the baptism dated back to Leonardo's Florentine upbringing. Later,
however, relationships between children became more direct and emotionally charged. Leonardo responded to it through substitution; the
adolescent John became the sacrificial lamb in the painting with Saint
Anne, the Virgin, and the Child. When he painted the Baptist for the last
time, the cross emerged as the instrument of the passion. Since the heavenward parallelism of arm and cross kept John and Christ together, the
symbolic carriers of baptism, passion, and resurrection stood side by side
to the end. The myth thus bore on a return to what Meister Eckhart
would have called the "sheer pure absolute One, sundered from all
twoness."[13] Like Tiresias, the Baptist shared with mythic seers the ability
to see detail and context, inside and outside, parts and wholes. If we
accept the view that anatomy is destiny, then androgynous wholeness
also implied a prophetic overview of events seen from beginning to
end.[14]

5

The ambiguity of the Baptist's pointing finger also rounds out a "symbolic recurrence" in Leonardo's art, and more comments are in order.

To start with, a similar gesture was to be repeated in the canvases of El
Greco, and Rudolph Wittkower considers pointing a descriptive marker
of literary themes. In the *Baptism of Christ* (1614, Fig. 22), "the angel's
right hand, interpreted on the descriptive level, points to the Baptism; his
right arm and hand, interpreted on the level of rhetoric, make an ex-

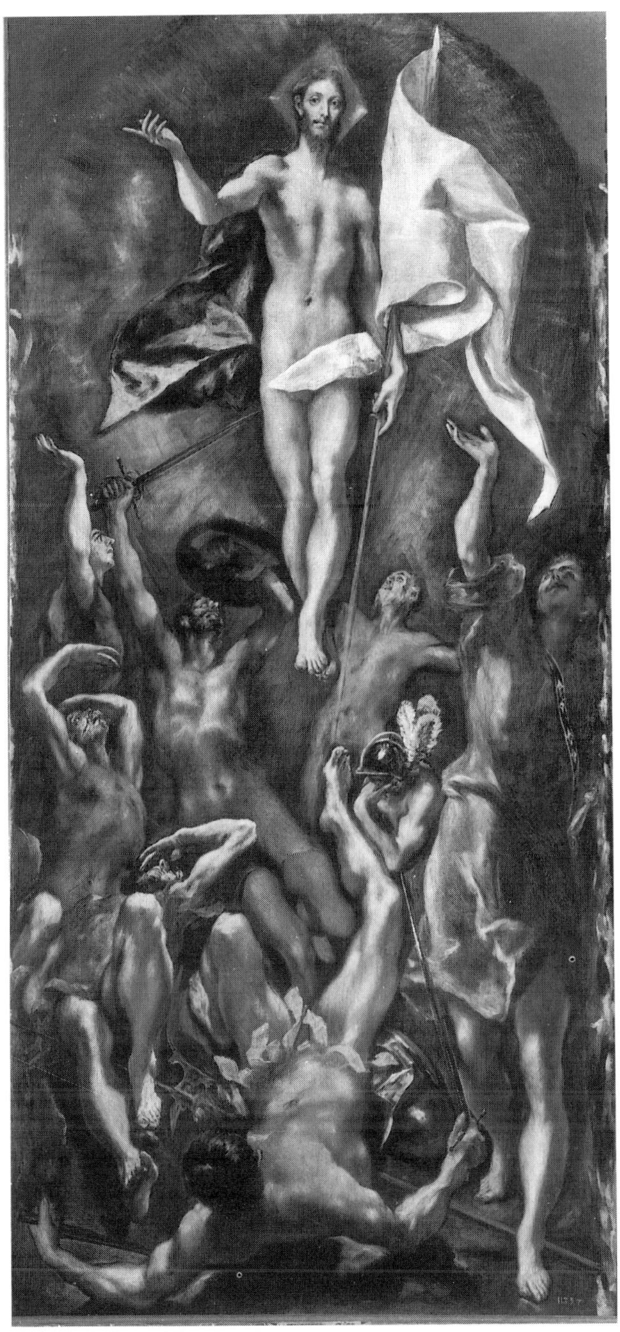

FIG. 22. El Greco, *Baptism of Christ* (1614)
Hospital of San Juan Bautista, Toledo

clamatory gesture, charged with emotion . . . both gestures seem to have also a symbolic meaning. The gesture of the pointing hand is that of recommendation and supplication,"[15] which is suggestive rather than demonstrative; emphasis is placed on prophetic ambiguity. Because it holds the cross, the Leonardesque symbolism of the Baptist's arm adds narrative significance to its elusiveness.

As a counterthrust to the sloping arms of Christ in Leonardo's *Last Supper* (see Fig. 14), Thomas's pointing finger steers the allegorical narrative toward mute forebodings of death. His gesture is decisive because it draws on foreknowledge. Like the Baptist, he does not doubt any longer, for his mind is already turned toward the afterlife. To find proof, he does not need to touch. Human betrayal in the Milan fresco shocks hearts and shakes bodies around the table. Its horizontal plane weighs on the earthbound, while food bears forth the ritual consumption of beginning and end; a foreshadowing of the Savior's own sacrifice and entombment. John and James back away, but Thomas leans toward Jesus. As a sign of betrayal, Judas's hand reaches for the bowl. That of Thomas, instead, points heavenward; he seems to know that he is attending a fateful event. "Last" therefore edges on a new beginning, whose radiance filters in through the open window. The very sacrament of the eucharist is about to take the past of Christ into the future of mankind's salvation. And the pointing finger marks an earth-shaking shift from the insecurities of the known toward belief in the unknown, from fact to faith.

To heighten the uplifting significance of the Baptist's hand amid the gestural iconography of Leonardo's paintings, we ought to turn to his allegorical drawing of Envy (Fig. 23), which presents an old and seminaked woman riding death and holding her right arm up with a clenched fist. Openness stands against closedness. The note explains that envy "must be represented with a contemptuous motion of the hand toward heaven because if she could she would use her strength against God" (677). Symbolism refers to man in the midst of earthbound struggles for predominance, and Envy's defiant gesture reminds us of earlier challenges by the Dantean Vanni Fucci as well as of mythic giants out to defy the deity around Babel. On matters of unity, the drawing to the right shows the twin figure of virtue and vice: "No sooner is Virtue born than Envy comes into the world to attack it; and sooner will there be a body without a shadow than Virtue without Envy" (677). The very emergence of human values entails dualisms. And the only way to overcome such divisions is to reestablish an androgynous state.

Whether in the form of El Greco's baptism or of eucharistic ritual in Raphael's *Disputa,* the mystery of transcendence was a revealed one for

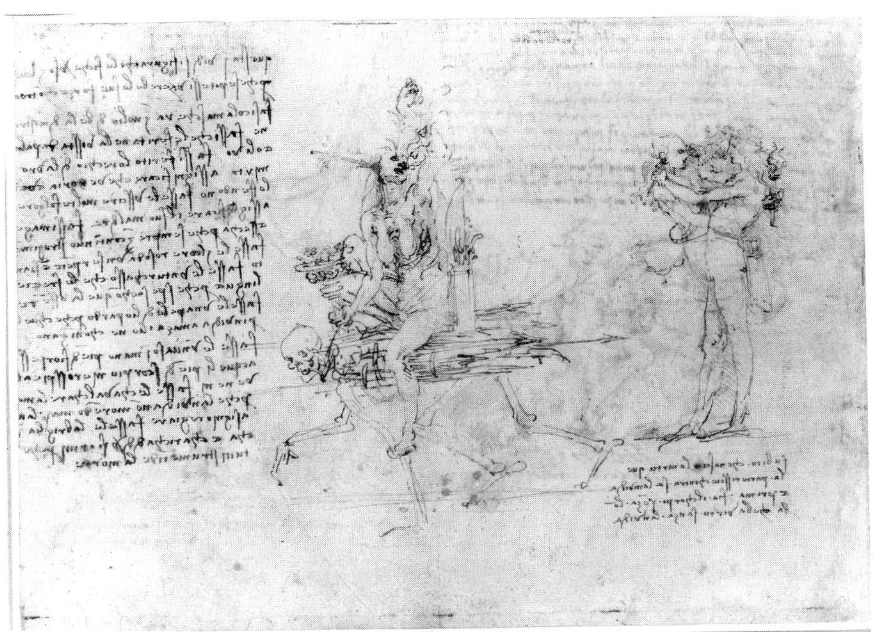

FIG. 23.   Leonardo da Vinci, *Envy*
Library of Christ Church College, Oxford

Christians who believed that the other side was where the best had
gained eternal bliss. The other side remained a realm whose forms could
not be visualized in Leonardo's last canvas. Rather than a symbol of
ethical preparation for the kingdom of God, the Baptist's gesture was
one of forthcoming deliverance, at once hopeful and obscure.

6

Leonardo followed tradition when he painted the Baptist as a wild man
with skinlike robe and wiry sheeplike hair. His bent for solitude and
prophecy was intense. The very fact that John was covered with, and
emerged from, an animal skin would point to the attainment of a higher
harmony of body and soul, which implied baptismal renewal and the
shift from Judaism to Christianity. In the wake of that tradition, Michelangelo put him behind a parapet that set the holy family apart from

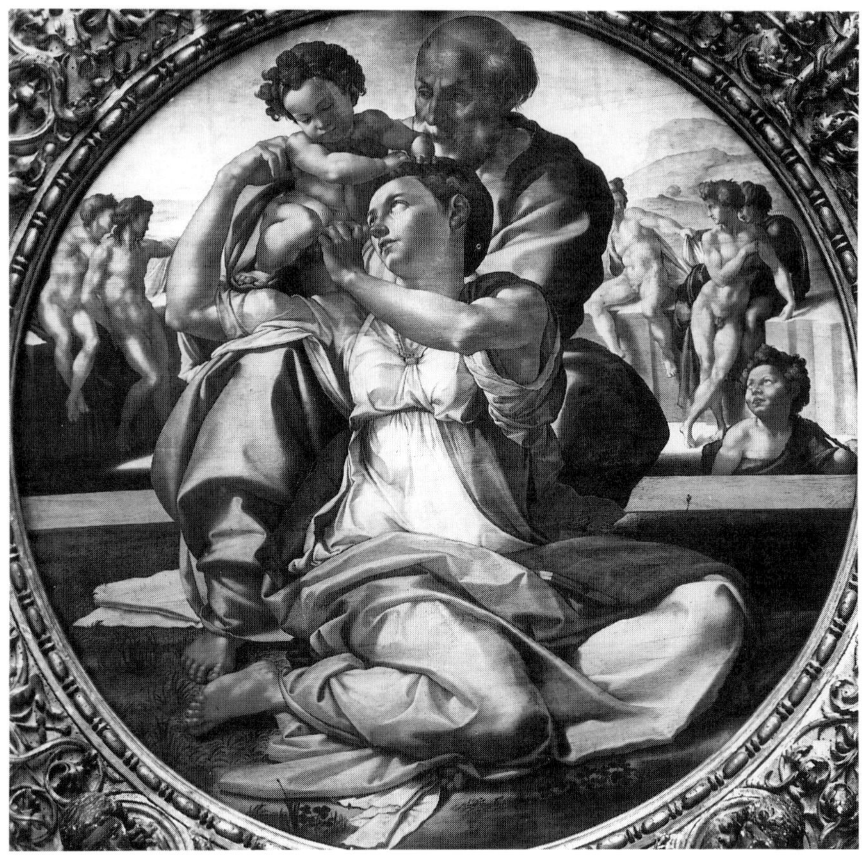

FIG. 24.   Michelangelo, *Madonna Doni* (1503?)
Uffizi, Florence

pagan nudes waiting to be baptized in the *Madonna Doni* (1503, Fig. 24). John did not uphold regressions to primitivism, but hopes of transformation.[16] It was in the wilderness that Christ faced temptations before the crucifixion. And it was in the harsh solitude of the Syrian desert that Leonardo painted Jerome's longings. Such a cluster of symbolic echoes came together in *Saint John the Baptist.*

After disturbing scenes of human drama in the *Adoration* and the *Last Supper,* the Baptist's hand at long last found the way of the spirit amid a darkness no longer bound to landscapes of reality. The pointing finger seems to initiate a gesture of divination. Giambattista Vico reminds us that "divinity" refers to *divinari* (to divine), "which is to understand what is hidden *from* men—the future—or what is hidden *in* them—their consciousness" (*New Science,* par. 342). In that sense, the Baptist turned the problematic toward some sort of archetypal yearning.

Saint Jerome craved spirituality in solitude, and Leonardo's early representation of the Church Father brought forth a testing experience. The Baptist, instead, was set in a lightless void. *Sfumato* has consumed the pictorial evidence of things by enacting the Nicodemean paradox of "seeing in darkness." At last, *sfumato* adumbrated a higher mystery at the edge of a more transcendental light.[17] Having cherished processes of growth and expansion throughout his works, Leonardo finally took up spiritual concerns that led him to steer process toward consumption.

Leonardo thus faced a dilemma that would torment Michelangelo's *Captives* and erode the *Rondanini Pietà* to the very end of his long life. For both of them, to unravel growth and move away from the world of things and deeds became as imperative as it had been for John the Baptist, whose words seem to have paved the way for what the sculptor called *discresce:* "He must increase, but I must decrease" (John 3:30). In a biblical spirit, John had to "decrease" his spiritual influence; that is, he could not lead his followers to believe so much in him as to slight the coming of Christ. By way of prophecy, he insisted that pride could not interfere with Christian destiny. The text presents a fateful moment; the epiphany of self-illumination moved the Baptist to seek a transcendental kinship with the Lord. The sculptor found a way of physical consumption in his last *Pietà,* whose uplifting thrust pointed toward redemption. The painter, instead, let the Baptist himself "show" the way, much as the cross he holds points symbolism toward paths of death and resurrection. However ambiguous or tormented their artistic forms, both artists confronted matters of ultimate beginnings at the very end of lifetime trials. We do not know, in a Leonardesque mode, what the Baptist is trying to suggest, but we do know that he has survived human tests. Because he has not failed, we should be encouraged to enter the wilderness trying to come out at the other side of the world on faith alone. Finger and cross, therefore, edge on a watershed experience; nature and history have been obliterated, and the visual mimesis is about to reveal a vision.

At the end of his life, the Baptist linked the mystery of the self to that of the cross, which ended Christ's separation from the Father. In that sense, the cross he is holding complemented the androgynous symbolism insofar as sexual unity overcame the godlessness of division. In a medieval spirit, Scotus Erigena would have linked the cross to the birth and death of the human Christ, who was resurrected free of sexual division (*De divisione naturae* II, 12, 14).

7

The Baptist is One and Many, figure and landscape within an anthropomorphic image whose male and female cells have fused together. In Ficino's *Commentary on Plato's Symposium,* in fact, androgyny reconciled male Courage with female Temperance in the bisexual Justice. Likewise, the sun is male and the earth female, while the moon, which gives and receives light, is bisexual.[18] Androgyny thus stood for unity at all levels, and Leonardo's French protector, Francis I, was represented by Niccolò da Modena in an androgynous portrait that was meant to praise his harmonious soul through a combination of the warring Hermes with the pregnant Venus.[19] It was only later that hermaphroditic descriptions of Henry III set forth a grotesque sexuality symbolic of a cultural shift toward the bizarre and the dreamlike figures of Ronsard and d'Aubigné.[20]

Wildness and androgyny precede history, and prophecy has promised us that they also survive it. As a matter of fact, Hayden White would suggest that wildness represents a kind of dialectical antithesis to civilization.[21] Yet the absence of background in the Leonardesque picture of the Baptist would infer that primitivism has lost the physical presence of Jerome's desert enclave. The transcendental symbols of cross and pointing finger have internalized space. In a way, the Baptist is a Christian androgyne. While rejecting civilized comforts, he holds the cross gently, gently smiles, and gently points the way. He has renounced the ways of the world, but not the life of the spirit.

Although in a more enigmatic key, Leonardo paved the way for Swedenborg, Coleridge, and Balzac, who saw the androgyne as the exemplary image of the perfect man, what German Romanticism called the ideal man of the future. On German grounds, Novalis identified androgyny with primitive man before the Fall—*der himmlische Urmensch.* He is the total person who unites sexes, body and soul, self and nonself, spirit and nature, subject and object. He embodied mythic ages of innocence and gold. Eventually, they came to an end through a split between man and nature that Novalis pinned to a cataclysm. Very much in the spirit of Leonardo's *Deluge* sketches, such a disruption broke down that archetypal unity. As a result, nature itself became inhuman, as it appears to be in the background of *Mona Lisa* as well as of *Saint Anne, the Virgin, and Child.* Reunion would occur in an androgynous body:

> Einst ist alles Leib,
> Ein Leib,
> In himmlischen Blüte
> Schwimmt das selig Paar
> (*Geistliche Lieder* xiii)

"One day all will be one body; in heavenly blood the blissful couple will float."[22] And that one body could as well have been Leonardo's Baptist, much as pictorial darkness would testify to the reintegration of man and nature through the symbolic copresence of Baptist and Wild Man. Along the thematics of hope, we need only mention that Jules Michelet ("*Je suis un homme complet, ayant les deux sexes de l'esprit*") and Virginia Woolf have lodged the sex of spiritual fullness in a realm of androgynous solitude.

Fullness, solitude, and self-sufficiency could edge on narcissism for Novalis, and so they did for Leonardo. As a portrait of the mind, therefore, the Baptist bodied forth the image of the most enigmatic and exclusive Academy of One. Leonardo sealed it on a drawing whose ornament is honeycomb and cobweb, nature and artifice (see Fig. 58). In other words, the emblem of a self-contained labyrinth at the center of which was the Minotaur—who embodied the archetypal denial of androgynous synthesis—was displaced to make room for the Daedalian mind, which Leonardo lodged in a body that united male and female sexuality.

At the spring of memory, Leonardo's Baptist stood as an image of origin and resolution, a primeval symbol to which I would like to relate the core of the artist's concept of human destiny:

> Hope and longing for repatriation and return to the primal chaos is to man what light is to the moth. With a constant joyous longing he awaits the new spring, always the new state, always the new months, the new years; for always it seems to him that the things longed for come too late, and he fails to realize that he is wishing away his own life. This same longing is the quintessence, the spirit, of the elements, which finding itself imprisoned in the soul of the human body, it longs always to return to its emitter. (Arundel 156v)

As a wild man, John is the primal myth of origin, but he also is the prophet of the everlasting way at the end of time. Criticism has debated whether the cross was part of the original conception of the picture. Historically speaking, it is inconsistent, since the Baptist died before the Crucifixion. Yet, the cross confirmed the pseudonymity of apocalyptic visions that tradition pinned to people like Gioacchino da Fiore on the assumption that later events had been determined far back in the past.[23] The cross created a liturgical context in which time and space nestled spirituality. In such a transhuman setting, a prophet was about to fulfill his faith and an androgyne longed to recover wholeness. At last, Leonardo sealed the story of Christ from birth in the *Adoration* and childhood in the *Virgin of the Rocks* to maturity in the *Last Supper* and death on the cross in *Saint John the Baptist.*

Within the broader perspective of Western culture, Gilbert Durand draws a line between two types of symbolic individuals. Civilized man tests tradition and transcendence alike. It is "as if possession of the earth by the laborer, Cain, as also by the Stealer of fire, were connected with the loss of transcendental hope." His operative mode is that of "exile." And Daedalus, the prototype of the laborer, started his technological career in exile from Athens, where envy had led him to harm his nephew. By contrast, the traditional man leads an existence whose acts and thoughts are meant to guide him back beyond the Fall: "Certainly he is liable to have myths of back-sliding, of a fall . . . which may seem close to those of banishment. But these myths are duplicated by, and make no sense without, those of promise and alliance. . . . In fact, the Fall can only be conceived against a background of recurrences and references to 'before' the Fall." As figures of exile, Prometheus, Daedalus, and Cain were Leonardo's technological Other. The Baptist, instead, offered him an image of return and reintegration; he was the "Man of Promise." Rather "than establishing order himself," he renewed the "Principle of Order."[24] He was Leonardo's spiritual Other.

8

For Leonardo, the original profile of myth absorbed enigmatic smiles, androgynous glow, and disquieting looks. Where did such unprecedented features come from? Whether ancient or medieval, no tradition offered direct precedents. Once again, the pre-Socratic frame of mind seems to call for comparison. The oracular nature of the Baptist's pointing finger recalls Heraclitus: "The lord, he whose oracle is the one in Delphi, does not speak or conceal but gives a sign" (B, 93). The Baptist gives us a sign, which indicates a direction. We confront a mythic gesture, which points to the power of origin and the nature of primeval relationships. It is a gesture of "mediation" between man and deity that paves the way for a metamorphosis into the archetypal unity of being.[25]

Darkness in the pictorial background tells us that mythic consciousness has relinquished concepts of linear time. In a way, the Baptist has drawn nature into his own wildness. At their most minute, his hair curls are texturally echoed in the pelt, the fluidity of movements, and an interlocking system of spirals along both arms and the animal skin. Circular and meandering patterns have been narrowed down to the human figure, much as hair curls recall Leonardo's flowers, water, and deluge studies. As a most anthropomorphic landscape, the Baptist carried the classical and humanist concept of man as a microcosm of reality beyond those structures of harmonious correspondences that inspired *Mona Lisa*.

The Baptist is about to reach back toward the beginning, where Adamic dreams would finally trade memory for truth. However vague, his enigmatic posture combines riddle and androgyny. In Heraclitus's words, "they do not know what is borne apart is borne together, a back-turning harmony, as in the bow and the lyre" (B, 51). The androgyne is bow and lyre; he is the embodiment of a supernal reconciliation toward which he himself is pointing.

Ancient and modern precedents aside, could Leonardo have found any of them within his own self? He pretended to be on the verge of revealing the origin "of the first or perhaps second cause" of mankind's existence (841). At the edge of prophetic ambiguity, he stopped short of revealing final truths. Yet did he really discover the cause? There lies the enduring mystery of a visionary *sfumato* at the limits of visual darkness and intellectual explanation. Smile and gesture heighten values insufficient to either clarify or "name" themselves. Since it points but does not tell, connotation validates the Baptist's prophecy, which brings Christian discourse to its longed-for closure. "With its designating, silent movements," Roland Barthes writes, "a pointing finger always accompanies the classic text." Within the connotative outreach of John's life and thought, Leonardo touched on a range of sedimented meanings, contradictions, and riddles that have burdened the discourse of truth since Oedipus. Mythic riddles aimed at revealing "names" yielded to the image of a spiritual mystery pointed toward revelation. In the verbal world of texts, connotation is the tip of the tongue from which the name, the truth, will later fall.[26] In the visual world of painting, the tip of the Baptist's pointing finger was about to foreshadow the "first cause."

Archetypes of Power

6

The Art of War and the
Inventor's Rhetoric of Power

*The only branch of technology which has never become
inactive is the art of warfare.*

—George Sarton

It was out of his knowledge of the way things were that Leonardo drew
the matter and tone of his letter (probably written in 1483) to the powerful duke of Milan. The Moor, as he was called, could in fact provide new
opportunities for an artist who had always been at odds with the Florentine establishment.

At the end of Leonardo's Tuscan upbringing, warfare turned from
images of art to matters of practical employment. In real life, war demanded that invention be steered toward the production of weaponry,
and commitments to the art of war spurred a dialogism that tested
humanist potential and antihumanist empiricism.

Appealing to the duke's need for security, Leonardo offered new weapons in a style that was apparently rooted in the factual power of technology. At no point did his letter weigh matters of principle. He accepted
the operative institutions of the time, aware as he was that today's lion
could become tomorrow's lamb. For him, war was neither the cause nor
the expression of higher principles. From Florence to Milan, strong men
knew by experience what he wrote: "Courage imperils life, fear protects

it" (1200). That axiom could not fail to impress the Moor, whose greed was—and had to be—as rapacious as his foes' ambition. Amid endless struggles for territorial expansion, weaponry and military manuals were earmarked at the top of any priority list.

Long before Leonardo, there were inventors who circulated note-books with drawings of machines, many of which were military. In 1268 the engineer Assaut tried to show a collection of military drawings to Alphonse de Poitiers, who was about to embark on a crusade. In 1328 Guido da Vigevano tried to do the same with Philip VI. Undertakings of that sort were in the background of what would later be called "theatres of machines." Above all, Roger Bacon's *Epistola de secretis operibus* (c. 1260) lists technological wonders that seem to anticipate Leonardo's tall order, from chariots and bridges to engines and instruments used to scale walls and walk under water. One could guess that the literature of inventions had established a mode and a nomenclature of its own. It is in the wake of this tradition that Leonardo's letter ought to be considered.

2

As a master strategist, Leonardo alerts the Moor to the urgency of his offer:

> Having now sufficiently considered the specimens of all those who proclaim themselves skilled contrivers of instruments of war, and that the invention and operation of the said instruments are nothing different to those in common use: I shall endeavour, without prejudice to any one else, to explain myself to your Excellency showing your Lordship my secrets, and then offering them to your best pleasure and approbation to work with effect at opportune moments as well as all those things which, in part, shall be briefly noted below.

Secrets of difficult execution could be reduced to a matter of boastful rhetoric, much against what one would expect the factual nature of the offer at hand would entail. The speculative word "secrets" stands up as a metaphorical point of transfer from literary description to visual fore-shadowing. We ought to bear in mind that the letter does not deal with the language of scientific information, but with the visual makeup of technological forms disguised under literary verbiage.

At issue here is a rhetoric that aims at being presentational in a literal sense, even though its matter is largely potential. The literary strategy is at once assertive and hypothetical. Although objects do not exist, language foregrounds the inventor's rhetoric, which had to reconcile the declarative optimism of a culture that fostered panegyrical gestures with the exploratory thrust of a writer out to translate science into technology. Their linkage echoed ingrained prejudices that dated back to Archimedes. Plutarch made it clear that the ancient scientist despised practical inventions; as a matter of fact, the "machines he had designed and contrived" were "mere amusements in geometry" (*Lives of the Noble Romans*, Marcellus). Only out of necessity did he comply with requests that his talents be put to practical use. His geometric fantasies were upgraded at the turn of the sixteenth century. Since he had to trade aloofness for employment, Leonardo was bound to make those amusements more convincing but not altogether plausible. To weigh the unique appeal of Leonardo's project, one might refer to the rather primitive character of the literature on the subject. Valturio's *De re militari*, written in 1462 and commissioned by Sigismondo Malatesta, was a tract on ancient Roman warfare whose illustrations resembled ancient cameo decorations but fell short of practical efficiency.[1]

On technological grounds, secrets point to objects that are, or could be, available. Because they are "secrets," they ought to be within reach of production, if not use. The term *secret*, however, refers to something beyond reach, but not too far if it needs to be kept out of sight. By toying with exposure and concealment, rhetoric heightens promise by withholding appropriation. Since he understood that the progress of technology could quickly turn choice into necessity, Leonardo resorted to expressions loaded with a sense of impending urgency. Because his inventions teased the humanist pursuit of theoretical "planning," the secretive and at times outlandish nature of such instruments edged on travesty.

The letter to the Moor centers on the moment of unchecked inventiveness. Its potential mode, however, is not expressed in the conditional. Even virtual contingencies ("if") rest with the certainty of the indicative mode, which points to what already exists: "*Ho modi*" (I have plans). Actually, "secrets" stood next to what Machiavelli called *castellucci* (castles in Spain, or virtual plans); both of them severed potentiality from "testing."[2] One note reads: "To devise is the work of the master, to execute the act of the servant" (McCurdy, 88). Alberti would not have taken issue with that stand. Both of them were setting the classical idea of the architect—as it had been formulated by Plato, Cicero, and Pliny—against medieval counterparts, namely masons and builders.

At the end of his letter, Leonardo insists, "If any one of the above-named things seem to any one to be impossible or not feasible, I am most ready to make the experiment in your park, or in whatever place may please your Excellency—to whom I commend myself with the utmost humility." Since it was expected of military experts to be original, such a rhetoric of exclusivity could not fail to entice the recipient's ambition. For Machiavelli, inventiveness "brings honor. We see that everything invented, even though slight, is praised by historians" (*The Art of War* 7).

Even as orthodox a humanist as Alberti could not help emphasizing the almost miraculous function of the architect in times of armed conflicts. His peacetime achievements would be supplemented with

> ballistic engines and machines of war, fortresses and whatever else may have served to protect and strengthen the liberty of our country, and the good and honor of the state, to extend and confirm its dominion. It is my view moreover that, should you question all the various cities which within human memory have fallen into enemy hands by siege, and inquire who defeated and conquered them, they would not deny that it was the architect. . . . Should you examine the various military campaigns undertaken, you would perhaps discover that the skill and ability of the architect have been responsible for more victories than have the command and foresight of any general; and that the enemy were more often overcome by the ingenuity of the first without the other's weapons, than by the latter's sword without the former's good counsel. And what is more important, the architect achieves his victory with but a handful of men and without loss of life.[3]

Such a magical role had been established by the time Leonardo took advantage of its prestige.

At the very beginning of his treatise, Vitruvius had demanded that architects be excellent in matters of theoretical knowledge (*ratiocinatio*), technique (*fabrica*), and letters (*litterae*), that is to say, history, philosophy, music, medicine, and astrology. And Alberti echoed those very requirements in the preface to his own *De Re Aedificatoria,* in which the architect's Daedalian expertise extends from water systems for personal health and agricultural benefits to "ballistic engines and machines of war." Those details are introductory to a rhetoric of praise whose social and civic range fell beyond Daedalian accomplishments: "Let it be said that the security, dignity, and honor of the republic depend greatly on the architect: it is he who is responsible for our delight, entertainment, and health while at leisure, and our profit and advantage while at work, and in short, that we lived in a dignified manner, free of any danger. . . . He should no doubt be accorded praise and respect, and be counted among those most deserving of mankind's honor and recognition."[4] The architect was recognized as the fulcrum of communal life, and it seems as if Leonardo read the Albertian text before writing his letter to the Moor. Once in Milan, he probably modeled much of his social, professional, and artistic activities after the humanist idealization of the Daedalian archetype.

The Platonic concept of the architect as "the ruler of workmen" (*Politics* 259) had been Christianized in the hands of Jerome and Augustine, who applied it to the great builders of the faith: one refers to "Paulus architectus" (*Letters* 48, 2) and the other to Christ as "architectus ecclesiae" (*The City of God* 18, 48). Isidore of Seville finally sanctioned the architect's mythic descent from Daedalus (*Etymologies* 20) right before the medieval mind would proceed to combine classical and Christian thought. Within the Latin tradition, even medieval buildings carried inscriptions that paid homage to individual talent: *magistri doctissimi, nobilis et doctus,* or *romana mastria.*[5] Before Michelangelo and Raphael would be called *divini* as artists, Francesco di Giorgio had claimed similar attributes in the name of a new Promethean fire that had given inventors Faustian powers. At his most authoritative, Alberti bestowed the attributes of "divinity" and "universality" on the architect.

3

Political strife was a permanent fixture throughout the Italian peninsula, where the progress of military technology was at once a matter of advantage and survival. We only need to read Guicciardini to weigh a tyrant's state of mind when the pope and King Alfonso of Naples agreed with the Florentines to rally against the king of France, who enjoyed the Moor's favor. Convinced that his safety rested on their ruin, the Milanese strong man left "no stone unturned" to bring French troops to Italy (*History of Florence,* chap. x).

As a master strategist, Leonardo alerted the Milanese ruler to the urgency of his offer at the very start of his letter. Neither favors nor privileges were called for. It was a matter of course that superiority in the open market of bloodshed would be brutally evident, and the competitive field obviously enhanced the quality of the services offered. On literary grounds, Leonardo shifted the humanist tradition of boastful praises that "deified" Cosimo and Lorenzo de' Medici toward a rhetoric of power that was both factual and suggestive. In an antihumanist key, emulation turned from matters of inherited ideology to the discharge of practical tasks. By choice, the prince could call on the courtier-soldier for counsel, but he could not delay—let alone brush aside—the services of a technician whose inventions were "secrets" of a kind different from any instrument "in common use." Mechanization was in the air, and it improved the competitive edge at a time when patrons were usually deep in military emergencies.[6] Leonardo joined Machiavelli in exposing flaws at the heart of men as determined as Moors and Borgias; their power, however, was more precarious than it could be suspected. Privilege would quickly turn into threat the moment the Moor realized that the offer could be handed over to his foes.

It was a time when the art of war thrived in muddled waters. Political alliances were unreliable, and manpower was mercenary by trade. Survival dictated suspicion of everything and everybody. Even military technology did not pledge exclusive loyalties. On the subject of poisonous powders to be launched over enemy galleys, Leonardo wanted to make sure that shifting winds would not asphyxiate foes and friends alike. In instances of that sort, it was mandatory to cover "nose and mouth with a fine cloth dipped in water so that the powder" (McCurdy, 846) would not filter through.

Machiavelli himself wrote about tricks and new warfare devices in his *Discourses on the First Decade of Titus Livius* (III, 14). By general consensus, *The Art of War* (1) recognized that power rested with arms in republics and tyrannies alike. Yet he underestimated gunpowder. A new technological expertise was called for, and Leonardo had no doubts that the scientist-inventor would play an ever more important role. Whereas one linked warfare to political ideology, the other made of technology an autonomous field of endeavors that suited man's "bestial madness."

In spite of its dispassionate tone, Leonardo's request was compelling, and what he had to offer touched on instincts of predominance. The terseness of his style rested with the axiomatic evidence of machines so well fitted to their function that value was implied. Since power could be persuasive just by exposure to it, the literary text exploited a rhetoric of advantage that was at once concise and hortatory.[7]

Although Leonardo was looking for a patron, the epistolary strategy made his request indispensable to the duke. The literary artifact turned into a treasure chest whose wealth of new marvels was put up for auction. Such a cornucopian ingenuity, I would like to suggest, found visual expression in a little-known drawing roughly entitled *Instruments Fallen from the Sky* (Fig. 25), which shows a rain of tools and utensils. In a spirit of almost surreal absurdity, the fantastic shower of man-made objects quantifies its useless abundance once we read the inscription at the bottom: "Oh slave to human misery, of how many things are you willing to become a servant for money" (*O miseria umana di quante cose per danari ti fai servo*). It seems to be a comment on things and servants of different sorts who would fall from prominence to demise as

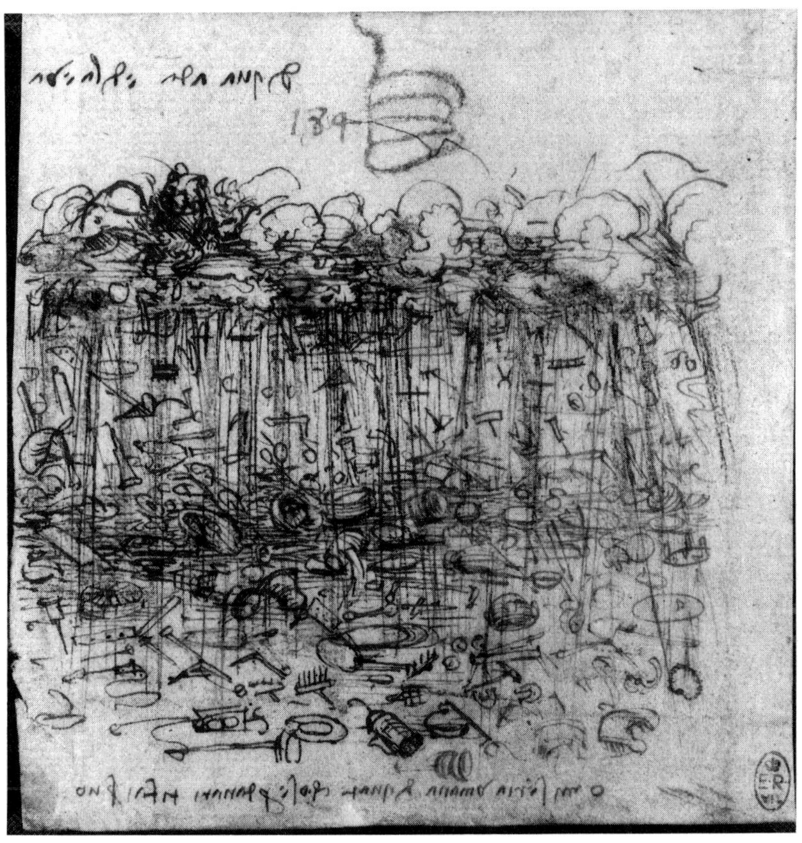

FIG. 25.   Leonardo da Vinci, *Instruments Fallen from the Sky* (c. 1498) Royal Library, Windsor Castle

fast as the political fortunes of Moors and Borgias. I cannot help linking that visual multitude of things to emergent measures of wealth based on manufactured goods that Alberti had called *masserizia*.

On artistic grounds, Leonardo's outpouring of forms pointed to an aspect of his art that also produced the *Adoration,* whose wealth of figures inspired Raphael. Moreover, correlations have been made between literary and visual language in the water drawings, which try to match the engrossing flow of fluvial streams with a suitable vocabulary. It suffices to quote part of a long passage: "*Risaltazione, circolazione, revoluzione, ravvoltamento, raggiramento, sommergimento, surgimento, declinazione, elevazione, cavamento, consumamento, percussione, ruinamento, discenso, impetuita, retrosi, urtamenti, confregazioni, ondazioni, rigamenti, bollimenti, ricascamenti . . .*" (MS I, fols. 72r, 71v).[8] We find many such passages in the Leonardesque notes, which push the vernacular to accommodate the literary demands of scientific progress. We look at a massive commitment to make of single words descriptive tools endowed with scientific reliability. By the same token, the narrative units of rhetorical discourse were largely rejected. By so doing, Leonardo gave full exposure to the vernacular range of his antihumanist vocabulary.

In a humanist mode, Alberti had written the first grammar of the Tuscan language, which he meant to set into a paradigmatic frame. Leonardo, instead, did not concern himself with rules, but set out to let language give verbal form to the mental flow as it responded to visual images and external processes. Rather than legislating on itself, there were instances when language confronted the mimesis of both thought and vision as nonlinguistic forms of experience.

At once presumptuous and patronizing, the inventor did not fail to expose the frailty of political might. Earlier, Alberti had linked the fickleness of power to the lure of ambition. His assessment of the development and consequences of the art of war paved the way for Machiavelli:

> In the recent age of our fathers, Italians employed hired troops and foreign armies rather than conscripted citizens, as had been our ancestors' custom. They did this by prudent choice, I believe, since exposing the lives of ignoble mercenaries to the perils of battle seemed more practical than risking the lives of citizens in the fortunes of war. They may also have wished to prevent Italian troops from taking up arms only to abuse them later to the ruin of their homeland, as in fact happened.[9]

The art of war lost its grandeur once it became a means for settling problems that interfered with the more serious business of business itself.

While Machiavelli saw in mercenary troops a sign of the moral failure of citizens unwilling to shed their blood for the fatherland, Leonardo severed ideology from the art of war. He was neither interested nor duty-bound to test the morality of historical events. Instead, he took up the task of improving military efficiency, whose dynamics called for technological advantage.

At the turn of the sixteenth century, Machiavelli's empirical *verità effettuale* made it clear that talent and circumstance—whether they be called *virtù* and *fortuna* or paired with Kairos and Tyché—so affected behavior that antihumanist rhetoric fell back on the crudity of need. Granted that the oratorical gestures of discourse are part of language, words must find equal strength in their utility. At that "administrative" juncture, Leonardesque letters and Machiavellian speeches stood side by side. And it is on antihumanist grounds that Ezio Raimondi refers to the episode of the Ciompi revolt, which led Machiavelli to invent a speech (by the Unknown) that proclaims an axiomatic truth: "The only teacher is necessity" (*io credo certamente che la necessità ci insegni*), much as "circumstance offers fleeting opportunities one cannot let pass by" (*le opportunità che dalla occasione ci è porta, vola, History of Florence* 3, 13). It is pain and injustice that make victory even more compelling.[10] To them, Leonardo would have added ambition and fear.

4

Adding to the deeper layers of his literary *sfumato*, Leonardo then proceeded to detail his secrets through a breathtaking list of military hardware. In the process, he set morphological archetypes of the modern art of war.

Artillery rushed in an unthought-of potential for carnage, and often was orchestrated as a flamboyant spectacle in which the show of power did not call for proportional body counts. In 1520 Mercurio Gattinara, who was Charles V's chancellor, claimed that twenty cannons would be enough to protect Milan from the French. His estimate was reasonable insofar as it was fair to guess that it stemmed from psychological fear as much as from actual firepower. Since it was largely mercenary, the profession of war demanded to raise costs and cut losses. Because he was professionally competent, Machiavelli saw the need of armies that would fight real battles. He also set moral worth at the core of *The Art of War,* whose very title bears out the duplicity of *arte* as a skill at once creative and utilitarian. To it, we ought to add the chivalric tradition of princely duels meant to settle judicial and political disputes. Their pomp was ostentatious and fictional. Combats were prepared, staged, and recorded up to the actual clash, which rarely took place.[11]

Below art, Machiavelli never tired of writing about battles in which only handfuls of soldiers died. At Zagonara, three men were lost; one was killed, and the other two drowned in mud after falling from their horses. That "great defeat" was "reported everywhere in Italy" (*History of Florence* 4, 6). The historian kept on repeating that wars were commenced without fear, continued without danger, and concluded without loss. For many, the very subject "battle" did not hold any real sense, to the extent that Michelangelo's would-be fresco of the Battle of Cascina washed down the story into bathing nudes. As a matter of fact, warfare widened the gap between technological and theoretical abstractions. Since ideology did not motivate them, it was impossible to make soldiers "carry food for two or three days." Even worse, they would not abstain from "gaming, from whoring," and "from cursing" (*The Art of War* 7).

Closer to Leonardesque grounds, Machiavelli introduced the "bloodless victory" at Anghiari: "In this great defeat and long fight lasting from two until six 'clock, not more than one man died, and he perished not from wounds or any honorable blow, but by falling from his horse and being trampled on. At that time men fought with such safety because, all on horseback and covered with armor and safe against death whenever they surrendered, they had no reason for dying, since they were protected during the fight by armor" (*History of Florence* 5, 33). Actually, more blood was shed than the writer was ready to admit. Although the battle did not amount to more than a skirmish by a bridge, the clash left more than one hundred men either dead or wounded according to Flavio Biondo's more reliable account in *Historiarum ab inclinatione Romanorum* (libri dec. iv, lib. 1). Yet the description is typical inasmuch as battles were calculated risks aimed at gaining advantage.[12] The decisive strategy was to outmaneuver the enemy. Annihilation on either side was incompatible with the economy of mercenary *condottieri* who needed competition to keep their business going.

Concerns with losses and tricks had been prominent since antiquity. Mardonius, counselor of King Xerxes of Persia, criticized the fairness of Greek warfare, which caused great losses to both sides. Later, Polybius set such an honorable way of conducting warfare against the deceitfulness of his own times, when war came to rely on secret weapons and stratagems. In 1361 Petrarch wrote that "the question is no longer how a man fights, but how he drinks; the only valiance is pot-valiance, the only battle is with the bottle."[13] The dialectic of wars fought either for honor or convenience could claim a long past, and Petrarch shared Polybius's divided views. The wars that *condottieri* waged on behalf of Milan, Florence, or Venice often were games of chess in which checkmate was accepted with little acrimony, and still less bloodshed. The Medicis of Florence rallied belligerence around tournaments that scaled down the art of war to ludic performances.[14] Books and battlefields did not warrant the ferocious struggles that Leonardo painted in the central episode of the Battle of the Stendard (in Rubens's copy, Fig. 26) and wrote about in his descriptions of battle scenes.

Because of such concerns, literary and visual images of warfare are unconvincing in fifteenth-century art. Piero della Francesca's battles are relatively bloody by humanist standards, but they are fought by ancient warriors. Paolo Uccello's *Battle of San Romano* (c. 1445), instead, was fought between Florentines and Sienese in 1432. Niccolò da Tolentino

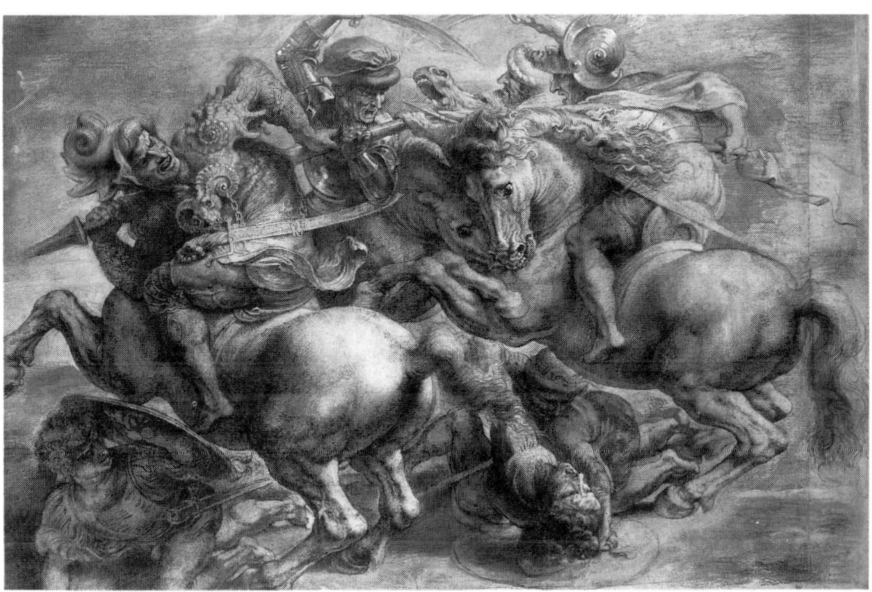

FIG. 26.   Peter Paul Rubens, *The Battle of the Stendard* (c. 1615) Cabinet des Dessins, Louvre, Paris

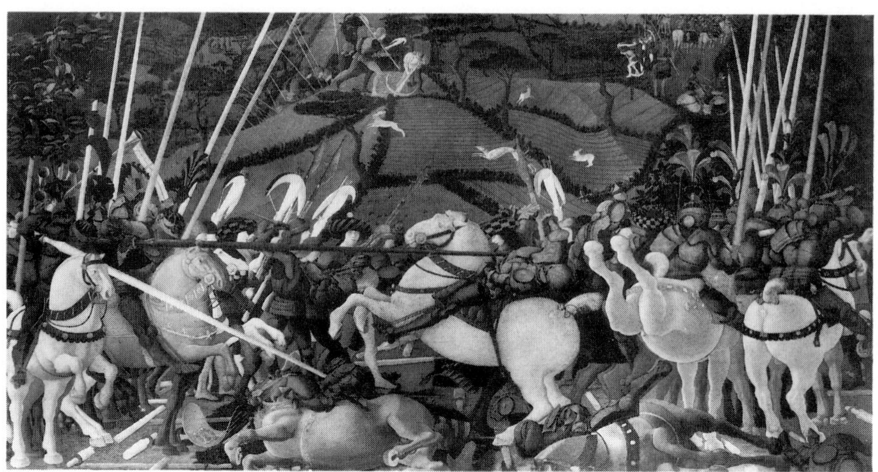

FIG. 27.   Paolo Uccello, *Battle of San Romano* (c. 1445)
Uffizi, Florence

led his men amid an array of broken weapons with only a few dead
soldiers in sight (Fig. 27), even though records tell us that he had been
able to hold off the enemy for eight hours. Any notion of serious killing
is downplayed by background groves of oranges and roses that produce
the effect of a garden more than a battlefield.[15] Either by defect or
excess, violence remained a predominant concern. Leonardo fell back on
animal-like caricature and inhuman ferocity, much as Machiavelli often
gave a caustic tone to military reports. At issue was the value of action
itself. First and foremost, action meant engagement for Leonardo and
Machiavelli, who were equally attracted to the Moor, Julius II, and
Cesare Borgia. By contrast, inanity was lethal to meaningful forms of
life; even misdirected deeds were better than no activity at all.

5

Leonardo's persona in the letter to the Moor is that of an inventor whose
public activities combined epistolarity with historiography. In the humanist mode, he would be expected to mix fact with fiction on the
assumption that narrativity was meant to be inspirational. As such,

Leonardo's inventions were plans (*modi*) of a rather extravagant kind. Artillery, in fact, had become so expensive that only the very powerful could afford it. At any rate, selfishness—not religion or patriotism—was at the core of the art of war.[16] The numerous items listed in the letter elevated the Moor to the aristocracy of financial might, which also shouldered the humanist splendor of the Montefeltro court at Urbino. Duke Federigo was a warlord whose reliability commanded such high fees that he could keep taxes low. The display of power was to be intimidating rather than destructive. It was a time when assassination, bribery, and marriage were more effective in making political gains than make-believe wars in which the opponents paraded strength, maneuvered for position, but rarely engaged in actual combat. Hence we should not overestimate the rugged grimness of equestrian *capitani* such as Gattamelata and Colleoni.[17]

Likewise, much of Leonardo's heartless approach to the lethal efficiency of his "plans" needs to be limited to an epistolary gesture; his machines—if ever built—could carry a destructive potential in excess of what customary practice would call for. The escalation of technology was aimed at raising fear, while its rhetoric was meant to disarm violence. The warrior's rhetoric in Machiavelli's *Art of War* no longer voiced heroism, but its surrogate.[18] Words foreshadowed the presence of things. Because the staging of might by far exceeded its usage, gaps between discourse and action would be ever more difficult to bridge.

The letter to the Moor, in fact, is not a bill of sale, but an estimate of services to be rendered. Visually, Leonardo's numerical list points to inventorial items ready for marketing, if not delivery. What follows, instead, is an outline of devices that exist either as linguistic constructs ("secret passages underneath rivers, plans for destroying every fortress or other strongholds unless they have been founded upon rock") or tentative sketches. Occasionally, factual references are given. Item 7 refers to "big guns and mortars," which, in item 4, "would be most convenient and easy to carry." In fact, big cannons and mortars were hard to move along the roads of the day. In March 1500 the Moor had six pieces of heavy artillery brought to Milan from Germany; two of them broke on the way and incidents of that sort were common. Yet heavy hardware was important. Leonardo knew the facts, but he did not make his plans any less hypothetical. The inventor's rhetoric was—and still is—that of an opportunist who kept up with workshops and battlefields to know what could be marketable. As a symbol of active and contemplative life at its best, Pedro Berruguete painted Federigo da Montefeltro in full armor and reading a book (Fig. 28); one stood for *armas,* and the other for *letras.* Yet we may

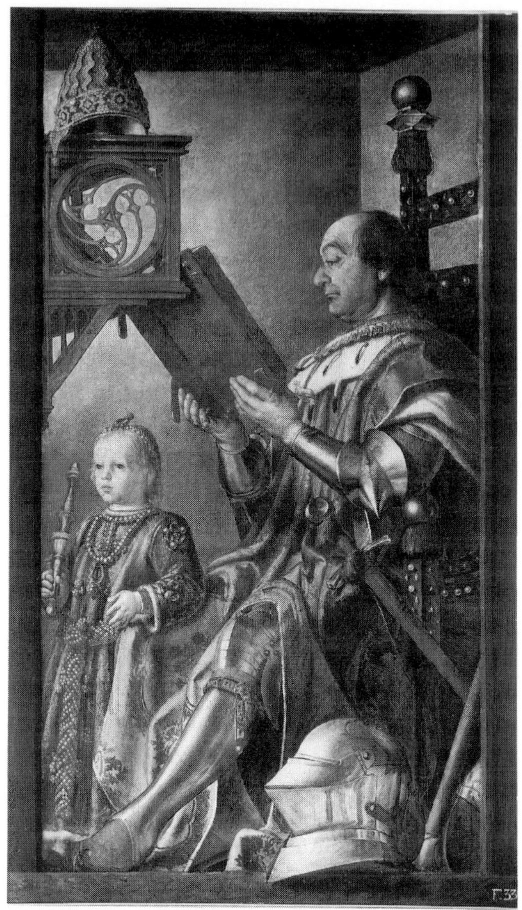

FIG. 28.   Pedro Berruguete, *Federigo da Montefeltro and His Son Guidobaldo* Palazzo Ducale, Urbino

wonder if that book was one on the art of letters or of war, since texts of that sort were indeed prominent in his *studiolo*.[19] Either way, the picture secured their coexistence.

Frederick L. Taylor wrote a while ago that "to the Italian condottieri who fought so sparingly belongs the honour of originating the modern theoretical study of warfare." The new enthusiasm for "abstract discussion accentuated military dilettantism." By the end of the fifteenth century, Italy resembled a military academy. The comparatively bloodless campaigns that *condottieri* waged were practical demonstrations "by professors of the art of war."[20] Much warfare was resolved into tactical moves; theoretical advantage on the battlefield did not call for actual combat. In a way strangely analogous to the animal world, violence was ritualized into moves that flaunted strength without testing it to any lethal extent. Weight and size needed only be paraded, and real engagements were mostly inconsequential. South of the Alps, the economy of professional warfare equated apparent advantage with victory. The hypothetical bent of the humanist mind projected an irresistible spell. One of man's most cruel endeavors often fostered elegant exercises.

With an eye to the practice of art, Leonardo preferred painting over sculpture also because the former did not entail massive physical efforts. Furthermore, it could be discharged in beautiful rooms where music would accompany artists dressed in fashionable clothes. Likewise, I cannot help picturing captains clothed in spectacular uniforms making tactical moves on the chessboard of colorful maps. Indeed, the Italians knew how to diffuse tensions into flamboyant images of beauty! From academies to battlefields, the Italian bent of mind kept a hold on theory—whether it entailed literary genres, social behavior, or the art of war. Like humanist treatises on princes, courtiers, and family leaders, Leonardo's inventions fell in the basket of forthcoming promises and hypothetical models.

6

Then as now, warfare made concrete demands, and Leonardo knew it. Whenever unfeasibility staked its claim, "realistic" details added to the rhetorical cover-up, which rendered the improbable credible. Although 145 military books were printed in Venice between 1492 and 1570, "secrets" in the art of warfare were either eccentric or easily available. Revolving gun turrets and grappling devices were equally improbable in Valturio's *De re militari,* which defied common sense by showing an underwater trooper in full armor. Nevertheless, credulity played a role everywhere. Even dispassionate historians saw it fit to link Lorenzo de' Medici's death to ominous forewarnings of howling wolves, restless lions, and thunderbolts (Francesco Guicciardini, *History of Florence,* chap. 9). It is a fact that some items in Leonardo's letter point to performances as virtual as the preposterous deeds that often were envisioned in humanist treatises.[21]

It would be unfair, however, to tone down the lure that technology spelled at a time when man-made machines offered more power than people and animals could ever provide. Machiavelli himself conceded

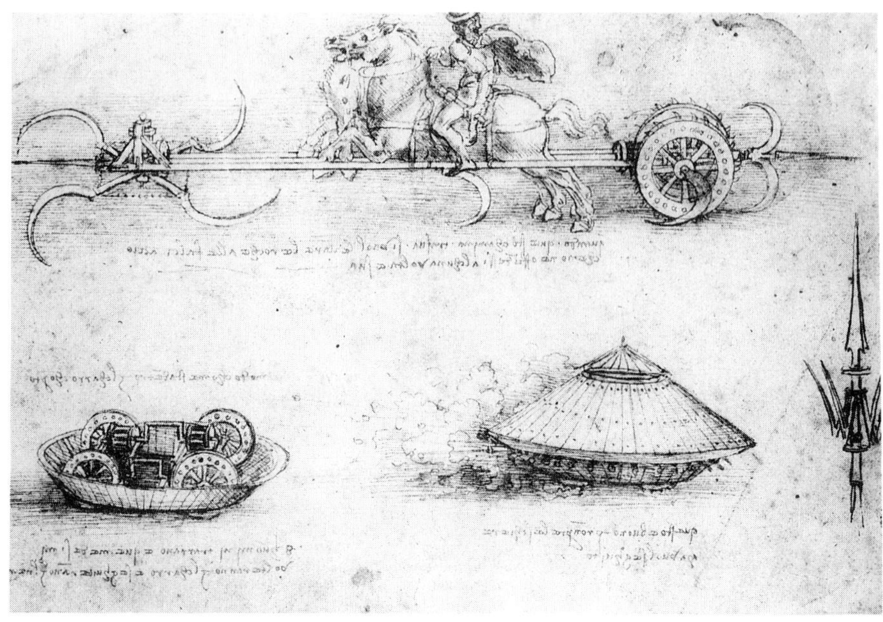

FIG. 29.   Leonardo da Vinci, *Armored Car*
British Museum, London

that "many times a spirited man will be on a cowardly horse and a cowardly man on a spirited horse; such disparities of spirit must cause disorder. Nor should anybody be astonished that a knot of infantrymen can resist any charge of cavalry, because the horse is a perceiving animal which recognizes dangers and is unwilling to enter them" (*The Art of War* 2). However hypothetical, Leonardo's sketches of the tank (Fig. 29) offered alternatives to the historian's cautious appreciation of gunpowder: "As to the army's artillery, ten cannons are enough for the siege of towns, not exceeding fifty pounds weight; these I use in the field rather for the protection of the encampment than for carrying on battle" (*The Art of War* 3). On the technical grounds of *poemi cavallereschi*, Ariosto believed that the gun was a cowardly invention: "Through thee is martial glory lost, through thee / The trade of arms becomes a worthless art" (*Orlando Furioso* xi). From Ariosto to Cervantes, nostalgia of chivalric deeds remained at odds with firearms that made knights and villains equally competent. Hierarchies of individual merit were undermined; emulative paragons waned, and weaponry traded distinction for uniformity. The undiscriminating availability of technological power cut so deeply into the "grand illusion" of knighthood that Chinese and Moors were blamed for the invention of those satanic weapons.

As such, Leonardo's plans were not less real than his sketches for moving under water and over clouds, or his fame as a master of gadgetry. Quickly, therefore, he took on the role of a magician entrusted with a militaristic horn of plenty: "In short, according to the variety of cases, I can contrive various and endless means of offence and defence." Even if some of his inventions seemed "impossible or not feasible" at that time, there were some that could be carried out. In the case of armored cars, it suffices to say that the rhetoric of fiction was prophetic.

Although based on available technology, the very core of Leonardo's inventions was but a cluster of forms bound to bestow a legendary epiphany on modernity. At least psychologically, the more "fantastic" aspects of his weaponry were meant to play a role in the "seduction" of the Moor, who would be lured into a realm of technological marvels. That kind of technology would make it possible for him to control the future. Once we gain insight into the overtones of Leonardo's letter, his literary style proves to be as shaded and suggestive as his pictorial *sfumato*. At work here is the twofold mode of rhetorical privilege and intimidation, what has been called the double intentionality of language.[22]

7

Because the inventor took precedence over the artist, Leonardo forced readers to measure the potential of technology against artistic achievements. And the very fact that he staked his reputation on elusive "plans" could not but add validity to his bombards, whose firepower was changing the art of war. Flaws in the documentation of "secrets" were somehow toned down when the letter turned toward peacemaking activities such as painting, sculpture, and architecture. Although aware of the Moor's interest in an equestrian piece, Leonardo did not seek a commission he had been longing for since Verrocchio had cast the Colleoni statue for the Venetians. And the warrior type so attracted him that it became a model for heads of soldiers, apostles, and ugly types.[23] Actually, the Moor could dispense with statues but not with cannons. The artistic coda to the letter heightened the inventor's role within a sociopolitical agenda that limited artistic endeavors to interludes.

The closing paragraph was therefore meant to reassure the Moor that preferences had been stated and priorities could be met. In the spirit of

Kenneth Burke's "administrative rhetoric," Leonardo proved that he knew how to draw a line between need and choice.[24] On the issue of the Sforza monument, he wrote: "Of the horse I will say nothing because I know the times." Indeed, he knew the times, and his reference to "immortal glory" was an afterthought, a kind of indulgent luxury the duke could afford only after power had been secured.[25]

Yet one cannot help noticing Leonardo's subtle—if not insolent—manipulation of a reader whose survival was made to depend on his talents. The almost ostentatious absence of a motivational force that could justify might beyond sheer predominance is explicitly premonitory and implicitly judgmental. Since questions of "why" are not addressed, means of military security may satisfy contingent needs, but to no moral avail. The letter does not contemplate the Moor's "proper" use of his inventions in any humanist or at least humane sense. Leonardo's implied cynicism was not excessive if we measure it against the Machiavellian *Prince*. On ideological grounds, "the only sound, sure, and enduring methods of defense are those based on your own actions and *virtù*" (chap. 24). That was wishful thinking. In reality, circumstances changed so fast that it had become impossible "to find any man shrewd enough to know how to adapt his policy in this way" (chap. 25). Instability could not be defeated; it was there to stay beyond Moors and Borgias, who were but flimsy markers to be eventually—and conveniently—disposed of. The letter seems to draw sender and receiver within a sort of militaristic *carpe diem* psychology validated by its own resilience. Perhaps the only form of stability one could hope to achieve was an equestrian monument *post mortem*. Long ago, Thucydides told us that war provides dreadful instructions, but fear is a quick and efficient teacher. And human intelligence was developed largely through fear.[26] That logic would make Leonardo's epistle exemplary.

In the antihumanist mode, the "factual" style of Leonardo's letter could be paired with the dedicatory epistle to *The Prince*, which, in Thomas Greene's recent comments, "repudiates rhetoric; the clipped opening chapter repudiates the graces of humanist elegance; from the beginning, the book refuses to be literature." The ending, however, "restores the book to cultural discourse, 'literary' discourse, as against that ulterior, detached, purely analytic discourse it had seemed to claim for itself."[27] Even Leonardo went back to art at the end of his epistle. As if moved by a cunning duplicity, he gave the Moor power without enticing him with promises of greatness, which was reserved for the dead. Yet fame rested with partisan favor, if we only think of the popular acclaim that moved the Florentines to build funerary monuments to honor their chancellors.

In the case of the Sforza project, was the endurance of art meant to shed an oblique light on the inevitability of human misfortunes?

The technological pride of the *homo artifex* came through when Leonardo expected the Moor to believe that he could "contrive endless means of offence and defence." Maybe the artist was challenging himself, smitten as he always had been with a love of the impossible.[28] For certain, he followed in the Petrarchan tradition of self-fashioning and self-crowning. As a renowned scientist, he noted that people would bring sackfuls of corals and shells to his workshop in Milan. And there may have been times when his inventions made him as proud as he was of his art. While the poet's *Letter to Posterity* (1350?) shaped the ideal of scholarship, the epistle to the Moor outlined that of the new inventor, whose rhetoric ranged from disturbing depths to boastful heights. At a rather hypothetical best, Leonardo might have seen himself as a sort of cultural counselor to the Moor, a role that Petrarch and Castiglione would have approved of.

It was a fact that in matters of war the military engineer combined the offices of the civil, the mechanical, and the mining technician.[29] Yet Leonardo never linked technology to macrocosmic matters of historical progress and social harmony. Unlike Daniel Webster and his American cohorts, he would not have resorted to the rhetoric of the technological sublime.[30] For him, technology was not the hope of the future, but a better tool for coping with a reality blurred by ever-shifting interests.

Michelangelo worked for Clement VII; then helped the Florentine republic (1527–30) with fortifications against that pope; and finally went back to work for the Medicis, who would not dispense with his services. To survive, he trusted art. To survive, Leonardo put his trust in technology. After the Moor's fall, he found immediate employment with Cesare Borgia, whose ruthless activities made no impression whatsoever on him. Some have found it revealing that, on the day when the murdered bodies of Astorre Manfredi and his brother were found in the Tiber, Leonardo wrote that carts with different wheels were used in Romagna. While the Manfredi murder precipitated a wave of speculations, he concluded that carts of that sort were an absurd construction according to the laws of physics.[31] Carts were just objects, and so had been bodies hanged in the Bargello at an earlier time. In 1479 Leonardo made a drawing of the dead body of Bernardo di Bandino Baroncelli, who had been executed after his attempt on Giuliano de' Medici's life. The sketch (Fig. 30) is accompanied by handwritten details that suggest an inventory for a possible commission. Leonardo could deal with carts, corpses, and tyrants in cold blood, since they were just vectors and

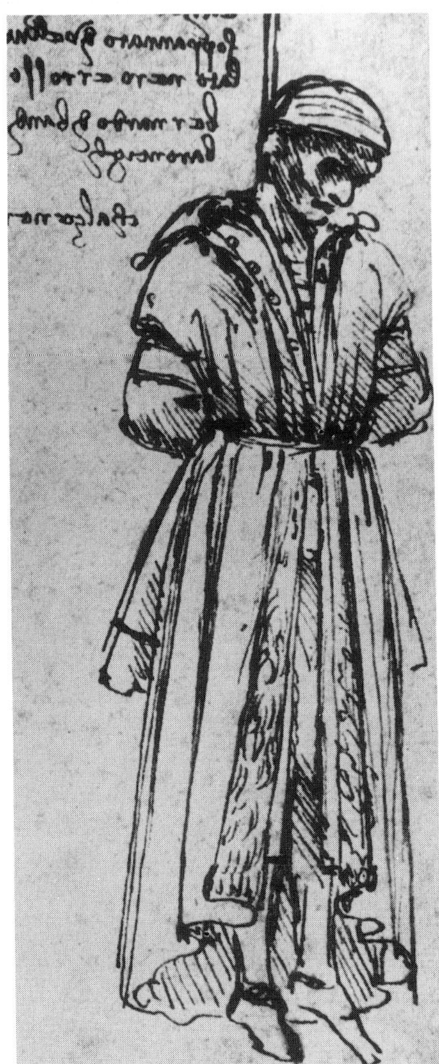

FIG. 30.   Leonardo da Vinci,
*Drawing of Bernardo di Bandino
Baroncelli Hanging* (1479)
Musée Bonnat, Bayonne

victims of a blind inevitability that leveled historical fortunes. I cannot help thinking of his Petrarchan quotation (Windsor 12349v): "*Passano nostri triunfi, nostre pompe.*" Art in general and painting in particular were but screens through which Leonardo could look at life with detachment. That posture brought safety to an artist who lived at bay of everyone else's rise and fall.[32]

Among "primitive" people such as Eskimos and Australian aborigines, so we are told, there is no proper word for war; there could have been fights, but not wars. By contrast, it seems that war not only originated with the high cultures but seems inseparable from them.[33] It would therefore be safe to assume that it will also end with them. Nowadays, "to civilize" implies the epiphany of technology, which has showered much art of war. Once again, Leonardo was prophetic when he linked the two to humanity's fateful demise.

8

Yet how would Leonardo have painted a battle? His fresco in Palazzo Vecchio melted down, but his literary descriptions have been preserved. In the multilayered tapestry of his literary endeavors, the rhetoric of power remained just as suggestive. Foreshadowing became pictorial: "First you must represent the smoke of artillery mingling in the air with the dust and tossed up by the movement of horses and the combatants" (601). Leaders do not stand out, and only an insignia rallies warriors to a point of even greater violence. Man's lethal efforts at wasting human lives are obscured by atmospheric disturbances that cover up the deadly struggle. At the same time, cannon balls with "a train of smoke following their flight" (602) trace the destructiveness of artillery. The dusty blanket does not discriminate between victors and vanquished; it trails after brutal deeds and is pierced through by the "crying out and lamentations" (602–3) of the wounded. The story breaks down amid the turmoil of a human carnage we can catch glimpses of through ominous perturbations of air and dust. The literary image becomes a phenomenon.

For Machiavelli, smoke and dust weigh on tactical concerns, since "many strong armies have been routed when their vision has been obstructed by the dust of the sun. . . . To blind a hostile army about to fight a battle with him (Epaminondas), he had his light cavalry gallop before the front of the enemy to raise the dust high and obstruct their view; this gave him victory in that battle" (*The Art of War* 3). Nature must be controlled, and hopefully turned to one's advantage through staged descriptions that comply with standards of order: "You see with what valor our men fight and with what discipline, as a result of the training that has made it their habit and of the confidence they have in their army; you see how at its own pace and with the men-at-arms on its flanks, it moves on regularly to come to close quarters with the adversary" (*The Art of War* 3). At the beginning of most sentences, the verbs "you see," "observe," and phrases such as "do you not see?" set a visual point of view through which we look down on the battlefield, where "discipline," "training," "order," and "habit" describe maneuvers as flawlessly geometric as the perspectival environments that fifteenth-century art has made us familiar with. Under such conditions, victory would be "certain," and literary texts would be expected to stage exemplary *istorie*. At the end of his description, Machiavelli notes that "with still greater success we would win if I were permitted to put it into action." We edge here on the humanist threshold of virtual accomplishments. As a most attractive form of wishful thinking, the *istoria* could only flow out of the writer's pen and be fought on the battleground of written pages.

For those who survive in Leonardo's notes, the end of the battle gives them a chance to clear their eyes: "You would see some of the victors leaving the fight and issuing from the crowd, rubbing their eyes and cheeks with both hands to clean them of the dirt made by their watering eyes smarting from the dust and smoke." A moment too soon, however; for beyond the thickness of dust other soldiers guess the progress of the combat, ready to move in and renew the struggle: "The reserves may be seen standing, hopeful but cautious; with watchful eyes, shading them with their hands and gazing through the dense and murky confusion, attentive to the commands of their captain. The captain himself, his staff raised, hurries towards these auxiliaries, pointing to the spot where they are most needed" (602).[34] Action speaks for itself, and officers need not exhort their soldiers with rhetorical weapons of a kind familiar to Machiavelli's warrior-orator.

On the subject of warfare, rhetoric was but a metaphor for desire, as impressive as the engrossing belligerence of Leonardo's own *Battle of the Stendard* (see Fig. 26). Its rhetoric of exaggeration was deliberate, since battle scenes called for "an infinite number of distortions and contortions of those who take part in such discord or, you might say, most brutal madness." Man's irrationality broke down measures of restraint, and discordant styles of excess emerged. Leonardo's narrative is expressionistic, to say the least: "He who weeps also tears his garments and hair with his hands" (McMahon, 266, 420, 423). The rhetoric of war confronts readers with the unraveling of a systematic assault on life. Soldiers can clear their eyes but not their ferocity, which trades compassion for bestiality. In one case, a beaten warrior shields "his terrified eyes with one hand, the palm towards the enemy, while the other rests on the ground to support his half raised body." Others, instead, are shown "disarmed and beaten down by the enemy, turning upon the foe, with teeth and nails, to take an inhuman and bitter revenge" (602). At that moment, humanity and inhumanity cancel each other out. Pity is out of place, and revenge stirs further aggression.

9

Paolo Uccello resolved war into games of linear clashes on chessboards where dead horses are as stiff as fallen statues. Form and feeling somehow could not come together but through the staging of a kind of puppet show we could best phrase in the poet's words:

> As if the soldier died without a wound;
> As if the fibers of this godlike frame
> Were gored without a pang; as if the wretch,
> Who fell in battle, doing bloody deeds,
> Passed off to Heaven, translated and not killed.
> (Coleridge, *Annus Mirabilis*)

Leonardo, instead, centered on the tragic and yet creative paradox of violence, which is at once destructive and life-sustaining.

Only if we were to take Leonardo's literary *ekphrasis* and the cartoon of the central episode of the *Battle of Anghiari* as indications of what the painting in Palazzo Vecchio might have been, can we begin to value the loss of an artwork that would have rushed in much of the baroque language of art, as Rubens well understood.

7

The Daedalian *Artifex:*

Myth, Technology, and Doom

*I am a technician but I am also a legend so that I survive
suspended in a solution of memory.*
—Michael Ayrton

In 1959 C. P. Snow stirred controversy in a lecture on the twentieth-century gap between art and science. Criticism of the split between the "two cultures" fostered dialogue, which raised hopes that "the clashing point of two subjects, two disciplines" would produce "creative chances."[1]

This is not the place to measure the distance between art and science in our modern age, when the scientist has been called a learned ignoramus by José Ortega y Gasset; when Philip Frank has taken the philosophy of science to be the missing link that could secure the unity of knowledge; and when Michel Serre has maintained that art, science, and philosophy are still bound by common goals. But this is the place to remind ourselves that watersheds of that sort did not exist at the time of Leon Battista Alberti and Leonardo da Vinci, when creative activities of all sorts enhanced each other in treatises and works of art. In the aftermath of the debate on the two cultures, some have defended the manifold modes of a tradition whose unity has become ever more complex. Life is wider than science, art, philosophy or all of them together. The fact is that mind encloses science, not the other way around.[2] Alberti and Leonardo never doubted that, even though they inherited a conflictive view of the relationship between *artes mechanicae* and *artes liberales*. The Hellenic habit of thinking in terms of axiological antitheses, in fact, never bridged the gap between Diogenes the philosopher and Daedalus the technician.[3]

2

In antiquity, Archimedes discriminated between mental and manual labor. Since he regarded "as ignoble and sordid the business of mechanics and every sort of art which is directed to use and profit" (Plutarch, *Lives of the Noble Romans,* Marcellus), only need could put mathematics to practical use. While the education of the master was mainly concerned with words, slaves were occupied with things; and knowledge of the nature of things was institutionally unworthy.[4] However admirable their achievements, Euclid and Archimedes did not promote progress in a modern sense, and the secondary role that technology was allowed to play in Greek culture was a factor in its decline.

By contrast, slavery had faded in the "New Athens," where technology made an impact on business, banking, education, and household management. However ironic the narrative mode of his *Momus,* Alberti praised the *homo artifex* as a builder. In Jupiter's own words, "we tried to build a new world, as if we could not tolerate our eternal serenity, which we thought we had to earn." It was a mistake, but the urge to "make" overrode the bliss of the "given." Work had become a measure of human divinity. From art to technology, man's ingenuity leaned toward mythmaking. The Renaissance output of mechanized artifacts, in fact, would have endorsed Gabriel Marcel's contention "that in its peculiar way technology is an heir of idealism."[5]

In that climate, Leonardo bridged the gap between theory and practice through mechanics, which "are the paradise of mathematical science, because here we come to the fruits of mathematics" (1155). In turn, technology put scientific ideas to practical use: "Science is the observation of things possible, whether present or past" (1148). To that effect, he recommended to "have Avicenna's work on useful inventions translated" (1434). Yet he did not want to "mix up practice with theory, which would produce a confused and incoherent work." Therefore, "the Book of the science of Mechanics must precede the Book of useful inventions" (5, 7).

Leonardo understood that the progress of technology was bound to strain the link between form and function: "Beauty and utility cannot exist together, as seen in fortresses" (1445). In our own day, efforts have been made to sort out what is distinctive about art, science, and technology. Briefly put, the aesthetic attitude is inquisitive, and it seeks satisfaction. For its part, science seeks knowledge regardless of practical goals. Since it constructs bridges, bombs, and a thousand mechanisms for controlling nature,[6] technology brings satisfaction, which in turn stirs knowledge; they can hardly be set apart. Leonardo already had faced a similar dilemma when he realized that technology could develop unnatural forms. Our very concepts of imitation, scale, and proportion could be changed forever. Efficiency no longer accepted reality as a world of images loaded with inviolable values. A new aesthetic consciousness was about to emerge, and knowledge at large would be affected by it.

At that early stage, relationships between technology and reality often stirred antagonism. At the source, technology proved to be self-referential. Leonardo never thought of integrating machines with nature. "Antipastoral" dialogues between locomotive and landscape would have been unacceptable to him. Nor would he have let technology pitch myth against the unknown just to set the imagination free.[7]

Throughout the Renaissance, however, the growth of technology kept at pace with a mythology that the humanists rooted in a kind of metahistorical modernity. Mythmaking no longer was an act of prehistorical remembrance, but a process that found its very point of origin in the present. Leonardo's "bird" therefore refers to Icarus only in the mode of poetic referentiality. In the mode of mythmaking activity, it is the "making" that makes myth modern. And technology often provided the means for meeting that challenge.

3

On technological grounds, the Renaissance *condottiero* was a sort of mathematical warrior. The texts of Valturio, Pacioli, and Ascham tell us that he arranged troops and fortifications with scientific accuracy. In the preface to the English translation of Euclid, John Dee later coined the term *stratarithmetrie*, which applied mathematical principles to military tactics. Yet it was not until the late sixteenth century that the rise of technology drew scholar and craftsman together.

Because its means and ends are man-made, technology is other, if not better, than nature; its novelty tests invention in much the same way as art can produce images unknown to nature. The *homo faber* could build a universe of his own making at a time when culture favored modes of creation that pitched *imitatio* against *aemulatio*. At all times, technology claimed priority for the present over the past.[8]

4

Inasmuch as the inventor can alter the order of nature, myth has linked technology to Daedalus, who designed the equipment that made it possible for Pasiphaë to couple with a bull. To keep their hybrid offspring in a suitable place, he also built a labyrinth to house the Minotaur. In the poet's verse, "He turned his thinking / Toward unknown arts, changing the laws of nature" (Ovid, *Metamorphoses* VIII, 190). We find here early warnings against the progress of technology, whose dynamics call for control and transgression alike. Invention edged on astuteness. Daedalus's very name means "cunningly wrought," an attitude of mind that was to bear on Leonardo's military inventions. One of Daedalus's most celebrated works was the Golden Honeycomb in the temple of Venus at Eryx in Sicily. His link to a master bee therefore was intentional. It suffices to mention that he had grown wings to escape the labyrinthine hive of many cells.[9] As a sculptor, Daedalus invented bronze casting, a technique that Leonardo hoped to raise to gigantic heights in Milan.[10] On either mythic or anthropological grounds, early man was at once cave artist and toolmaker. He was a technician out to master reality on the trail of Daedalus, and a dreamer driven to share eternity with the gods on Hermes' wings.

In myth, Daedalus was careful to build wings that were accurate, and was just as cautious to fly halfway between sun and sea. He meant to follow the natural order. It was assumed that birds only flew in the lower air, which was the most suitable to breathe. By and large, the more powerful gods rarely resorted to wings in their heavenly migrations.[11] While it was not typical of Attic Greek imagination, flight with wings attached to the body emerged through contacts with Asia and Middle Eastern mythology. Even though Plato noted that "the natural function of the wing is to soar upward and carry that which is heavy to the place where dwells the race of the gods" (*Phaedrus* 246d–e), the Greek notion of flight was horizontal; it conformed with the order of nature. The vertical thrust of Icarus was punished as an act of antinatural hubris.

Later, Christian ascents and descents tested natural gravity in the paintings of Tintoretto. On more spiritual wings, Giordano Bruno's Icarus stood a better chance to soar toward infinity at the end of the sixteenth century.

The Daedalian mode of flight emerged at the watershed between myth and science. Beyond legends, no aeronautical artifacts survived antiquity. As a painter and an inventor growing up in the culture of humanist *aemulatio,* Leonardo had to outdo the ancients, but he could count only on a few legends. Among literary reports about mythic exploits toward the middle of the fifteenth century, Giovanni da Fontana refers to Alexander the Great's flight on a sort of chariot powered by griffins, which he coached by maneuvering pieces of meat held in front of them.[12] The narrative praises human genius, but it also recognizes an excess of daring in man.

Daedalian efforts to follow the given order of nature presumed that man's subjection to gravity was but a measure of his fallen state. The idea of human flight stemmed from immoderate pride, which the legendary Faust was to steer toward the magical powers of aeromancy.[13] The earliest myths and legends about bird-men concern magicians, men of exceptional gifts like Daedalus, or kings like Alexander, whose fame gave him reasons for defying the God-ordained nature of things.[14] Usually transgressions of that kind led to broken legs and deadly falls. Even the latter-day "Daedalus of Perugia," Giovanni Battista Danti, dared to fly too high and fell on a roof, hurting his leg (about 1498/99). Technological progress was ominous and its transgressive mode exacted a price on human daring.

Leonardo set his studies of bird wings against a peculiar model: "Remember that your bird should have no other model than the bat, because its membranes serve as an armour or rather as a means of binding together the pieces of its armour, that is the framework of the wings. . . . Dissect the bat, study it carefully, and on this model construct the machine" (McCurdy, 489, 437). The reference is revealing, for the bat is a kind of hybrid—half bird and half rat—very much like the ornithopter wings Leonardo made so many drawings of. He also wrote about the bat as a symbol of "unbridled lust," since it pairs promiscuously as it may happen (1234), and of blind vice that shies away from the virtues of the blazing sun (1238). Symbolism becomes sinister, and indeed appropriate in the case of a nocturnal animal charged with devilish attributes. On archetypal grounds, in fact, excess and hybridism are crucial to the technological frame of mind. The moment he lifts off in Ovid's *Metamorphoses,* man is birdlike for the gods and godlike for people on earth; yet his condition is metaphorically unbirdly, ungodly, and inhuman even though he somehow shares in all of them. Daedalus, therefore, defied the order he wanted to imitate by the act of imitation itself.[15]

Because transgressions were their trademark, inventors often had to face an adverse fate. Prometheus stole fire and got eternal punishment for it. Daedalus harmed his nephew, and Leonardo was accused of sodomy and other crimes. In a wider cultural framework, we edge on a shift from the Aristotelian concept of nature as an ideal model which art can fulfill to the post-Cartesian belief that art, with the help of science and technology, can be as exemplary as nature itself.

Leonardo studied air currents and the flight of birds before he designed a flying machine, which he based on the imitation of nature. Man powers the wings by standing horizontally (Fig. 31) like a bird: "A bird is an instrument working according to mathematical law, which instrument it is within the capacity of man to reproduce with all its movements. . . . We may therefore say that such an instrument constructed by man is lacking in nothing except the life of the bird, and this life must needs be supplied from that of man" (McCurdy, 493).[16] The inventor soared from scientific instructions to mythic enthusiasm: "Tomorrow morning on the second day of January 1496 I will make the thong and the attempt. . . . To make the paste, strong vinegar, in which dissolve fish-glue, and with this glue make the paste, and attach your leather and it will be good" (McCurdy, 513). The notation of day and month indicates an event that deserved to be marked down on the calendar of technological endeavors. At the same time, the minute list of materials heightens both speculation and expectation.

As such, the text unravels a prosaic narrative that is merely documentative. Yet it also gives the forthcoming deed an aura of plausibility. The test is so important that a recommendation is made: "See tomorrow to all these matters and the copies, and then cancel the originals and leave them at Florence, so that if you lose those that you take with you the invention will not be lost" (McCurdy, 451). The chronological notation takes on a symbolic tone when Leonardo points to the need of keeping a record of the event; originals and copies have to be secured, so that history will remember it. The bureaucratic procedure of dispersing records implies measures of care that betray value. The event about to take place will be worthy of celebration. Rhetoric shifts from the literal to the panegyrical. Just as the actual deed is overshadowed by a deed that is willfully uplifting, the literary form unravels the Daedalian fashioning of a memorable experience.

Life is force, and Leonardo designed mechanisms that would take

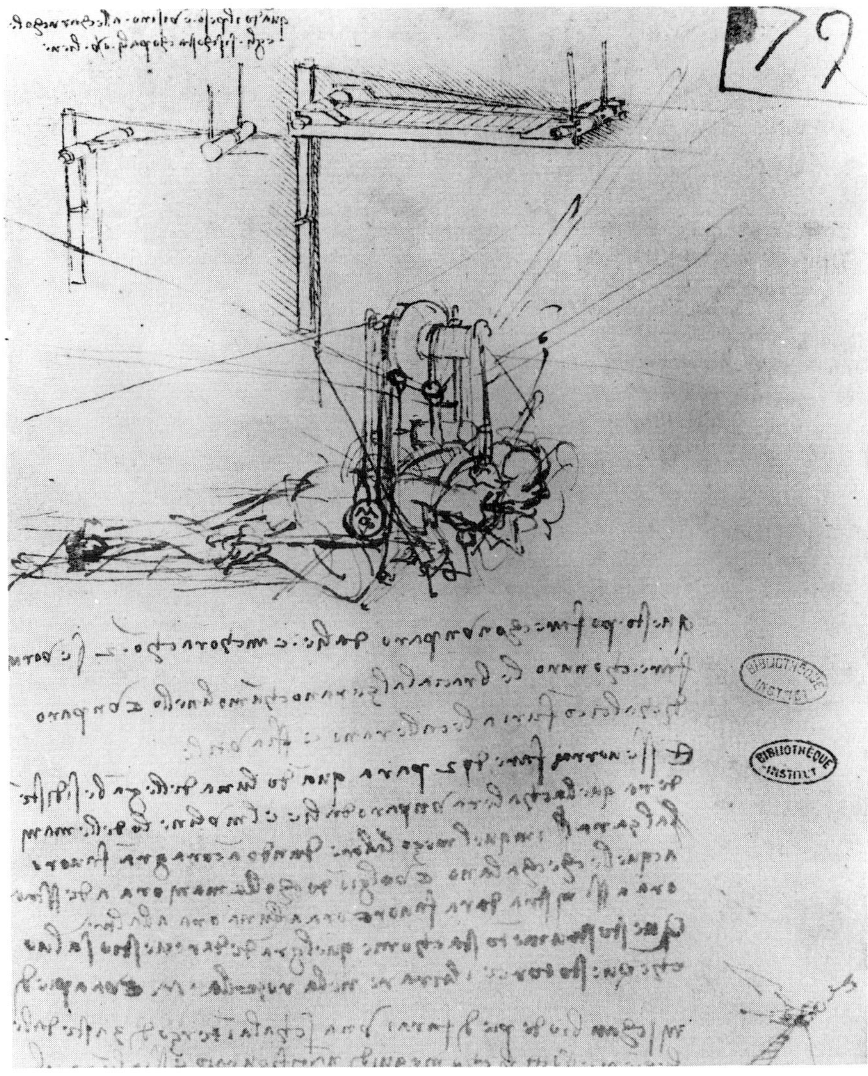

Fig. 31. Leonardo da Vinci, *Type A Ornithopter* (1486–90)
Institut de France, Paris

maximum advantage from the power lodged in man's lower limbs. Yet force "lives always in hostility to whoever controls it . . . without it nothing moves. . . . Power is only a desire of flight. Always it desires to grow weak and to spend itself" (McCurdy, 510–11). Human power is congenitally limited, and desire is equally temporary. Machines could defy the gods, but technological dangers were significant. Leonardo knew it; he therefore made cautionary statements and sketched safety devices. One was the parachute, which would allow the aviator to "throw himself down from any great height without sustaining any injury." Furthermore, the flying machine was to be tried over a lake, and the aviator would carry "a long wine skin as a girdle" (McCurdy, 498) so as not to drown in case of a fall.

Whether in Grecian waters or over Tuscan hills, aviational archetypes would take a toll on human daring. It was myth as much as observation that spurred the inventor. Hephaistos was the god who made weapons, and he was lame. Such a handicap made it impossible for him to run away from warriors who needed his services. Perhaps even the gods thought of craftsmanship as dangerous, though necessary. Mythic warnings must have become all the more meaningful for latter-day inventors whose pride tested heavenly privileges. Anyone who had not learned from the Muses' song but by the Muses' anvil deserved to be either chained or maimed. The Olympian gods did not create the world; they conquered it. Unwillingly, they set a model whose emulation was to be met with brutal punishments. Yet man would never relent in his attempts to usurp their powers.

Leonardo did not resort to any kind of inspired language in his notes on the helicopter (Fig. 32), an idea that was scientifically superior to his bird-man. The point is that the helicopter—and fixed-wing drawings of gliders—had no mythic model. The ornithopters were the least scientific machines that Leonardo invented. He knew better about aviary motion and human power. Yet he was driven by a symbolic commitment to the idea of flight.[17] He had to triumph where Icarus had failed and turned the Daedalian legend into fact. His challenge was myth more than science.

To a substantial extent, Greek myths have given form to creative ideas. Leonardo knew it and bent those exemplary markers to his advantage. Scholarship has wondered about a detail in Leonardo's sketch of a semi-prone ornithopter, which shows a mysterious device that dangles a bell-like object in front of the pilot's nose. I cannot help thinking of Alexander holding pieces of meat in front of his griffins. The motif was there, and Leonardo probably turned it into a bell to wake up the heavens and make sure that the gods would take notice of a new deity flying by. Details of that sort were technologically useless but mythically relevant. The standing ornithopter in a bowl-shaped spaceship was nothing short of a chimera (Fig. 33).[18] Yet it was of the same kind that produced

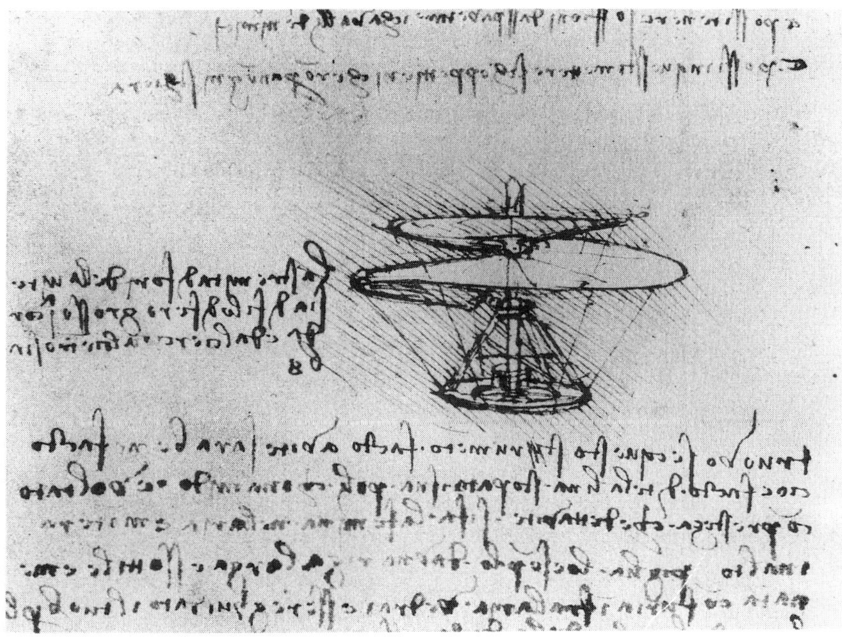

FIG. 32.   Leonardo da Vinci, *Type I Helical Screw Helicopter* (1486–90)
Institut de France, Paris

Alexander's flying basket (*Alexander in Flight,* attributed to Hans Leonhard Schaufelein, 1480–1539).

Chimerical lures have tested human resilience as much as technological ingenuity. A few years ago, a team of MIT graduates brought a man-propelled plane to Crete. They called it "Daedalus" and planned to make a flight to the island of Santorini, about sixty-two miles northeast; an exercise in futility nowadays. After years of planning, weeks of waiting, and numerous attempts called off at the last moment because of adverse weather conditions, the "Daedalus" finally took off. At about fifty yards from shore, gushes of wind broke a wing and the plane fell; Daedalus turned into Icarus. Nevertheless, the flyer survived and made it to land in about four hours. Nature took only a symbolic toll for man's challenge. The plane had kept near sea level throughout, while jets that crossed the skyways above remained unnoticed. It is almost a matter of general indifference that high-tech aviational wonders are produced every day. When the "Daedalus" took off, however, Cretans were out to celebrate,

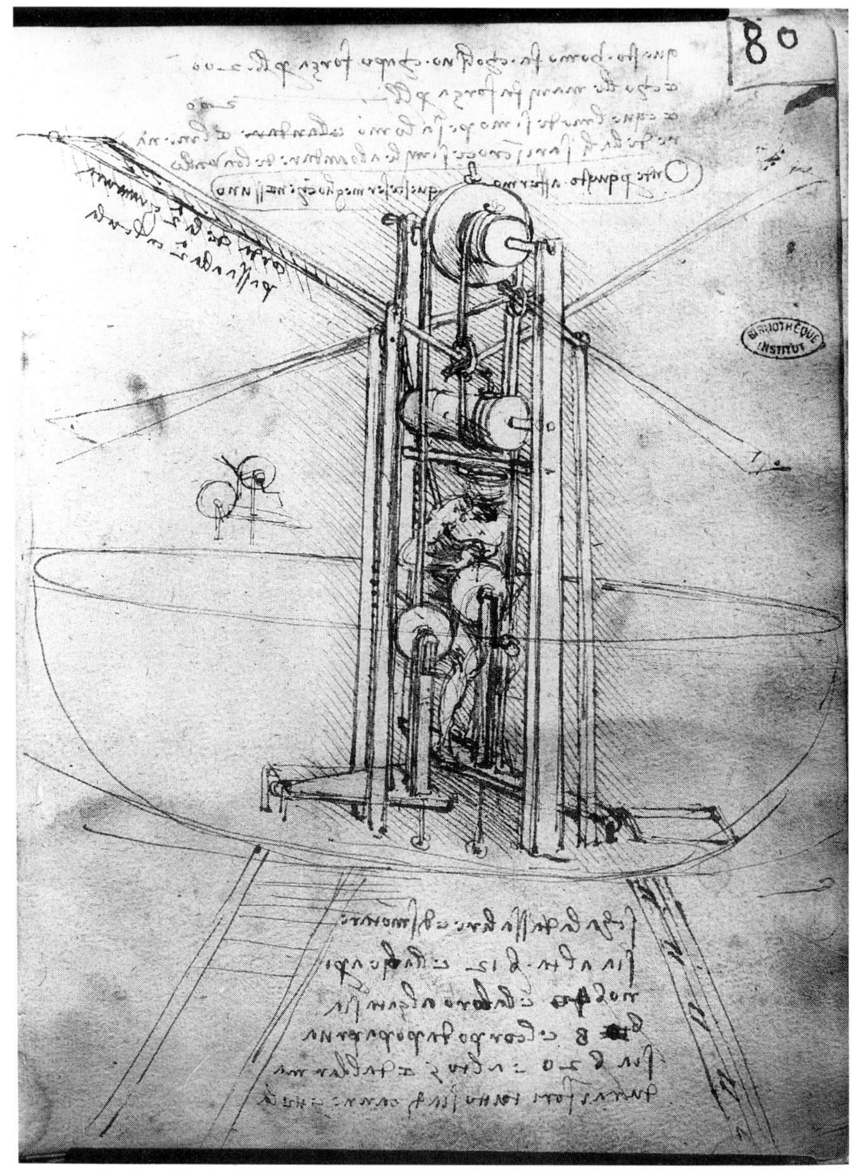

FIG. 33. Leonardo da Vinci, *Type C Standing Ornithopter* (1486–90)
Institut de France

and Greeks everywhere rejoiced at its success. The question is, Why? Sir Edmund Hillary climbed Mount Everest because it was there. It could be argued that the MIT crew took up the Daedalian challenge because the myth was there. Insofar as our Western makeup is classically oriented, myth brings up tests of human excellence as towering as the highest mountain peak. To answer what he has asked of himself since time immemorial, man fulfills myth, and by so doing he takes stock of his godly sparkle.

At the boundary of a mythmaking language of epic majesty, Leonardo wrote: "The great bird will take its first flight upon the back of the great swan, filling the whole world with amazement and filling all records with its fame; and it will bring eternal glory to the nest where it was born" (McCurdy, 420). Praise is bestowed on the great bird, and glory will be brought to its nest. Language presents a bird supported by another bird in a flight of fantasy. The imagery is cognizant of a fateful transgression that cannot let the human artifice flaunt its man-made nature at the most literal level. Form and meaning have been released to "winged words" that thrive on the transferential power of metaphor; its etymology, after all, points to a "change of place." Even prophecies add to a riddle-like turn of mind: "Feathers shall raise men towards heaven even as they do birds: —That is by letters written with their quills" (McCurdy, 1115). *Metaphora* could make men fly on technological and literary wings alike.

However unwittingly, Leonardo took metaphor as an archetypal figure of speech stemming right from an itinerant mode that started with Adam's displacement from Eden. Metaphor was but the verbal form of our myth of origin.[19] Language transferred the timid jump from a Tuscan slope to a Daedalian feat of aviational temerity. Technology, art, and writing joined forces in spelling the emergent language of infinity. The text thrived on a panegyrical vocabulary as hypothetical as the humanist rhetoric of praise. In the Promethean mode, however, personal thoughts and ancestral heritage uttered a language that partook of myth as much as of science. That kind of fateful rhetoric touched on events that would change human nature. Promethean feelings, in fact, entail a sense of the risk of experience, which often has underrated scientific plausibility.[20]

Yet Leonardo's flying machine was not a way station between Icarian feathers and the fixed wings of airplanes. While drawing knowledge from birds and strength from gods, he believed that technology could fulfill mythic beliefs and scientific hypotheses. Martin Heidegger reminds us that technology involves two meanings: skill and knowledge. One refers to the "making" of craftsmanship. The other links *techne* to *episteme,* which refers to a knowledge that provides an opening up, a bringing forth; in other words, the knowledge that presides over the skillful "making" of ships, chalices, or houses. What is decisive in "*techne* does not lie at all in making and manipulating nor in the using of means, but rather in the aforementioned revealing. . . . Technology is a mode of revealing."[21]

We seem to be edging here on mythic archetypes that favor ideation over execution. In terms of the house, plan is more important than construction. In that sense, the teleological thrust of technology was akin to the humanist emphasis on theoretical drawings that Alberti found more satisfying than actual construction.[22] Leonardo's sketches, therefore, are epistemological exercises in the knowledge, rather than the practice, of technology. They are annotations replete with mythic referentiality.

Leonardo's flying machine did not take off; or maybe it did, if we believe Gerolamo Cardano, who refers to two unsuccessful attempts (*De Subtilitate*). Both of them would have been as fascinated as Petrarch by the story of "a man who soared toward heaven on his wings, and another who survived beneath the waves." Those were rare cases, and there were "many things we could do if we didn't renounce them in despair without making the effort."[23] At any given point, technology, faith, or the gods may fail man. His fatal demise, however, can only occur when he fails to believe in the power of myth. At the beginning, there was a quest, whose metaphorical symbolism has made of myths of origin our latest, and our last, hope. The loss of myth, therefore, would entail the loss of both origin and destiny.

5

Because he had found life at the edge attractive, Leonardo was critical of people who "possess information of those things of which the human mind is incapable and which cannot be proved by any instance from nature"; instead, we should not "desire the impossible." Yet his drawings of the flying machine, the helicopter, the submarine, underwater equipment, and other attempts at working out "miracles" in mechanics and anatomy prove that his lifework was a quest after the impossible. His driving commitment to the progress of knowledge would be echoed in Nicolaus Steno's much quoted line: "Beautiful is that which we see, more beautiful that which we know, but by far the most beautiful that which we do not comprehend."[24] If only on paper, and if only in the mode of either hope or remembrance, they updated the Heraclitean core of mythic longing: "If he does not hope for it, he will not find then unhoped for, it being uninvestigated and unapproachable" (B, 18). Perhaps Leonardo's classical counterparts were those half-fabulous Palamedean artist-craftsmen—the *technitai*—headed by Eupalinos. It may not be accidental that Leonardo and Eupalinos became central to Paul Valéry's mythmaking architecture of art. In his own notes on the *Notebooks,* the Frenchman wrote that "Leonardo was the first to understand that *knowing* and *making* cannot long remain separated without damage." The Frenchman was probably right in guessing that an abyss would challenge Leonardo to "think of a bridge."[25]

A generation after Leonardo, Niccolò Tartaglia praised the scientist's power to remake creation:

> Chi brama di veder nove inventioni
> Non tolte da Platon, ne da Plotino,
> Ne d'alcun altro Greco, over Latino,
> Ma sol da l'arte, misure, a Ragioni,
> Lega di questo le interrogationi

> (Whoever desires to see new inventions
> Not taken from Plato or Plotinus,
> Nor by any Greek or Latin,
> But solely from art, measurement, and reasoning,
> May he read the inquiries of this person).

Invention suffered no anxieties of influence in the realm of technology, whose ground-breaking dynamics stood on equal footing with transgressions in art. It has been asked whether the discovery of the New World could have taken place without the discovery by artists, poets, and philosophers of man as an individual whose inquisitiveness had become unrelenting. Pico della Mirandola's rhetoric of praise in his *Oration on the Dignity of Man* was as significant a testimony to human ingenuity as Christopher Columbus's seafaring journey or the flying machine that Leonardo conceived in order to fulfill one of man's oldest quests. Endeavors of that kind gave man power over the world. It is less than a coincidence that the quantitative nature of technology became a challenge at a time when geographical discoveries were well on their way to double the known surface of the earth.[26] The words of authority were set next to the deeds of men who tested boundaries of all sorts.

Much of the humanist rebirth of antiquity rested with atemporal analogues that favored "spatial sameness" over "temporal growth." Aristotle's biological interests could have led him to take notice of time-space, but he did not. Even his logic was a spatial logic that proved to be inadequate for expressing the dynamics of time.[27] The growth of technology remained minimal until the thirteenth century, when the recovery of Greek and Arabic science together with Aristotelian and Euclidian texts spurred activist leanings that led to the experimentalism of the School of Padua, where Cusanus, Regiomontanus, and Copernicus preceded Galileo.[28]

Leonardo's axiomatic belief in motion as the source of life, and in man as an inventor out to shape things in spite of final doomsdays, drew temporality into his worldview. At a macrocosmic level, motion generates "force," which is "the mother and origin of gravity ... force is unlimited, and by it infinite worlds might be moved if instruments could be made by which the force could be generated" (McMahon, 7, 859). In the same breath, study and speculation energize each other. At first, faith in the instruments of knowledge seems to verge on a godlike utterance of Faustian might. Upon reflection, however, why should one make instruments for shifting the order of the whole cosmos? Perhaps this is a personal insight into the self-fulfilling potential of a technology by far more hypothetical than the one Leonardo offered to the Moor.

Since births and rebirths were forms of ceaseless growth for Leonardo, his technological sketches bear out a phantasmagoric vocabulary of activity. If humanist scholarship was past-oriented, Leonardesque experimentalism began to look on science not as a set of findings but as the search for them.[29] That search implied labor, which antiquity and early Christianity disparaged. It was the Benedictine rule *ora et labora* (work and worship) that paved the way for a "work ethos" rooted in the symbolism of Saint Joseph as laborer. To weigh the progress of technology on a comparative scale, the Greek-born Neoplatonist Gemistos Pletho was so impressed by Italian crafstmanship that he called for young Greeks to be trained in Venice, where they could learn ironworking and shipbuilding better than anywhere else.[30]

6

The challenge of the "new" led Leonardo to take technology where it had always been needed: the art of war. The very idea of progress, which Francis Bacon would link to navigation, gunpowder, and the printing press, echoed Leonardesque ideas that best vindicated the scientific heritage of Abelard and Roger Bacon.

Leonardo's drawing of the Scythian chariot went back to accounts of Alexander the Great's campaigns. In earlier illustrations such as Valturio's, heavy wagons were drawn by oxen, which pulled mobile artillery almost to the end of the fifteenth century. That technology changed when Charles VIII invaded Italy. By contrast, the Leonardesque drawing is "modern" in style and function. The sheer beauty of its dynamic thrust (Fig. 34) seems to go back to ancient race chariots, which were used for combat occasionally.

Here the ambiguities begin. By Leonardo's own admission, the chariot was actually useless. It was not difficult for the Romans to "spread panic among the horses," which would "charge at their own side in frenzy, despite the efforts of their drivers" (McCurdy, 813). More often than not, mobile chariots would harm their own foot soldiers. As a protective countermeasure, Leonardo designed blades that could be lifted among friendly troops. Although exact, Leonardo's information raises questions. Only the Egyptians and the Mycenaeans used massed chariotry armed with long thrusting-spears and bows. Homeric heroes used chariots for

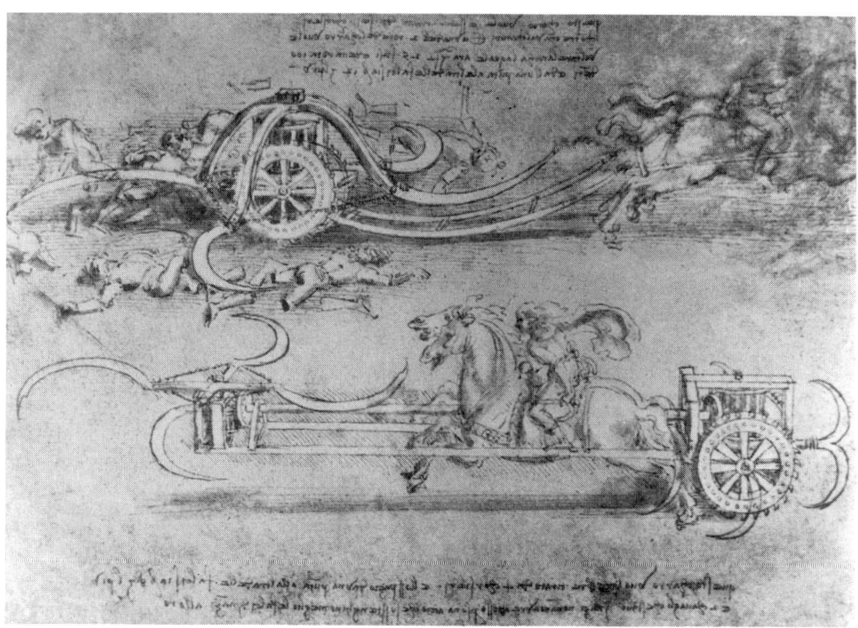

FIG. 34.   Leonardo da Vinci, *Chariot Armed with Scythes*
Royal Library, Turin

transportation to and from battlefields, where they usually fought on foot. Even in the mythic Atlantis a large number of war chariots were used for transportation. Horsemen would fight on foot "carrying a small shield and having a charioteer who stood behind the man-at-arms to guide the two horses" (Plato, *Critias* 119). The exception was the Theban Sacred Band of pairs of "charioteer" and "crew," who later ended up fighting on foot. Darius's scythed chariots required that the ground be leveled. Alexander's troops opened ranks, let them pass through, grabbed the horses' reins and dragged the drivers down. When he painted the *Battle of Issus* (1528), Albrecht Altdorfer presented Darius on a magnificent chariot running away from Alexander, who pursued him on horseback.

For the Romans, chariots were mostly ceremonial and agonistic; they were not important in an army that relied mostly on foot soldiers. The Seleucid king Antiochus used scythe-wheeled chariots against them at Magrasia in Asia Minor (191 B.C.), and Caesar fought British chariots in England (54 B.C.). Because he knew that his soldiers were infantrymen, he relied on the cavalry of Spanish, Gallic, and German allies. Little attention was therefore paid to chariots as major instruments of war.[31] As ceremonial vehicles, however, they carried warriors to their triumph in Rome, and they did it again at a much later time, at least in the paintings of Piero della Francesca and Dürer's drawings.

Technological advantage could be easily reversed. In the mythic tradition of Daedalus, wings could carry to freedom and death alike. While it owes neither loyalty nor exclusivity, technology is available for use and abuse. Functionally, therefore, the Scythian chariot was as impractical as the flying machine; at heart, they were artistic forms. In the world of myth, the Phaedran charioteer heralded a Platonic image of heavenly grandeur. From Plato to Ficino, classical and biblical chariots translated the horizontal warrior's onslaught into vertical flights; they were symbols of transcendence,[32] and raised fact to fame.

As a war machine, the chariot combined human with natural power. The epic charioteer mastered horses, speed, and spear. In the Leonardesque drawing, instead, he does not even stand on the chariot, which becomes a rotary chopping machine whose multiple blades could spin their deadly efficiency beyond the singleness of epic endeavors. Technology plays center stage; man is either subordinated as rider or victimized into chopped body parts. The drawing therefore made of the past a matter of apparent idealization but of actual compromise. After all, how could heroism retain its epic grandeur in a nonepic age? In spite of sustained efforts to the contrary undertaken from Petrarch to Ronsard, the technological crisis of the "epic mode" from books to battlefields was but a sign of its obsolescence. There were traditions that no longer could endure. The descent from classical heavens affected literature and technology alike. The march of progress called for altogether new concepts of beauty and power.

Technology absorbed much of the humanist longing for an antiquity modeled after modern ideals. In the 1430s Mariano di Jacopo, known as Taccola, aspired to become the "Sienese Archimedes," and Leonardo brought classical references to bear on his own future. "Although he had greatly damaged the Romans in the siege of Syracuse," Archimedes "did not fail in being offered great rewards from these very Romans." When Syracuse "was taken, diligent search was made for Archimedes; and he being found dead greater lamentation was made for him by the Senate and people of Rome than if they had lost all their army; and they did not fail to honour him with burial and with a statue" (1476). In a wishful bent of mind, Leonardo may have hoped that Moors and Borgias would have treated him in a similar manner. But they did not, and he knew it. Desire and memory enhanced each other, and the result was a panegyrical vision of the technological *artifex*. In those days, the word *ingegno* was associated with "genius" and "invention"; it qualified architects and builders of machines from Brunelleschi to Alberti. Repeatedly, Francesco di Giorgio Martini, a respected military engineer, had voiced concerns about the devastating power of gunfire. And Leonardo's insistence on "bombardment," "mortar," "artillery," and naval vessels impervious to the attack of the largest guns calls to mind Francesco di Giorgio, who believed that whoever could provide defenses against such weapons of offense surely was endowed with a divine more than human talent ("*Colui adonque che a questa offensione trovasse la defensione, più presto doveria essere chiamato divino che umano ingegno*").[33] For him, architects were Daedalian heirs.

That heritage, we can bet, stood at the forefront of Leonardo's mythmaking mind. Archimedes' military inventions were as mysterious as they were effective. The Roman general, "deriding his own artificers and engineers," was so impressed that he thought of surrendering to that "geometrical Briareus." In fact, Archimedes "plays pitch-and-toss with our ships, and, with the multitude of darts which he showers at a single moment upon us, really outdoes the hundred-handed giants of mythology." Even Roman soldiers had come to believe that, because of Archimedes, they were not fighting Syracusans, but "the gods" (Plutarch, *Lives of the Noble Romans*, Marcellus). Leonardo's machines kept the lure of that godly challenge alive in a world from which Alexander and Marcellus were long gone. In the pit of Machiavellian survival at its worst, he did not let the inventor's knowledge become a fatal liability; unlike Archimedes, he did not become a victim to his own ingenuity, for he knew that it was not worth dying for a bunch of villains. Cannons became a status symbol, and beauty veiled their deadly efficiency in Pisanello's drawings for Alfonso I of Aragon. Pius II named his native town Pienza, after his humanist name; he also named two cannons Enea and Silvia after his own name (*Commentaries 5*). Charles V and Henry VIII had gun batteries known as the Twelve Apostles. At the battle of Ravenna (1512), Alfonso d'Este wore a cuirass with the emblem of a flaming bombshell. And Titian later painted him with his arm resting on the muzzle of a cannon. Toward the end of the sixteenth century, theorists of gunnery put their art on a par with music, medicine, astronomy, and mathematics. Dekker wrote a stirring "Praise of the Shotte" in *The Art of Artillery,* whose gunfire became the soldier's choicest music.

7

As a painter, Leonardo wanted judgment to be ahead of execution. As an inventor, he also thought of machines to solve problems that had not yet entered the realm of concrete possibilities. The scientist studied the present, and the inventor built the future; the artist-scientist set out to create technological icons. And so did most humanists with their images of flawless excellence. If we just look at the monumentality of Leonardo's *Giant Ballista* (or *Giant Crossbow with Six Wheels*) and the cannon in *Rhythm in the Workshop* (or *The Courtyard of a Foundry*), we are struck by their kinship with Bramante's Nicchione in the Vatican and the equestrian statue of Colleoni by Verrocchio in Venice.

The man on the *Giant Ballista* (Fig. 35) looks like a minuscule being inadequate to operate a weapon so big that it is more apt to be aimed—like other drawings of giant cannons and multibarreled guns—against groups rather than individuals. At its very inception as a modern myth, technology broke "human measures." In fact, the sheer magnitude of some artillery pieces would have been unfit for transportation on the roads of the day. Enormous bombards were built in the fifteenth century. Some of the heavier ones were German and were almost impossible to move. To a considerable extent, power was a matter of psychological intimidation. Whether artistic or technological, the measure of myth tended to be monumental.

Leonardo's *Rhythm in the Workshop* (Fig. 36) showcases nudes who

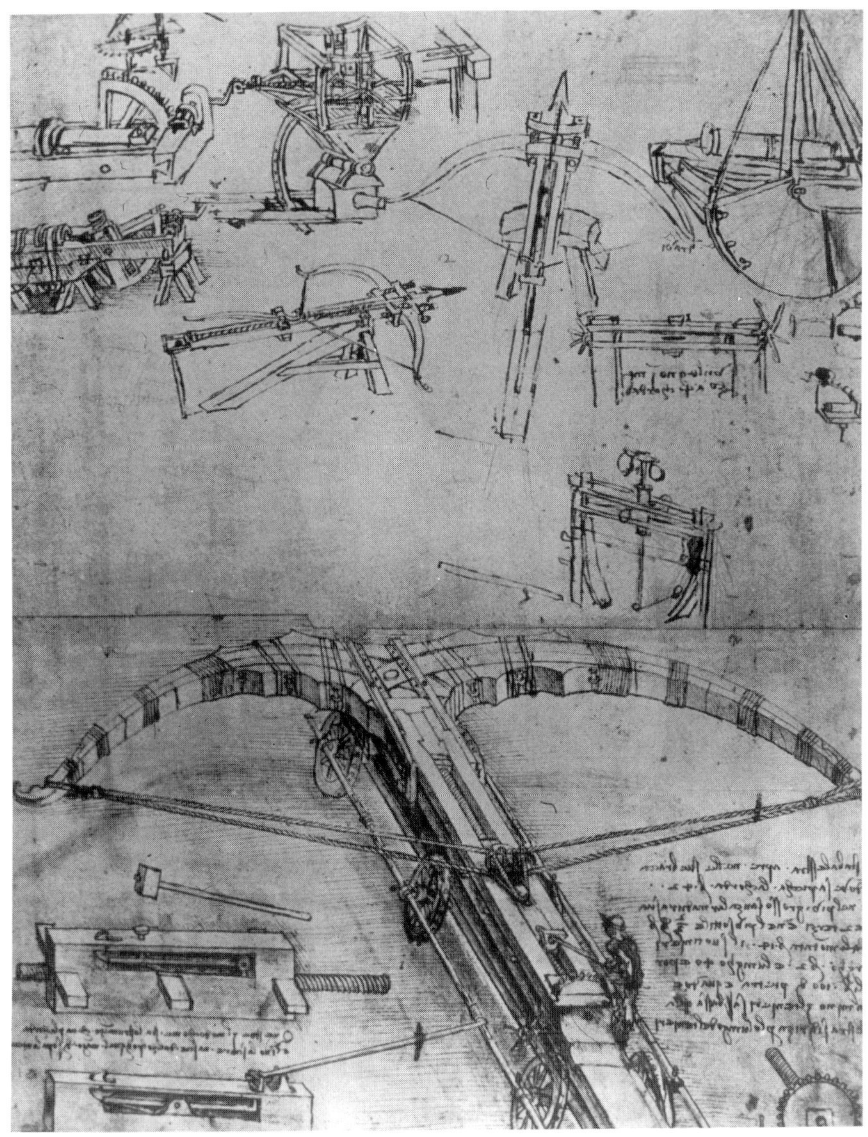

Fig. 35. Leonardo da Vinci, *Giant Ballista*
Biblioteca Ambrosiana, Milan

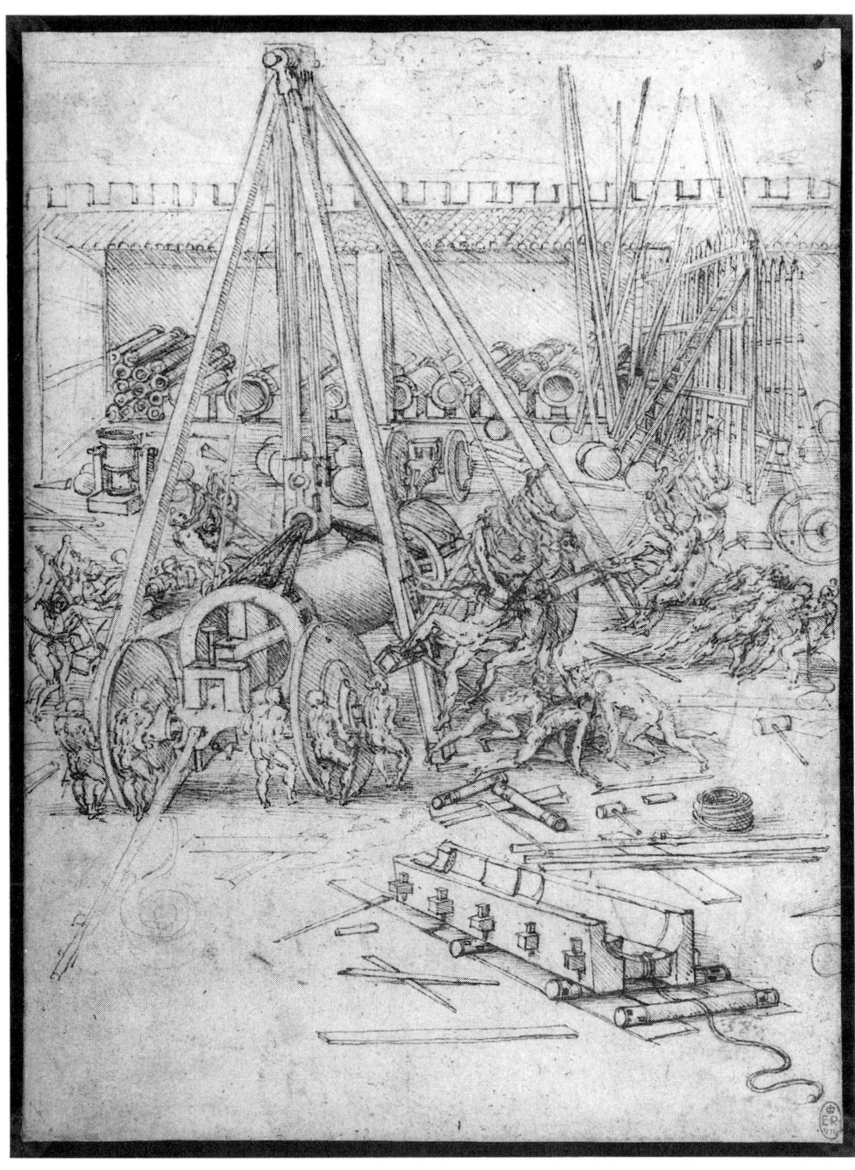

FIG. 36.   Leonardo da Vinci, *Rhythm in the Workshop*
Royal Library, Windsor Castle

struggle to cope with military ingenuity. The gigantic machine dominates the scene amid a vermiculate crowd that toils to make it operational. Construction gadgets and gun barrels are stacked up in the background, thus heightening a quantitative mode of production. Since superiority on the battlefield called for numerical advantage, success rested with novelty as well as with output; technology had to be cornucopian. Assemblage foreshadows usage. However rhythmic, toil in the workshop forewarns doom on the battlefield, while nudity links up to the "wasted" bodies chopped down by the Scythian chariot. Once parts are raised on the carriage, it becomes clear that something in excess of human measure has been created. Cannons and ballistas are sleeping Goliaths too strong for the mightiest David. The image rests on a paradox; it celebrates the inventor's ingenuity, but the very monumentality of the object belittles human presence. To phrase it in Francis Bacon's guarded assessment of mechanical experiments, those laborers would "neither raise their minds nor stretch out their hands for anything else" (*Novum Organum*, aphorism 99). They embody sheer manpower out to counter a greater force they have just manufactured. However powerful, they are too small for the task at hand. Yet their despair is our hope, even though the many gun barrels suggest that the mechanical giant is there to stay. Technological drawings of that sort do not urge viewers to recall the way warriors fought in the traditional battle scenes of Piero della Francesca, Paolo Uccello, or Leonardo's own sketch for the *Battle of Anghiari*. Rather, they challenge us to imagine new tactics and unprecedented casualties, much as they alert us to the bitter irony of men's dependence on his mechanical servants.[34]

The humanist cosmos was abstract, selective, and other than nature. It could be expected to function only in light of man-made criteria that had to be other-than-natural. As a more empirical *omo sanza lettere* who worshiped nature and the dynamics of living processes, Leonardo took a critical stand vis-à-vis the philosophy and poetics of Humanism. As a scientist and an inventor, however, he shared its theoretical stand and deductive method. Invention, in fact, presumes a body of knowledge and a methodology for translating ideas into actual forms more functional than, but just as abstract as, humanist constructs. Alberti did not particularly mind that many of his projects were neither executed nor completed; likewise, Leonardo might have been quite content with his paperbound machines. For certain, both of them settled with the unflawed completeness of their drawings. On such grounds, humanist and antihumanist standpoints were dialogic.

In the place of work, Leonardo's nudes are so mechanized that the

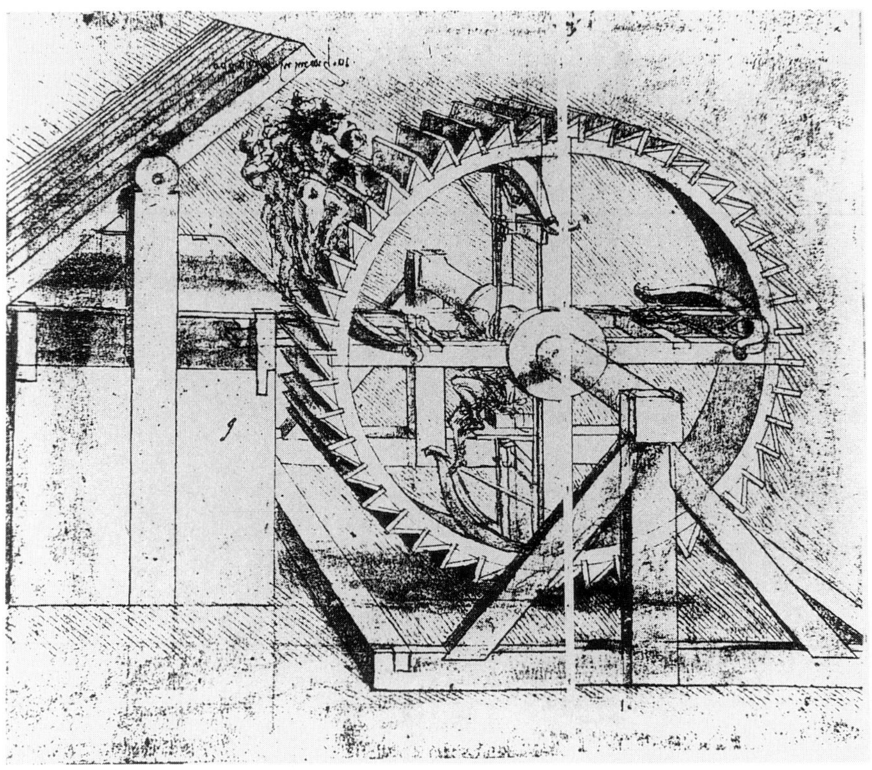

Fig. 37.   Leonardo da Vinci, *Machine Gun with Archer and Threadwheel*
Biblioteca Ambrosiana, Milan

drawing with archers and threadwheels (Fig. 37) makes of man a functional part inside machines that force him to move "technologically." The archer's task is to trigger each crossbow as it descends the quadrant before him, shooting through the slot at given times. We are nearing the concept of automation, which Leonardo reinforced in his drawing of the file maker (Codex Atlanticus 6r) through a sequence of interdependent acts that would minimize decision making. Human actions only enforce the inventor's search after more efficient ways for using the human motor. To that effect, Ladislao Reti tells us that Leonardo measured the force of every muscle. He "was the first engineer who tried to find a quantitative equivalent for the forms of energy available. . . . Often, he compared the human body with a mechanical system."[35] The clockwise precision of war machines in which man had to operate at pace with timed motions brought to the fore a regularity that was compatible with humanist treatises in which human conduct was meant to conform with theoretical plans.

At the turn of the sixteenth century, there were activities—ceramics, textiles, printing, weapons—that employed men in repetitive operations. In Milan, the arms industry kept over one hundred shops busy. Since it employed over two thousand men, the Venetian Arsenal could either build or repair many galleys at one time. Mass production was beginning to emerge. The urge to improve quantitative output was pervasive, and Leonardo invented multibarreled machine guns and rapid-fire guns.[36] As an artist, however, quantification was not a criterion of excellence for him.[37] Painting "cannot be copied as can words and phrases, where the copy is worth as much as the original. It cannot be cast, as sculpture can. . . . It does not have an infinite progeny as does the printing of books. Painting alone remains noble, it alone honors its author and remains precious and unique, never bringing forth children equal to itself" (McMahon, 18). Painting was quality that could not be serialized; it was inimitable.

8

Human actions in Leonardo's technological drawings seem to be paced by clock-measured time, which stood at the other side of the agricultural and seasonal "time of the Church." A shift was taking place from the Julian to the Gregorian calendar (1582). It was in the fourteenth century that time based on the canonical hours of monastic life gave way to clocks whose regularity was more in tune with the demands of bourgeois sectors. We thus confront a rather modern concept of production time. Church bells, sundials, and clepsydras gave way to technological ways of measuring time. Mechanical clocks made their appearance toward the end of the thirteenth century, and spring-driven clocks were manufactured at the beginning of the fifteenth century. Giovanni Tortelli was amazed that clocks work on man's behalf by synchronizing human actions.[38] Alberti praised the emergence of an intensely functional use of time, which even Petrarch had appreciated. The emergence of mercantile economies increased the tempo of life; time was well on its way to becoming a commodity in the art of war, in business, and even in scholarship.[39] Vergerius recommended that a clock be kept in every library, for it added dignity to man's labor; even sixteenth-century portraits began to display clocks.

It was in a room filled with the noise of printing presses that Erasmus and Aldus Manutius worked on the Venetian edition of the *Adages*. Upon reflection, the humanist scholar wrote that, whereas the libraries of princes and scholars were set in enclosed walls, Aldus's production of books was "delimited only by the ends of the world itself." One of Erasmus's lifelong friends was Johann Frobenius, a Swiss who printed the classics, especially those of medicine. From Aldus to Frobenius, the happy passion of printers made its mark on the page almost as powerfully as knowledge itself did.[40]

Although Vespasiano da Bisticci remained forever proud that the Montefeltro library owned books written only with the pen, "and had there been one printed volume it would have been ashamed in such company," the future belonged to printed paper.[41] Rabelais, in fact, demanded that visits to shops of goldsmiths, printers, and watchmakers be a requirement of any liberal education (*Gargantua and Pantagruel* 17). Only in the utopian landscape of Rabelais's golden primitivism could Gargantua have no doubts that the greatest loss of time was to count the hours.[42]

The "time of the scientist" and the "time of the merchant" began to converge. Businessmen found it mandatory to serialize commercial techniques through double-entry bookkeeping—the *partita doppia*. They also resorted to gauging in order to calculate the volume of barrels, which would not be standardized until the nineteenth century. Piero della Francesca wrote a handbook for merchants (*De abaco*), and Leonardo made accurate estimates of labor costs for engineering projects.

9

Because technology tended to produce hardware that was bigger and faster than anything invented before, destruction could be spectacular. As an aloof scientist, Leonardo wrote on the movement of projectiles: "I wish to know what weight ought to be that of lead which will drive a ball of a pound of lead a greater distance from itself than any other weight which is also of lead, the said movers having also the same movement" (McCurdy, 577). The drawing of cannon balls shot through the air by huge bombards (Fig. 38) traces explosions that seem to generate a festive shower of firecrackers. During the last quarter of the fifteenth century, artillery bombardments tested the vulnerability of fortified towns. In Fernand Braudel's happy phrase, ramparts were demolished like " theatre sets."[43] On theatrical grounds, firepower had become part of mock battles, parades,

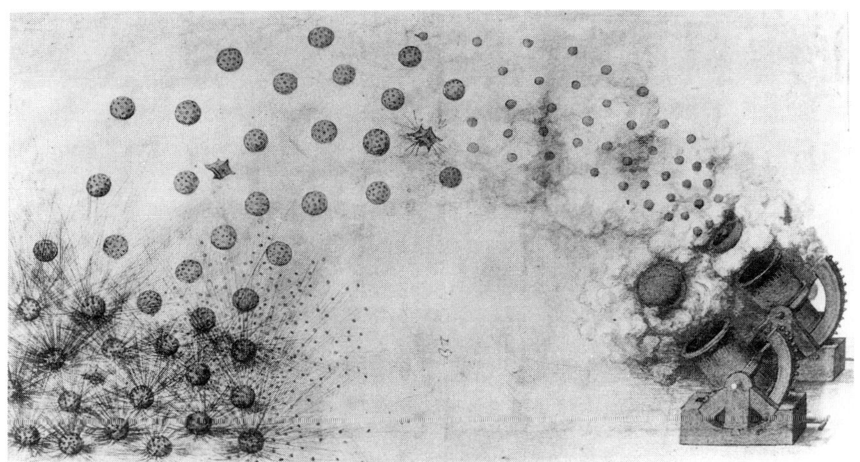

FIG. 38.   Leonardo da Vinci, *Bombards Firing Shrapnel Shells*
Biblioteca Ambrosiana, Milan

and celebratory events in which it mingled with fireworks. Artillery produced a phantasmagoric spectacle that ignited Leonardo's imagination long before Apollinaire and the Futurists would admire the blasts of ever more lethal explosions.

With a passion, Leonardo centered on the dynamics of functionality. He also understood that efficiency was a matter of "how much" as well as of "how fast"; and there were no limits to improvement. Unquestionably, the drawing of the huge bombards was made by an artist who took pleasure in the dynamics of forms whose trajectories and fragmentation reveal as much care as the studies of flowing water or undulating leaves. In the same breath, the beauty of technological motion could be set against natural movement: "The fine drops of rain water seem continuous threads descending from their clouds" (McCurdy, 575). Form unfolds like filaments that are at once point and line, very much like the flight of birds that Leonardo's exceptional eye could catch with comparable keenness. At all levels, he studied and represented the figurative potential of *forza*.

Yet Leonardo was ahead of himself. The point is that mortars could not shoot as many projectiles at one time as the visual image would have us believe they could. His organlike piece of artillery had thirty-three guns; they would be fired eleven at a time, but only on paper. It was technology as it could be at an automated stage which, though thinkable, was unfeasible at that time. For certain, technology thrived on excess and intimidation. Its pictorial rhetoric echoed literary statements that the artist made on the art of war in his letter to the Moor.

Leonardo's sketches set a disproportion between man and man-made objects that I cannot help linking to Piranesi's *Prisons* (Fig. 39). Giant

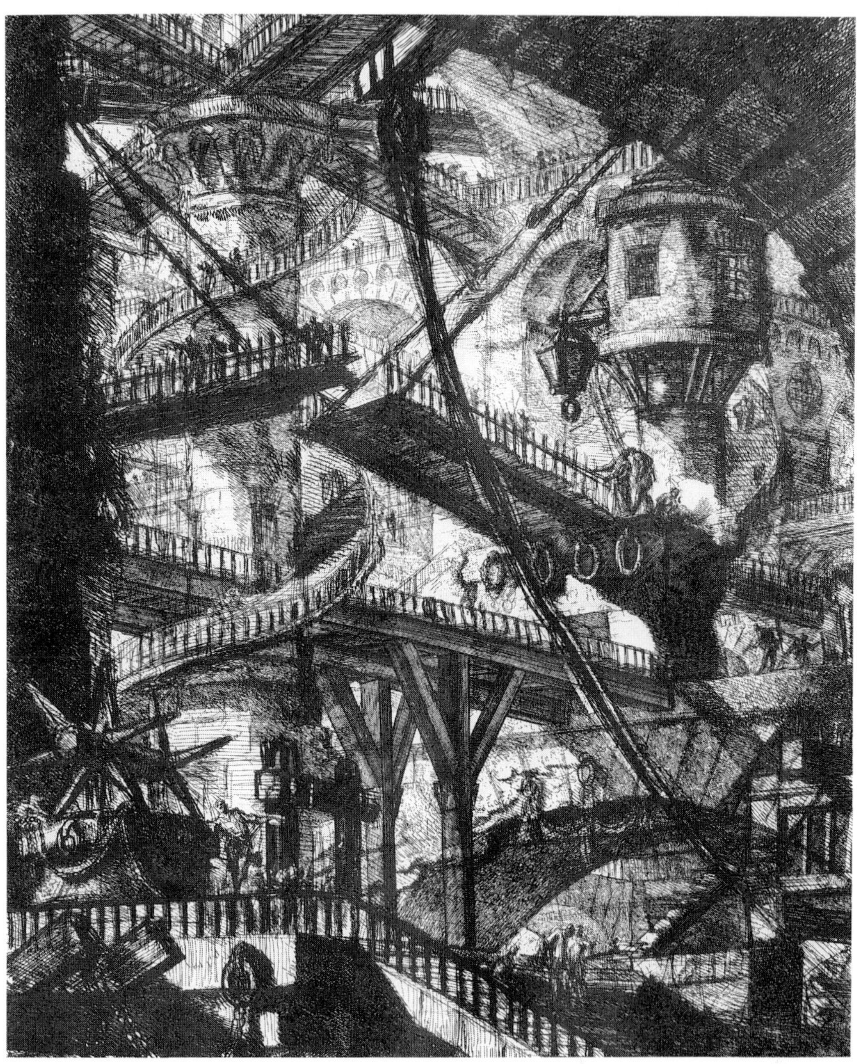

FIG. 39.   Giovan Battista Piranesi, *Prisons* (c. 1761), plate 7, second edition Metropolitan Museum of Art, New York

wheels and screwlike staircases map out the abysmal madness of human ingenuity. Dehumanized silhouettes wander aimlessly as if to expiate the mortal sin of technological pride in their own man-made underworld. Thomas De Quincey and Samuel Coleridge took those images to be "dreams"; better yet, nightmarish gothic halls with machines that had been turned into instruments of torture. Piranesi himself could be identified with one of the minuscule human shadows that reappear on every floor without hope of escape.[44] We are looking at a latter-day Daedalus imprisoned in his own labyrinth. What the *Carceri* and *Rhythm in the Workshop* bring to the fore is the overwhelming predominance of technology, whose power of endless growth victimized operators and inventors alike.

10

Leonardo's prophecies finally took up man's ill-fated abuses of his own talents. The proliferation of metals from prehistoric times to the age of gunpowder updated a devastating march: "That shall be brought forth out of dark and obscure caves, which will put the whole human race in great anxiety, peril and death. . . . This will lead to the commission of endless crimes . . . this will make men torment each other with many artifices, deceptions and treasons" (1295). Such a dim view brought out an unchallengeable sense of inevitability that left no room for doubts, let alone alternatives. We face the prediction of nightmares which the indicative mode—"shall be"—draws within our ontological, if not chronological, reach. Unlike nature, man could be his own mortal enemy. The proud inventor began to reflect on the long-range effects that the abuse of metals was rushing in.

Metals were brought out of womblike caves through acts of transgression that violated the secrets of nature. Since Tibullus, lands of milk and honey were there because gold and iron had not been dug up. Man's proper place, in fact, was at the surface. Leonardo turned toward the future what Ovid recollected from the mythic Age of Iron, when

> The rich earth,
> Good giver of all the bounty of the harvest,
> Was asked for more; they dug into her vitals,
> Pried out the wealth a kinder lord had hidden
> In Stygian shadow, all that precious metal,

> The root of evil. They found the guilt of iron,
> And gold, more guilty still. And War came forth
> That uses both to fight with; bloody hands
> Brandished the clashing weapons
>
> *(Metamorphoses* 136–44)

Metals were forbidden fruits whose usefulness could be lethal. From Ariosto to Spenser, weaponry was consistently linked to images of depth whose darkness was symbolic. In *Les Armes,* Ronsard presumed that whoever invented iron feared no guilt for having killed his whole family.

Once metal was used to make instruments of death, the earth became a living hell where technology and ecology would be locked in a deadly struggle for ages to come: "Animals will be seen on the earth who will always be fighting against each other with the greatest loss and frequent deaths on each side. And there will be no end to their malignity; by their strong limbs we shall see a great portion of the trees of the vast forests laid down throughout the universe. . . . Nothing will remain on earth, or under the earth or in the waters" (1296). Leonardo foregrounded the nightmare of terminal violence, which nuclear power has made all the more total. We confront an early instance of what Margot Norris has called a biocentric vision, which "eschews realism in favor of new, experimental modes that are easily confused with the visionary, the allegorical, or the satirical." Such texts are self-reflexive metaphors that force us to listen "to the voice of our own beast," which mumbles sounds of the anthropocentric demise of traditional worldviews.[45] On balance, the upheavals that we bring down on ourselves can be as destructive as natural floods. And we have been told that civilization at its best is extraordinarily inventive in devising means of killing, but it has no resuscitating forces in it.[46]

The fig tree tells the chestnut tree in one of Leonardo's fables that man is endowed with "such ingenuity that with rods and stones and stakes" he will take their fruits. Nature is helpless, whereas man is dangerous to himself; the day will come when "men shall sleep, and eat, and dwell among trees," and they "will hear every kind of animals speak in human language" (1293). Such landscapes of destruction brought out the monstrosity of perverse idealizations of power. Judas's betrayal of Jesus in the *Last Supper* was but a further proof that man is again and again failed by mankind. Yet Leonardo seems to suggest that Judas was as much an individual as the symbol of knowledge gone astray. Eventually, abuses of technological power would forbid humankind to fail man one more time. Prophecy could draw present and future on a plane where a degenerative permanence would prevail. The natural order of things would be so upset that evolution itself could be either halted or reversed.

The next prophecy is set under the sun, where man's predatory instincts do not spare the utopian-like order of bee societies: "And many others will be deprived of their store and their food, and will be cruelly submerged and drowned by folks devoid of reason. Oh Justice of God! Why dost thou not wake and behold thy creatures thus ill used?" (1293). The collapse of reason is then shifted toward a dream world whose irrationality has shaped a most implausible landscape. Men "will instantaneously run in person in various parts of the world, without motion. They will see the greatest splendor in the midst of darkness. . . . You will speak with animals of every species and they with you in human speech" (1293). Humanity is brutalized and animalism has become human. We seem to be wandering amid beasts of the modern imagination. It seems as if one could cross paths with images of violence Francisco Goya and Max Ernst have impressed upon the modern mind. While assaulting the very concept of representation, grotesque expressions of that kind bore on transgressions of normative categories; evolution edged on involution.

Leonardo's prophecies checked Judas's betrayal of humanity against behavior in the natural kingdom. The traditional idea has been that dog does not eat dog; man, instead, attacks man. In the footsteps of Aristotle and Seneca, Erasmus wrote in *The Education of a Christian Prince* that the tyrant "who is a man, turns his bestial cruelty against his fellow men and fellow citizens." To man, no wild beast is more deadly than man himself. Animals fight singly and have never been slaughtered on battlefields by the thousands. But humans have, and Leonardo gave a prophetic slant to that standing tradition.[47]

Physical laws have run amok. But Leonardo's text is a dream. Out of the dream, however, he insisted that even nature is a "tender and benign mother" for some, and a "cruel and pitiless stepmother" for others (1293). Rhetoric shifts from the future of dreams back to the present of observation. Apocalyptic strains therefore take on the immediacy of a transgressive constant. Violence plagued the Italian peninsula, where the doomsday language of the time drew from Savonarola's burning of books, Machiavellian analyses of human greed, and lingering beliefs in millennial reform or damnation. Let us not forget that Michelangelo's fresco cycle on the Sistine ceiling ends with Noah's drunkenness and the Deluge. With an eye to apocalyptic nomenclatures, there were a few who believed that human progress had become pathological.[48] By so doing, Leonardo placed himself between the intolerance of Savonarola and Guicciardini's fatalism. The world of the spirit was not an alternative for the man of science, who could neither accept nor tolerate nature's unreliability. Images of cosmic devastation ran along patterns of mythic upheavals that have been recurrent in the West.

11

For Leonardo, man is reproductive and destructive; at all times, he is deficient in both humanism and humanness. The biological transformations of things eaten by other things betrayed the sheer animalism of a human race whose hell had come to the surface. At the end of civilization, we find a mad giant who destroys humankind on Armenian mountaintops, where Leonardo's visionary gaze became literary: "His eyes were as red as a burning fire and he rode on a big stallion six spans across and more than twenty long; with six giants tied to his saddle bow and one in his hand which he gnawed with his teeth" (McCurdy, 1056). We can see in that final image of bestiality forewarnings of Goya's *Saturn Devouring His Sons*. They are monsters because of their gigantic size. They also are monstrous because they have undermined the Heraclitean harmony of parts and whole; their disproportion is physical as well as moral.

A primeval archetype therefore destroyed its own kind; the very structure of our Western fabric was assaulted at its core. Man was about to be taken out of history, and chaos would soon stake claims. Leonardo's prophetic range exceeded mankind and pointed toward the transhuman story of the earth. He had lost hope. The generative force of life's "moisture" would turn into "mire" (*fanghi*) so deep that men would be forced to "walk on the trees of their country" (1295). While the sun's heat would drive its nourishing warmth out of control, water itself was bound to become putrid lime before erupting into a deluge.

The *Deluge* drawings (Fig. 40) rounded out Leonardo's literature of doom by depicting the final moments before the earth would shape itself back into some sort of primeval stillness. From fetal cells to the concretion of liquid matter into solidity, Leonardo dealt with natural and human beginnings. His prophecies of doom gave visual form to the final breakdown of matter long after human presence had been wiped out from the face of the earth. Together with the water studies, the *Deluge* drawings embodied the autonomous dynamics of process, whose earth-shaking discharge of power (*forza*) claimed chaos's primeval authority over its own "fragmentation" into the manifolds of things. While some

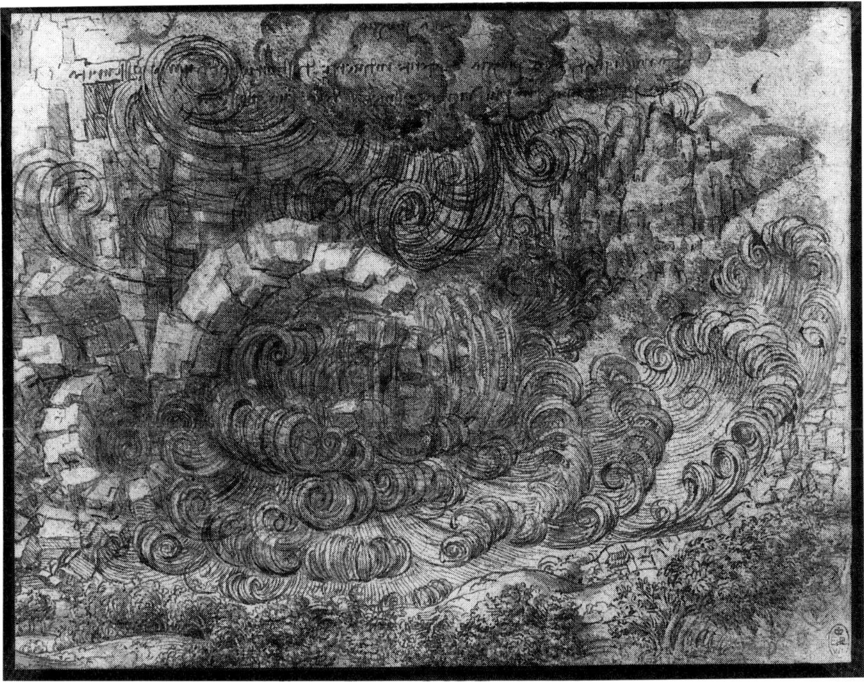

Fig. 40.   Leonardo da Vinci, *Study for the Deluge* (c. 1515)
Royal Library, Windsor Castle

sketches still show horses and crumbling towers, others bring demise to a posthuman world in which waves and whirlwinds can hardly be set apart. Rock formations seem to melt into water twirls, and solid matter dissolves into primordial fluidity. We look at the final act of a posthuman process of upheavals about to exhaust the last remnants of force. Perspective, depth, and lines collapse, and with them the idea of human-bound spaces.[49] At last, Leonardo shattered matter on a cosmic scale. The forms of life were annihilated into the original chaos, even though the end of humanity would not mark the end of life on earth.

Studies of allegory and prophecy in the ancient world note that the power of the word is God's, not the prophet's. Deuteronomy, in fact, prescribes the death penalty for anyone who prophesies falsely, that is, speaks by himself. The Word gave authority to Jeremiah, Isaiah, and Paul.[50] Leonardo, instead, spoke in his own voice, which split prophetic authority between myth and science. At all levels, however, his visual nomenclature of pointing fingers (John the Baptist) and heavenward gazes (Jerome) favored prophetic forewarnings over the certainty of demonstration.[51]

At the turn of the sixteenth century, Michelangelo, Raphael, and Castiglione brought ancient and modern humanism to a standstill. By contrast, the prophets of technology are agents of ceaseless progress; they strike the dissonant chords of what is not, and yet might come to be. Leonardo's prophetic voice could not settle with any achievement. Science, which is ever unfolding, stood at the source of his prophetic authority. By its very nature, however, technology often furthers progress by destroying the future it claims to build. To control technology, it may take more than faith in science, and Leonardo's workers are so constricted into those war machines that hopes could not be raised.[52] Technology spurred apocalyptic inevitability.

12

Leonardo was not a specialist in the modern sense of the word, and he could not stay with a single problem for too long. Had posterity taken his lead, the progress of science would have been more cautious. He cherished experience and experiment, but with a prudent sense of responsibility toward all forms of life. His critical distance returned with Francis Bacon, who wisely wrote: "I foresee that if ever men are roused by admonitions to betake themselves seriously to experiment . . . through the premature hurry of the understanding to leap or fly to universals and principles of things, great danger may be apprehended" (*Novum Organum,* aphorism 64). The universalist therefore kept the specialist's instincts in check long before some would think that the quest for truth is an absolute that must be honored even if it leads to destruction.[53]

The future belonged to technology, and Leonardo probably knew that pure research could take on an ominous life of its own. While maintaining that the machine is a material expression of the human spirit, recent criticism of modern automata has taken to heart warnings against technological excess. And it is by turning to Leonardo for inspiration that hopes have been raised about the birth of a new humanism in which moral and technical progress would keep pace with one another.[54] Technological inventions presumed their own transgression. It was through Adamic and Promethean disobedience, in fact, that man became a "maker" of civilization.

In a humanist mode, peace was mythic. From fact to fiction, Leonardo split his interests between projects of war—tanks, cannons—and activities of peace—canals, pulling machines, printing press—that tangled technology into the gloom and glory of its own success. The inventor's epistemology was inscribed in ambiguity. Derek de Solla Price tells us that dialogism between scientists and technologists has produced a long and honorable tradition about lying for the sake of pure science. Whenever he wanted to pursue pure geometry, Archimedes asked his uncle for financial support with the excuse that he would be a useful man to have around in time of war. When war came, he started something that was unrelated to pure science and burned the enemy fleet. "Leonardo da Vinci had the same technique: promise them technology, make good if you must, but really give them the pure learning that you want and you know they will need in the end."[55] Leonardo promised the Moor a world of wonders, but gave him a world of words. He promised technology, but delivered either entertainment or nothing at all. As a military mind, Leonardo described underground passages, even though he might have been thinking about mining or transportation. In a military mode, he planned to flood the Arno Valley around Pisa, but he might have been thinking about canals for irrigation during peacetime. The technologist promised, and the scientist dreamed. At heart, he did not harbor enough faith in people to use his talents beyond the pursuit of a personal mythology.

In the end, mankind would get what it deserved: doom. Leonardo's apocalyptic prophecies tell us that destruction would be caused by a natural upheaval unleashed after the rise and fall of man-made technology. Without any doubt, "Nature desires to exterminate the human race, as a thing useless to the world and the destroyer of all created things" (McCurdy, 1112). Like the modern Prometheus, he was not fond of man, but he loved "what devours him. Now, what devours Man? His eagle. . . . Everyone should have an eagle" (André Gide, *Prometheus Misbound*, 5). What devoured Leonardo was his quest for knowledge, and his eagle would lift him from the dreadful realities of warfare to fulfill a mythic longing for human flights of body and soul. He did not love man, but he cherished those redeeming forms of myth that man had been able to explore and exploit in spite of himself.

13

Either via rebirths or survivals, myth and prophecy took on modern guises. In the realm of science, the echoes of tradition had to make room for a daring individualism. Fifteenth-century praises of the *homo artifex* were metahistorical for Pico della Mirandola and metascientific for Leonardo; one fell under the aegis of Orpheus and the other of Daedalus. By reenacting myths, Mircea Eliade has taught us, man "is able to repeat what the Gods, the Heroes, or the Ancestors did *ab origine*. To know the myths is to learn the secret of the origin of things."[56] To know the myths as a modern inventor was for Leonardo a way of mastering the beginning and fulfillment of things. And the Daedalian mode established technology as the bridge between the legends of myth and the facts of reality.

In antiquity, the gods did not love the restless industry of man the maker. They punished Prometheus and crushed the revolt of the Giants. Yet all technology is of a titanic mold, and man the maker, we have been told, belongs to the race of the Titans. His delight in towering works that impress by their massiveness explains why man the technician so often lacks a sense of beauty and proportion; he is not an artist.[57] Leonardo was an artist; yet it was not enough.

The Forger of Experience

8

The *Vitruvian Man:*

At the Navel of Life's Compass

Leonardo's drawings of the fetus were about the beginning of life. Those of belaboring nudes were about the beginning of technology, which in turn affected the representation of man. As a result, the very concept of man was split between the organic and the mechanical, the birth of a single man and the construction of prototypes. Better than most, the theorist Filarete intertwined the two modes through a comparison that mixed the natural with the artificial. In his opinion, the building is like a man: "First it is conceived, using a simile such as you can understand, and then is born. . . . Since no one can conceive by himself without a woman, by another simile, the building cannot be conceived by one man alone. As it cannot be done without a woman, so he who wishes to build needs an architect." Under the titular rubric of "geometry and nature reconciled," attention has been paid to the implications of linear perspective in the body of Leonardo's work. As a test for mastering the new technique, Paolo Uccello, Piero della Francesca, and Leonardo exploited the circular form of the *mazzocchio.* Unlike his peers, however, Leonardo put that form to technological use by turning it into cylindrical shapes, wheels, ground plans for circular objects, and drawings of military devices.[1] Technology was the myth of the future, but it also fulfilled archetypal longings drawn by a pantocratorial compass that God handed down to humans as a symbol of rational and scientific modes of creation.

Daedalus used technological ingenuity to construct a labyrinth in Crete. And Plato tells us that Daedalus the sculptor made statues that could walk (*Meno* 97). Some say that he also built a gigantic automaton meant to stand guard over the island; its name was Talos, and it spit fire from its mouth.[2] Minos's kingdom, therefore, housed the first breed of legendary automata that have been with us ever since.

From Cretan labyrinths to Mondrianesque grids, intellectual juxtapositions between pulse and measure have been central to the Western nomenclature of the ego. As a matter of fact, Filarete had no doubts that the rationale for architectural measurements was taken from the best-formed man, who must have been Adam, "because it cannot be doubted that he was handsome and better proportioned than any other man who has ever lived, since God formed him." Leonardo's *Vitruvian Man* (Fig. 41), therefore, bodies forth his humanist quest of an archetypal figure which, fitting as it does square and circle, falls within a tradition of proportional aesthetics whose anthropomorphic guise has spawned confidence and discomfort alike. Set as he is at the center of a geometric field, the nude amounts to no more than an anatomical configuration. Its character is measured down to a geometrized self that has not experienced the mystery of growth because it has never known the warmth of a maternal womb. It is neither Minotaur nor automaton, since it has been conceived by a maze maker who has circumvented, but not challenged, the secret of birth. The difference between the Vitruvian Man and Saint Jerome—not to mention Leonardo's own "caricatures," the giants of Luigi Pulci, or Rabelaisian bodies—is one that would set the geometric space of *logos* against the heartbeat of a more obscure *bios*.[3]

It would seem that Leonardo abused the powers of the compass at a point in time when its radius was about to meet the challenge of modernity's openness. And one could agree that the Leonardesque drawing foregrounds an image of transition from construction to growth. As such, technique tends to open a cleavage between flesh and spirit by transforming organic into organized bodies.[4] There is indeed a cleavage between body and being in the *Vitruvian Man*. A stranger to the breath of life, he has been born to a scheme of order. His past is cultural, not genetic; he is one of those orphans of the gods that utopian minds have always dreamed about.

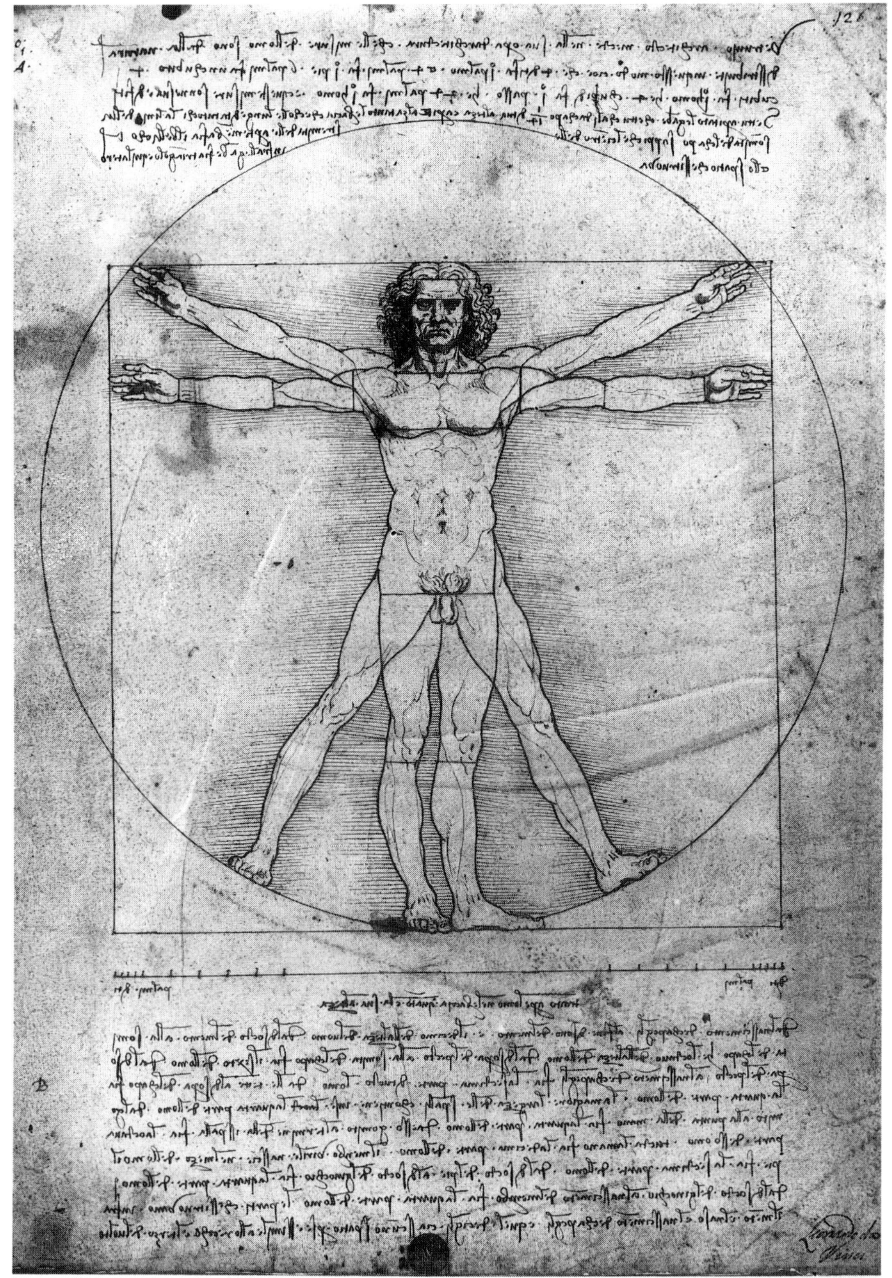

FIG. 41.   Leonardo da Vinci, *Vitruvian Man* (c. 1485–90)
Accademia, Venice

2

Leonardo's "historical" attribution makes it clear that the lure of creating "organized bodies" was to be traced back to Vitruvius and Daedalus himself. The breath of life is a sign of mortality in postlapsarian worlds, whereas the compass can draw figures of eternity. Blakean juxtapositions between serpent and compass updated that tradition. The organic grows and dies, but construction lasts forever.

Vitruvius linked "anthropomorphic measure" to architectural symmetry, which was taken as a cornerstone for quantitative concepts of beauty throughout the Renaissance. Having stated that "proportion is a correspondence among the measures of the members of an entire work," he pinned symmetry to architectural relationships, "as in the case of those of a well shaped man" who can fit a square and a circle (*De Architectura* iii, 1). It would appear that nature has designed the well-shaped body, whose proportions reflect a complex system of mathematical ratios that operate at the physical surface.

It is significant that such a statement on the human figure appears in a treatise on architecture. And we should find it equally indicative that Alberti waged ten books on the subject against the three short sections of his treatise on painting. The implication is that harmony and proportion find better expression in buildings. Insofar as pictures are concerned, Francesco di Giorgio's *Vitruvian Man* is a nude not quite foursquare and with a foot out of the circumference. For some, he is merely human, suggesting as he does some stretching in a faint weariness. Because it presents only a circle, the drawing shows a variation on the Vitruvian paradigm. Later, Leonardo took the square out of the circle. He therefore set anatomical proportions into a more complex geometric system. Awareness of, and return to, the classical source steered away from mere imitation, which was traded for a more meaningful *nostos,* that is to say, a "corrective return" loaded with the experiences of modernity. Unlike Vitruvius, Leonardo made drawings of proportions whose source was the human body itself, and the Vitruvian figure brought together a systematic description of anatomical proportions. To fit the circle, the feet have to be set apart so as to reduce the height by one-fourteenth. Such innovative adjustments could suggest that square and circle might be derived from the human figure itself.[5] Amid modern drawings, schematic heads and limbs proliferated. Francesco di Giorgio, Piero della Francesca, Dürer, and Leonardo himself were obsessed with measurements symbolic of perfection.

Hybridization emerges from Leonardo's reference to Vitruvius, who "states in his work on architecture that the measurements of a man are arranged by Nature" in mathematical ratios: "and these measurements are in his buildings" (McCurdy, 211). Man was subordinated to the contextuality of architecture in the ancient text, just as the system of linear perspective would reduce him to a proportional element centuries later. Geometrizations of nature thus became anthropomorphic, and Leonardo wrote: "The centre of the circle formed by the extremities of the outstretched limbs will be the navel" (McCurdy, 211). At the navel of the Leonardesque drawing, the creational metaphor doubles back on itself. It seems to be at once organic and constructive, but it is neither. Or it could be a hybrid of both, and Dürer's *Man Inscribed in a Circle* (after 1521, Fig. 42) made the point forcefully. He knew the classical passage, which he illustrated with two small drawings of a nude man inscribed in a circle and a square. In the footsteps of Vitruvius and the Albertian *De statua,* the German master applied the "exempeda method," which measured the body by a rod divided into ten "numbers," in turn subdivided into ten "parts" and again into three "bits."

Nature creates the human body, but geometric verification gives it artistic status. Vitruvius said so, long after Plato had made similar statements on the symbolic value of geometry at large. Insofar as anatomy was concerned, the generative seed of the marrow "solidified" into bone structure, which "gave to the marrow as many and various forms as the different kinds of souls were hereafter to receive" (*Timaeus,* 73). What emerged was a principle of individual diversity that Vitruvian prototypes were to shift toward modular uniformity. For Plato, the neck was central to the division of body and soul, whose noble marrow is of round shape. In turn, the brain was protected by "a globe made of bone." While the human focus is on the head, "the part of the soul which desires meats and drinks and the other things of which it has need by reason of the bodily nature" was "placed between the midriff and the boundary of the navel, contriving in all this region a sort of manger for the food of the body" (*Timaeus,* 73, 70). Since it belonged to the lower body and because its value was strictly functional, the navel was taken to be the center of physiological sustenance.

In turn, Leonardo's *Vitruvian Man* altered the Platonic hierarchy of body and soul. The navel is the visual marker of man's emergence into life out of a spherical womb. Once into the world, he is sheltered under a heavenly dome of ideas that put him at the center of a geometric universe. The circle into which he is inscribed carries forward a shape of inclusion at once symbolic of origin and destiny; it is egg and cosmic sphere, to which Christianity added the wholeness on divine circularity. By contrast, the

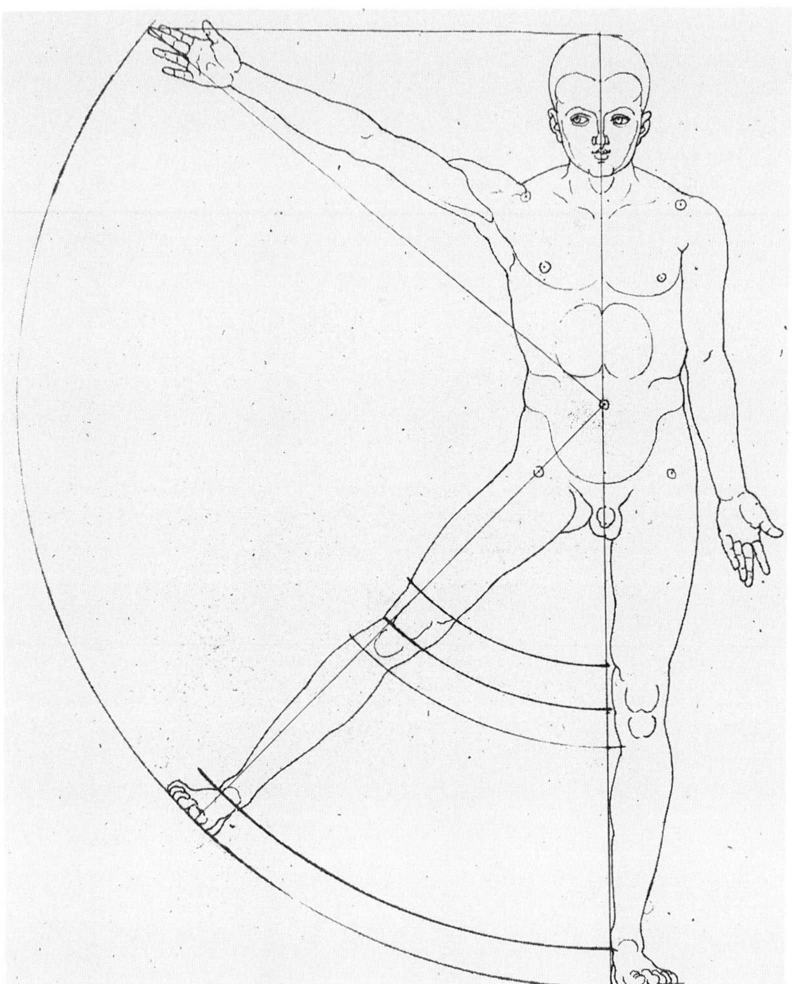

FIG. 42.   Albrecht Dürer, *Man Inscribed in a Circle,* front view (after 1521)
Sächsische Landesbibliothek, Dresden

physiology of matter is contained within a foursquare microcosm whose center is sexual and gravity-bound. Almost by way of paradox, physiology seems to have been reconciled with idealism.

The *Vitruvian Man* echoed a referentiality ingrained in the aesthetic sense of Western culture. At the root of that tradition, Rudolph Wittkower has told us, was the conviction that "if infinite space is ordered according to immutable metric laws, all objects perceived in finite space must be subject to unchanging optical laws."[6] Such a universal harmony pointed toward a cohesive system of common measurements that included music, architecture, the visual arts, and Christian symbolism.[7] If some are right in seeing a Christ-like pose in the figure with outstretched arms, then one might agree that he has been crucified to the merciless demands of geometric perfection.

Although they were set at the roots of the humanist vision, unchanging optical laws ran against Leonardo's atmospheric perspective, which subordinated perception to an array of variables. Yet there were instances when the antihumanist chose to meet his call in a humanist frame of mind. Instead of setting his Vitruvian nude against a natural background, Leonardo placed it in a world of linear abstractions as autonomously humanist as the architectural text he drew from. In that sense, the artist still operated in a mode that was at once archaeological and antiquarian; a mode that had produced ornate helmets (see Fig. 26) as well as elaborate sarcophagi (see Fig. 10).

3

Yet centuries of referentiality have not resolved the original ambiguity. Is the Vitruvian Man well shaped because he fits standards of geometric proportion? In that case, why should abstract criteria determine the value of human beauty? And why should the compatibility of anatomy with geometry warrant standards of artistic excellence? In terms of method, did Leonardo draw square and circle around the human figure, or did he fit the nude within them? In other words, was his procedure inductive or deductive? So phrased, the issue is not one bearing on futile matters of chicken-egg priorities, but one that weighs on modes of creation and criticism. The procedural riddle is conceptual as well.

For sure, Vitruvius reduced a living organism to an anatomical map that lodged a quantitative system of measurements: "For if a man be placed flat on his back, with his hands and feet extended, and a pair of compasses centered at his navel, the fingers and toes of his two hands and feet will touch the circumference of a circle described therefrom. And just as the human body yields a circular outline, so too a square figure may be found from it" (*De Architectura* iii, 1). The human body is literally flattened out on the two-dimensional surface of a planimetric surface. Such a dependence bore symbolic forebodings.

When man stood up on the perspectival plane of humanist space, he found himself to be no more than a "relational element" amid a contextual whole. Whether ancient or modern, the symbols of humanist constructs could not—or would not—resolve tensions between individualism and individualities, the ideal One and the phenomenal Many.

In spite of organic functions and volumetric appearances, the deeper structures of nature were presumed to be geometric. Below the surface, all forms partook of a constant and proportional system that could dictate anthropomorphic standards as well. The humanist distortion of empirical observation led to paradoxical results. For its own "better," if not "best" good, the nonhuman was to be humanized. To do that, man had to lie down in a dehumanizing posture, which would pave the way for man's later subjection to his own humanist "plans." The navel had always been the archetypal marker of beginning; in the Vitruvian mode, it also became a point of measurement. Embedded in man's attempt to humanize reality was the potential for reducing him to a measurable concept. Geometric ratios of order overcame him. He got trapped in his own net.

However tentatively, Leonardo could not ignore the fact that his Vitruvian Man set a prototype at once mechanical and quantifiable. He understood that the Albertian concept of beauty as an assemblage of parts into a superior whole could turn out to be either a mechanism of transcendence or a technological model. The typical and the individual stood next to each other; they could even merge together, as they did in the columnar types of Piero della Francesca and the puppet-figures of Paolo Uccello. Leonardo found that there were too many people "who only study the measurements and proportions of the nude, and do not analyze its variety, for a man may be well proportioned and be fat and short, or tall and thin, or average. And he who takes no account of these differences makes his figures as if they had been turned out by a stamp, so that they all seem sisters. Such a thing merits grave reproof" (McMahon, 97). The humanist worldview was indeed geometric, and therefore mechanical at heart. However critical, Leonardo felt its lure.

If we were to compare Michelangelo's Adam on the Sistine ceiling (Fig. 43) to Leonardo's Vitruvian Man, a common emphasis on the harmonious excellence of human proportions would emerge. Yet the Adamic nude draws his dignity from a godlike condition to which Pico della Mirandola had given panegyrical form in his *Oration on the Dignity of Man*. The nude celebrates the divinity of man because he is an

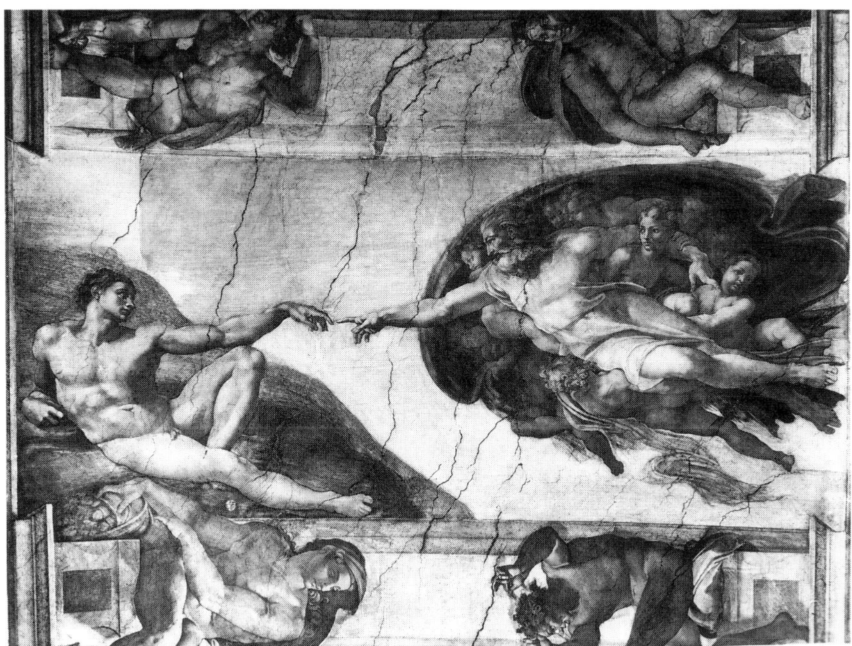

FIG. 43. Michelangelo, *Creation of Adam* (1511)
Sistine Chapel, Vatican, Rome

image of the divinity that has just created him. He lies on the ground in the natural position of the first human awakening to life, and he stands reassured that the deity would not lose sight of his hand.

Such a spiritual contextualism becomes geometric in the *Vitruvian Man,* even though mythologers have told us that the square cross enclosed in a circle was a symbol of authority in Minoan Crete.[8] Dependence on a transcendental system is turned within a design of rational self-sufficiency. The heavenly cosmology has been reduced to an intellectual graph that checks human ingenuity against its own standards. Adam is created out of nothing and without a specific name. By contrast, the Leonardesque nude draws from a visual and onomastic nomenclature that is more artificial. One has borrowed God's features of beauty, while the other seems to have stolen the method of his compass. He could demonstrate theoretical systems akin to linear perspective, whose abstractions would measure dehumanized figures. Born out of an artistic text, he has come to light as a pictorial figure bound to, and restricted by, geometric figures drawn on paper. The closure of square and circle frames intellectual self-containment, which outlines forms of abstraction. He is Vitruvian at conception, referential at birth, and prototypical at maturity.

By way of a self-fulfilling circularity, the Leonardesque artwork updated artistic tradition. The autonomous geometry of a man-made universe retained its lure. At that juncture, mythmaking traced its roots back to a momentous statement that Pliny made about Polyclitus. Among other sculptures, he "also made what artists call a 'Canon' or Model Statue, as they draw their artistic outlines from it as from a sort of standard; and he alone of mankind is deemed by means of one work of art to have created the art itself" (*Natural History* xxxiv, 55–57). That statue was the Doryphoros. The canon of art was art itself, and the means for achieving it were left rather vague by Pliny, Galen, and Plutarch. For sure, it was substantially numerical, and it took the name of *lineamenta, symetria, concinnitas,* or *dimensio.* Fifteenth-century artists did not possess so accurate a replica of the Doryphoros as we do. Yet Lorenzo Ghiberti acknowledged that Polyclitus *"fece regole e liniamenti dell'arte"* in his *Commentari.* And Alberti had made of *lineamenti* a fundamental term for art theory in his treatise on architecture. However unwittingly, Leonardo's mathematical studies of human anatomy were also meant to confront a gap in the classical source. Pliny, in fact, did not spell out the system of measurement in the Greek canon. To a certain extent the *Vitruvian Man* set out to reconcile canon with number, Polyclitus with Plato. And if one were to juxtapose the Vitruvian figure to some of the grotesque drawings (see Fig. 47) then it would become clear that Leonardo tackled what has been called the contrast between the Platonic/Vitruvian tradition of the perfect cosmic body and the Ovidian/Dantesque tradition of changed and warped bodies.[9]

If he were to step out of the circle that frames him, Leonardo's Vitruvian Man at first would walk right into a building designed by Luciano Laurana and erected after Vitruvian proportions, then he would get up on a pedestal, and thereafter stare into the void of spherical emptiness. And were he to utter words, they probably would be mathematical numbers of a geometric language incompatible with historically bound expressions of prose and poetry. If at all necessary for public purposes, he would speak unflawed Ciceronian Latin, a language that could afford the same clarity and stability as the linear outlines that define his body. Much as linearity denies "pictorial pulsations," so would Latin deny the transformational nature of modern vernaculars, which Leonardo's own "caricatures," we can bet, would twist and flaunt with the gusto of shameless accents.

The Vitruvian Man is a "demonstrator," or a builder who has erected himself into master and prisoner of his own construction. His gaze projects the fixed stare and glacial coldness of a body drained of life. Neither the sparkle of discovery nor the obliqueness of memory have crossed his mind. In the humanist mode of an intellectual paradigm, he is an image of human power drained of bodily warmth. The miracle of birth has yielded to the norm of intellect. He was, is, and shall be what he appears to be: an anatomical prototype exuding a spectral intensity. At a more personal level, the Vitruvian figure is the "other" of Leonardo's inquisitive attempts at guessing what he might find inside a cavern. His fears and Jerome's longings stirred inquiries that would have to be relinquished outside the Vitruvian perimeter, which delimited an enclave of rational certainties.

In a significant way, the single *Vitruvian Man* and the groups of nudes in *Rhythm in the Workshop* (see Fig. 36) show a uniform type of man that called for the quantitative output of mechanical or organiclike modulors-automatons-robots of a kind that Dürer, Cambiaso, Bracelli, and Le Corbusier have surrounded us with. That development offered Lewis Mumford and Roderick Seidenberg precedents for their criticism of technological—or posthistorical—men bound to lead a uniformly predictable existence.[10] And if one could ask Carlo Carrà to find a human form symbolic of what the *Engineer's Muse* could produce, he would find *Vitruvian Man* satisfactory. It is no sheer coincidence that Carrà's technological deity flaunts a compass.

4

At the navel, creation breeds birth, and birth causes separation; two crucial moments in the drama of individual life forms. For Vitruvius, instead, the navel was only a point at the core of figures that edged between the organic and the geometric. However linear and two-dimensional, proportional uniformity was achieved, but at what cost?

The Vitruvian model added to the aesthetic bent of humanist ideology. Man remained the microcosmic center of a universe whose cosmology was compatible with the classical concept of "symmetry" as the fundamental principle of aesthetic perfection. The fact that man could fit not only a circle but a square as well shifted the symbolism of the Vitruvian Man to matters more rigorously humanist. Because it has neither beginning nor end, the circle has always represented eternity: "God is a circle whose center is everywhere, but whose circumference is nowhere," so we have been told over and over again. And the navel has served to pinpoint concentric circles of symbolic systems since the earliest times. Within the larger context of the heavenly spheres, man would stand at the center of similitudes studded with astrological signs. Beyond the thrust-pull of phenomenal tensions, the Vitruvian Man was set at the still center where all directions met and where the world found a point of rest.

Still at a macrocosmic level, the square also accommodated the Pythagorean theory of the tetraktys, which based reality on the four elements—hot, cold, dry, moist—fixed at the four corners of a square. That tetrad was the root and foundation of all nature. The four elements also reflected the four letters that made up the Hebrew word for God, the tetragrammaton. The classic statement of such a tetrad was Oronce Fine's *Protomathesis,* which projected the archetypal idea in the mind of the creating deity.[11]

At a microcosmic level, Agrippa accompanied his *Three Books of Occult Philosophy* with illustrations. One of them apportions man within a square that approximates the tetrad: "The four square measure is the most proportionated body; for, if a man be placed upright with his feet together, and his arms stretched forth, he will make a quadrature equilateral, whose center is in the bottom of his belly." It has been noted that the two diagonals from the corners of the diagram intersect at the genitals of the body. Since it is reminiscent of the tetrad, that position calls forth the elementary world of physical nature; man, therefore, has sexual organs as the center of his being.[12] Leonardo's Vitruvian figure anticipated that visual symbolism.

Moreover, the square points to human constructs such as architecture, building forms, lettering, etc. In terms of shelters, we ought to remember the angular perimeter traced by the mythic founders of Rome. Figuratively, Vitruvius confirmed that the four-sided square outlines the square form of man when his arms are outstretched. There are four cardinal points, and four is the number of moral perfection, for the man who is morally fortified stands foursquare against attacks. During the Middle Ages, the macrocosm-microcosm symbolism put out the *homo quadratus,* whose four sides reflected the quadripartite divisions of elements, regions of the earth, and phases of the moon. That tradition endured, and George Puttenham referred to the Aristotelian *Ethics,* which refers to "a constant-minded man, even egal and direct on all sides, *hominem quadratus,* a square man" (*The Arte of English Poesie,* 1589, bk. 2). Furthermore, the squared man could be pentagonal, since five was a circular number of arcane perfection; five were the essences of things and the genera of living creatures. Leonardo's own drawing has been linked to the pentagon that would form if one were to join by straight lines the extremities of man's body.[13] At that point, it would seem, *natura naturans* and *natura naturata* could coalesce; as in a Blakean vision, the living symmetry of the organism would merge with the dead symmetry of the diagram. But it was only wishful thinking.

The moment we sharpen our critical focus on the square, details and context demand more comments. By taking the square out of Vitruvius's circular enclosure, Leonardo added to the earthbound symbolism of the angular figure; no longer pinned to the circle, it rests on the ground. The modern text mistranslated its ancient source. For Leonardo, the cubic shape emphasizes the volumetric nature of the human body: "The face in itself forms a square, of which the breadth is from one extremity of the eye to the other, and the height is from the top of the nose to the bottom of the lower lip, and what is left over above and below this square has the height of a similar square" (McCurdy, 208). Since individual expression has to conform to geometric measurements, the Vitruvian mindset turned out to be on its way toward robotlike forms of behavior.

Quite literally, Dürer transformed man into a cubic automaton: "At first, position two cubes as the two sections of a man you wish to draw. . . . Once this is done, the two cubes seen from the front can be moved along their joints. But wherever they join, the contours of the body, if these are added, must be divided."[14] The modern mind cannot but ask, What for? Was it not enough to know that the archetype was there? Such an artificial image no longer was a knight in armor, since man himself had become the armor by a process of dehumanization that produced ominous-looking automata (Fig. 44). At long last, geometry fulfilled one of its legends; the stereometric man had been created, and we have been burdened with his heritage ever since.

The linearity of square and circle heightens the support function of space, whose external grid is reversed in the skeleton's parallel function inside the human body. The Leonardesque drawing therefore heightens tensions between the mechanics of bones and the dynamics of muscles, both of which are exploited by the nude's bifocal stand. If muscles cannot flex, the whole body either shifts position or rotates on its axis in another Leonardesque drawing (Fig. 45). The *Vitruvian Man* gives us two fixed positions, but we can imagine four as well as additional stages in between. And Marcel Duchamp's nude descending a staircase could help our shift from juxtaposition to sequential movement.

Caught in that bifocal stand, the Vitruvian nude seems about to project a personal posture, but it does not. Its contrapposto position sets

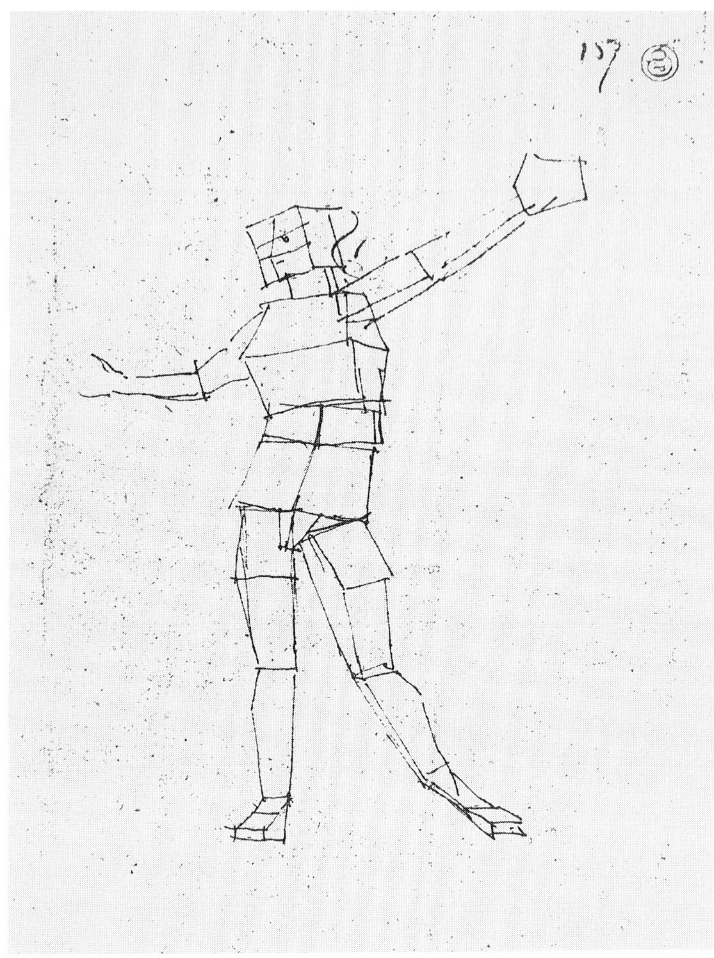

FIG. 44.   Albrecht Dürer, *Stereometric Man* (before 1519)
Sächsische Landesbibliothek, Dresden

abstract contextuality against organic weight. Anatomically, it still
seems to carry over the stiffness of fifteenth-century nudes in the tradition of Luca Signorelli's frescoes at Orvieto and Antonio del Pollaiolo's
Battle of the Ten Nudes. Because they drew from the study of corpses
whose weight and gravity had been severed from the dynamics of movement, their figures are anatomical bodies free-standing but yet to conquer a more relaxed composure.[15]

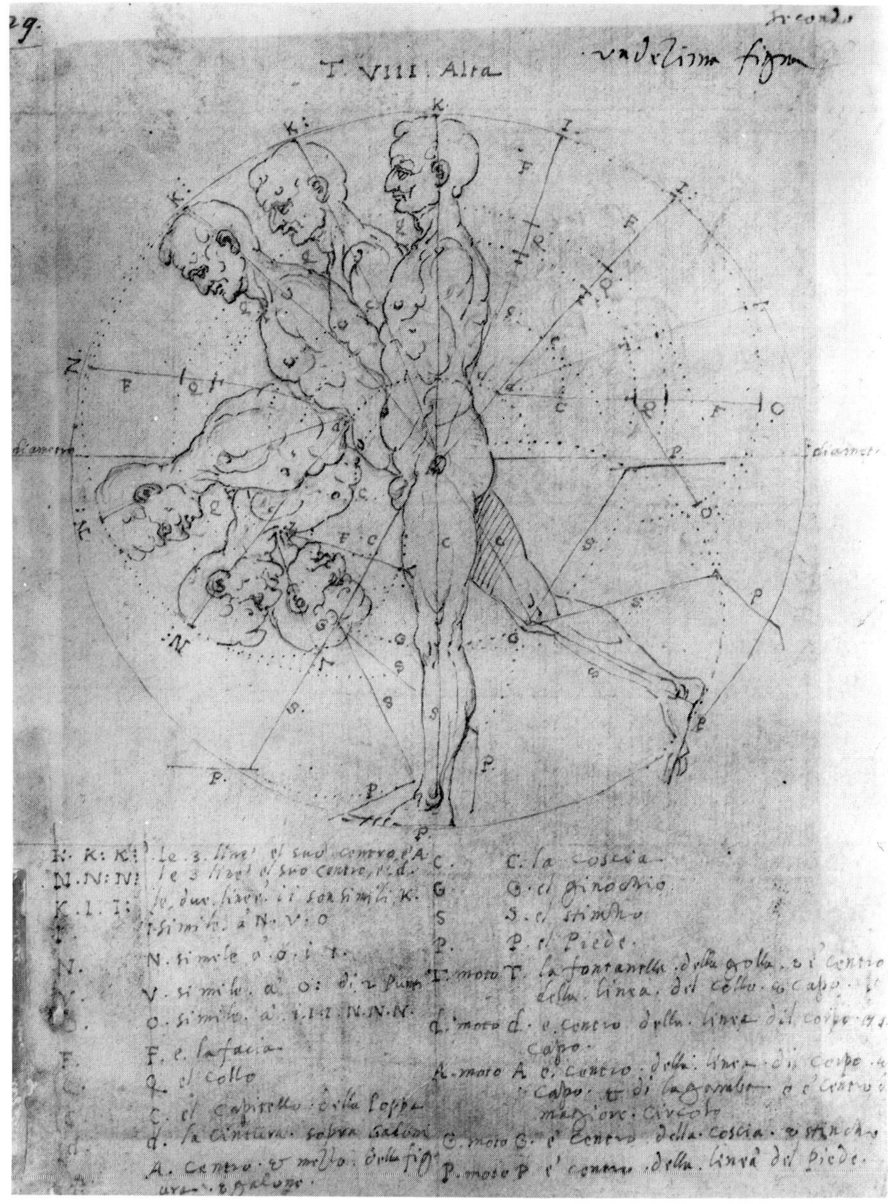

Fig. 45.   Leonardo da Vinci (or Leonardesque), *Study of Nude*
Morgan Library, New York

To an extent, even the circle could be viewed within a microcosmic perspective that fostered the expansion of knowledge. As Nicholas Cusanus put it, "human activity consists in unfolding everything beyond itself into its own circular field, in making everything come forth from the virtuality of the center."[16] At a symbolic level, the Vitruvian Man would seem to fit human and spiritual frames. The "squaring of the circle" was not only a mathematical challenge, but also an ideological attempt to reconcile humanity with spirituality.

5

Having made a direct reference to Vitruvius, Leonardo wrote, "The geometer reduces every surface surrounded by lines to the shape of a square and the volume of every object to the shape of a cube." Geometry and arithmetic in fact deal with continuous and discontinuous quantities. They "are not concerned with quality, the beauty of nature's creations and the harmony of the world" (McMahon, 15). Since geometrical approaches to reality are criticized, beauty and harmony ought to be other than abstract principles. Having made a critique of his own humanist leanings, Leonardo focused on the umbilical vein, by which "is composed the life and body of every animal of four feet. . . . The navel is the gate from which our body is formed by means of the umbilical vein" (McCurdy, 113). We are back to the mystery of birth.

Once Leonardo acknowledged biological functions, fixed measurements flaunted their futility. Since the body is in a constant state of growth, "veins are extensible and expansible" (McCurdy, 115). The emergent description is organic: "Make first the ramification of the veins by themselves, then the bones by themselves, and then join the bones and the veins together. . . . The plant never springs from the ramification for at first the plant exists before the ramification, and the heart exists before the veins" (McCurdy, 117). Muscles also go through stages of growth "such as infancy, childhood, adolescence, youth etc. And in all you should describe the changes of the limbs and joints and show which grows fat and which thin" (McCurdy, 188–89). The human body is not a construct, but a transformational organism that led Leonardo to draw fetuses and make ground-breaking annotations on gerontology.

On the subject of Vitruvian figures set against geometric backgrounds, Kenneth Clark finds Cesariano's "Vitruvian Man" an unfortunate exercise in imitation: "From the point of view of strict geometry a gorilla might prove to be more satisfactory than a man."[17] To fit linear intersections, the figure is awkwardly stretched out on the canvas. Leonardo's Vitruvian nude, instead, bears its own weight on square and circle. Even though the Pythagorean emphasis on structure is predominant, man still consists of a substantial nude set at the core of a cosmos whose intelligent nature Plato could place only into a living creature. Such an interactive stand also took up concerns with individual flaws: "By all means remember the defects that are in your person, and defend yourself against them in the figures you compose." The painter must not fall "into the same faults in the figures created by him, which are found in his person. You must know that you have to fight to the last against this bad habit, since it is a defect that was born at the same time as your judgment" (McMahon, 56). The *Vitruvian Man* was the embodiment of manly power at its most mature, steering as it did Leonardo's knowledge of geometry and mathematics toward the equally rational basis of humanist aesthetics. Clarity of meaning and linearity of form merged into a unified symbolism.

6

Musculature is proportional in the Vitruvian drawing, and it calls to mind Pollaiolo's nudes and forthcoming "musclemen" in Vesalius's illustrated *De Corporis Fabrica* (1543). Drawings of skulls, muscles, and veins were models for students of anatomies. They used scalpels to cut through skin surfaces and get to the mute truth of internal forms. Whether it was muscles sheathed in skin or seashells embedded in rocks, pioneering probings of that sort drew strength from the Heraclitean dictum "Nature loves to hide" (Frag. 10).

With equal love, knowledge had to unconceal the depths of nature's hidden structures. Leonardo's notes on anatomy, in fact, plan descriptions of "the fully grown man and woman, with their proportions, and the nature of their complexions, colour, and physiognomy." Moreover, four drawings will "represent four universal conditions of men," namely Mirth, Weeping, Contention, and Labor. The human personality was geometrized into categorical types fit for the "mechanism of man" (797). From Leonardo to Vesalius, anatomies shifted from dissertations on first principles to quantitative lists, tables, and diagrams. Human nature became visually stretched out on paper, and the *Vitruvian Man* somehow paved the way for theoretical synopses of that kind.[18]

At first, Leonardo undertook the study of anatomy as a painter. Unlike Michelangelo, however, he soon made ground-breaking drawings of scientific validity, and his notes blended empirical achievement with scholarly demonstration. As a man of science, he shared with fellow anatomists a loathing of dissection. They all were haunted by "the fear of living in the night hours in the company of those corpses, quartered and flayed and horrible to see" (796). Rhetoric centered on an under-world where secrets were stolen by individuals who could be uniquely unemotional. In the verses of a modern commentator, "Macabre beauty of the skeleton / Endures his lonely inquest, head to foot." To unearth the body's insights, the scientist had to be artist and teacher. God-given talents helped him to confront daring undertakings: "If it pleases our great Author, I may demonstrate the nature of men" (798). Having drawn the heart as delicately as a rose, Leonardo smilingly let "his sinister hand unglove, / Startling, bizarre, the Anatomy of Love."[19]

The Age of Discovery also started with microcosmic voyages inside the human body. Skin surfaces no longer set barriers against entering "the cosmography of this lesser world" (*la cosmografia del minor mondo*). The journey was proving to be endless, since "this amount of knowledge will not continue to satisfy you." The deeper order verged on chaos:

> And the veins, which discharge this blood, are not discerned by reason of their smallness. Moreover integrity of the tissues, in the process of investigating the parts within them, is inevitably de-stroyed, and their transparent substance being tinged with blood does not allow you to recognise the parts covered by them, from the similarity of their blood-stained hue; and you cannot know everything of the one without confusing and destroying the other. Hence, some further anatomy drawings become necessary. (798)

Drawing brought clarity to the apparent confusion of research. The later Middle Ages produced anatomical dissections in Bologna, and Mondino dei Liucci's *Anothomia* (1316) stood as a text for the following two centuries. Within the artistic tradition, the figures of Bartholomew and Marsyas offered iconographic materials for nudes dead beyond hopes of resurrection. It was in the middle of the fourteenth century that Giovanni da Milano painted *Sun Bartolomeo scuoiato* (predella of the Polittico della Galleria Comunale, Prato). The fifteenth century then ranged from Masaccio's skeleton under the *Trinity* of Santa Maria Novella to Do-

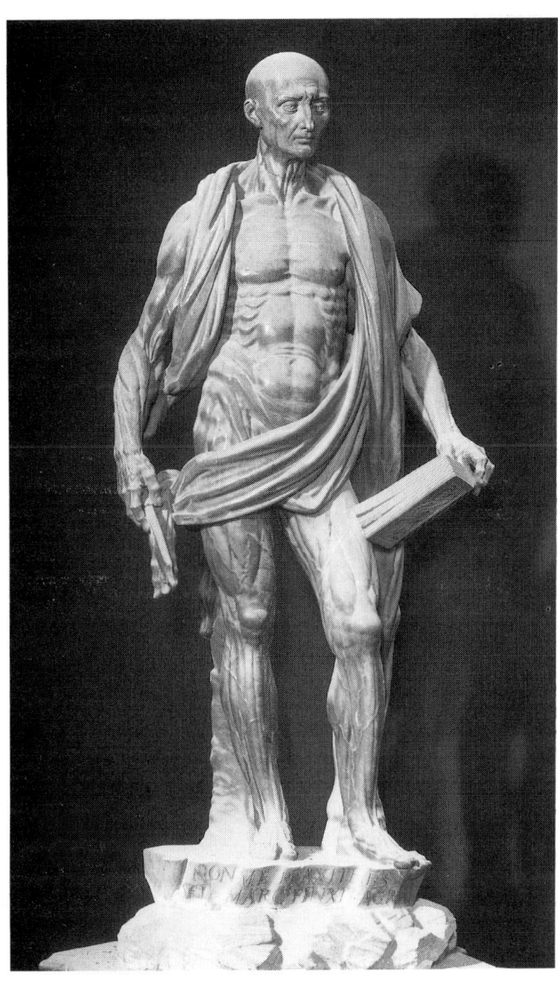

FIG. 46.   Marco d'Agrate,
Flayed Saint Bartholomew
Duomo, Milan

natello's *Anatomy of a Miser's Heart* (1450, Basilica San Antonio, Padua). For reasons as yet unclear, sixteenth-century artworks on anatomy such as Marco d'Agrate's *Saint Bartholomew* (Fig. 46) flaunted flayed bodies. At the turn of the seventeenth century, the working conditions of anatomical artists such as Ludovico Cigoli—who also sculpted a bronze *Scorticato*—had not improved. And Gaetano Zumbo's *cere* of the *Peste* added decomposed bodies to Leonardesque experiences.[20] Throughout, knowledge pushed willpower to the edge of revulsion.

Activities of that kind were not discharged in elegant attire amid musical accompaniments in the manner that Leonardo deemed appropriate for painters. Neither did they produce anatomical lessons in which professors read books while "demonstrators" cut corpses, on the assumption that discrepancies between book and scalpel would be settled to the former's advantage. By and large, much effort went into memorizing Galen rather than dissecting.[21] Clearly, that was not medical research in the professional ambiance of Rembrandt's anatomy lessons. At issue here are solitary endeavors that traded disgust for discovery. At best, anatomical studies led artists to cut through the superficiality of representation, probing into the unbookish and unwordy nakedness of substantial forms. To Leonardo's delight, there were men of science who either believed in images more than words or foreshadowed Bacon's suspicion of verbal communication. At its best, the anatomist's commitment to investigation unsettled epistemological assumptions. Vesalius's preface to his treatise calls for theory and observation to converge in medicine, after they had been split for centuries.[22]

Out of such experiences came the clarity of Leonardesque drawings in which art and anatomy joined forces. By and large, the body had to be physiologically utopian. Once he removed a man's skin, however, Leonardo unlocked the drawn-out effects of use and abuse. Underneath, "the muscles were worn down and remained in a state like thin membrane" (804). More than most, the anatomist was aware of process. Note 814 lists a project for the study "of the causes of" physiological functions, but illness evidently falls outside legitimate pursuits. Actually, "sickness is the discord of the elements infused into the living body" (853), an intrusion to be taken as an act of fate. Leonardo's anatomical studies were split between analysis, which probed below the order of surface appearances by means of dissections, and synthesis, which rounded details into a whole. Antagonistic relations between anatomical parts and systematic order has led anatomists to insist on dissections.[23] We have been told that fragmentation is a means of getting at a unified truth. As a result, an idealized body is destroyed, but a new field of knowledge is opened up for the creation of a scientific order of knowledge. A dialectic was thus enforced. In Vesalius's case, it led to skeletons poised to retain human suffering within the tradition of *memento mori*. Since they were medical-naturalistic nudes set in a landscape, those "musclemen" were figures consciously unique though placed amid forms borrowed from tradition. While dehumanized parts were not quite that, the boundary between living and dead matter was blurred.

The *Vitruvian Man*'s outstretched arms are not gestural in any narrative sense. Yet they are symbolic inasmuch as they are measured against the presumed perfection of the geometric frame. In fact, human forms can be geometric whenever one chooses to take a posture of stylized order—a posture that Piero della Francesca and Paolo Uccello would have admired. Accordingly, man happens to be as proportional as the square-circle. Since adjustments to criteria of beauty were not strained, the intended effect was one of utopian correlations. Because science mingled with art and metaphysics, the ideal body of the mature man came to fit the context of abstract symbols of beauty. Nowadays, the *Vitruvian Man* has become the universal logos for concerns with health. That symbolism thrives on attitudes that are at once classical and modern. Whether or not Leonardo meant it, we could be led to believe that his drawing embodies the ancient dictum *mens sana in corpore sano*. The body is undeniably healthy, but what are we to make of its spectral stare? If the eyes are the window of the soul, what kind of unbearably distant personality should we expect to confront? The question is, at what price health?

In a classical mode averse to growth and decay, disease was a pathological condition that could not be accepted; there was nothing romantically attractive about it. Amid the Apollonian solarity of heroic maturity, health was the only standard. Sickness was either cured or eliminated by means as natural as plagues or as drastic as death itself. The Vitruvian Man's unblemished condition is not derived from harmonious relationships with nature, but from a radical separation from it. He has not been endowed with a natural immunity system. Instead, he stands at the core of a geometric vacuum free of natural bacteria and impervious to either processes or contaminations. The figure betrays the ominous price that health could exact whenever well-being tends to be equated with anatomical integrity. The anthropomorphic vision of humanist idealism resurrected one of its last ghosts, whose transparent—and paper thin—beauty was its whole and yet mysterious truth.

Untroubled by ambiguities, Leonardo was at once responsive and resistant to the anthropomorphic lure of humanist geometry. His studies of the scientific ratios at the heart of natural shapes and human proportions make one wonder whether naturalism and abstraction could have merged together through an inductive approach as well. Criticism confims that Alberti and Leonardo were equally determined to raise the theory of proportions to the level of an empirical science. Hence they disregarded tradition in favor of experiences that could be supported by studies of nature.[24] It is as if they sought the ideal in order to define the normal. Dependence and coincidence overlapped in the Vitruvian drawing, which linked the knowledge of natural laws to definite rules of thought. To phrase it in modern terms, Leonardo exploited the abstract dimension of figurative shapes.[25] I cannot but think of Kepler's axiom: "Where there is matter, there is geometry."

7

In his final comments on the development of the theory of human proportions, Erwin Panofsky writes: "In Egyptian art, the theory of human proportions meant almost nothing; it was doomed to sink into insignificance as soon as this relation was reversed. The victory of the subjective principle was prepared, we recall, by the art of the fifteenth century,"[26] when individualism claimed godlike powers for subjectivity. Yet even a cursory look at the visual nomenclature of humanist forms cannot but recognize the geometric angularity of stereotypical figures in the works of Piero della Francesca, Andrea Mantegna, and Paolo Uccello. From Roberto Longhi to Bernard Berenson, scholars have noticed the paradox of an objective typology that stemmed from the artist's individual projections. The subjective was indeed on its way toward victory, but had not quite conquered it.

Leonardo's Vitruvian Man appeared at a point in time when the revival of antiquity had not yet spent its momentum. It was a reading of the past in praise of classical intellectualism. Just as science was beginning to break the circle of Ptolemaic enclosures, the *Vitruvian Man* invited readings as well as misreadings about would-be certainties. He could not fail to bring up concerns with man's position at the center of a universe in which he appears to be at once enclosing and enclosed. A warning was sounded against humanist quests of an order so impeccable that it would lead to dehumanized—though flawless—constructions. I cannot but return to Nietzsche, whose cutting remarks on modern man also apply to the intellectual nudity of the Leonardesque figure. Over and against the unity of myth, miracle, and religion, Socratism demands that we "consider abstract man stripped of myth" and an "artistic imagination unchanneled by any native myth" (*The Birth of Tragedy* xxiii). Indeed, the modern text seems to comment on the geometric and anthropomorphic abstractions that Alberti embodied in the metaphorical network at the center of which he placed the family leader. Like the Albertian spider, the Vitruvian Man was ready to spin a paradigmatic web inside his perimeter of perfection.

Like Piero della Francesca and Dürer, Leonardo applied linear perspective to inorganic objects as well as to organic forms; wheels, cylinders, heads, and limbs stood next to each other. The goal, perhaps, was to reconcile geometry with nature or to order nature's powers; or to do both. Accordingly, Leonardo moved from linear perspective to model making, which reduces the complexity of the organic world to essential lines that can readily be translated into geometrical figures. Because of the median position they hold between abstract geometry and concrete nature, models link the ideal to the actual. As a result, geometry could be seen naturally and nature geometrically.[27]

The time for synthesis had come. Plato and Aristotle stood next to each other in Raphael's *School of Athens,* and it was Pico della Mirandola's project to reconcile a cluster of religious schools. To highlight the resilience of the Vitruvian paradigm through the sixteenth century, Fernán Pérez de Oliva updated the Piconian oration by presenting man as a proportional being whose harmonious nature—*de hechura hermosa y conveniente*—is exquisitely Vitruvian.[28] God does not speak to Adam in the Spanish text, which presents a dialogue between two men about the beauty and excellence of the prototypical human being. His raison d'être is not a matter of archetypal origins but of intellectual achievements grown out of the mind's collective experiences. First and foremost, therefore, man is a human postulate replete with spiritual and cosmological symbolisms.

Panegyrical enthusiasms aside, the *Vitruvian Man* could be taken as a two-dimensional model that yielded problematic results. The drawing tested the concepts of integration, reconciliation, and complexity. As for synthesis, one may wonder; for sure, abstraction could not foster birth. The initial juxtaposition between the painterly Jerome and the linearity of the Vitruvian Man comes back. Both of them link selfhood to contextuality. In both of them, the body is origin and center of outreaching coordinates. Everything circles around it and is seen through it. But whereas one is a rational center, the old man, to borrow from William James on the experience of activity, is "the storm center . . . the constant place of stress."[29] For Jerome, as for Leonardo's poetics at large, stress is spiritual as well as physical, since the body's own metabolism is teleological. Anatomies aside, students of philosophical biology tell us that no living organism can be statically self-reflexive.[30] The very concept of man is that of wholeness-in-action; it could not be reduced to a statuesque body constructed according to the concept of organic unity.[31] In the painting, "organic" is literally applied to physiology whereas the drawing links it to the mechanical assemblage of parts into a superior whole.

Even as passionate a student of Leonardo's method as Paul Valéry may have read in the Vitruvian figure a warning that could be called antihumanist. In the classical dialogue on Eupalinos the architect, Phaedrus finds the "incorruptible wealth" to be "perfection" in the harmonious union of mind and body: "We wrought each of us in his own sphere; thou by living, and I by dreaming." Reconciliation was to lead them to "interchange fitness and grace, beauty and lastingness, if they barter movements for lines, and number for thoughts." They would then discover "their true relationship, their act." Since its proportional nature would guarantee immunity to circumstance, the body brought stability to that venture. Admiration broke into open praise: "Perishable as thou art, thou art far less so than my dreams. Thou endurest a little longer than a fancy; thou payest for my acts, and dost expiate my errors." Short of that dialogic synthesis, the *Vitruvian Man* knows no natural secrets, and he neither acts nor expiates; he is himself the shell of dreams without depth. Motions and lines never established organic relationships, and that very flaw could utter Eupalinos's dream. "By dint of constructing," he put it with a smile, "I truly believe that I have constructed myself."[32] At the navel of his cobweb, the Albertian spider would have nodded approvingly. The illusionistic process of humanist abstraction could not have gone any farther.

Yet to be seduced by experience, Leonardo paid homage to humanism past and present, since he was yet to take full pride in his lifelong sketch of the antihumanist *omo sanza lettere*. Like a Janus image of divided consciousness, his artistic self-portrait was at once a form of affirmation and of denial. On the surface of visual forms, the Vitruvian diagram rested on a proportional harmony of lines, angles, and human limbs; a harmony as mysterious and charismatic as the *concinnity* that Pythagoras, Leonardo Bruni, Pomponius Gauricus, and Francesco Lancilotti set at the core of humanism ancient and modern. All that was in Leonardo's background; to which we ought to add Archimedes' last request. Upon his death, friends were asked to "place over his tomb a sphere containing a cylinder, inscribing it with the ratio which the containing solid bears to the contained" (Plutarch, *Lives of the Noble Romans,* Marcellus). On a planimetric surface, sphere and cylinder could be circle and body; in both of them, the *ratio* was the very secret of the Vitruvian logos, and of all those spherical shapes-within-shapes that so fascinated Piero della Francesca and Leonardo da Vinci, Paolo Uccello and Luca Pacioli. His polyhedric figures in *De divina proportione,* we might add, were probably executed by Leonardo himself.[33]

However unwittingly, humanists and antihumanists alike had unearthed the Archimedean epitaph, which translated one man's request into the symbolic cornerstone of an enduring worldview.[34] At the Vitruvian juncture, Leonardo held man hostage to the legend of geometry and to the promises of technology. At least for a chosen moment, the Vitruvian navel could be zenith and nadir.

"Stripped of myth," Nietzsche would comment on the Vitruvian drawing, "man stands famished among all his pasts and must dig frantically for roots" (*The Birth of Tragedy* xxiii). Below the fascination with linear surfaces and the intriguing patterns of paper-thin cobwebs, Leonardo had to break the spell of the Vitruvian moment, for experience demanded that he keep digging beneath history and at the other side of books. Certain as he was that any past would uncover figures drawn in the sand, he was committed to disinter mythic roots that would let growth break through the nostalgia of order.

9

"Biological Inventions":

Ludic Grotesque or Forbidden Myth?

Daedalus was the first to demonstrate that the scientific worker is not concerned with gods.

—*J.B.S. Haldane*

In the age of the gods, Daedalus's fabulous automata were imitations of nature, and so was his legendary bird-like flight. Yet he was not deified.

Daedalus also made it possible for Pasiphaë, queen of Crete, to couple with a bull and thus conceive the Minotaur. While stirring Minos's hate, success in experimental genetics gained Daedalus humanity's agelong reprobation. Yet he was not damned.

The mechanical, the organic, and mixtures thereof were all contained in the primeval myth of the maze maker, who created men-animals as well as men-machines. At the archetypal source, Daedalus was the universal man, the culture of one.

Because he was responsible for the actual or attempted murder of his nephew in Athens, Daedalus went to Crete, only to escape once again to Sicily, where he was honored by King Kokalos of the Sicans. To discover the maze maker's whereabouts, Minos put out a riddle that only a most astute mind could unravel. When the riddle was solved, Minos knew that he would find Daedalus on the western shores of the Italian island, where he rushed to take revenge. And we could bet that Daedalian ingenuity on matters of hydraulic engineering played a role when bath-water boiled the king to death. Minos was Zeus's son; yet the artist-inventor was not smitten by a thunderbolt.

Leon Battista Alberti reminds us that "Daedalus received much praise from his contemporaries for having constructed a vault in Selinunte where a cloud of vapor emanated so warm and gentle that it induced a most agreeable sweat, and cured the body in an extremely pleasant manner." His talent for using water could restore health or cause death. From the very beginning, therefore, the architect's genius was double-edged. Even as a military engineer his ingenuity was provocative. "It is written," Alberti goes on, "that Daedalus founded the town of Agrigentum on a steep rock, which was so difficult to enter that it could be guarded by only three men—an effective defense, provided that the exit could not be blocked by a small band of armed men with equal ease."[1] At any rate, there seems to be no evidence that he ended up either in Elysium or Tartarus. Like his moving sculptures, he walked away with his own legend. His myth had no ending.

Whether for good or evil, Daedalus invented things that were accepted because they satisfied needs, as technology has always done. The fact that he was unworthy of heaven and hell tells us something about talents that could make unexpected things, as technology has empowered us to do.

Although at odds with the cosmic order of things that classical tradition and Ptolemaic science had set for ages to come, the Daedalian art of "making" could not be halted. However transgressive, a new mode of creativity claimed the status of a myth of origin; its forward-looking thrust was to grow ever more relevant for modernity. Daedalus's archetypal powers were not lost.

Long after the age of legends, Leonardo multiplied Daedalian exploits. In Milan, his automatalike figures for the Feast of Paradise stunned the audience. From Boboli to Pratolino, mechanical wonders of that sort colonized Italian gardens. Reality became an object of manipulation in the hands of the technological *artifex*. Human ingenuity tested the boundaries that had separated art, nature, and technology. Whether Daedalian or Leonardesque, man's flight with batlike wings was a hybrid that challenged the given order of things.

In Leonardo's hands, manipulation could make mimesis artificial. His eclectic frame of mind was at once empirical and experimental. Although it took on naturalistic guises and disguises, willful distortions of the mimetic tradition stemmed from the same intellectual core that produced forms of humanist aloofness. One was ludic and the other idealistic. Both of them altered nature once creation was thrown to the other side of *imitatio*. Among such deviations, the grotesque and the technological were meant to be other-than-natural. Whether playful or utilitarian, mimetic transgressions soon claimed legitimacy.

2

It is now a fact that the fantastic Middle Ages rejoiced in grotesque and surreal distortions. To his dismay, Saint Bernard could not deny that Romanesque art valued "unnatural" inventions. Unwittingly, he coined the phrase *deformis formositas ac formosa deformitas* (deformed beauty and beautiful deformity), which put in a nutshell the definition that would govern much grotesque art. By the early sixteenth century, it has been noted, *invenzione* challenged nature and pushed art beyond imitation.[2]

After Leonardo had written that "the painter strives and competes with nature" (662), Pontormo praised in 1546 the artist's ability to represent "life in two dimensions, whereas God had needed three to create it." And Ludovico Dolce insisted in 1557 that painters should not only imitate, but surpass nature. At the same time, Benedetto Varchi drew a line between substantial (nature) and contingent (art) forms, whose origin "is not in the things that are made, but in him who makes them."[3] Because it exceeds the uniformity of nature, contingency falls back on fantasy, which has been described as a mainspring that mixes sensory impressions so as to create new compounds in unending abundance. Emulation yielded a cluster of bizarre forms that were called *capricci, ghiribizzi,* and *grottesche;* they all flaunted artificiality through an array of ugly and deformed guises.

Since antiquity, fantasy spurred license when Philoponous referred to the "hyppocentaur" and Socrates led centaurs and Gorgons to populate the world of the imagination (*Phaedrus* 229c–d). Later, Albertus Magnus mentioned two-headed men, and Augustine wrote about distortions due either to defect or excess. He surmounted the theological problem of the grotesque as either an error at Creation or an anti-Creation vis-à-vis the idealized human body made in the image of God. Monsters were a proof of God's mastery of anatomy, which would reassure mankind about his competence in resurrecting the body Christian at the end of time.[4]

The Renaissance appreciation of pagan and modern eccentricity made of the grotesque a carrier of ludic virtuosity, critical reflections, and visionary concerns. As outstanding rungs in the development of the

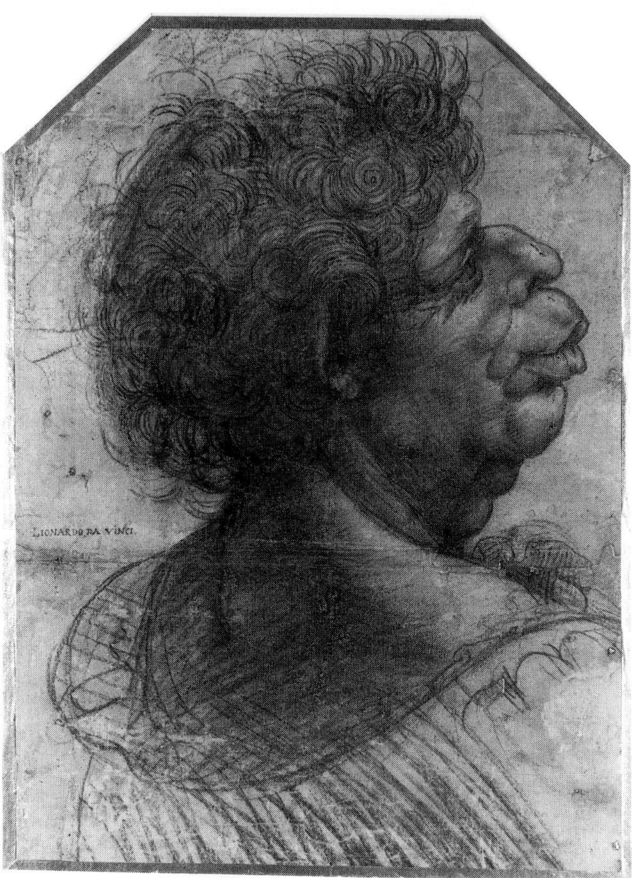

FIG. 47.   Leonardo da Vinci, *Scaramuccia* (1503–4)
Library of Christ Church College, Oxford

genre since antiquity, it suffices to mention Vitruvius, Horace, Cennini, Mantegna, Dürer, and Bosch.[5]

Familiar as he was with a standing tradition of human monstrosities, Vasari found the Leonardesque head of Scaramuccia (Fig. 47) very attractive. And Leonardo led the way toward the grotesque when he wrote that "if the painter wishes to see monstrous things that frighten, or those that are grotesque and laughable, or those that arouse real compassion, he is their lord and creator." As an alternative to the facial stereotypes of Botticelli and Piero della Francesca, he unveiled a world of monstrous things that might have echoed one of Alberti's less orthodox precepts:

"You will see some whose nose projects and is humped, others will have flaring nostrils, others pendant lips, still others the adornment of thin little lips. . . . All these things the studious painter will know from nature, and he will consider most assiduously how each one appears" (*O.P.*, 92). Much like Dürer and Northern fifteenth-century art, Leonardo could operate, to follow Erwin Panofsky,

> in two spheres, both outside Goethe's "natural" or "noble" nature and, for this reason, complementary to each other: the spheres of the realistic and the fantastic, the domain of intimate portraiture, genre, still life and landscape, on the one hand, and the domain of the visionary and phantasmagoric, on the other. The world of mere reality, accessible to subjective sensory perception, lies, as it were, before "natural" nature; the world of the visionary and phantasmagoric, created by equally subjective imagination, lies beyond "natural" nature.[6]

Within the context of Leonardo's stand against humanist canons of beauty, the grotesque evolved through stages of ugliness, caricature, and monstrosity.[7] At the first level, one finds volumetric drawings of ugly types whose expressions show forth "the purpose in their minds" (593). The old woman with colossal chin and enormous cheeks (Fig. 48) wears a self-complacent smile of undaunted pride. Attention has been called to a sketch for the *Battle of Anghiari* in which the heads of man, horse, and lion share "symptoms" of a dreadful fierceness (Fig. 49).[8] At that initial stage, Leonardo was conquering the idea that the interplay between beauty and ugliness would enhance expression. Taking on basic precepts of humanist art, he wrote that even "in narrative paintings one ought to mingle contraries so that they may afford a great contrast to one another, and all the more when they are in close proximity; that is, the ugly next to the beautiful, the big to the small." Because it shares details "drawn from life," diversity in art and nature—like father like son—is inherently transitive. In fact, "there is no figure of a woman so ugly as not to find a lover, if she is not monstrous" (McMahon, 277, 271, 87). A limit was set; beyond ugliness, proportion fostered excess, whose dissociations from the operative reality of mimesis could lead to the autonomous world of the grotesque.

At the second stage, distortion tested the border between men and animals. Monstrosity betrayed lack of proportion, and Leonardo wrote about "one who has a very large head and short legs" (McCurdy, 906). In *Five Grotesque Heads* (see Fig. 1), the female profile shows reptilian eyes

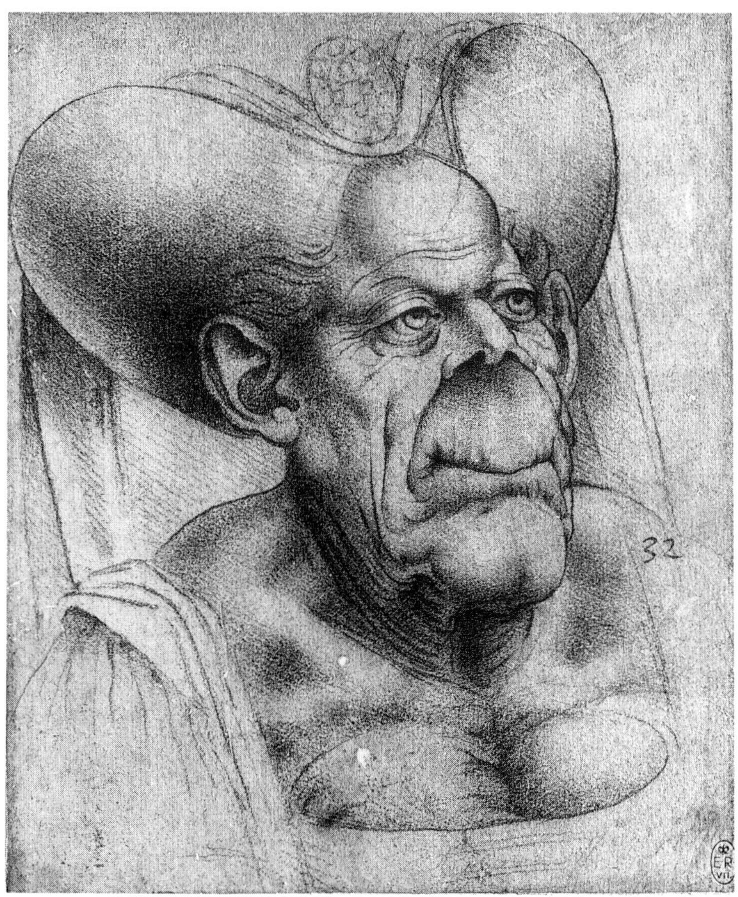

FIG. 48.   Leonardo da Vinci, *Grotesque Head* (c. 1492)
Royal Library, Windsor Castle

and a froglike mouth, while the male faces with ornithic and primatelike features are as stereotypical as the old nutcracker head and epicene youth (*Old Man and Youth*, Fig. 50).[9] At the edge, Leonardo seems to have tested the potential for morphological distortions of various kinds. Before engaging in artificial mixtures, he may have foreseen biological developments as distant in the future as the geological mutations that had come down to him from the Alpine past. At both extremes, diversity would reach back toward a primeval unity that could be regained through metamorphic processes in excess of Darwinian evolution.

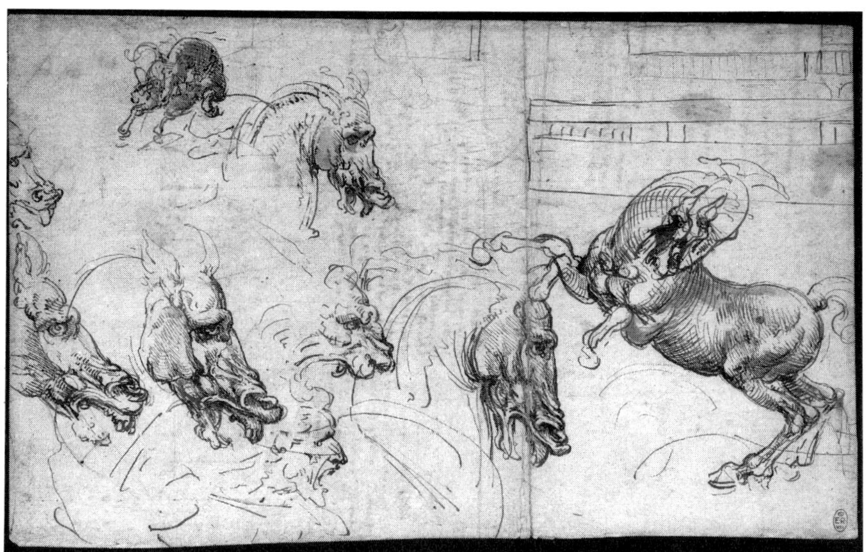

FIG. 49.   Leonardo da Vinci, *Horse, Lion, and Man* (c. 1504)
Royal Library, Windsor Castle

Inevitably, Leonardo's interest in comparative anatomy toyed with fantasy and nature: "You know that you cannot invent animals without limbs, each of which, in itself, must resemble those of some other animal. Hence if you wish to make an animal, imagined by you, appear natural—let us say a Dragon, take for its head that of a mastiff or hound, the eyes of a cat, the ears of a porcupine, the nose of a greyhound, the brow of a water tortoise" (585). The painter-scientist mixed parts, and his compound animal mocked the concept of organic unity. In a ludic vein, he displaced and reassembled animal parts (Fig. 51); yet he violated the forms of the animal kingdom neither in words nor images.

Transgressive modes date back to Ovid's *Metamorphoses*, whose predominant pattern is that of animate forms turning into inanimate objects. Medusa turns men into stone, and the vanity of Medusa-like thoughts would lead to Dante's memorable lines:

> io veggio te ne lo 'ntelletto
> fatto di pietra e, impetrato, tinto,
> si che t'abbaglia il lume del mio detto

(I see your mind has turned to stone,
and, like a stone, is dark and, being dark,
cannot endure the clear light of my words)
(*Purgatory* xxxiii, 73–75; trans. Mark Musa)

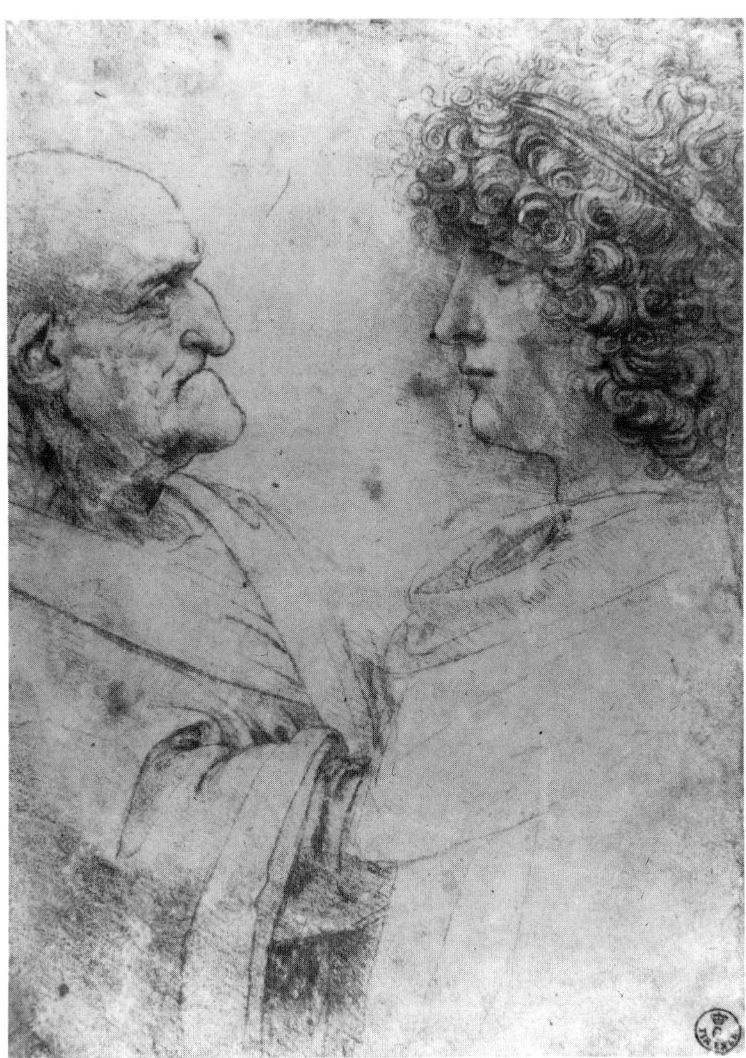

FIG. 50.   Leonardo da Vinci, *Old Man and Youth* (c. 1500)
Uffizi, Florence

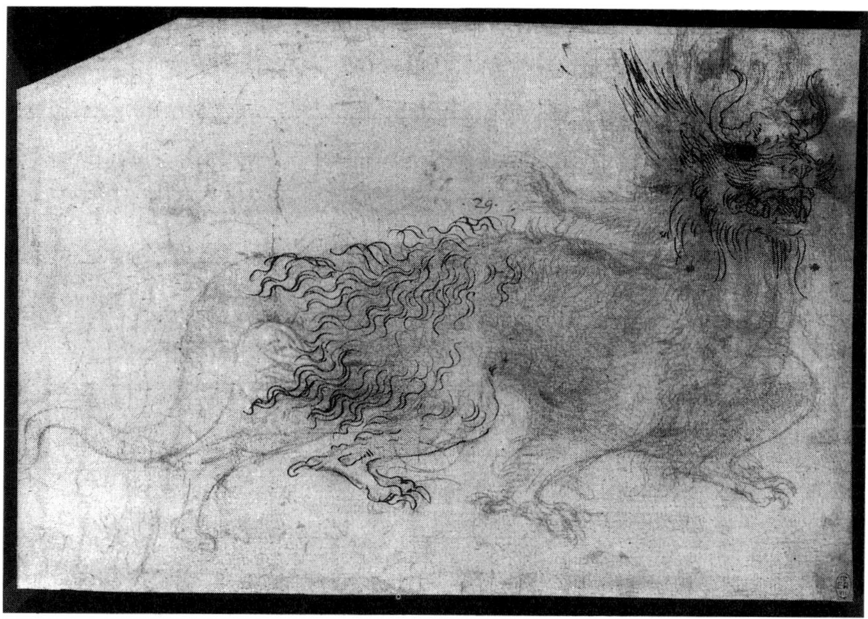

FIG. 51.   Leonardo da Vinci, *Dragon* (c. 1505)
Royal Library, Windsor Castle

Sensual beauty could petrify man into a haunting art object. And the Petrarchan pun *Lauro-Laura* (tree-woman) updated the petrifying effects of the artistic process. The poet fell in love with his own creation, which in turn paved the way for the poet laureate. Because he finally saw the truth, Francesco confessed his sin of idolatry, which led him to equate Laura with the Medusa in the closing prayer of his collection of poems.[10] Spiritual help did not let the poet turn himself into a statue. Beauty could take a dreadful toll, but it did not.

The reverse also occurred in myth. Pygmalion, in fact, brought an inanimate statue to life; with the help of the gods, Galatea was born, and she would bear children (*Metamorphoses* 10, 243–97). The figure of speech that carries forward both metamorphoses is *prosopopoeia*. While literalizing allegory, *prosopopoeia* exploits linguistic propensities toward tropological substitution. In the humanist mode, mimesis offered organic forms that artists simplified into the rather geometric mannequin-like or columnar figures of Piero della Francesca and Paolo Uccello, whose interest in perspectival constructs and geometric shapes never relented. By means of a more subtle art that "conceals art,"

Pygmalion brought to life the inanimate Galatea. Ancient myth therefore offered two modes of creation: Medusa drained life from bodies turned into stone, whereas Pygmalion gave life to statues. Antiquity itself was split between the philosophic axiom that art imitates nature and the mythic belief in the power of art to create rather than to portray. Modern versions of the myth by Burne-Jones and Daumier aside, we have been told that Donatello wanted his *Zuccone* to speak and spit. Leonardo himself wrote: "It happened to me that I made a religious painting which was bought by one who so loved it that he wanted to remove the sacred representation so as to be able to kiss it without suspicion. Finally his conscience prevailed over his sighs and lust, but he had to remove the picture from his house" (McMahon, 33). In the end, E. H. Gombrich writes, Leonardo fixed wings and a beard on a lizard, which turned into a dragon. "It was only a whimsical footnote to a Promethean life. The claim to be a creator, a maker of things, passed from the painter to the engineer—leaving the artist only the small consolation of being a maker of dreams."

Daedalus, however, had gone beyond dream making. He made statues that walked and cowlike constructs that facilitated, so to speak, the birth of the Minotaur. Leonardo was attracted by both. But he was too much of a scientist to try to meet Pygmalion's challenge, which edged dangerously between art and life. As Jean-Jacques Rousseau was to write in his own *Pygmalion,* "I adore myself in what I have made." To that extent, narcissistic self-love was externalized into a hyperbolic mode that has been called pygmalionism; self-involvement yielded to self-projection. Human creativity thrived on excess and self-deification.[11]

Antiquity was crowded with monsters of the human imagination. One of them was Medusa, whose hair of snakes attracted Leonardo's attention as well as that of Mannerist and baroque artists from Cellini and Caravaggio to Rubens, who made a copy of it. Like Shelley and Walter Pater later on, some of them might have believed that the artwork now in the Uffizi was by Leonardo. To follow Vasari, the painting put forth a visual thematics replete with bats, snakes, and toads that would have enticed Leonardesque curiosity.

Young Leonardo, Vasari tells us, set out to paint the buckler his father had given him with a subject that would produce the same effect as the head of the Medusa. He thus

> carried into a room of his own, which no one but he himself entered, crawling reptiles, green lizards, crickets, snakes, butterflies, locusts, bats, and other strange species of this kind, and by

adapting various parts of this multitude, he created a most horrible and frightening monster with poisonous breath that set the air on fire. And he depicted the monster emerging from a dark and broken rock, spewing forth poison from its open mouth, fire from its eyes, and smoke from its nostrils so strangely that it seemed a monstrous and dreadful thing indeed. And Leonardo took such pains in creating it that out of the great love he felt for his profession, he did not smell the overpowering stench that arose from the dead animals.[12]

Vasarian distortions notwithstanding, this passage brings out essential features of Leonardo's poetics at the very beginning of his career. First, he foregrounded a faithful adherence to the imitation of natural forms, which he then rearranged into grotesque compounds. Likewise, the slow pace of his working habits is measured by the mounting stench of his models, which would "educate" him to environments where he would cut up corpses later in his life.

At a more speculative level, Vasari's wishful *ekphrasis* exceeded even Leonardesque ingenuity. The assemblage of the monstrous creature with poisonous breath that set the air on fire points to an organism whose "biological birth" is closer to romantic than Renaissance ingenuity. We might suspect that Vasari got so carried away that he himself brought to life the Leonardesque artifacts, which, however, remained just artifacts. Percy Bysshe Shelley also focused on the Leonardesque Medusa at the beginning of his poem on the Uffizi picture (Fig. 52). Yet he quickly shifted from representation to re-creation. As a result, the artist would be a new Perseus who, having lost Athena's mirror, goes against the monster with naked eye.[13] For Shelley, Medusa was "an uncreated creature" that Perseus had killed and poetry would bring back to life. According to myth, she could petrify humans; yet, modern man was bound to make of her a source of art that would awaken monsters of the imagination.[14]

As to the grotesque character of the Medusa-like subject, we might agree that it tested the range of possibility.[15] By that, the artist might have meant the transhuman, the unmimetic, and the anticanonical. To kill the monster, Perseus was given wings by Hermes. Once slain, the Gorgon's blood generated Pegasus, the winged horse that would incite flights of the human imagination.[16] Mythic flyers found a counterpart in the Uffizi picture, which presents a bat next to the severed head. The bat draws the Leonardesque cluster of organic grotesques into a convergence of myth, technology, and transgressions thereof. The bat, in fact, was the

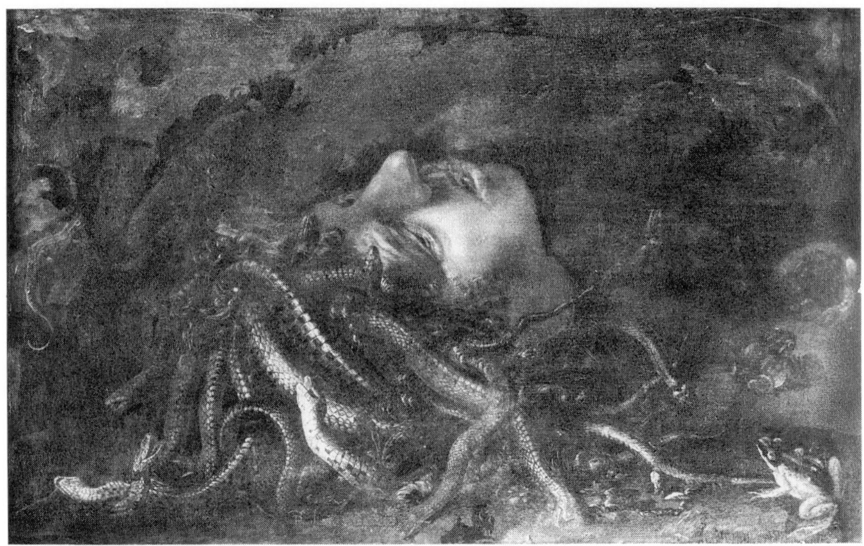

Fig. 52.   After Leonardo or Flemish School, *Head of Medusa*
Uffizi, Florence

model for Leonardo's flying machine. Mythmaking ancient and modern, technological and biological, mimetic and grotesque seems to have exploited the whole range of artistic ingenuity. Whether they be Arabian tales or Quixotic legends, literary descriptions have always rejoiced in crowding the skies with a flying horse or a mechanical Pegasus. While Regiomontanus is said to have built an artificial eagle that flew to salute Emperor Maximilian, Ariosto conjured up a flying hippogriff born by an ass to a griffin (*Orlando Furioso* 2).

From words to images, Leonardo's drawing of the *Monster of Ravenna* presents a man half human, half birdlike, with batlike wings and a horn on his head, not to mention a kneecap that looks like an eye.[17] That hybrid was a more stationary version of the Icarian birdman; as such, it came closer to transpass natural kingdoms. It is even more revealing that Leonardo rounded into a single sheet of paper drawings of a bat, a dragonfly, a flying fish, a butterfly, and a human grotesque (MS B fol. 10 v). The accompanying words refer to *"animal che fugge dell'uno elemento nell'altro."* Interest is centered on forms of life that cross natural boundaries in order to become other than what they are. Emphasis is placed on organic adaptations that include man as well. At its most extreme, the antihumanist grotesque spawned forms at the edge of physiological mutations. Beyond the untamed vitality of early medieval grotesques, Leonardo's monsters fell short of either metamorphosis or any "collapsed" evolution. His caricatures pushed mimesis toward disproportional profiles whose lack of depth flaunted their "fabricated" makeup. Originality therefore spawned forms of unsightly artificiality.

As one of the more magical branches of technology, alchemy seems to have made it possible for Albertus Magnus to discover an elixir that animated statues. Yet they took on so many human habits that their chatter became intolerable. Technology also produced water tricks at Pratolino, automata at Boboli, and E.T.A. Hoffmann's later fictions about human machines in *Automatons* (1812) and *The Sandman* (1814). In a world of creatures that can be reduced to machines, we have been warned, technocrats would indeed be gods.[18] At the other side of nature, man no longer was bound to the proportional standards of godlike analogues.

While Pythagoras drew on a slate ratios of musical harmonies that brought concord to heavenly spheres in Raphael's *School of Athens*, Leonardo probably played ludic notes on a lyre that he built as a monstrous hybrid. From instrumental grotesques to pictorial unnaturalness, he may have crossed the boundary of mimesis but once, if we give credence to Melzi's copy of one of his sketches (Fig. 53). Conversely, his drawing of *Leda and the Swan,* as well as Raphael's version of it, leads the hybrid union to produce eggs that contain human babies. The myth is at once transgressive and corrective.

3

Like Daedalus, Leonardo was a technician and an artist. He dared to gaze beyond technology and never tired of asking himself: "What think you Man! of your species? Are you as wise as you set yourself to be?" (McCurdy, 85). That dilemma voiced the mythic split of scientific knowledge, which could be divided between forethought (Prometheus) and afterthought (Epimetheus).

Challenges to human wisdom in the name of technological ingenuity must be traced back to Crete. At the birth of Western culture, Crete stood as a place of divided origins, and Dante called it a "wasteland" (*Inferno* xiv, 94) where Daedalian cunning would test the resources of the human species. Having helped Pasiphaë to bring the Minotaur to life, Daedalus, so the story goes, gave Ariadne a ball of thread that helped

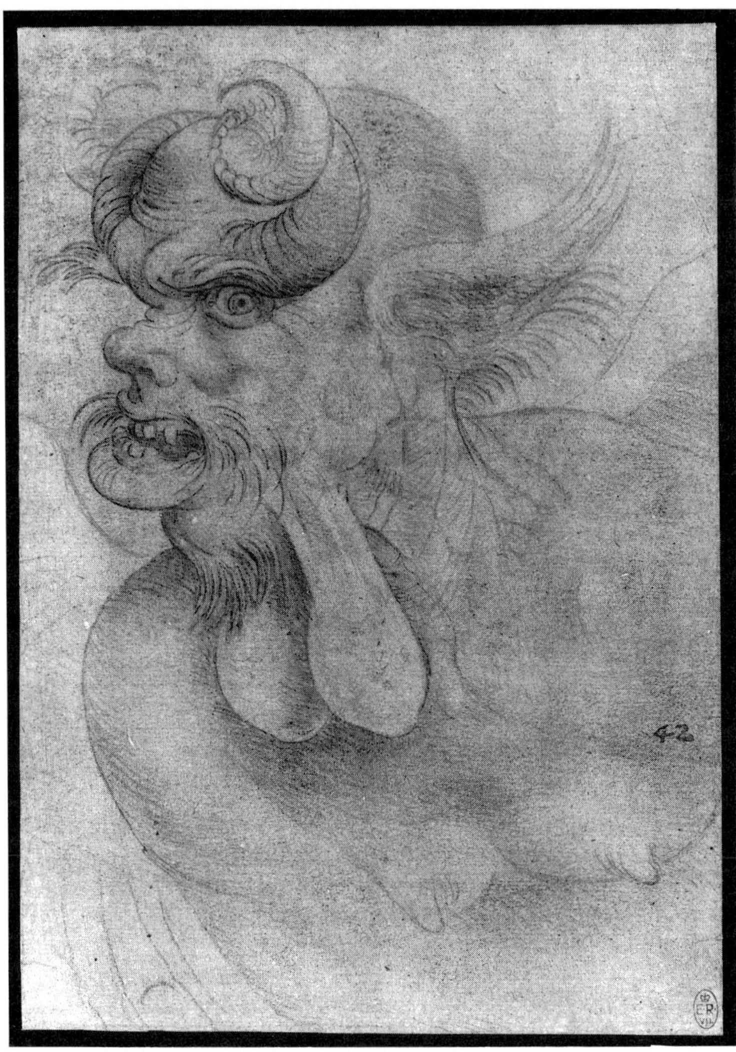

FIG. 53.   Melzi's copy of Leonardo's drawing, *Monster* (c. 1513)
Royal Library, Windsor Castle

Theseus to escape from the labyrinth. Daedalus was crucial to the birth
and death of the monster, as well as to the invention and violation of
labyrinthine impenetrability. In the end, he had to run for his life. The
myth thus raised the question, Can the mind control its own fantasies?

Can the intellect curb its own pride? The thread of experience may have led Leonardo to master his own Minotaur. Later, however, labyrinths without many walls hid ever more voracious men-Minotaurs. Goya was not the first to concede that the historical nightmare of reason generated bestial hybrids of the human imagination.

Soon enough, Daedalian transgressors hid in the labyrinth of experimental "alchemies" that could produce monsters in the Faustian womb of scientific laboratories; Pasiphaë's sin would become man's proud enterprise. Through magic, it seems, she burdened Minos with a sexual anomaly. In case of intercourse with another woman, he would generate snakes and other horrible animals that bodied forth biological deviations.

Again, myth was there to sound a warning. Once he pitted human ingenuity against nature and the gods, Daedalus would never be the same. He was instrumental in creating a bull-like hybrid that killed youths; he himself harmed his nephew and contributed to his son's death. The "artificer" could fly away from the labyrinth, but a monstrous talent had taken up residence in the citadel of his own mind.

Back in Crete, Theseus killed the Minotaur. His heroic deed, however, exacted a price. Quickly, he gave in to sexual excess and abandoned Ariadne. On the way back home, he also forgot to replace black with white sails. His oversight failed to signal victory to King Aegeus, who drowned in the sea that would be named after him. In a way that bore sinister forebodings, Daedalus and Theseus became victims of their own achievements.

4

Did Leonardo foresee the possibility of overstepping the kingdoms of nature and of tampering with the human species? As a scientist, he raised a question that Rabelais, a humanist and humane writer, would translate into paternal warnings half a century later: "Knowledge without conscience" ruins the soul (*Gargantua and Pantagruel* 2, viii).

Leonardo did not engage in what J.B.S. Haldane has called "biological inventions," the "most monstrous and unnatural action."[19] Since antiquity, however, mechanistic inventors stood next to artificers who tried to simulate biological forms. Artificial heads made oracular pronouncements in Greece, and Christian texts record mummified faces that spoke. Throughout the Middle Ages, alchemists and kabbalists hoped to build automata of flesh and blood, with Paracelsus's Homunculus at their forefront.[20]

Forms of genetic manipulation usually lead to sterility in the world of nature, where mules do not reproduce. As a biological invention, therefore, the grotesque in the mode of cross-fertilization defies the limit of its transgressive potential. However artificial its appearance, the grotesque could not be allowed to produce living hybrids. It could be less than coincidental that the Minotaur-like figure Leonardo designed in one of his emblematic drawings steers a ship out to sea, perhaps toward Cretan islands where a labyrinth would shut it out of the civilized lifestream.

Technology helped Daedalus to take his "forbidden" knowledge elsewhere, even though he did not use it again. Equally talented, Leonardo checked his overreaching talents against strategies of restraint; sketches and outright silence withheld information about things to come. He was a technician and became a legend that has survived in our memory. He also built himself into a fabulous figure whose Daedalian profile took features from Hermes and Prometheus.

At the outer limits of human experience, Leonardo shared with the humanists the belief that man wants "to be everywhere. . . . He is content with no frontier. He yearns to command everywhere and to be praised everywhere. And so he strives to be as God everywhere" (Marsilio Ficino, *Theologia platonica* XIV, 5). Like Ficino, he knew that excessive ambition could be ruinous. Yet they neither could nor wanted to curb their yearning for more knowledge. As a Faust who never sold out to the devil,[21] Leonardo became his own emulative paragon. The Neoplatonists made of Icarus a symbol of transcendental longings. Because he was Daedalian, Leonardo did not become an overreacher whose "waxen wings did mount above his reach / And melting, heavens conspired his overthrow (Marlowe, *Doctor Faustus* prologue, 20–21).[22] Matters of anxiety were self-reflexive and future-oriented for Leonardo. Like Daedalus, he survived his own darings.

5

After a lifelong interest in Daedalus, Michael Ayrton equated the myth with a category of the human spirit. Icarus lived for a single moment, and death became a monument that made the boy immortal, though he never became a man. Daedalus, instead, chose cognition, and his modern worshiper so worded his testament: "In my view the valiant act is to live as long as possible, but then I am a maker of things and that takes time."[23] When the two myths came together, father and son also gave a parental guise to the dualism of *kairos* and *chronos,* that is to say, heroic moments and empirical vicissitudes. As a technician, the maker takes on responsibility for the quality of other people's lives. In a thoughtful moment, Daedalus may have uttered: "I triumphed in the knowledge that I had contrived this possibility of flight. Yet I knew, as I watched him swim in his new dimension, that I had destroyed my own son."[24] At all levels, Daedalian creativity was ominous. As a sculptor, his violent envy turned the mythic role of the artist as teacher into a crime.[25]

Even the Promethean criminal invented ships and lit the fire of knowledge, but he was punished: "For I myself am without contrivance / to rid myself of my present affliction" (Aeschylus, *Prometheus Bound* 470–71). It is the affliction of pagan transgression and Christian fall, of knowledge as curse and conquest; indeed, the Daedalian wound.

As an inventor, Daedalus could not stop Icarus from abusing the potential of human flight; and he lost his son. As an architect, he built such a complex structure that he almost could not find his way out of it. At the mythic point of origin, technology turned into a mode of construction and transgression that could overwhelm its own creator.

It is perhaps in such a spirit that Leonardo paused with a sense of sinister foreboding on the misuse that his inventions could have entailed; his reservations about probable abuses of the submarine by reckless people led him to withhold information and interrupt research. Leonardo knew that technology could make us either super- or subhuman. For certain, it would test humaneness; and it did. Flight was Icarus's glory and doom. Had he survived, would he have wanted to walk again?

6

Moral boundaries often collapsed when human ingenuity used technology to tamper with nature. In a Daedalian spirit, grotesque hybrids were deviations of a metamorphic mode that stood at the core of mythology. In Ovidian poetry, Olympian transformations were complete and reversible. Metamorphosis was metamorphic; at any moment, forms could turn into other forms.

With the passing of time, metamorphoses became difficult. It was only by hiding in a wooden cow that Pasiphaë could couple with the bull.[26] Transformation carried a deception whose shameful outcome had to be hidden in an equally deceptive environment. In turn, the Minotaur could change neither into a beast nor into a man. Metamorphoses got stuck halfway and often created monsters. The would-be epiphany had become a curse.

Because he could unravel the most difficult riddles, Daedalus probably learned the myth's lesson. But posterity did not take it to heart. At the turn of the nineteenth century, "biological inventions" lured scientific minds. Johann Friedrich Blumenbach came up with a way of growing human embryos resembling frogs, while Johann Friedrich Meckel thought of tampering with fetal growth in order to produce monstrous children. From Faust to DNA genetic codes, scientific overreachers, so we have been told from a feminist perspective, have always sought to usurp the generative powers of the womb.[27] The Minotaur was a hybrid that could not reproduce, but who can say that biological engineering could not make monsters fertile?

Perhaps Leonardo was not unfamiliar with strange thoughts of that kind. His notes on anatomy open with an axiomatic commitment "to work miracles," which he linked to the metamorphic creativity of "alchemists, the would-be creators of gold and silver, and to engineers who would have dead water stir itself into life and perpetual motion" (796). His passionate and yet ambiguous attacks against necromancy uncovered fearful longings at the watershed between humanity and divinity. With spite, he warned against the necromancer's power over the forces of nature: "In truth, whoever has control of such irresistible forces will be lord over all nations, and no human skill will be able to resist his destructive power" (McCurdy, 82). At that point, the Daedalian mythmaker could usurp divine privileges.

Leonardo's indictment of the Faustian ethos was deliberate. Yet he could not help laboring over the many privileges that such a forbidden achievement would entail. For sure, a whole spectrum of possibilities was open to man: "He will cause himself to be carried through the air from East to West, and through all the uttermost parts of the universe" (McCurdy, 82). Leonardo could be seduced by the dynamics of his own rhetoric. He could become the cause of his own flying in a godlike freedom unburdened by either wings or chariots.

Beyond Daedalian technology, Leonardo would soar on his own power, like Zeus himself. It was a forbidden thought, and he knew it: "But why do I thus go on adding instance to instance?" (McCurdy, 82). The inventor, the artist, and the mythmaker could not but face up to their ultimate potential. They spearheaded a quest that traced effects one by one—"instance to instance"—back to the revelatory mystery of their cause. Its lure almost overwhelmed him. It was a struggle to keep it under control; unlike later overreachers, Leonardo succeeded.

7

While Pico della Mirandola and Michelangelo celebrated the dignity of youthful maturity, Leonardo's panegyric to the miracle of human birth thrived on scientific observation: "This work must begin with the conception of man, and describe the nature of the womb and how the foetus lives in it, up to what stage it resides there, and in what way it quickens into life—*vivificarsi*—and feeds" (797). *Vivificarsi:* the word almost captures the very emergence of life. The rhetoric of science spilled over into poetic reflections. Anatomy led to physiology, which energized knowledge: "I reveal to men the origin of the first, or perhaps second cause of their existence" (841).

As a scientist, Leonardo wrote on the unity and reciprocity of mother and fetus: "One mind governs two bodies, inasmuch as the desires and the fears and the pains of the mother are common with the pains, that is, the bodily pains and desires of the infant lying in the body of the mother."[28] Observation takes on a more human tone when we are told that the umbilical cord carries dangers and responsibilities that affect the sacredness of life: "A wish, a strong craving or a fright or any other mental suffering in the mother has more influence on the child than on the mother" (837). Notations of that sort betray humane concerns for the unborn, whose dependence on the mother is physical as well as psychological. They share bodily functions and attitudes of heart. Personal concerns are so transparent that parental responsibility must offset the fetus's helplessness. At once artist and scientist, Leonardo gave a description of human bondage that was both medical and poetic. His primordial respect for life filtered love through the womb, where life unseen is affected by the toils of life seen. The umbilical cord became a primeval "line of life." Within the larger context of human sacredness, even the "marvellous works of nature" pale "compared with the soul that dwells within" the human body, which "is a divine thing" (McCurdy, 80).

Later maze makers stood against Leonardo's own respect for the sacrality of mother and fetus. In the middle of the nineteenth century, the evolutionary biologist T. H. Huxley asked at the end of *Man's Place in Nature* (1863): "Where, then, must we look for primaeval Man?" His answer was some kind of an intermediary being between man and ape, a "blurred copy" in the semblance of the Antropomorpha of Linnaeus. The primeval man could be a monster we might look for in the wilds of South America or at the North Pole. Leonardo, instead, countered monsterism with the androgyne of archetypal reconciliation, Saint John the Baptist.

8

Daedalus was not punished by the gods, because he punished himself by destroying what was most dear to him, his own son. He was instrumental in inventing a biological hybrid once and did not try experiments of that sort again.

But posterity did. Believing as he did in his "unhallowed arts," Victor Frankenstein dared beyond Renaissance anatomists: "I collected the instruments of life around me, that I might infuse a spark of being into the lifeless thing that lay at my feet." The humanoid was assembled with parts coming from charnel houses, slaughter pens, and dissection rooms. Their assemblage produced a monster who was neither half human nor half machine; he was endowed with human feelings. The romantic quest for transgressive myths of origin fell back on Prometheus, Cain, and Hyperion while the hope of creating spirit out of matter inspired Novalis, Hoffmann, and German *Naturphilosophie*. In their path, Mary Shelley belittled the challenge of writing a ghost story and took up the romantic quest of making the inanimate animate. While keeping abreast of current debates in the sciences, she gave artistic expression to the belief that scientific inquiry would have to be pursued regardless of any spiritual or secular authority. The devil's doctrine, so we are told, commands that what can be done must be done.[29]

Leonardo's fetus was born because of a force or "motive power" (1139) that was spiritual. Frankenstein's monster, instead, came to life through the electric power of galvanic charges. The Promethean scientist of modernity helped to create a "new species" that would venerate him as "creator and source." A reader of Milton, the monster stated: "Remember, that I am thy creature; I ought to be thy Adam; but I am rather the fallen angel." He wanted to legitimize man's ascent to the role of an alternate divinity.[30] However well-intentioned his attitude toward society might have been, he terrified people. At the end, he could not but paraphrase Milton's Satan: "Evil thenceforth became my good." The romantic monster shared with the Renaissance Adam the belief that language is a "godlike science." Pico's word was born with the myth of creation, but it could not redeem the monster's accursed origin, to which language itself refused to give a name. The onomastics of modern automation, however, named Golem a machine made of dead matter. The living spirit, Ernst Fischer warns, "resists the metamorphosis which turns it, not into a laurel tree like Daphne fleeing from Apollo, but into an automaton, a machine fleeing from the self."[31] Hence the fateful question, What will the outcome be, man-as-object or a humanized product?

9

The alliance between technology and the grotesque remained peripheral during the Renaissance, but it seems to have become central in our own days; throughout, they have never been too far apart. The intransitive could become transitive, and anatomy could turn into physiology. We have grown accustomed to believe that most science fictions turn into prophecies of the future; and too many of them are one prolonged horror story.[32] Leonardo's own prophecies were but compelling chapters of that unfolding narrative.

We know Frankenstein as fiction, but could a latter cohort of his transgress the boundaries of art and point toward biological inventions? After all, investigations into modern technology and human values bearing the titular marker of Herbert J. Muller's *Children of Frankenstein* (1970) have raised a preliminary question, Can man control technology? Can he direct the extraordinary power he has achieved to sensible, humane, and civilized ends? At the end of another landmark study, Jacques Ellul's *Technological Society* (1964), recommendations have been made to cage the Frankenstein monster, who was about to get out of control.

After Leonardo, even as wise and thoughtful a humanist as Michel de Montaigne took up matters of creation and procreation. Toward the very end of his essay "Of the Affection of Fathers for their Children," the Frenchman begins to wonder whether Augustine would bury his writings or his children. Likewise, would Virgil have been prouder to have fathered the *Aeneid* or the handsomest boy in Rome? Such issues are linked to the Ovidian text about Pygmalion, which closes the essay. By letting Pygmalion bring to life an artistic creation, myth set man's godlike talents at the boundary between resemblance and identity. As for himself, Montaigne wrote: "I do not know whether I would not like much better to have produced one perfectly formed child by intercourse with the muses than by intercourse with my wife."[33] Human conscience at its most humane thus spoke.

Well in excess of nature's own ingenuity, Philip Sidney's *Defence of Poetry* insisted that the artist can invent "Cyclops, Chimeras, Furies and such like . . . freely ranging within the zodiac of his own wit." In myth, Galatea came to life with Venus's blessings. At the turn of the sixteenth century, Raphael did not ask for Olympian dispensations when he painted her in a Roman palace. And he could find a model for her only in an idea born from his own mind. Within the zodiac of the artist's own wit, therefore, invention became autonomous. While disregarding nature and gods alike, the artist could push originality and emulation toward unknown, if not altogether forbidden territories. In the Ovidian text, Galatea gave birth to a girl named Paphos. An island was named after her, and

> Her son was Cinyras; had he been childless,
> He might have been a happier man. The story
> Is terrible, I warn you. Fathers, daughters,
> Had better skip this part, or, if you like my songs,
> Distrust me here, and say it never happened
> (Metamorphoses 10, 298–302)

Cinyra's daughter was Myrrha, who fell in love with her father. Myth did not fail to sound a warning, to which Leonardo could have added cautionary forebodings drawn from scientific and technological research.

At present, the primacy of mathematical physics as the science of sciences at the core of progress since the seventeenth century has been waning. The new hub is that of the life sciences.[34] Because of technology, forbidden myths of the past could indeed become reality in the future. Since we have engineered just about everything else, should we leave humans out? That final step would lead to genetic alterations capable of transforming the biological stock of mankind. At that point, genetic manipulations would force people to confront problems with which they might not be prepared to cope.[35] Just as war is too important to be left to generals, so the future form of the race is too important to be left to professionals in the life sciences.

In chapters yet to be written, it would be wise to build on lessons we have learned about forbidden knowledge. For certain, we know that it is not ludic, and technology itself has become a labyrinth in which it is not clear whether anyone is safe, trapped, or both. On the subject of extraterritorial lifelines, George Steiner has reached a thoughtful conclusion, which is a prediction as well. Since the Renaissance, Western civilization has operated on the assumption that, by and large,

> man and truth were companions. Certain trends in the life sciences now cast doubt on this assumption. It is as if the bio-

chemical and biogenetic facts and potentialities we are now beginning to elucidate were waiting in ambush for man. It may prove to be that the dilemmas and possibilities of action they will pose are outside morality and beyond the ordering grasp of the human intellect. . . . The forward-vaulting intelligence of our species, which is so intricate yet so vulnerable a piece of systematic evolution, finds itself in front of doors it might be best to leave unopened. On pain of life.[36]

Leonardo's prophecies went back to the stealer of fire, whose few words told "the whole story: all arts that mortals have come from Prometheus" (Aeschylus, *Prometheus Bound* 504). And it was fitting that his son Deucalion would bring together Prometheus, the creator of human life out of clay, Pygmalion, the creator of human life out of marble, and Frankenstein, the transgressor of creative mysteries:

> If I only had the power, I would restore
> The nations as my father did, bring clay
> To life with breathing.
> (Ovid, *Metamorphoses* I, 362–64)

The story of Deucalion and Pyrrha, so we have been told, is one that moves from chaos to creation.[37] Long after myth, however, could anyone be sure that "re-creations" of man by man at crucial moments in the development of modernity would not plunge us back into chaos?

Iconographers have traced the change that the figure of Prometheus underwent at the dawn of the Renaissance, when emphasis shifted toward the man-making artist. Boccaccio drew a line between two creations; one into existence and the other into the life of culture. Bovillus insisted on the growth of value from the man of nature (*primus homo*) to the man of art (*secundus homo*): "The second in time becomes first in value." As a utilitarian form of art, technology has upheld the thesis that *homo* is *sapiens* because he is *faber*. The Christian tradition, however, could uphold neither the idea that natural man is exempted from original sin nor that scientific creation is morally neutral. Rather than indicting pursuits of knowledge, the tale sounds a warning against scientific interests at variance with ethical responsibility.[38]

Whether pagan or Christian, Nietzsche would insist that cognition is an act of sacrilege, which entails either imprisonment or exile. That was the lot reserved for Prometheus and Adam; that was Daedalus's destiny—and Leonardo's own. His early interest in the Medusa could be severed from the creature's symbolism on matters of creation. As mythographers tell us, Athena attached the head of the monster to her aegis so as to warn people not to probe into the divine mysteries hidden behind it.[39] For Leonardo, creation and transgression, knowledge of natural laws and defiance of divine ones were intertwined. And so they remained for centuries to come. As the most creative form of Joycean mythography, Stephen Hero was a "re-named" Dedalus, which the modern artist took as a prophecy: "At the name of the fabulous artificer, he seemed to hear the noise of dim waves and to see a winged form flying above the waves and slowly climbing the air . . . a hawklike man flying sunward above the sea, a prophecy of the end he had been born to serve and had been following through the mists of childhood and boyhood, a symbol of the artist forging anew in his workshop out of the sluggish matter of the earth a new soaring impalpable imperishable being" (*A Portrait of the Artist as a Young Man*). In the Joycean workshop, the forger named names. As long as man would strive to forge the sluggish matter of the earth into higher forms of life, however, Daedalian prophecies came to pass. In the Leonardesque workshop, talent could not be allowed to be otherwise. While nobody would invent Faustian instruments to assault the sun, wings would be made for hawklike minds bound to fly sunward.

Experience and foresight have made it clear that the Daedalian myth is at once a model and a force; it is not unresolved, but unfolding. The Daedalian *artifex* was not one of the gods of creation; he was one of the postlapsarian deities of progress.

The Minotaur's mindless appetite was contained in a place symbolic of man's lowest soul, namely the "gut" part of the body below the waist. Such a maze, in fact, imitated intestinal windings. As a human creation, however, its meandering passages also were a model of the brain's convolutions, the "citadel" at the top of his body. With an eye to anatomies of myth, the labyrinth was a representation of Daedalus's mind, the daedalia of his own ingenuity.

As a postlapsarian artist who cherished myths of origin, Leonardo created beauty. He did not bestow bliss because he was an inventor, not a healer. As a Daedalian mythmaker, he spearheaded a tradition of return that would be forever divided and reconciled through exchanges between the progress of technology and the worship of prestigious beginnings.[40]

Trailing as we do in the train of progress, we now know that Daedalus's legend will never end. We also have grown to understand that he could be neither in Elysium nor in Tartarus. He is in our midst now, and we all bear scars of his wound.

Dialogism

10

The Dialogic "Mean" in the *School of Athens*

The peculiarity of man is to create in two kinds of time, one of which runs on in the domain of pure possibility, in the very heart of that subtle substance which can imitate all things and combine them with one another to infinity. The other time is nature's. It in one sense contains the first, and in another sense, is contained in it. Our acts partake of both.

—Paul Valéry

At the turn of the cinquecento, Raphael gave visual form to the dialogic tensions of fifteenth-century culture in the *School of Athens* (1510–11, Fig. 54), which is much less Athenian than one might suspect. We need only say that the arched structure is a tribute to Roman more than Athenian architecture, which was one of planes rather than volumes.[1] The Pantheon, in fact, celebrated man's successful attempt to contain space within human bounds, and the vault overarching the figures in the Vatican fresco was probably modeled after a cluster of Bramantesque experiences that pointed back to the Roman temple.[2]

The Greeks were thinkers, the Romans were builders, and the moderns set out to be both. It is against such a background that the Greek substructure of the *School of Athens* enhances a modern mythology whose ranks enlisted Michelangelo, Bramante, Raphael himself, Sodoma, and Leonardo. They are presented in ancient disguises that locked in a flawless system of correspondences, with Plato and Aristotle set in the midst of talent ancient and modern. Enough has been said about the Plato-Leonardo juxtaposition. But more ought to be said about Aris-

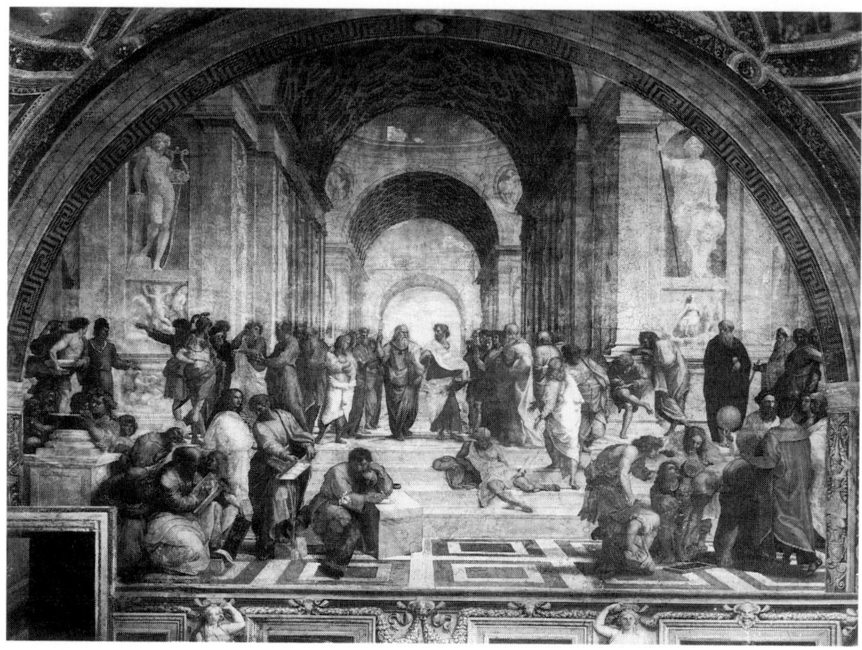

Fig. 54.   Raphael, *School of Athens* (1510–11)
Stanza della Segnatura, Vatican

totle, since his modern analogue is just as crucial to the philosophical content of the fresco.

2

Leonardo's famous drawing of himself in the guise of an old bearded man (Fig. 55) has been taken as a counterpart to the equally old and bearded Plato. The physical resemblance might have been there, but we should not underrate the rather archetypal nature of that figure. There is a drawing of Giovanni Bellini and innumerable images of Jerome that are quite similar, not to mention Leonardo's own insistence on the old man type. In a preliminary way, I would like to suggest that such elusive matters are less relevant than stylistic indebtedness. Furthermore, all of them are ancillary to the ideological relationship between ancient and modern figures.

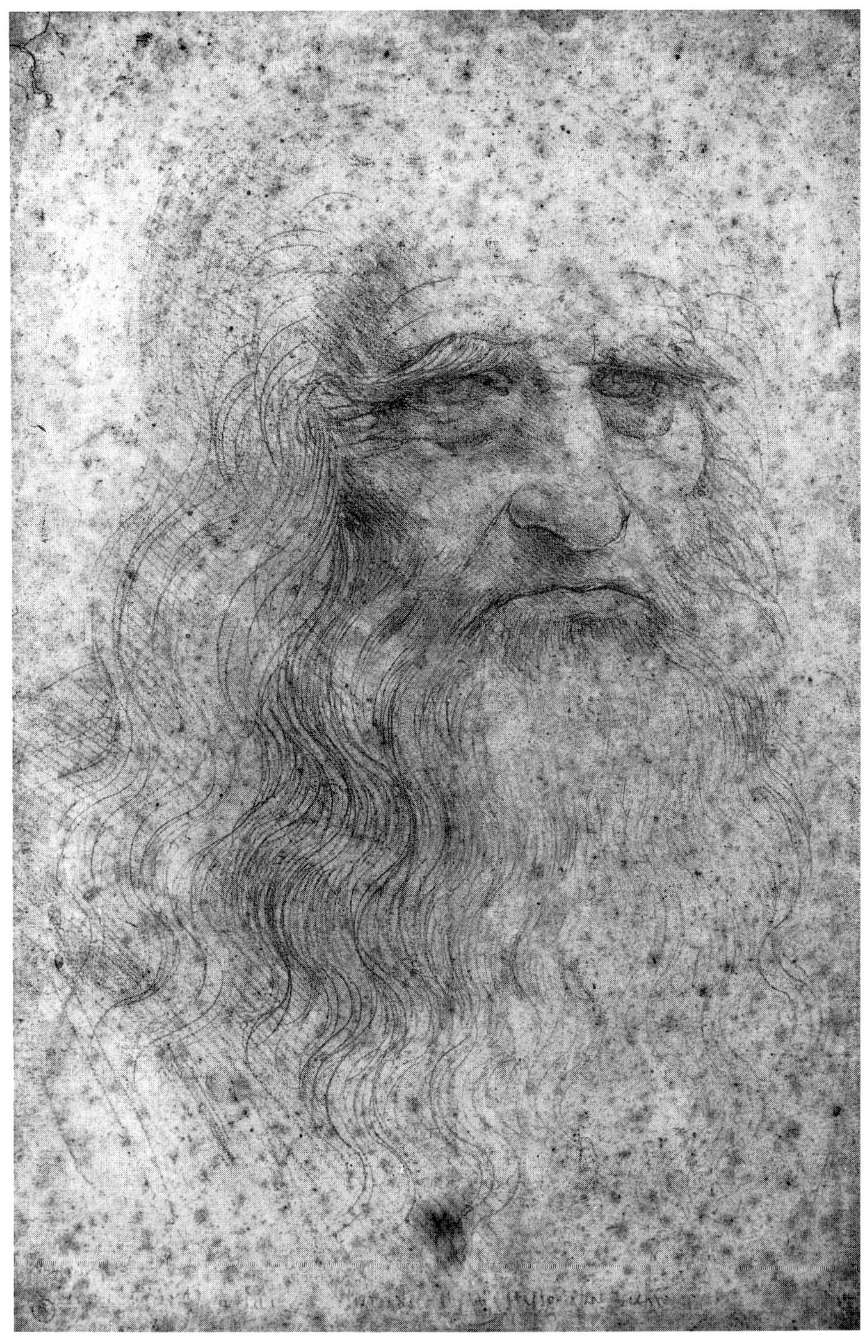

Fig. 55.   Leonardo da Vinci, *Self-Portrait* (1512)
Royal Library, Turin

On the subject of stylistic indebtedness, it has been argued that Raphael borrowed from the "dark manner" of Leonardo's early works (*Adoration, Virgin of the Rocks,* and *Last Supper*) in the *School of Athens* and the *Transfiguration. Chiaroscuro* aside, outstanding borrowings could be pinned to heads of bearded old men, contrasting types of youth and age, and the pointing gesture.[3] Indebtedness ranged from emulation to outright envy, to the point that Michelangelo patronized Sebastiano del Piombo in the hope that a Venetian colorist could somehow contain, if not challenge, his rival. Raphael, instead, acknowledged his sources, and he probably met Leonardo in Rome between 1513 and 1516—or even earlier. If Michelangelo could be considered a competitor, Leonardo was the old master from whom no rivalry had to be feared and much could be learned. It therefore stands to reason that the younger artist would find a place for him in his fresco.

The figurative argument gains strength when we move to matters of content. To focus on the symbolism of the two central figures, I propose to center on the books they hold, which are the *Timaeus* and the *Ethics.* A few samples from the Platonic dialogue will justify Leonardesque references. Timaeus himself is "the most of an astronomer amongst us, and has made the nature of the universe his special study" (27). The cosmological range at issue would obviously point to Leonardo, who also updated the Platonic emphasis on human anatomy. As to the phenomenal instability of creation, Critias states that "there have been, and will be again, many destructions . . . the greatest have been brought about by the agencies of fire and water, and other lesser ones by innumerable other causes" (22). Parallels with Leonardo's notes and *Deluge* sketches are blatant. And a look at the *Adoration* will suffice to visualize Timaeus's words: "As being is to becoming, so is truth to belief" (28). To a more substantial extent, it seems to me, the Leonardesque association ought to be focused on time and its phenomenal implications.

The older Leonardo was not alone in educating Raphael to appreciate a more dynamic approach to form, whether pictorial or architectural. Maurizio Calvesi has in fact underlined a substantial difference: "The conception of Brunelleschi and Alberti reflects the moral certainty, the synthetic structure of humanist thought . . . whereas that of Bramante already presents the antitheses and contrasts of Renaissance thought and configures its dialectics in dynamic forms."[4] It is quite clear that Raphael chose to link the more transformational aspects of Platonic cosmology to antihumanist postures.

3

Obviously short of any figurative evidence, it is my contention that the Aristotelian *Nicomachean Ethics* is linked to Alberti, the foremost architect, moralist, and theoretician of "modern" Humanism. We could consider this parallel symbolic of a frame of mind that was crucial to Humanism as well as to Leonardo's Anti-Humanism. I need only mention that formal and philosophical parallels between Aristotle's text and the Albertian *On the Family* are remarkable, and it is a fact that one's name and thought are present throughout the other's opus. On humanist grounds, it suffices to mention that Coluccio Salutati had come in contact with the *Nicomachean Ethics* during the 1390s. In *De nobilitate* (1399), the intellect is expected to prevail over the will on the Aristotelian assumption that theoretical knowledge is essential to man's pursuit of happiness. Actually, Lorenzo Valla was not alone in attempting to reconcile Christian with Peripathetic ethics. His disciple Leonardo Bruni, scholarship tells us, regarded Aristotle's ethical doctrine as a natural system appropriate for the lay life and free of theological restrictions. Such a selective attitude toward the natural world marked a crucial difference between trecento and quattrocento Florentine humanism.[5] Moreover, references have been made to Politian's public readings of the Aristotelian text, which Pico quoted in his *Commento sopra una canzone d'amor*. By and large, the *Nicomachean Ethics* was centered on nature, extending divine presence horizontally toward the world of man. That cluster of humanist texts implemented a *"concordantia Aristotelis et Platonis"* that would secure philosophical peace.[6]

On matters of universal concord in the Vatican fresco, Raphael inscribed on a Pythagorean slate (Fig. 56) a figure with the ratio of geometric, architectural, and musical congruity that governs the harmony of the spheres. By so doing, Rudolph Wittkower points out, the artist gave us "in an ingenious diagrammatic design of the four strings of the ancient lyra, the whole system of the Pythagorean harmonic scale." Above "Pythagoras appears the heroic figure of his great pupil carrying the *Timaeus* in one hand and pointing heavenward with the other hand. This is Raphael's interpretation of the harmony of the universe which Plato had described in the *Timaeus* on the basis of Pythagoras' discovery of the ratio of musical consonances."[7] It need only be mentioned that several artists were skilled musicians. Outstanding among many were Giorgione and Leonardo, who ranked music

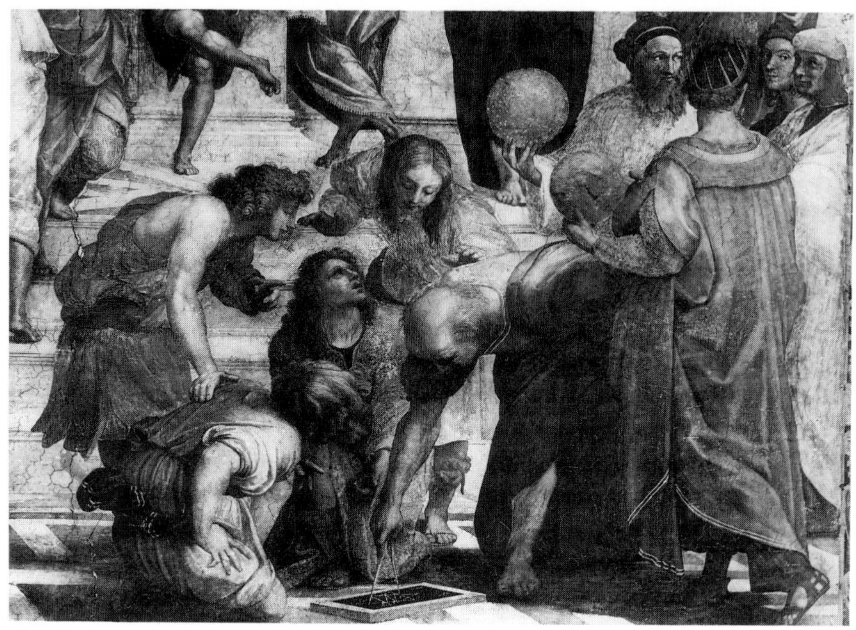

FIG. 56.   Raphael, *School of Athens,* detail (1510–11)
Stanza della Segnatura, Vatican

right after painting in his *paragone*. Music created harmony through "the conjunction of proportioned parts sounded at the same time" (McMahon, 25), and Alberti believed that music is geometry translated into sound. Together with arithmetic, geometry, and astronomy, music was part of the educational curriculum known as quadrivium. Shared principles of harmony governed music, architecture, and geometry, much as they shared in the standards of linear perspective and harmonic chords. The theoretical nature of Pythagorean music led to the Renaissance *musica speculativa,* whose intellectual character did not call for any actual performance. By contrast, Aristotle linked music to perception and human activity, since its function was to provide "remedy to pain caused by toil" (*Politics* 1339b15). Its pleasurable relief would foster ethical growth as a counterweight to the abstractions of theory.

Recent scholarship has followed the modern retreat from the word as a narrative unit up to Ludwig Wittgenstein, whose *Tractatus* is built on aphorisms and numbers just like Leonardo's own oeuvre. The proximity of music and mathematics within a meaningful universe of concordant, though nonnarrative, analogues is defined as the "Pythagorean *genre*," which harks back to a Heraclitean time when metaphysics and mineralogy spoke verse.[8] And so did Leonardo's breathtaking list of verbal and yet nonnarrative attributes meant to present fluid mechanics in the guise of foam, waves, currents, and whirlwinds.

4

Within the visual nomenclature of the Vatican fresco, Aristotle's outstretched arm is not simply earthbound, but demonstratively relational. It stands midway between Diogenes' downtrodden cynicism and Plato's heavenward turn; at its junction, idea and action are symbolically reconciled.

The very text of Aristotle's *Nicomachean Ethics* (1105–7a25) describes the "mean" as a point of equilibrium between the extremes of excess and deficiency on artistic and ethical grounds alike: "For temperance and bravery are destroyed by excess as well as by deficiency, but they are preserved by moderation (or the mean)." For the Magnanimous Man, "the ethical virtue is a mean . . . that is a mean between two vices, one with respect to excess and the other with respect to deficiency; and that it is such a mean because it aims at what is moderate in feelings and actions" (1109a20). Moreover, the "mean" cannot be divorced from the particular and it therefore rests with "perception," to which reasoning gives a selective thrust.

It has been pointed out that Plato alone insisted on the imitation of the measurable and the true as opposed to the imitation of appearances. By contrast, Aristotle placed a certain *ratio* at the doorway of intellection. Actually, the sense of sight itself was considered to be a *ratio* of a kind that Leonardo trusted wholeheartedly when, among other things, he set out to reconcile mathematical with atmospheric perspective.[9] To that extent, Aristotle did not oppose Plato, but set a complementary standard through the dialogism of humanist and antihumanist standpoints.

Parenthetically, it is worth noting that the predominance of mathematical knowledge, which Leonardo took as a prerequisite for reading his treatise on painting, had been part of humanist culture long before Raphael. By the end of the fifteenth century, Jacopo de' Barbari painted Luca Pacioli demonstrating a mathematical problem surrounded by the tools of the trade (Fig. 57). The slate bears the name of Euclid. The

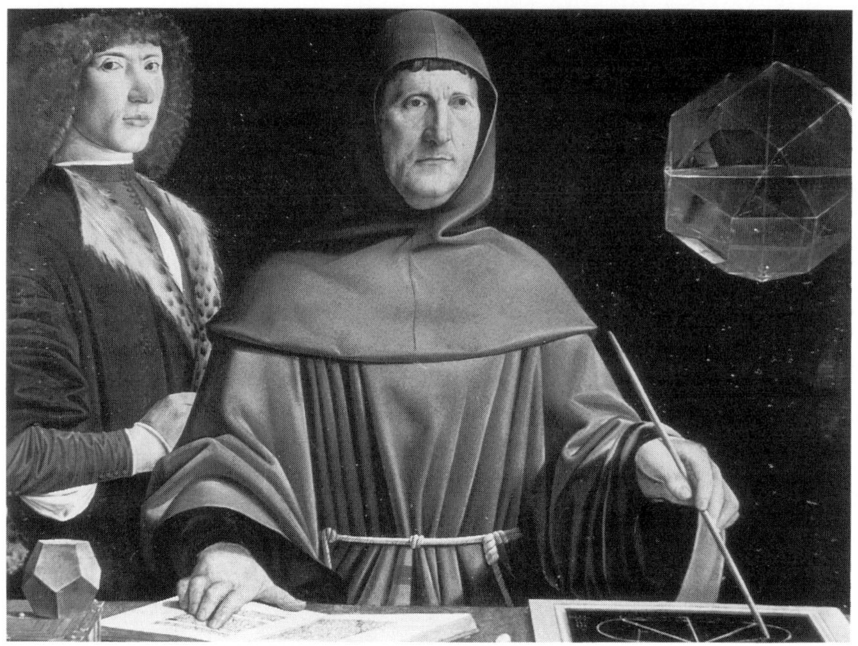

Fig. 57.   Jacopo de' Barbari, *Portrait of Luca Pacioli with Guidobaldo da Montefeltro* (1495?)
Galleria Nazionale di Capodimonte, Naples

source is a book, probably one of Pacioli's own—either the *Summa de arithmetica geometria proportioni et proportionalita* or *Divina proportione*. Names and titles betray their cultural kinship with the Vatican fresco. Pacioli had been a friend of Piero della Francesca and had worked in Milan with Leonardo on problems of construction.[10]

Alberti made the classical reference explicit: "I affirm again with Pythagoras: it is absolutely certain that Nature is wholly consistent. . . . The very same numbers that cause sounds to have that *concinnitas*, pleasing to the ears, can also fill the eyes and mind with wondrous delight. From musicians therefore who have already examined such numbers thoroughly, or from those objects in which Nature has displayed some evident and noble quality, the whole method of outlining is derived."[11] Numerical certainty was linked to the clarity of outlines. A student of Leonardo and a thoughtful lover of architecture, Paul Valéry so rephrased the kinship of the arts: "The hero, whether he combine octaves or perspectives, conceives outside the world. . . . He assembles and fecundates that which exists neither elsewhere nor before him, and often takes pleasure in rejecting the precise memory of nature."[12] Ethics was part of such a concinnity, and it is revealing that Alberti wrote some *Sentenze pitagoriche* that took up the ethical implications of Pythagoreanism. To start with, man was conceived as a social being whose identity had to be linked to *amici*. Their common ground was based on *concordia: "Per fare una discordia, vi bisogna due. A perseverare in concordia, basta che uno de' due sia savio"* (to cause discord, you need two people. To prosper in concord, it is enough that one person be wise). Excellence thus demanded that individual talent be dedicated to the dialogic maintenance of human fellowship. To secure that, Alberti turned to the Aristotelian emphasis on reason: *"In ciò che tu fai o pensi, obbedisci alla ragione"* (in whatever you do or think, you should follow reason). And reason would affect behavior according to restraint and measure—*misura*. Likewise, the ideal leader (*iciarca*) was to handle the heterogeneous nature of humankind "by resorting to an excellent and pliable reason." Even the wise Theogenius referred to Aristotle, who said that "a happy country is that which is excellent; excellent is he who does well; and nobody will do well who is not endowed with virtue."[13] The dialogic "mean," therefore, was contextual and exemplary.

What humanists ancient and modern shared was an overriding belief in the visual nature of epistemology. Sight was knowledge. And sight could bring within reach all that is measurable in nature; in fact, it served Plato and Aristotle as a model for the mechanism of thought itself.[14] Gestural epistemology in the *School of Athens* therefore "enacted" the meaning of the Greek verb *noein,* which defines "to think" as an act of vision, a seeing with the mind.[15] By the same token, visual language did not fail to comment on the stylistic opposition between Plato's towering posture and the slouching body of Diogenes, whose lack of composure points to mental aimlessness. Between them, Aristotle's outstretched arm gives the figure a propulsive *impetus* that pushes him toward the foreground and amid his cohorts. He is the link and the visual "mean" that reconciles philosophical diversity. Most of the philosophers that Raphael grouped on the left side of the *School of Athens* also appear as a group in Alberti's *Profugiorum ab Aerumna,* in which everyone turns to Socrates on the subject of man's capacity to withstand fortunes and misfortunes. He did not find such power "in the skies, but in himself; because he willed it, he did do it. Nor can we cite Socrates as worthy of praise in such matters; but we also have been told of many others whose spirit was equally upright. Amid such a group we can count Diogenes the cynic, a man reduced to extreme poverty, humiliated and at times downcast; yet he could whenever he so wanted endure his misfortunes and other peoples' injuries." Pyrrhus and Heraclitus are also included with them.[16] In their very midst, therefore, Aristotle's hand gathers the visual epistemology of the whole fresco to a focal point where contrasts yield to interactive modulations.[17] That focal point became symbolic of an emergent synthesis unknown to antiquity and forewarned in the dialogism of humanist and antihumanist thought.

The optimistic aura that exudes from the Vatican fresco echoed the unrestrained faith in human dignity that Alberti projected in *Della famiglia, De Iciarchia,* and *De Re Aedificatoria.* Cecil Grayson's comment on those humanist cornerstones is memorable: "What he had striven to achieve as a moral architect out of the elusive qualities of the mind, he now attains as a practical architect out of the more tangible and stable medium of stone and the perennial principles of mathematics." However virtual his artistic program, Alberti did not warrant "learning or eloquence for its own sake or for the narrow pursuit of personal fame, but the application of accumulated wisdom and practical experience for the greater beauty and happiness of human life."[18] One cannot but be reminded of Leonardo's insistence on the practical applications of any form of knowledge. It is on the basis of such an aesthetic and philosophical kinship that the two modern artists relate in a significant way to Plato and Aristotle. As an image of the synthesis that Raphael drew from Florentine Humanism, the *School of Athens* exemplifies a cultural portrait of the mind that could indeed bear the parental names of Alberti and Leonardo.

5

On matters of humanist "outdoing," the architectural grandeur of Raphael's fresco embodied a progressive break with Platonic discriminations between liberal and mechanical arts, which even Hugh of Saint Victor had upheld during the Middle Ages. Yet attention has been called to another twelfth-century writer, Dominicus Gundissalinus, who drew the arts of civil and family government within the province of the practical sciences. Their welfare was to be secured through the mechanical arts, one of which was architecture.[19] Since antiquity, Vitruvius had sanctioned that the architect put to the test all the work done in the other arts. Once Christianity took over, Jerome presented Paul as a Christian architect, and Paolo Toscanelli described Brunelleschi as Paul reborn—at least so Vasari says.

It is in the prologue to *De Re Aedificatoria* that Alberti outlined his concept of the architect, who stood as a cultural symbol akin to the concept of "universal man" as it was applied to Leonardo:

> Let it be said that the security, dignity, and honor of the republic depend greatly on the architect: it is he who is responsible for our delight, entertainment, and health while at leisure, and our profit and advantage while at work, and in short, that we live in a dignified manner, free of any danger. In view then of the delight and wonderful grace of his works, and of how indispensable they have proved, and in view of the benefit and convenience of his inventions, and their service to posterity, he should no doubt be accorded praise and respect, and be counted among those most deserving of mankind's honor and recognition.[20]

Since the architect emerges as a figure of ethical and artistic inclusion, we may begin to understand why Raphael painted himself next to geometers and mathematicians in the *School of Athens;* the builders of antiquity had found a worthy heir.

It is indeed significant that Alberti first wrote on the family and then crowned his literary and artistic achievements by writing a treatise on architecture. Both establish the guiding principles of an ethical framework centered on the pursuit of the Aristotelian "mean," which was taken to be the fulcrum that energizes practical and moral alertness. In *Momus,* Jupiter blames himself for having failed to call on architects to design a new world order. For Alberti as well as for Leonardo, the architect emerged as a towering figure, and the grandiose architecture in the *School of Athens* did nothing but sanction his charismatic role. What I find more Albertian than Aristotelian in the architecture of the Vatican fresco is its heroic grandeur. It exceeded classical and medieval Stoicism, as well as Aristotelian *mediocritas.* The monumental proportions of Raphael's construct are indeed Albertian if one thinks of the gigantic Roman arch that frames the facade of his San Andrea church in Mantua.

Vitruvius had located the temple of architecture at the top of a lifelong training in, and knowledge of, the arts and sciences. Later, Leonardo Bruni opened his panegyric to Florence by praising its buildings, whose proportional forms reflected the city's harmonious institutions. The fundamental symbolism of architecture, therefore, was one of synthesis,[21] which would gather a republic of intellectuals. Raphael's Vatican fresco gave visual form to that project.

6

At the center of his labyrinthine pattern of arboreal intertwinings in the Sala dell'Asse, Leonardo wrote *"Academia Leonardo da Vinci"* (Fig. 58). *Academia* pointed to an architectural form that could house structures of human excellence amid cohorts of one's own kind. Raphael's school stood as a transhistorical image of humanist achievements. Aware as he was that he had ventured beyond most, Leonardo moved to the Daedalian grounds of the maze maker, where he created the antihumanist academy of a most exclusive One.

It was in his dialogue on Eupalinos, "or the architect," that Paul Valéry pitched the time of nature against that of art. Since "centuries cost nothing" in nature, processes of erosion and corruption can change forms, and one would eventually see in them whatever he could imagine. Such a concept of "indefinite time" runs against the forms of art, which

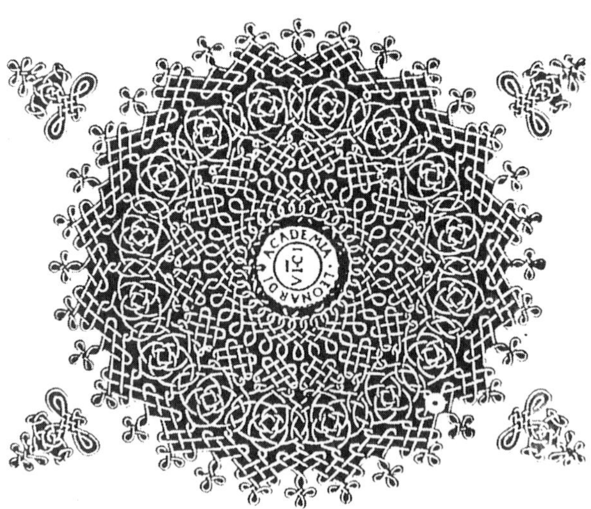

FIG. 58.   Leonardo da Vinci, Sala dell'Asse, decoration Castello Sforzesco, Milan

are created rather instantaneously, as "though acts illuminated by a thought abridged the course of nature; and so we may safely say that an artist is worth a thousand centuries."[22] Eons of cultural time have suddenly sprung to life in the *School of Athens,* which could make us wonder when, or whether, the future ever came to be.

11

The Dialogism of Humanism
and Anti-Humanism

> *The picture displayed by the Renaissance is one of transfor-*
> *mation and hesitation, one of transition and of intermixture*
> *of cultural elements. Anyone seeking in it a total unity of*
> *spirit capable of being stated in a simple formula will never*
> *be able to understand it in all its expressions. Above all, one*
> *must be prepared to accept it in its complexity, its heteroge-*
> *neity, and its contradictions, and to apply a pluralistic ap-*
> *proach to the questions it poses.*
> *—Kenneth Clark*

The humanist *Kunstwollen* fostered images of the way things should have been, which demanded control over light, color, movement, and the human will itself. From the family to the arts, Albertian models of virtual perfection halted the process of life, and intellectualism carried the day.

By contrast, Leonardo's interest in the way things are drew strength at the turn of the sixteenth century, when Machiavelli and Guicciardini studied human nature for what it was. However heterogeneous their fields of investigation, they all realized that neither the linearity of drawing nor the semantic clarity of language could do justice to the complexity of life. The order of things had to confront the facts of human experience.

Leonardo's criticism of humanist erudition was one-sided inasmuch as the rebirth of antiquity spurred conformity as well as originality. From treatises to panegyrics, the imitation of the classics was but a step for setting paradigms of a higher order. At least on hypothetical and artistic grounds, the humanists outdid the achievements of the Graeco-Roman world. By and large, it was understood that it was un-Greek just to copy the Greeks. The predominant tendency was to dissolve experience into art and history into metahistory.[1] Yet originality affected humanist intellectualism as well as Leonardesque empiricism. Interactive contacts between *imitatio* and *aemulatio* fed the dialogism of Humanism and Anti-Humanism.

There were artistic reasons behind Leonardo's attack against those who found his proofs inconsistent with the "authority of certain men held in the highest reverence" (12). His polemical stand operated within a sphere of activity whose roots were quite immune to matters of ancestry and indebtedness. We move here on grounds where Alberti and Leonardo shared archetypal attitudes. God created out of nothing, and so did the *artifex* in the world of art. Pliny the Elder reports that Lysippus, who had no teachers, decided to become an artist when he heard that the painter Eupompos identified his predecessors with an anonymous crowd of people: "Nature, and not the manner of some other artist, is alone worthy of imitation" (*Historia Naturalis* 34: 61). Autodidacticism was emphasized, and natural talent replaced artistic legacies.[2]

In the preface to *On Painting,* Alberti noted that the ancients could rely on "masters," whereas the moderns had to start anew. In one stroke, origin and originality were made to stem from within the humanist experience itself. The founding fathers of the "new" art were immediately acknowledged: Masaccio, Donatello, Ghiberti, Brunelleschi, and Luca della Robbia. By the time he wrote about them, Alberti himself had become the authority on art theory, and the follower he calls on at the end of the treatise would be there only to uphold his paradigmatic endeavor.

Leonardo's incomplete treatise on painting fulfilled a similar task for posterity. Except for spurious references to Giotto and Masaccio, he ignored ancestry. His source truly was nature, which offered Alberti raw materials: the shapeless. Leonardo, instead, saw an inspiring wealth of forms around himself: the shapely. In a way, notes and sketches disclosed mental powers to the endlessness of research. The tradition of foreclosed systems aside, his incomplete writings gave form to processes that thrived on the resilience of mind and nature alike.

2

Standards of perfection inspired the birth of Adam in Michelangelo's fresco as well as in the panegyrical literature of Pico della Mirandola, who brought to fruition seeds embedded in the writings of Ghiberti, Bruni, and Alberti. The rhetoric of praise became an ideological imperative in the Stanza della Segnatura, where Raphael's Muses legitimized a world of refined education; where origin was not located in caves but in the *polis;* and knowledge was kindled in the *scuola* rather than outdoors. Because it was pointed neither toward primitivism nor dark ages, history lodged cultural fulfillment in the House of Fame.

Leonardo's first and last works, instead, center on figures who tested the learned core of civilization. Jerome left Rome and went into the desert, where the Baptist had been foretelling a revolutionary future. Geographical dislocations of that sort were challenging; aestheticism tested asceticism, and Jerome experienced both. Penitential contemplations exposed the flair of urban discourse. Recently, Geoffrey Harpham has written that the ascetic imperative "is always marked by ambivalence, by a compromised binarism." The ascetic experience fosters "an ambivalent yearning for the precultural, postcultural, anticultural, or extracultural." It could therefore be suggested that Leonardo's figures also set "an opposition within which dialogue and dialectic can occur."[3] At times partial and partisan, he was finally able to forge a concept of culture at once antagonistic and complementary, that is to say, dialogic.

3

It is quite obvious that criticism has acknowledged, if not exploited, the role that contrast and complementarity have played in the culture of the Renaissance, whose development has been earmarked with "anti," "counter," "early," "high," or "late" period concepts.[4] We have been taught that events ought to be read in sequence as well as in breadth, since history is not unilinear. In the world of science, synthesis and opposition are active at any given time. The Byzantine mind cherished trinitarian theology without slighting chariot races, much as later developments in atomic physics have not discredited astrology altogether.[5] Yet it would be fair to say that one style of art has been predominant at any given period. Transitions and diversity notwithstanding, the recurrence of binary phenomena has favored dialogism. Ernst Cassirer sees man's unity as a functional one that does not "presuppose a homogeneity of the various elements of which it consists. Not only does it admit of, it even requires, a multiplicity and multiformity of its constituent parts.

For this is a dialectic unity, a coexistence of contraries." On matters of culture, in fact, "the dissonant is in harmony with itself."[6]

Having started from dialogic opposites, Leonardo and Piero della Francesca found in art the higher truth of a harmonious worldview. Indeed, one could not but agree with the other that "what is fair in men passes away, but not so in art" (651). And many humanists would have shared the belief that "whatever exists in the universe through essence, presence, or imagination," the artist "has it first in his mind and then in his hands" (McMahon, 35).[7]

4

At the turn of the sixteenth century, Anti-Humanism gained strength on its own merits as well as from the unfolding crisis of Humanism. In spite of visual and literary output, humanist dreams had soared so high in the Stanza della Segnatura and in the pages of *The Book of the Courtier* that the whole "baseless" edifice of culture was bound to collapse once gravity staked empirical claims. While Castiglione built his model of excellence on a defensive posture that Alberti would have not justified a few decades earlier, Ariosto hid wisdom on the moon and let chivalric heroes go mad on earth in his *Orlando Furioso*. Criticism was rampant, and Guicciardini set Machiavellian idealism against life's disheartening details (*particolari*). Much literature either failed to sustain theory or succeeded in testing it.[8] Recent scholarship on crisis and evasion in the Italian Renaissance tells us that the Greek etymon of crisis means both "separation" and "judgment" or "interpretation." As a rupture, crisis threatens meaning; as interpretation, it discovers it.[9] On such interactive grounds, Albertian treatises brought forth canons that legislated on the arts; yet they could not mute self-assertiveness vis-à-vis more unselective views of reality.

On matters of referentiality, the future-oriented *Adoration* emphasized both "judgment" and "interpretation"; much like Giorgione's *Tempest,* it exploited the range of meaning. Novelty spawned the uncertainty of *sfumato,* Venetian *poesie* without definite narratives, and atmospheric perspective. Leonardo was not alone in warning that "the supreme misfortune is when theory outstrips performance" (McCurdy, 900). As a result, the antihumanist mind paved the way for the baroque coexistence of creation and criticism within the same artwork.

It is indicative that Alberti's treatise on painting opens with a praise of artists and ends with a statement of faith in theoreticians: "Perhaps someone will come after me who will correct my written errors. In this most worthy and most excellent art he may be more helpful and useful to the painters than I (have been)." Forebodings of the great age of criticism hover over the closing remarks on technique, for individual genius was to give way to an "art well governed." By the turn of the sixteenth century, emulation had caught up with its own possibilities. As it had happened at the close of Hellenism, a kind of learned taste muted much of the path-breaking ardor of adventure,[10] which Leonardo never lost sight of.

5

At this point, insights into the dialogism of Humanism and Anti-Humanism could profit from Alfred North Whitehead's view of a universe pivoting on interactions between the "world of activity" and the "world of origination." The timelessness of value is typical of the latter, which stands at bay of need and circumstance. It was a classical and humanist misconception that such a world could thrive on self-enjoyment independent of "any reference to effectiveness in action." Only dialogic relationships can overcome polarity: "When we enjoy . . . possibility as an impulse toward realization, we are then stressing the ultimate character of the Universe, which rests on interactions between Harmony and Frustration, Beauty and Ugliness, Attraction and Aversion."[11] Leonardo made a compelling case for dialogic exchanges between artistic choices and scientific undertakings, convinced as he was that progress would call for balance between them.[12]

Beyond the Ptolemaic isolation of Humanism, Anti-Humanism spearheaded progress under the infinite skies of a Copernican vault about which Leonardo had understood that "the sun does not move" and the "earth is not in the centre of the Sun's orbit nor at the centre of the universe" (858, 886). The diachronic complexity of the Renaissance notwithstanding, sixteenth-century culture sponsored academic tradition with the Carraccis; Caravaggio's art at the fringe, which later criticism has labeled with such terms of exclusion as "anti" or "counter"; and a *maniera* style that steered the more formal concerns of humanist poetics toward a self-complacent aestheticism.

Criticism has pointed out that whereas Botticelli brought to a close the fifteenth century, Leonardo opened the sixteenth, and we owe to him the modern conception of art as inquiry, investigation, and personal quest. That ideal led to Caravaggio, who restated it in moral terms. Along the Anti-Humanism–Baroque trajectory, his criticism of the antique as a source of authority echoed Leonardo's attitude.[13] It is a fact that the clashing animation of the *Battle of the Stendard* (see Fig. 26) became a case study for baroque artists. As a matter of fact, the battle cartoons of Leonardo and Michelangelo started two styles, the baroque and the classical. Beyond the group of human figures in the foreground, the Louvre *Virgin of the Rocks* (see Fig. 13) went a long way in shifting composition toward depth. That development also involved Correggio, who acknowledged his debt to Leonardo.[14]

In a humanist vein, Carpaccio and Antonello de Messina portrayed Jerome as a scholar in his study. Leonardo, instead, led the saint to the liminal outdoors of the desert, where he bathed knowledge into ascetic experiences. The common goal, to paraphrase Dante on the subject of learning, was to teach *"Come l'uom s'eterna"* (*Inferno* xv). Knowledge had to be put on trial in enclaves of privileged seclusions. Jerome did that in life as well as in the Vatican painting, which staged an "incarnational test." Long before Don Alonso Quijano, he could not settle for the reading of books, for he had to take literary and spiritual passions to places as diverse as imperial Rome and the Syrian desert. Leonardo appreciated that choice and let him be driven by a will-to-action that foreshadowed baroque postures.

Keeping in mind the link between Anti-Humanism and the progress of science and technology, the concept of "current" is appropriate, for it points to a dynamic view of life.[15] The future-oriented potential of Anti-Humanism provided fertile grounds for the emergence of the Baroque, which made a synthesis of the dialogic heritage of Humanism and Anti-Humanism.

6

At the edge of the path leading toward the Baroque, Mannerism pointed to a dead-end of Humanism.[16] Moving from the laterality of Mannerist dead-ends to the mainstream of cultural growth at its transitive best, I would like to suggest that Anti-Humanism plunged the theoretical supports of Humanism into life's flux. It is a critical fallacy to presume that periods—or movements—follow one another as single links in a chain. As it later happened with Neoclassicism and Romanticism, contacts do not necessarily imply sequence or subordination. Culture, in fact, can thrive on dialogic progress, but it also can take an antagonistic stand toward stagnation.

In light of Mikhail Bakhtin's spatio-temporal chronotope, the literary dialogic of genre and countergenre could indeed measure cultural range.[17] I would claim validity for a similar dialogism even at the macrocosmic level of "currents" or "periods," as I believe that it was the case with Humanism and Anti-Humanism. Hence we could answer in the affirmative whether periods and currents are but different methods for the conceptual grasp of an identical chronology.[18] Concepts such as quattrocento or Siglo de Oro, in fact, stress the plurality of systems and durations within the same chronological unit.

Diachronically speaking, Anti-Humanism remained backstage during the quattrocento, but grew to prominence thereafter. In terms of synchronic *récupération de valeurs,* Humanism set up the building blocks of the Renaissance, whereas Anti-Humanism spearheaded a diachronic *reconstitution d'un devenir.*[19] At their dialogic best, Walter Pater would insist, they combined into "one complete type of general culture. The fifteenth century in Italy is one of these happier eras, and what is sometimes said of the age of Pericles is true of that of Lorenzo— it is an age productive in personalities, many-sided, centralised, complete."[20] With a dialogic nomenclature in mind, I would associate the cultural predominance of Humanism during the fifteenth century with the concept of period, whereas Anti-Humanism could be seen as a current that outlasted Humanism and made a fundamental contribution to the emergence of the Baroque.

7

To a crucial extent, the Age of Discovery drew from artists, inventors, and explorers. The symbolic "breaking of the circle" began long before Copernicus, and Leonardo himself was quite aware of heliocentrism. The Ptolemaic heavens broke open after a legion of navigators had dared beyond Hercules' pillars. A leader of journeys westward was Christopher Columbus, who trusted knowledge as much as emotional calls that linked the future to prophecy rather than to technology. While in Seville, he wrote a *Book of Prophecies* (1501), in which he made a statement that shed light on the dialogic circularity of human motivations: "It was by no means mathematics, nor the charts of the ancient geographers, nor the deductions of reason that helped me to accomplish that which I did accomplish; but solely the prophecy of Isaiah about a new heaven and a new earth."[21] Such a confrontational text went to the core of the fifteenth-century dialogism between rational measure and inner power. As such, classical and humanist notions of the "mean" implied a concept of reality based on the universal harmony of given concordances. Faith in the "mean" rested with the stability of a world order without any real sense of development. Since reality needed to be neither changed nor improved in any significant way, classical science and technology did not go very far.

After the discovery of the New World, Columbus believed that within seven years he would be duty-bound to lead an army to claim the Holy Sepulcher from the infidels.[22] His prophetic impulse found a context in the sermons and politics of Savonarola, Machiavelli's idealism at the end of *The Prince,* and Leonardo's literary prophecies and *Deluge* sketches. In the process, Christian progress moved toward apocalyptic fulfillment as well as toward the development of scientific thought. As such, prophetic impulses break limits and strive toward the exceptional. Above all, they cannot rest. After his first voyage, Columbus could have stopped, for he had obtained wealth and glory. But he could not. Gianni Granzotto reminds us that "there is no choice between wisdom and ambition for the sort of temperament that Columbus had in such abundance. The admiral had to keep riding his phantoms across the horizon, like Don Quixote his nag Rocinante. Both men saw things before them which no one else saw."[23] As an artist, a scientist, and a technician, Leonardo could be just as visionary. For all of them, glory called for more glory.

If mechanics was the paradise of the mathematical sciences, the *Deluge* sketches and fluid mechanics must have been Leonardo's nightmare.[24] Correlations of a similar kind could be drawn between his grotesque faces vis-à-vis the proportional features of his Vitruvian prototype and epicine youth. Along the whole spectrum of fifteenth-century experiences, prophetic impulses were liminal in a dialogic sense that unsettled the predictability of rational measures. Columbus found neither a new heaven nor a new earth; as a matter of fact, what he found was not what he had been looking for. Compared to his prophecies of doom, Leonardo's quests were more imaginative. He did not love humankind, but he cherished the myth of man. His prophetic and mythmaking impulses led him to steer mechanics toward the creation of the great bird, on whose wings he would try to fulfill one of the oldest prophecies about human immortality.

The Myth of Myths

12

Mona Lisa:

The Smile of Life

In the character before us, taste, without ceasing to be instructive, is far more than a mental attitude or manner. A magnificent intellectual force is latent within it. It is like the reminiscence of a forgotten culture that once adorned the mind; as if the mind of one, fallen into a new cycle, were beginning its spiritual progress over again.

—Walter Pater

Part I

For Baudelaire, portraiture could be understood either as history or fiction:

> The second method, the one characteristic of the colourists, consists in making a picture out of a portrait, a poem with its accessories full of space and reverie. This form of art is more difficult, because it is more ambitious. The artist must know how to bathe a head in the soft light of a warm atmosphere or bring it out from the depths of "chiaroscuro." Here imagination plays a greater part, and yet, just as fiction is often truer than history, so a sitter may be more clearly interpreted by the rich and skillful brush of a colourist than by the pencil of a draughtsman.[1]

One may wonder whether he had in mind portraits of the Salon (1846) or *Mona Lisa* (1502–4, Fig. 59). At any rate, Leonardo anticipated the

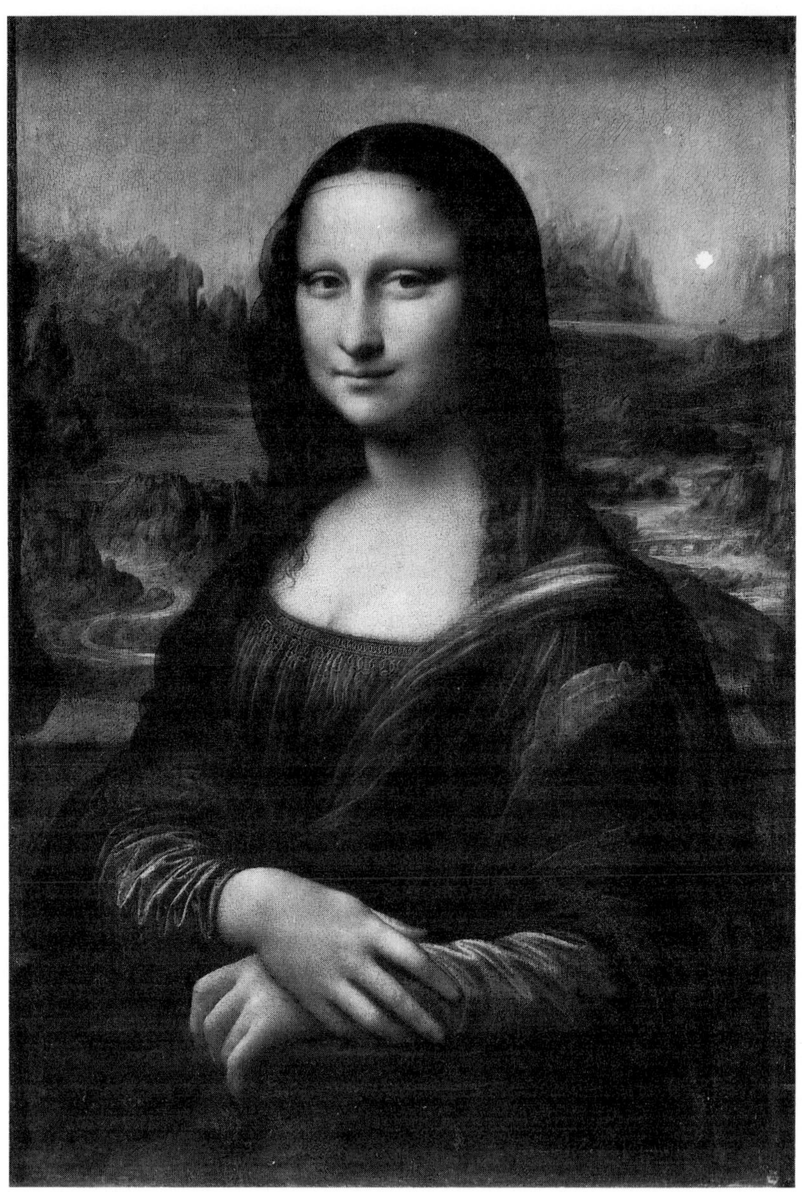

FIG. 59. Leonardo da Vinci, *Mona Lisa* (1502–4)
Louvre, Paris

method of the colorists, and succeeded better than most in making a picture out of a portrait.

Human and natural perpetuity took on a feminine guise in *Mona Lisa.* Her smile nestled an attitude of mind in the visual mode of everlasting ineffability. One of the artist's standing concerns emerged: "Just as iron rusts unless it is used, and water putrifies or, in cold, turns into ice, so our intellect spoils unless it is kept in use" (1177). At once, we confront the portrait of a woman and a posture of self-contentment that is best reflected in the Italian title, *La Gioconda.* As a rhetorical graph, her smile mutes discourse into a visual gloss. Presence becomes suggestive; while meaning is hidden the very moment it seems about to be unlocked, viewers undergo a progressive revelation.[2]

2

To comply with narrative demands, the humanists codified physical poise. Taking a more independent stand, Leonardo believed that painters would not consider a figure "praiseworthy if it does not, insofar as possible, express in gestures the passion of its spirit." Sketches and notes never fail to pin expression to movement, which could take the form of eighteen different positions (McMahon, 374). In a more restrained mode, references are made to the "contained motion" that "the animal makes within itself without change of place." Mona Lisa's smile fulfilled an artistic project: "Contained motion is infinite" (McMahon, 355) whenever it opens up to psychological restlessness.

Hands are prominent in Leonardo's multifigure paintings and portraits, whether they be *Lady with the Ermine* (Fig. 60) or the drawing of Isabella d'Este: "Hands and arms must, whenever possible, display in all their actions the intention of the mind that moves them." It is quite probable that the missing portion at the bottom of *Ginevra de' Benci* (Fig. 61) also included the hands.[3] As a recurrent motif in Leonardesque poetics, Mona Lisa's arms and hands fold into a restful posture free of specific concerns. Whatever they might be, emotions remain "without bodily action" (McMahon, 400, 396, 408); yet they do not fail to project the complexities of an enigmatic personality. Mona Lisa's hands would have satisfied demands that art theorists made later in the sixteenth century. For Agnolo Firenzuola, "the fingers are beautiful when they are long, trim, and delicate, and when they taper just a bit toward the tips . . . and the whole hand should as a result have a smooth softness

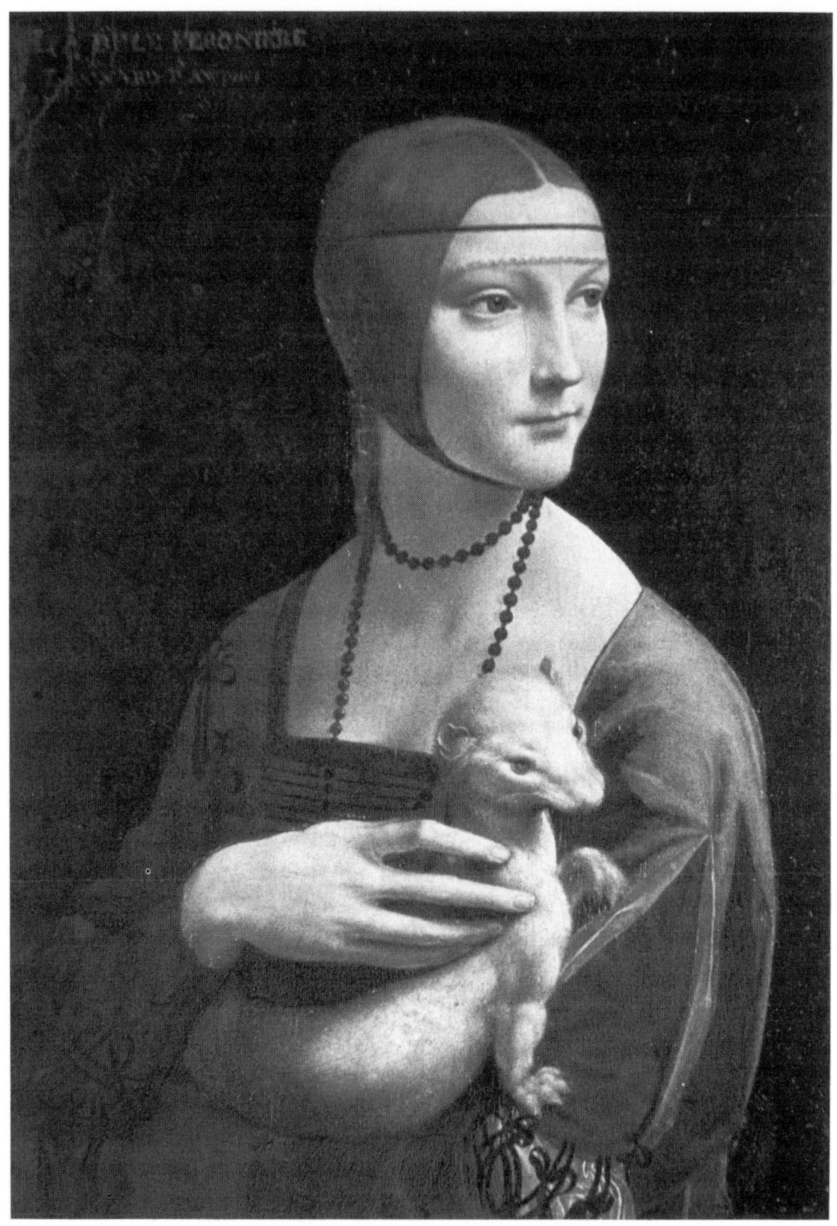

FIG. 60. Leonardo da Vinci, *The Lady with the Ermine* (1485)
Czartoryski Muzeum, Cracow

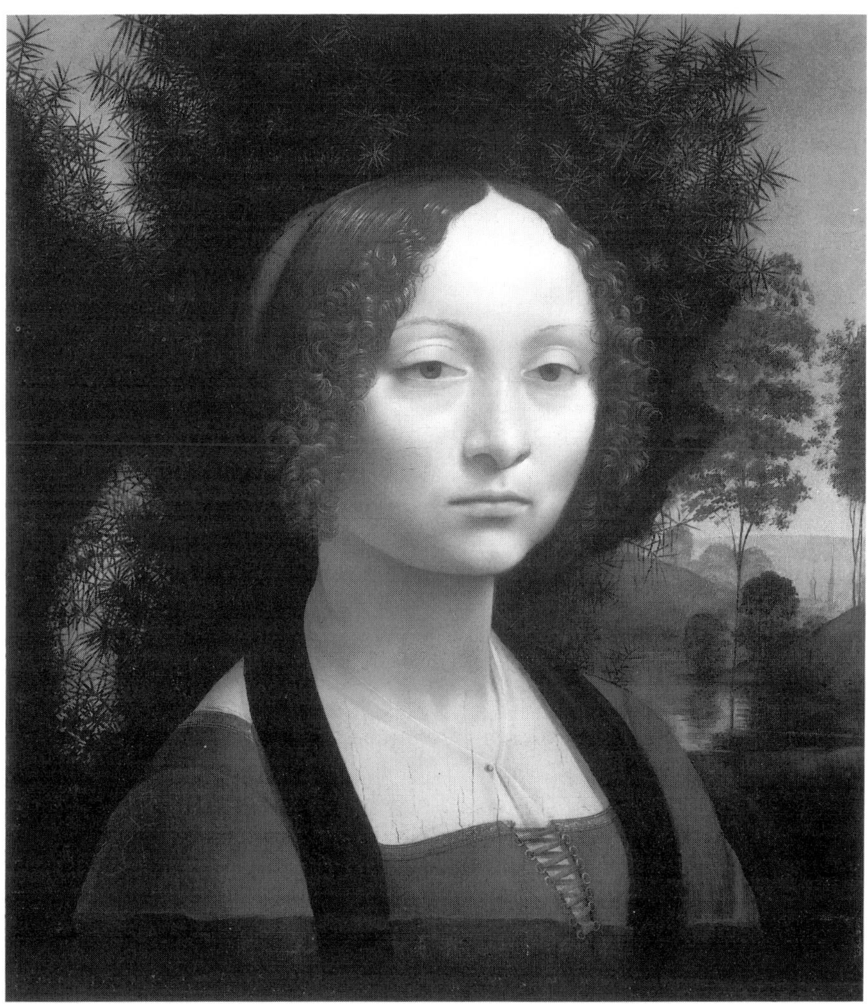

FIG. 61.   Leonardo da Vinci, *Ginevra de' Benci* (1475)
National Gallery of Art, Washington, D.C.

(*soave morbidezza*)."[4] First and foremost, Mona Lisa's folded hands assert human presence in the lower part of the canvas, where they rest amid what man has made: dress, parapet, and the other man-made details that have been left out. The chair's arm, on which Mona Lisa rests, sets a horizontal line parallel to that of the other artifact behind it, the bridge. The hands therefore relate to artificial shapes that point to manual "making."[5]

Slowly, Mona Lisa's arms raise our attention toward the head, which is set against organic forms whose beauty and function rest with natural vitality rather than with the order of historical "making." In the anti-humanist mode, ingenuity no longer could hold its grip on the power and mystery of an *un*measurable landscape that calls for discovery and understanding. Human features are as meaningfully "bare" as the primeval nature that surrounds them. Stylistic similarities have been drawn between the folds of the dress, the winding road, and mountain ridges. While the symbolism of natural processes is explicit, artificial details still remind us that human activism has been neither "lost" nor "returned" to nature. Although it seems just about vanished, civilization still links up to a road and a bridge. Conventional markers, I think, have become transhistorical, just as the smile exudes a kind of atemporal presence. Because they fade amid the fluid permanence of the landscape, colors intensify a phenomenal depth akin to the psychological fecundity that La Gioconda wears on her lips.

3

As a portrait, *Mona Lisa* projects her very selfhood in the form of a smile. Her restrained self-reliance gives presence to what the humanists treasured most about women. In the words of Francesco Barbaro (*On Wifely Duties* 2, 1415–16), "one's demeanor declares and manifests many things without the use of words. From the face and its movement the disposition of an individual may be known. . . . And her demeanor should not be clumsy but gracefully dignified. Moreover, I earnestly beg that wives avoid immoderate laughter," which is usually caused by immoderate speech. By contrast, women were to pursue concise discourse and outright silence.[6] Echoing Plutarch, the humanist wrote that "Epaminondas followed the excellent teachings of nature, the mistress of life, who has clearly made known her thoughts on silence. She has with good reason furnished us with two ears but only one tongue, and this she has guarded with the double defense of lips and teeth." Even Sophocles "has termed silence the most outstanding ornament of women. . . . Therefore, women should believe they have achieved glory and eloquence if they will honor themselves with the outstanding ornament of silence."[7] Mona Lisa's smile either follows or precedes speech; at least it suggests a mental process that is as elusively active as the atmospheric landscape behind her. Because the figure is seated, action is reduced to a speechless attitude typical of an age that appreciated the visual rhetoric of body language. *The Book of the Courtier* also takes up the contrast between discourse and gestures. While males resort to the first, females trust the second. Leonardo seems to have given a restrictive intensity to that convention.[8]

Whatever the circumstances, La Gioconda is an image of self-congratulatory happiness.[9] She exudes a personality at peace with nature, immune to the vicissitudes of history, and free of social demands whereby women "should be represented with modest gestures . . . heads bent and inclined to one side" (McMahon, 253). Among courtly standards of beauty, she complied with Castiglione's demands for a "jocund gaiety" (*giocosa ilarità*) and "a soft and delicate tenderness" (*una tenerezza molle e delicata*) (*Courtier,* 16, 206).[10] Her contentment shows forth womanly pride in spite of the ingrained misogyny of a Christian tradition that even the otherwise tolerant Boccaccio finally upheld. Mona Lisa seems to be toying with the witticism of courtly dialogues and "coed" *cenacoli misti* held by Veronica Gambara, Tullia d'Aragona, and Cecilia Gallerani, that is to say, Leonardo's *dama dell'ermellino.* Mona Lisa's indulgent omniscience echoed the aloof superiority of the ideal cortigiana.[11] Women are the *causa* of man's best endeavors: "I will not name you the bright talents that there now are in the world, and here present, that every day produce some noble fruit," and yet find their subject matter entirely in the beauty and virtue of womanhood. The courtly lady must be *"molto dissimile dell'omo"* (*Courtier,* 258, 206), so that she can complement him. And Leonardesque smiles would reward man's best efforts to suit her.

In terms of portraiture, the symbolic range of *Mona Lisa* ought to be measured against Raphael's *Donna velata* (c. 1514, Fig. 62), which flaunts ornaments from hair to shoulders. Her sleeve parades exuberantly errant folds that were to be fully exploited by baroque artists from Rubens to Bernini. Even *Maddalena Doni* (c. 1516, Fig. 63) shows off lots of rings, but few secrets and even less psychological insight.[12] Such portraits carry notions of rank, wealth, and fashion that Leonardo dispensed with. Mona Lisa's garments are less fluttering and they seem to be more functional than decorative.[13]

For Leonardo, "it is a very beautiful face and not rich ornaments that stops" passersby. "Women in the hills wrapped in plain and poor draperies" possess "greater beauty than those who are adorned" (McMahon, 442). Yet Mona Lisa's plucked eyebrows were contemporary in fashion; and so was the very thin veil with which married women usually covered their heads. James Mirollo has made it clear that Renaissance matters of

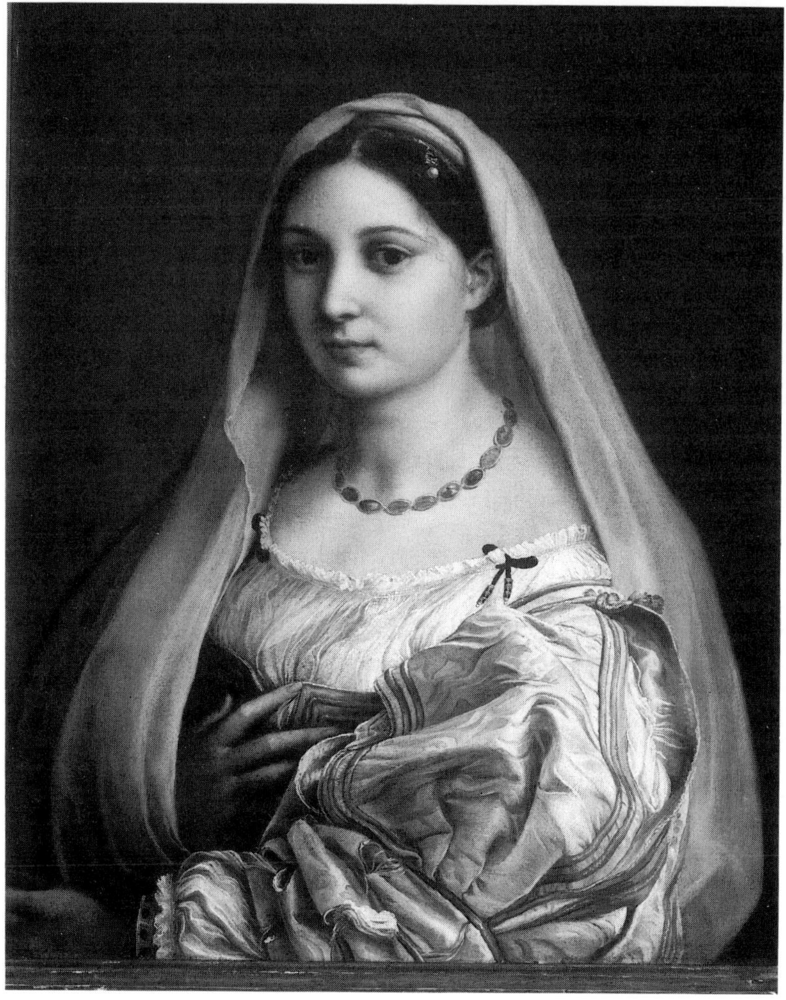

Fig. 62.   Raphael, *Donna Velata* (c. 1516)
Palazzo Pitti, Florence

fashion were physical as well as conceptual. In the symbolic relationship between visage and veil, the latter's symbolism has been predominant amid an array of Petrarchan love sonnets.[14] The same can be said of Mona Lisa. Although spare, such details were important, since they did not let history yield to vision altogether. Metahistorical images transcend history, which nonetheless qualifies their context.

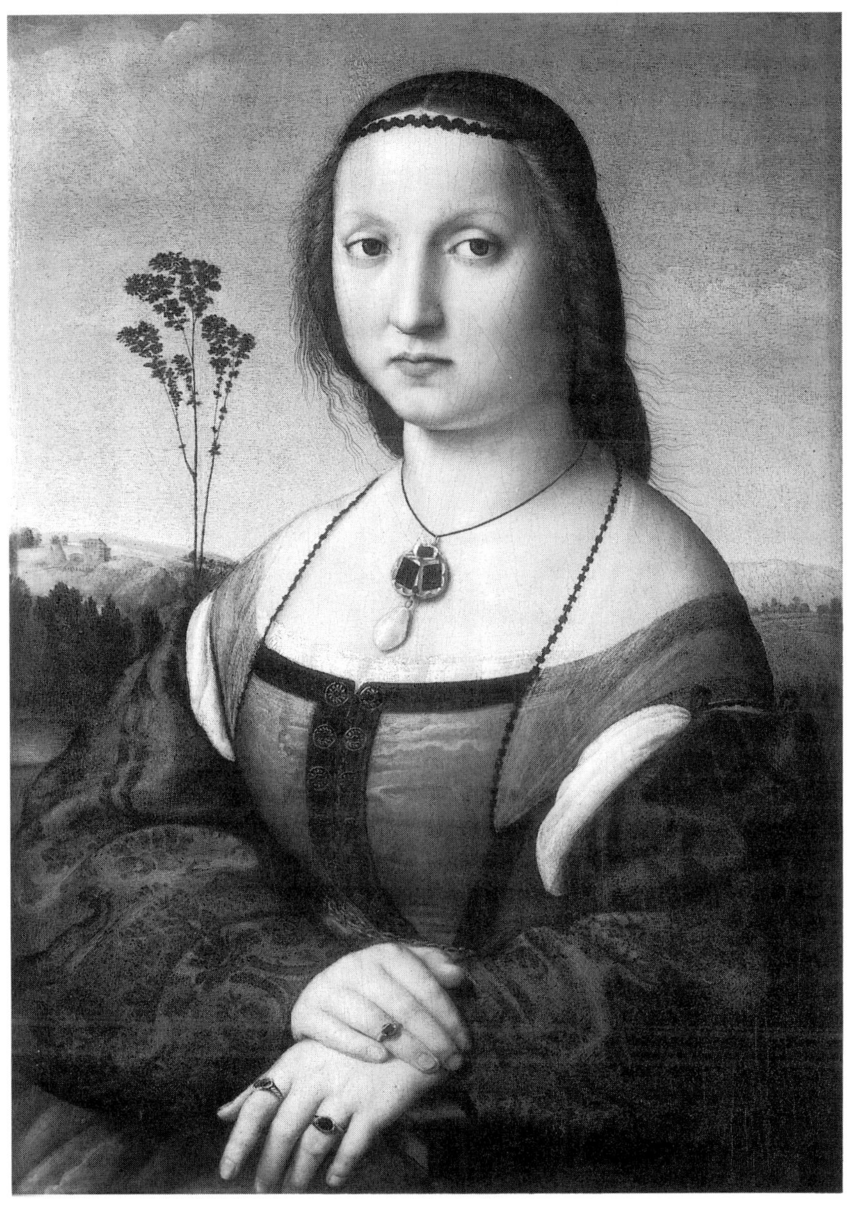

FIG. 63. Raphael, *Maddalena Doni* (c. 1506)
Palazzo Pitti, Florence

Leonardo was critical of contemporary fashion, which was bound to be "laughed at by our successors" (McMahon, 574). It seems as if Castiglione had reminded him to avoid sartorial extravagance. Like the courtier, Mona Lisa was not to be "overample" in the French style nor "overscanty" in the German manner. Moreover, clothes were supposed to "tend a little more toward the grave and sober rather than the foppish. Hence, I think that black is more pleasing in clothing than any other color; and if not black, then at least some color on the dark side" (*Courtier,* 121–22). That description would fit Mona Lisa as well as Raphael's portrait of Castiglione himself. The understated elegance of black attire was exemplary from Spain to the Netherlands. In portraiture, black highlighted faces rather than external details, and it suffices to mention that Rembrandt would master the art of portraits in black.[15]

4

Mona Lisa's graceful restraint was indeed familiar to the decorous laughter that moderates debate in *The Book of the Courtier.* Her smile gave a feminine form to *sprezzatura* inasmuch as it showed no "effort or care to be beautiful. Such is that careless purity (*sprezzata purità*) which is so pleasing to the eyes" (*Courtier,* 66). With an eye to the interdisciplinary nomenclature of the arts, ambiguity of context and conduct lies at the heart of *sprezzatura*'s artful artlessness, which affects action and language alike. To assert a mood of intellectual serenity, *sprezzatura* relies on play, which would tone down competition. Moreover, we ought to remember that *sfumato* and *sprezzatura* were cultural signposts that favored novelty and exploited anachronism. Painter and writer thus probed into a semantic density thereto unknown to life and art. Like the portrait's smile, meaning became elusive rather than demonstrative.

If we were to put the aloofness of La Gioconda into words, Castiglione's *gravità riposata* would shed light on it: "The calm gravity that is peculiar to the Spaniards is, I think, far more suited to us than the ready vivacity we see in the French." While censoring plucked eyebrows, he looked on affectation in matters of gestures and cosmetics as a foe to grace, which "is produced by simplicity and nonchalance" (*Courtier,* 135, 65). Actually, *grazia*'s unstudied but skillful spontaneity could be neither acquired nor taught; it was an epiphany as implausible as the lady's smile. Such a cluster of charismatic attributes refers to courtly acts which Mona Lisa has left behind. She does not act. Unlike Cecilia

Gallerani's petting gesture, her hands overlap in the inert casualness of a more aloof tranquility.[16]

Like the courtly lady, Mona Lisa flaunts an attitude that is altogether feminine. We must remember that Castiglione was critical of womanhood's "manly" attributes. The equation of feminine *virago*—Diana, Amazons—with masculine *virtù* did not appeal to him, just as the softness of Mona Lisa's hands dismisses any familiarity with "robust and strenuous manly exercises." We could guess that her actions would be carried out "in a measured way and with gentle delicacy." In the Italian text, gentle is in fact *molle,* which refers to something that is as tangibly soft as the agent's delicate hands. Instead of women who "play tennis, handle weapons, ride, hunt, and engage in nearly all the exercises that a cavalier can," Castiglione seems to prefer those who perform unspecified *esercizi* in a manner that is "gentle and grave" (*maniera mansueta e grave; Courtier,* 210–11). That description is a far cry from active personalities like Caterina Sforza. Accounts of her military prowess in defending Forli' impressed Jacob Burckhardt, who would have considered Vittoria Colonna's poetry "immortal" because of its "manly tone."[17]

Conversely, we can expect Mona Lisa's hands to enact a gentle behavior. Although joy and laughter call for bodily actions, there are emotions that "allow the arms to fall, and so the hands" (McMahon, 408). Movement has become a form of internal evaluation: "I would have her at least possess such understanding of them (exercises) as we may have of those things we do not practice; and this in order that she may know how to value and praise cavaliers more or less according to their merits." Men *do* things and *perform* deeds. The court lady, instead, should "have knowledge of letters, of music, of painting," and expression in her "talk, her laughter, her jesting" (*Courtier,* 211). Men are active; women understand, evaluate, and entertain. On her part, Mona Lisa has overcome courtly tensions between maturity of soul and youthfulness of deeds. Likewise, her pose has closed the gap between idea, act, and understanding.

As a portrait, Mona Lisa is herself at her best and has nothing else to prove. Like the perfect court lady of Castiglione, she projects a "soft and delicate tenderness, with an air of womanly sweetness." And she is to share with the courtier "virtues of the mind" and "a quick vivacity of spirit." Above all, "she must observe a certain mean (difficult to achieve and, as it were, composed of contraries) and must strictly observe certain limits and not exceed them" (*Courtier,* 106–7). Since she asserts herself as a symbol of implicit "self-knowing," her restrained smile stands between Bembo's serious contemplation in his *Asolani* and that open laughter lurking behind the playful witticisms of *The Book of the Courtier.*

References to smiles and laughter have been prominent so far. For Baudelaire, laughter stems from man's idea "of his own superiority; and in fact, since laughter is essentially human it is essentially contradictory." Laughter stands at the other side of sorrow and midway between superiority over animals and wretchedness in the face of divinity. Because it is at once angelic and satanic, Walter Pater would agree with Baudelaire that laughter is truly human.[18] At heart, laughter tends to express conflict, weakness, and dualism. Mona Lisa's composure, instead, remains equidistant from excesses she has learned to overcome. Like the court lady, she can be "most graceful . . . in her talk, her laughter, her play, her jesting, in short in everything" (*Courtier*, 211). The smile of La Gioconda therefore opens up to a kind of behavioral aesthetics.[19]

The courtier is a synthesis of Castiglione's experiences at court; he is type, history, and ideal. Likewise, Mona Lisa is type as the eternal feminine principle, history as Ser Giocondo's wife, and ideal as La Gioconda. Her *puissance de dissimulation* and *souveraine insensibilité* transcended Virgins and Venuses.[20] Like the courtier, she did not simply sit, but was enthroned above all the deeds that had gone into her making. Neither mother nor seer, La Gioconda projects a confidence that would enhance any challenge she might take up. Her artfulness is akin to *sprezzatura* insofar as it thrives on a kind of concealment that others must appreciate. To date, our own encounters with her gaze have never tired of undermining any presumption of knowledge.

5

Historically speaking, Piero della Francesca's portrait of Battista Sforza (c. 1465, Fig. 64) mirrors a worldview under the artist's control. Her profile looks nowhere, for it is fixed into a pose of aloof self-containment. Piero froze life within a flat outline, which defined a space that tended to drain figures of their emotional content. Existence, we can agree, was quite unthinkable.[21] The two-dimensional linearity of the duchess's head is typical of human portraiture. Before Leonardo's three-quarter profiles, artists were careful to avoid three-dimensional roundness. At that threshold, they could have shaped volumetric figures at unison with the mental depth of self-sufficient personalities. But they stopped; otherwise, the portrait would have been *released to life*. In Pirandellian terms, the figure would have taken on a life separate from its author.[22] Instead, she remained forever dependent on her creator for a raison d'être. At the edge

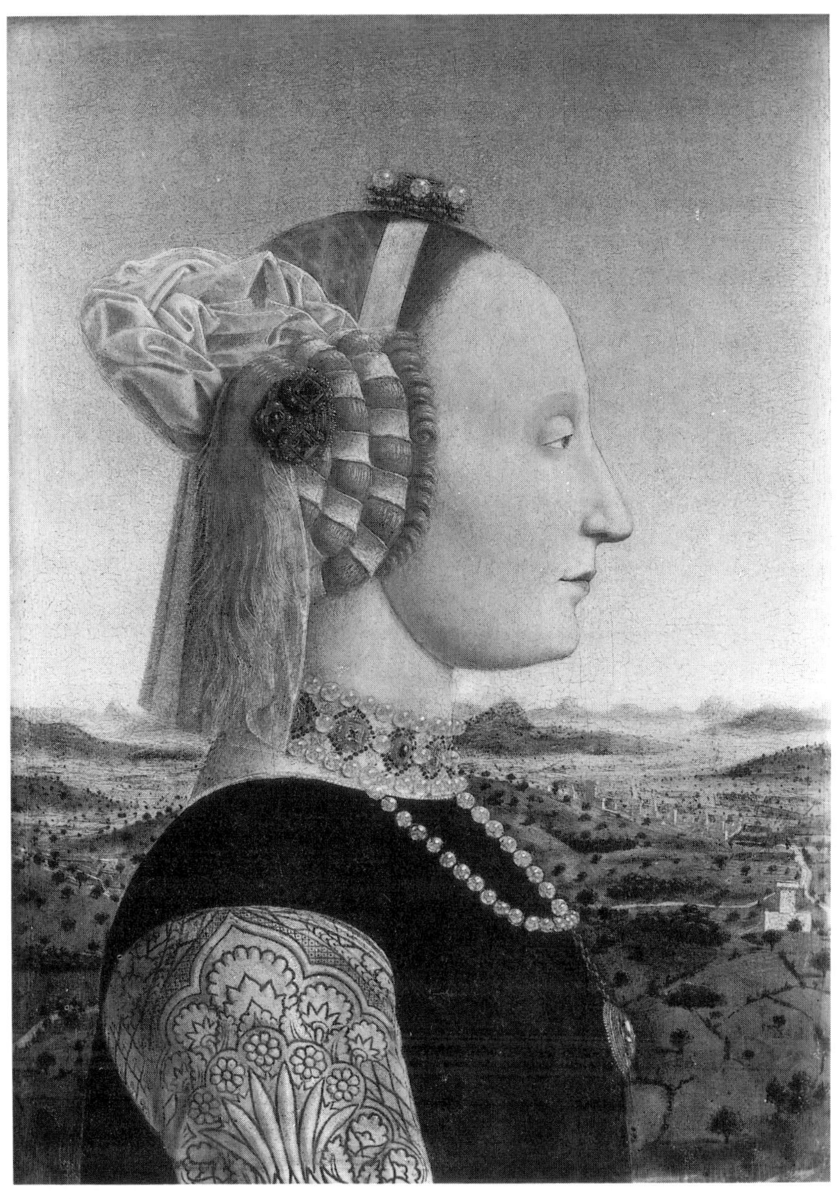

FIG. 64. Piero della Francesca, *Battista Sforza* (c. 1465)
Uffizi, Florence

between nothingness and eternity, Battista Sforza's profile remained as lifeless as an empty shell. The portrait has been read as an image of courtly marriage. It is not a study of human character, but the representation of a noble figure whose visual mimesis was drawn from recollection. In fifteenth-century art, in fact, the profile involved *donatori,* portraits for weddings, and genealogical representations.

The almost frontal view of Mona Lisa, instead, confronts us with the acknowledgment of value. She stares at us; imitation stands against expression. Scholarship tells us that profile and frontal portraits imply more than stylistic choices; one emphasizes what a person has done, while the other centers on what the figure is. In medieval art, the full face had no penetrating gaze, since physiognomic expression was yet to be discovered.[23] That discovery measured the progress of art that led to *Mona Lisa*. Alberti and Leonardo were familiar with the mythic origin of painting either as the imitative outline of one's shadow or of Narcissus's image reflected into a pool. In both instances, art revealed identity. Profile pointed to the memory of vanished subjects. Frontal positions, instead, stood for authority and uniqueness. Such a representation of the human character echoed the tradition of Byzantine, medieval, and early Renaissance images that ranged from God on portals of cathedrals to Dürer's ideal self-portrait as Christ. Mona Lisa's three-quarter figure mixed profile with frontality, type with individual. Her volumetric presence complements a face whose lips court and elude the grammar of human emotions. Piero della Francesca explains Battista Sforza, whereas Mona Lisa owes her unforgettable presence to herself alone. "If you are alone, you will be yours" (McMahon, 74), the artist wrote. She is alone, and she does belong to herself probably more than her creator could hope for himself. Leonardo released her to life, and she crossed the threshold of art with a personality of her own. In terms of critical appreciation, we shift from a Vasarian portrait of artistic skill to one of self-expression. For Walter Pater, Mona Lisa embodied the animalism of Greece, the lust of Rome, and the mysticism of the Middle Ages, for she knew the secrets of a human soul couched in memory and grown through experience.[24] I would like to think that she is what life was about to give, or shall never yield. Behind her smile, there lie unresolved hopes and lurking fears from which we shall never rid ourselves.

At his death, Leonardo still thought of the picture as unfinished. As a scientist, he could write with confidence that "the muscles which tighten the mouth lessening thus its length are in the lips themselves." The lateral muscles "extend the length of the mouth for the creation of laughter." And he was convinced that motions of that kind could be described "by means of mathematical principles" (McCurdy, 144). Yet confidence vanished at the tip of his paintbrush. Perhaps, he always hoped to find brushstrokes that could capture for him the secret of La Gioconda's soul. In his heart of hearts, however, he must have known that her secret had been lost to art.

The artist's life-giving powers exceeded his own ingenuity. "The painter who doubts not, attains little." *Saint Jerome,* the *Adoration,* and *Saint John the Baptist* made individual and collective cases for a creative doubting that Leonardo set at the core of his dynamic worldview. Yet *Mona Lisa* may have resolved all doubts. That was the masterpiece in which "the work surpasses the judgment of the painter," making the expressive "power of expansion" (McMahon, 54, 58) endless. She could be as alone as he would never be. Her smile left meaning at the edge of her lips, which held speech hostage to a magic instant and a composure for all time.[25] Words were not to be uttered, for her mystery could not fade into the prosaic details of language as either discourse or explanation.

6

In terms of creatures released to life and at ease in their environment, the landscape behind Mona Lisa takes us amid rivers and mountains through a foggy mist that enfolds fluvial and airy condensations. Leonardo proved that painters could show "mists through which visual images penetrate with difficulty" (McMahon, 55) at a time when Giorgione's backgrounds were equally replete with atmospheric effects. It is perhaps no sheer coincidence that the Venetian Pietro Bembo resorted to similar forms of expression when he described the verdant power of springtime regeneration: "*Ogni cosa che si vede è vaga; ride la terra, ride il mare, ride l'aria, ride il cielo*" (*Asolani* ii, 33). At that point in Renaissance culture, the earth's smile (*ride*) was one of concord amid the process of living things; a concord as pregnant as Mona Lisa's own smiling in the fullness of human growth.

There are many instances, Leonardo wrote, when "one and the same thing is attracted by two strong forces, namely Necessity and Potency. Water falls in rain; the earth absorbs it from the necessity for moisture; and the sun evaporates it, not from necessity, but by its power" (523). This passage seems to echo Aristotelian statements on the origin of rivers. Fluvial beginnings stem from a process whereby "small drops form in the region above the earth, and these again join others, until rain water falls in some quantity. . . . For mountains and high places act like a thick sponge overhanging the earth and make water drip through and run together in small quantities in many places" (*Metereologica* I, xiii, 349b–350a). Landscape in *Mona Lisa* represents the process whereby fluvial bodies of water first emerge and then dissolve. Art could transcend the erosion of time, which "must destroy all things and devour all things with the relentless teeth of years, little by little in a slow death. Helen, when she looked in her mirror, seeing the withered wrinkles made in her face by old age, wept" (412). Because the arrow of time has been bent toward circularity, mental and natural processes outlast decay. As such, landscape in the Louvre painting echoes the archetypal nature of the *Virgin of the Rocks* (see Fig. 13). The presence of a bridge and a road signal that human activity is less than an unstoppable *faciendum*. Instead, it is a bygone *factum* pointing toward a landscape that is at once "pre" and "post" historical.[26] In archetypal enclaves, *techne* could assert no more than faint presences.

La Gioconda's smile, therefore, wears a creational utterance that was preceded, and would be followed, by eons of time. Only art could trade the vicissitudes of life for the stability of primeval forms. That was the mimetic character and mythic outreach of "the divine science of painting" (McMahon, 42–43). It would be difficult to disagree with viewers who found that time is necessary to enter into communion with Leonardo's inexplicable faces, on which life has written its history in a way that all those who have had similar experiences can read and understand.[27] To understand Mona Lisa's smile is to understand much of life itself, as Leonardo retrieved it from the collective experiences of Helen, Lucrezia Borgia, and the Giocondas of his mind.

7

In the language of portraiture, Raphael's *Castiglione* (c. 1515) spells grace, seriousness, penetrating intellect, balanced temperament, and unrelenting self-control.[28] Indeed, these are the qualities of Mona Lisa. And it is perhaps by a happy coincidence that the two portraits stand side by side in the Louvre. Since the intellectual status of women fell short of parity, such proximity would have been deceptive in Renaissance society. Mona Lisa's matronly and maternal attributes echoed contemporary expectations. A woman's destiny was either *maritar* or *monacar*, to marry or become a nun. Otherwise, learned women were a threat to both male pride and traditional female roles they were tampering with.[29] From Costanza Calende and Elena Cornaro to Eleonora of Aragon, most of those women who pursued the life of the mind had to spend much time in the solitary chastity of book-lined cells of a kind more Spartan than male-inhabited *studioli.* At best, a girl like Cecilia Gonzaga could join her brothers as pupils of Vittorino da Feltre in the Casa Giocosa (Joyous House), a humanist school under the sponsorship of the marquis of Mantua. It was taken for granted that womanly pursuits of knowledge stemmed from masculine impulses; often, they were considered intellectual transvestites or outright sorceresses. Before the turn of the sixteenth century, Politian could praise Cassandra Fedele's intellectual distinction only by replacing male- with female-oriented objects— books instead of wool and a pen rather than a needle. By so doing, she either relinquished or overcame femininity. Praises of outstanding females produced paradoxical arguments. At best, some could do men's work, which implied that everything female was inferior. At once, women exceeded and violated nature. Because they were viewed as male by intellect and female in body and soul, learned women belonged to an amorphous sex of the third kind.[30]

The cultural makeup of the age tended to link womanhood to the elusiveness of Mona Lisa and the otherworldly ambiguity of Saint Anne. They embodied other-than-normal and other-than-natural human beings who exuded spiritual and intellectual attributes we would consider androgynous. In that sense, they offered a measure of Leonardo's response to the status of women in a society far less amicable toward them than the one portrayed in Castiglione's book or in Agnolo Firenzuola's *Delle bellezze delle donne* (1541–48). Whereas power and religion provided Isabella d'Este and her mother Eleonora with a privileged framework for the expression of their talents,[31] Mona Lisa stood in front of nature, where a wild man called the Baptist was to meet her in a spirit of androgynous fellowship.

Part II

*Anyone aiming at a comprehensive system of human
culture has, of necessity, turned back to myth.*
—*Ernst Cassirer*

If Adam were to proclaim and Mona Lisa to whisper the very secret of their souls, they would not do better than W. B. Yeats in loosing words to a paramount commentary: "Does one not hear those lips murmur that, despite whatever illusion we cherish, we came from no immaturity, but out of our own perfection?"[32] Because he reflects his maker's mighty grandeur, Adam is equally passive in Pico della Mirandola's oration. Adam cannot but look at God, for life and knowledge still belong to him.

Although quite young, Mona Lisa has tested existence. Like Adam, she has been created; after Eve, she has re-created herself by making natural perfection human. Enthroned as she is at the edge of an archetypal landscape, Mona Lisa is Promethean rather than Adamic. The fire of consciousness that the mythic hero gave to man was a stolen gift. But she no longer feels any guilt about it.

As Mona Lisa, her name pins identity to a specific time, and she belongs to the history of art. When she is called La Gioconda, however, her soul shows forth in its proper light. Although resembling her creator, the fire is hers alone; she is mirror and lamp, humanist ideal and antihumanist power.

8

In 1509 Carolus Bovillus wrote that "the world may be all things, but it knows nothing." Since he "knows all things," man can move from potency to act. There begins wisdom, which is the perpetual becoming of self-achieved perfection. Those who "know the causes of all things, what and why things are as they are; who know the dimension, order, number and place of all single things" get to master the cause of the substantial world. The wise man, "who knows the secret of nature, is himself secret and spiritual. He lives alone, far from the common herd. Placed high above other men, he is unique, free, absolute, tranquil, pacific, immobile, simple, collected, one."[33] We are told about a masterful secrecy that Walter Pater read in the subtle smile of Mona Lisa, who embodied a cultural ideal rooted in life, nurtured by nature, and entrusted to art.

Adam is about to get up in the Sistine fresco (see Fig. 43), and the test of choice awaits him. Yet his Protean freedom is theocentric; the moment he wakes up to life, God faces him. The model of imitation is immediately set. Adam looks at the source, pattern, and goal of his oncoming journey, which is expected to be a Christian one.

By contrast, the "absolute" and "immobile" composure of Mona Lisa does not point toward beginnings, but accomplishments. Her lifetime experience has been resolved into a contented (*gioconda*) human attitude, and it is toward mankind that she looks. She has neither lost nor regained Eden; yet she has walked with confidence on those solid grounds that humanity as a whole has treaded since the beginning. The quests of Adam and Aeneas were linked to appointed destinies, and even Ulysses at last found his way back home. Mona Lisa is seated, but she has traveled with her mind through our Western experience. Her journey has been Joycean rather than Homeric.

By way of comparison, Adam's potential being is predictable insofar as it rests with analogical models of humanist imitation. God explains Adam through words and gestures familiar to man. Since she has traded explanation for expression, Mona Lisa's smile points to a subtle utterance of the human character. It has even been suggested that her attitude is one of anticipated satisfaction and of hostile superiority.[34] She stands at the threshold of nature, and her smile edges on a private mood never to be spent through explicit gestures. Her arms are as solidly bound as the bridge behind her; one cancels out the gap between mind and matter, while the other arches over time and myth.

However unbridled, Walter Pater's memorable commentary measured the range of Mona Lisa's bottomless secrets when he found in her pagan goddesses, Christian madonnas, animalism, mysticism, and ten thousand experiences.[35] She is older than the rocks among which she sits because she embodies the fulfilled experience of human life. And because her knowledge is paramount, her smile will always mean too much for anybody trying to steal any one of its meanings. If the source and origin of all mythology is linguistic ambivalence, then we can agree that ambiguity triumphs on the lips of the "modern" myth.[36]

9

If we were to give perfection the dialogic guise of a culture at once split by history and reconciled through myth, we ought to ponder on systematic tensions between what we are and what we ought to be. To achieve wholeness, human nature ought to join the two together.[37] Leonardo and Mona Lisa did go together, for every painter paints himself under the guise of idealized images. In that sense, she is the portrait of the artist's autobiography of hope, which he penned with an elusive and yet inerasable signature. Creator and creation merged to a point where the myth of art shared in the pulse of its own source.

Between 1869 and 1919, an average of one full-length book per year was published in Europe on the subject of Leonardo da Vinci. The figure of Jesus aside, nobody else received so much attention during those fifty years.[38] We need only think of Walter Pater, Bernard Berenson, Sigmund Freud, and Paul Valéry, who wrote six different texts on Leonardo from 1894 to 1928. The centerpiece of Valéry's introduction to the Leonardesque method centers on a self-correcting mind capable of seeing relations "between things of which we cannot grasp the law of continuity."[39] The fact that Leonardo did not finish most of his undertakings because he never committed himself wholeheartedly to any one of them confirmed his ability to remain aloof from the world of time-consuming details. While "poor is the man who desires many things" (McCurdy, 1122), rich is the one who can master their unified conception. Valéry found Leonardo's mind to be imperially conscious of its own potential and disdainful of execution.[40] Beyond all divisions, promise and fulfillment could be reconciled through words imbued with mythmaking fervor: "The universal man can now be imagined. We have reached the point where a Leonardo da Vinci can exist as a concept in our minds."[41] As a figure of synthesis, he was artist, inventor, and the most daring of Daedalian makers.

As inventors, Daedalus and Leonardo exemplified myths of conquest. Their talents had to rely on the logic of *techne,* whose forward-looking hypotheses stirred hopes and doubts alike. Because it turned certainty and truth into values that were at once relative and provisional, *techne* forced the human mind to steer away from the traditional certainties of *episteme.* Its immutable truths, in fact, were entrusted to the "known" powers of a primordial past. Beyond the illusions crafted in Daedalus's *officina,* Leonardo never lost sight of Jerome's faith in the desert. Since time immemorial, his own sketches of the Deluge—which echoed the frescoes of Paolo Uccello and Michelangelo—would curb Promethean freedom. Adam's creation on the Sistine ceiling led to human toils, earth-shaking punishments, and Noah's drunkenness after the Fall. Michelangelo could not bear to tell us that the weight of knowledge had stirred hate, discord, and Abel's murder. Creation had started with the separation of light from darkness, to which man's story had quickly returned. Better than Jerome, Leonardo's Baptist had learned to tame wild impulses in the loneliness of the desert, and he could still point toward hope out of a dark void at last free of words, measures, and images. As an act of faith, some still believe that human creativity exceeds the mechanisms it invents.[42] Hopes of that kind should urge us to wish that Mona Lisa would outlast Daedalian challenges. In that spirit, her smile nestled the myth of the unconquerable core of human nature.

10

Leonardo's foremost concern was not with the created, but with the mind that makes creation possible. In his own words, "the divine provides that the mind of the painter in the science of painting transmute itself into a likeness of the divine mind" (McMahon, 280). He had no doubts that art was the instrument by means of which man could generate divinelike forms.

It was Leonardo's choice to identify divinity with human and natural archetypes immune to the time-bound likenesses of the empirical world. For him, art was an epiphany through which myth would be brought within reach. Art could spell the original grammar of divinity through an incomparable brew of history and myth that mixed the potential with the actual. To appreciate such a bent of mind, we have been told that history is our myth. It combines what can be thought, the "thinkable," and the origin.[43] In terms of humanist values, probability became certainty at the metahistorical level of Leonardo Bruni's panegyrical method, whereas the antihumanist Leonardo let myth bestow meaning on much of history.

Life has come and gone behind La Gioconda, who has confronted us with values of perpetuity.[44] We have been led to a point where the last Deluge has nurtured the source. River and road point both ways toward the last journey and the first daylight.

Leonardo placed Mona Lisa at the threshold of cosmic revolutions by far in excess of human millennia. Leone Ebreo voiced current speculations in astrology and philosophy when he wrote that "human life will continue for as long as the eighth sphere takes to make one revolution; and when this is completed all things will be dissolved, the Forms reverting to the Divinity, and matter to Chaos, its mother . . . and after the fifty thousandth year will return to her labour of conceiving the heaven and the earth together with the whole of the universe."[45] At the end of mankind's cyclic revolutions, La Gioconda's smile remains as enigmatic and noneloquent as experiences sunken below the cresting chaos. Likewise, the artist's *preimaginare* and *postimaginare* overlap amid outbursts of primeval creativity. His lifelong quest found at last the source of past and future, for she could be "Sister of the mirage and echo" (Robert Graves, *The White*

Goddess).[46] She was never born on Mount Helicon, nor was she a gifted sister at Apollo's patriarchal court in Delphi. She never remembered Mnemosyne, but Hesiod's cosmology would suggest that she walked matriarchal grounds among the daughters of Mother Earth. No Cuman sybil could explain her riddle-like smile, because she never uttered the divided language of either sisterhood or poetic otherness. Whether they came from Basilisks, the Sphinx, or Medusa, archaic gazes had the power of death. La Gioconda's gaze, instead, exudes a subduing strength, which is neither sinister nor punitive; rather, it is a visual sign of fulfillment inimical toward dreadful deities that have been stopping man at the crossroad of human dividedness. Perhaps she is the undivided Muse bespeaking an androgynous language to which John the Baptist alone could smile back.

Above an ever-growing myriad of meanings, La Gioconda remains the surviving goddess who does not speak. She is an image and a force, like Greek deities who were at once personal and impersonal.[47] Long after the immortals have descended from heaven, she still stands in the elusive and yet royal composure of the Louvre queen of painting. In the words of the Shakespearean verse, we shall treasure her smile "to the last syllable of recorded time."

11

As a testimony to life-giving images, Mona Lisa is all that we have been told she is, and more. For Oscar Wilde, Leonardo "may have been merely the slave of an archaic smile" that escaped him. Yet an "excess of intellectual intention" has set everyone else's imagination afire. "For when the work is finished it has, as it were, an independent life of its own, and may deliver a message far other than that which was put into its lips to say."[48] It took Pater—and every other beholder—to make La Gioconda older than the rocks among which she sits. And what we have been seeing in her smile has wrought layers of interpretations.

The myth of myths, in fact, does not draw its power from the heartbeat of life, but from life's legend. Although its slow pulse could grow faint at times, the spell of Mona Lisa's lure has challenged its own resilience through the ages. In the echoing plenitude of her human wholeness, she holds origin, destiny, and a thousand mysteries hostage to her lips. Her smile is that of a creature—perhaps the only creature—who has been able to experience a life of absolutes. For hers was—and still is—the beguiling smile of life.

Notes

Introduction

1. I take this phrase from Eliseo Vivas, "Myth: Some Philosophical Problems," *Southern Review* 6 (1970): 89. For a literary treatment of "myth-theory" and "theory of myth" that is both comprehensive and well thought out, see Jeffrey M. Perl, *The Tradition of Return: The Implicit History of Modern Literature* (Princeton, 1984).

2. At the two chronological poles of scholarship, see Louis Menard, *Du polythé-isme hellénique* (Paris, 1863), 58–59; and Eric Gould, *Mythical Intentions in Modern Literature* (Princeton, 1981).

3. See Jean Seznec, *The Survival of the Pagan Gods: The Mythological Tradition and Its Place in Renaissance Humanism and Art* (Princeton, 1961); my *Adam "New Born and Perfect": The Renaissance Promise of Eternity* (Bloomington, 1987), esp. chap. 6, 107–18; the opening chapter of John J. White, *Mythology in the Modern Novel* (Princeton, 1971), 3–31.

4. Paul Valéry, *Variety* (New York, 1927), 181–82.

5. See Carl Jung, *The Archetypes and the Collective Unconscious* (Princeton, 1969), 21–23.

6. *Petrarch's Bucolicum Carmen*, trans. T. Bergin (New Haven, 1974), 49.

7. See Thomas Bergin's bibliographical note, in ibid., 223–24.

8. John Hollander, *Vision and Resonance: Two Senses of Poetic Form* (Oxford, 1975), 23.

9. *Goethe's World View: Presented in His Reflections and Maxims* (New York, 1963), 61.

10. See Ernst Cassirer, *The Individual and the Cosmos in Renaissance Philosophy* (Philadelphia, 1972), 50; Eugenio Garin, *Scienza e vita civile nel Rinascimento italiano* (Bari, 1972), 74.

11. By and large, scholarship has set Leonardo's originality next to the last generation of fifteenth-century artists. Michael Levey includes the master's early paintings in the Early Renaissance (quattrocento), in *Early Renaissance* (Baltimore, 1967); Bernard Berenson splits him into halves (one for each century), in *The Study and Criticism of Italian Art* (London, 1916); and Frederick Hartt places him in the sixteenth-century context of the High Renaissance, in *History of Italian Renaissance Art* (New York, 1969). Perhaps less than unwittingly, Kenneth Clark is keen to detect Leonardo's "pre" or "proto" baroque leanings in *Leonardo da Vinci* (Baltimore, 1973); Ernst Cassirer has touched on his originality vis-à-vis Renaissance thought, in *The Individual and the Cosmos in Renaissance Philosophy;* for Giuseppe Saitta, the artist's earthbound sense of reality—*il senso della terrestrità*—took a confrontational posture against humanist learning in "L'*amor vitae* in Leonardo da Vinci," *Atti del Convegno di Studi Vinciani* (Florence, 1953), 147; Rocco Montano has linked the term "anti-humanist" to the *omo sanza lettere* in a brief study of Renaissance and baroque poetics, in *L'estetica del Rinascimento e del Barocco* (Naples, 1968).

12. See Umberto Bosco, *Saggi sul Rinascimento italiano* (Florence, 1970), 50–51; Eugenio Battisti, *L'antirinascimento* (Turin, 1962), 21; Hiram Haydn, *The Counter-Renaissance* (New York, 1950), xv. On Battisti's book, see Mario Apollonio, *L'antirinascimento* (Milan, 1970).

13. Leon Battista Alberti, *Theogenius,* in *Opere volgari,* vol. 2, ed. Cecil Grayson (Bari, 1966), 93; translation by the author.

14. See Pamela Major-Poetzl, *Michel Foucault's Archaeology of Western Culture: Toward a New Science of History* (Chapel Hill, 1983), 10–11.

15. On the critical debate and relevant references, see J. H. Whitfield's "Momus and the Language of Irony," in *The Languages of Literature in Renaissance Italy,* ed. P. Hainsworth, V. Lucchesi, C. Roaf, D. Robey, and J. R. Woodhouse (Oxford, 1988), 31–43.

16. See relevant chapters in Jacques Derrida's *Dissemination* (Chicago, 1981), 65–117.

17. Leon Battista Alberti, *Dinner Pieces,* trans. D. Marsh (Binghamton, 1987), 28–29, 33.

18. For more negative criticism, see Elizabeth A. Chesney, *The Countervoyage of Rabelais and Ariosto: A Comparative Reading of Two Renaissance Mock Epics* (Durham, 1982), 9.

19. See Mikhail Bakhtin, *The Dialogic Imagination,* trans. M. Holquist and C. Emerson (Austin, 1981), 426–27.

20. A Neoplatonic presence is underlined by Lionello Venturi in *La critica e l'arte di Leonardo da Vinci* (Florence, 1956). Giovanni Gentile, *Il pensiero del Rinascimento* (Florence, 1955), 144–49, maintains that Leonardo leans toward the metaphysical naturalism of Giordano Bruno and Tommaso Campanella, instead of Galileo's scientific naturalism. As to Leonardo's sources, see Eugenio Garin's review of the controversial scholarship (Duhem, Solmi, Cassirer) in his *La cultura filosofica del Rinascimento italiano* (Florence, 1961), 388–401.

21. See Michael Holquist's introduction to Bakhtin, *The Dialogic Imagination;* and Tzvetan Todorov, *Mikhail Bakhtin: The Dialogical Principle* (Minneapolis, 1984), 60. See also Thomas Greene, *The Light in Troy: Imitation and Discovery in Renaissance Poetry* (New Haven, 1982), esp. 16–19.

22. Michael Ayrton, *The Testament of Daedalus* (London, 1962), 56.

23. In his *Trattato dell'orificeria* in *Opere di Baldassare Castiglione, Giovanni della Casa, Benvenuto Cellini,* ed. Carlo Cordiè (Milan, 1960), 975.

24. In this context, I refer to Leonid M. Batkin's Italian translation of *Gli umanisti italiani: Stile di vita e di pensiero* (Bari, 1990), esp. 177–98. He also concludes his discussion of Italian humanism by centering on the *School of Athens.* By and large, Batkin's emphasis on heterogeneity, dialogism, and eclecticism supports my approach.

25. Octavio Paz, *The Labyrinth of Solitude* (New York, 1985), 292.

26. See George Sarton, *The Life of Science: Essays in the History of Civilization* (New York, 1948), 58.

27. Geoffrey Hartman, *The Fate of Reading and Other Essays* (Chicago, 1975), 18.

Chapter 1

1. Jules Michelet, *The Insect* (London, 1875), 218–19. Later, the spider became potbellied for having sacrificed "everything to a job, to need, to the industrial apparatus satisfying this need" (as translated in Linda Orr's *Jules Michelet: Nature, History, and Language* [Ithaca, 1976], 122). This study does not consider the more strictly artistic symbolism of the cobweb as an interlacing of plotting threads in chivalric works such as Ariosto's *Orlando Furioso* and Spenser's *Faerie Queene.* On the subject, see Judith Dundas's thoughtful, *The Spider and the Bee: The Artistry of Spenser's Faerie Queene* (Urbana, 1985). Figure 4 of the illustrations presents Veronese's *Industria* (1576–78), an allegorical figure that holds a spider's web, which she holds with a stick at one end and with her fingers at the other. Such a self-sufficient configuration was allegorical, and it did project much of the autonomous world of technology.

2. Ernesto Grassi, *Folly and Insanity in Renaissance Literature* (Binghamton, 1986), 17.

3. Carlo Dionisotti, "Leonardo uomo di lettere," in *Italia medioevale e umanistica* 5 (1962): 195. On Leonardo's sources, Garin, *La cultura filosofica del Rinascimento italiano,* 388–402.

4. See Battisti, *L'antirinascimento;* Alberto Tenenti, *Il senso della morte e l'amore della vita nel Rinascimento* (Turin, 1982), 189–90.

5. Petrarch, *De remediis contra utriusque fortune* (begun 1353), as partially translated in *Four Dialogues for Scholars,* trans. Rawski (Cleveland, 1967), 31, 51.

6. Alberti, *Dinner Pieces,* 62.

7. See Christian K. Zacher, *Curiosity and Pilgrimage: The Literature of Discovery in Fourteenth-Century England* (Baltimore, 1976), 18–20.

8. Politian, *Epistolae,* in *Prosatori latini del Quattrocento,* ed. Eugenio Garin (Milan, 1952), 894; translation by the author.

9. *The Letters of Machiavelli,* trans. A. Gilbert (New York, 1961), 185.

10. A. Bartlett Giamatti, "Proteus Unbound: Some Versions of the Sea God in the

Renaissance," in *The Disciplines of Criticism*, ed. P. Demetz, T. Greene, and L. Nelson (New Haven, 1968), 439.

11. From Petrarch, "On Our Own Ignorance and That of Many Others," in *The Renaissance Philosophy of Man*, ed. P. O. Kristeller, J. H. Randall, and E. Cassirer (Chicago, 1967), 107; *Letters from Petrarch*, trans. M. Bishop (Bloomington, 1966), 207; *Rerum familiarum libri I–VIII*, trans. A. S. Bernardo (Albany, 1975), 19.

12. *De vita solitaria*, in *Francesco Petrarca: Prose* (Milan, 1955), 292, 299, 328–30, 588; translations by the author.

13. Thomas Bergin, *Petrarch* (New York, 1970), 188.

14. *Letters from Petrarch*, 134.

15. Leon Battista Alberti, *De commodis litterarum atque incommodis: Defunctus* (Milan, 1971), 73; translation by the author.

16. *Letters from Petrarch*, 231.

17. Leon Battista Alberti, *Intercoenales*, in *Prosatori latini del Quattrocento*, ed. Garin, 644–46; translation by the author.

18. Alberti, *Dinner Pieces*, 21.

19. See George Holmes, *The Florentine Enlightenment 1400–1500* (London, 1969), 137–67.

20. Giovanni Papini, *Four and Twenty Minds* (New York, 1970), 33.

21. Lorenzo Valla, *De libero arbitrio*, in *Prosatori latini del Quattrocento*, ed. Garin, 528–30.

22. See Sam Lilley, "Leonardo da Vinci and the Experimental Method," in *Atti del Convegno di Studi Vinciani*, 414–15.

23. Moshe Barash, *Light and Color in the Italian Renaissance Theory of Art* (New York, 1978), 52–53.

24. *A Visual Dictionary of Art*, s.v. "sfumato" (Greenwich, 1974), 536.

25. Rhys Carpenter, *The Esthetic Basis of Greek Art of the Fifth and Fourth Centuries B.C.* (Bloomington, 1959), 108.

26. H. van de Waal, *Steps toward Rembrandt: Collected Articles 1937–1972* (London, 1974), 14–15.

27. Giovanni Papini, *Scrittori e artisti* (Verona, 1959), 1243–44, finds in Leonardo's *chiaroscuro* a carrier of "moral values" symbolic of his tendency to court mystery and ambiguity. Francesco Flora sees in the *sfumato* a symbol of Leonardo's moral and mental dialectic of the cycle of life and death, in "Unità dei linguaggi leonardeschi," *Raccolta Vinciana* 17 (1954): 4. Sidney Freedberg contends that *sfumato* is "a carrier of an attitude toward content," in *Painting in Italy 1500–1600* (Baltimore, 1971), 12.

28. Heinrich Wölfflin, *Principles of Art History* (New York, 1950), 237.

29. David Summers, *The Judgment of Sense: Renaissance Naturalism and the Rise of Aesthetics* (Cambridge, 1987), 15–16.

30. Sidney Alexander, *Lions and Foxes: Men and Ideals of the Italian Renaissance* (New York, 1974), 284–85, writes that Guicciardini's mind "portrays itself in its *sfumature;* the conditions, the exceptions, the modifications, the qualifications with which the author weighs every human act and motivation. He had not read, of course, but he was a fellow Florentine of Leonardo da Vinci." Also, Peter Bandanella, *Francesco Guicciardini* (Boston, 1976).

31. In *Il libro del Cortegiano del Conte Baldessar Castiglione, colla vita di lui scritta dal Sig. Abate Pierantonio Serassi* (Padua, 1766). See also J. R. Woodhouse, *Baldesar Castiglione: A Reassessment of the Courtier* (Edinburgh, 1978), 189.

32. See Alessandro Parronchi, "Passaggio della prosettiva da Firenze a Venezia," in *Giorgione: Atti del Convegno Internazionale di Studio per il Quinto Centenario*

della Nascita (Venice, 1979), 120. For Leonardo's "dark manner," see K. Weill Garris-Posner, *Leonardo and Central Italian Art: 1515–1550* (New York, 1974).

33. José Ortega y Gasset, *Meditations on Quixote* (New York, 1963), 67. Also, Claudio Guillén's remarks on the subject in his interdisciplinary essay, "On the Concept of Metaphor of Perspective," in his *Literature as System: Essays toward the Theory of Literary History* (Princeton, 1971), especially 306–7.

34. At a later time, the stylistics of *sfumato* came to bear on semantic transcendence when Josephin Peladan described the ambiguity of the Leonardesque *Saint John the Baptist* as a "*clair-obscur physique*" and "*animique*" (Epilogue, in *Leonardo da Vinci: conferenze fiorentine* [Milan, 1910], 308). See also Mario Praz's comments in *The Romantic Agony* (Oxford, 1951), 334–35.

35. Leone Ebreo, *The Philosophy of Love,* trans. F. Friedeberg-Seely and Jean H. Barnes (London, 1937), 318.

36. Ibid., 315.

37. See Elmer Belt, *Leonardo the Anatomist* (Lawrence, 1955), 3.

38. Leon Battista Alberti, *Apologhi,* ed. Marcello Ciccuto (Milan, 1989), 76; translation by the author.

Chapter 2

1. See Colin Eisler, "The Athlete of Virtue: The Iconography of Asceticism," in *Essays in Honor of Erwin Panofsky,* vol. 1, ed. M. Meiss (New York, 1961), 82–85. See also John M. Mecklin, *The Passing of the Saint* (Chicago, 1941), 8, 17. On Andrea del Castagno's Jerome, see Hartt, *History of Italian Renaissance Art,* 226–27; Edward E. Malone, *The Monk and the Martyr: The Monk as the Successor of the Martyr* (Washington, D.C., 1950), 64–76. Most humanist portraits of Jerome reconciled ecclesiastical with humanist knowledge, which however created tensions in the saint's mind. See Herbert Friedmann, *A Bestiary for Saint Jerome: Animal Symbolism in European Religious Art* (Washington, D.C., 1980), 32.

2. Peter Brown, *The Making of Late Antiquity* (Cambridge, Mass., 1978), 93–96; and "The Rise and Function of the Holy Man in Antiquity," *Journal of Roman Studies* 61 (1971): 80–101.

3. On the thematics of pride, see Robert Payne, *Hubris: A Study of Pride* (New York, 1960), 99–100.

4. See M.L.W. Laistner, *Thought and Letters in Western Europe: A.D. 500 to 900* (Ithaca, 1957), 276–85.

5. See Giulio Carlo Argan, *Botticelli* (Geneva, 1957), 78–80; and Millard Meiss, "Scholarship and Penitence in the Early Renaissance: The Image of St. Jerome," *Pantheon* 32 (1974): 136–40.

6. See Charles H. Haskins, *The Renaissance of the Twelfth Century* (Cambridge, Mass., 1971), 71.

7. See Jean Steinmann, *Saint Jerome and His Times* (Notre Dame, 1959), 57.

8. Eugene F. Rice, Jr., *Saint Jerome in the Renaissance* (Baltimore, 1985), 75–76.

9. See Marc Bloch, *The Historian's Craft* (New York, 1953), 31.

10. Geoffrey Harpham, *The Ascetic Imperative in Culture and Criticism* (Chicago, 1987), xii.

11. George H. Williams, *Wilderness and Paradise in Christian Thought* (New York, 1962), 10.

12. See Ferdinand Cavallera, "The Personality of St. Jerome," in *A Monument to*

Saint Jerome: Essays on Some Aspects of His Life, Works, and Influence, ed. F. X. Murphy (New York, 1952), 30–31.

13. See Edwin A. Quain, "St. Jerome as a Humanist" in *A Monument to Saint Jerome,* ed. Murphy, 201–32.

14. I follow here J.N.D. Kelly, *Jerome: His Life, Writings, and Controversies* (London, 1975), 47. In terms of geographical details, see ibid., 46–47; P. Monceaux and L. Brosse, "Chalcis and Belum: Notes sur l'histoire et les ruines de la ville," *Syria* 6 (1925): 341–50.

15. See Alison G. Elliott, *Roads to Paradise: Reading the Lives of the Early Saints* (London, 1987), 196–97; Beryl Rowland, *Animals with Human Faces: A Guide to Animal Symbolism* (Knowville, 1973), 121.

16. See Rice, *Saint Jerome in the Renaissance,* 85–86, 94; and Charles L. Stinger, *Humanism and the Church Fathers: Ambrogio Traversari (1386–1439) and Christian Antiquity in the Italian Renaissance* (Albany, 1977), 223–24. For artistic treatments of the subject, see Bernhard Ridderbos, *Saint and Symbol: Images of Saint Jerome in Early Italian Art* (Groningen, 1984).

17. Maurizio Calvesi, *Treasures of the Vatican* (Cleveland, 1962), 92.

18. See Richard Krautheimer, *Rome: Profile of a City, 312–1308* (Princeton, 1980), 30–31.

19. See Augusto Gentili, *I giardini di contemplazione: Lorenzo Lotto 1503/1512* (Rome, 1985), 175; John V. Fleming, *From Bonaventure to Bellini: An Essay in Franciscan Exegesis* (Princeton, 1982), 32–33, 35.

20. Steinmann, *Saint Jerome and His Times,* 41–42.

21. See *Selected Letters of Aeneas Silvius Piccolomini* (Northridge, 1969), 56. See also Alice A. Kuzniar, "The Temporality of Landscape: Romantic Allegory and C. D. Friedrich," *Studies in Romanticism* 3, no. 1 (1989): 69.

22. Aristides, *Panathenaicus,* in *The Civilizing Power,* trans. J. H. Oliver (Philadelphia, 1968), 89; "On Those Who Died in the War," in *The World's Famous Orations,* vol. 1 (New York, 1906), 26.

23. *The Letters of Marsilio Ficino,* vol. 2 (London, 1978), 37.

24. See B. A. Van Groningen, *In the Grip of the Past* (Leiden, 1953), 98.

25. See Joseph Campbell, *The Hero of a Thousand Faces* (Princeton, 1972), 319–27; Philip R. Hardie, *Virgil's Aeneid: Cosmos and Imperium* (Oxford, 1968), 253; Ernst Curtius, *European Literature and the Latin Middle Ages* (New York, 1963), 98–101.

26. Alberti, *Opere volgari,* vol. 2, 108.

27. Ibid., 114.

28. Ibid., 68–72.

29. On the formative nature of baroque art and thought, see my *The Cornucopian Mind and the Baroque Unity of the Arts* (University Park, 1990), esp. the chapters on formation and perfectibility.

30. Michel Foucault, *The Use of Pleasure: The History of Sexuality,* vol. 2 (New York, 1985), 26–27. See also Northrop Frye, *The Secular Scripture: A Study of the Structure of Romance* (Cambridge, Mass., 1976), 88.

31. "Of the Essence of Laughter," in *Baudelaire: Selected Writings on Art and Artists* (Baltimore, 1972), 142.

32. F.W.J. Schelling, *The Philosophy of Art* (Minneapolis, 1989), 99.

33. I follow Alice A. Kuzniar's thoughtful discussion of the subject, which she places in the context of German romanticism, namely Novalis and Hölderlin, in *Delayed Endings: Nonclosure in Novalis and Hölderlin* (Athens, 1987), 34–36.

Chapter 3

1. For a detailed discussion of religious symbolism in Botticelli's painting, see Rab Hatfield, *Botticelli's Uffizi "Adoration"* (Princeton, 1976), esp. 33–67.

2. See Hartt, *History of Italian Renaissance Art,* 394–96; Clark, *Leonardo da Vinci,* 37–43.

3. Martin Kemp, *Leonardo da Vinci: The Marvellous Works of Nature and Man* (London, 1981), 74. See Shirley J. Case, "The Study of Early Christianity," in *A Guide to the Study of the Christian Religion,* ed. G. B. Smith (Chicago, 1961), 244–46.

4. Carlo Pedretti, *Leonardo: A Study in Chronology and Style* (Berkeley and Los Angeles, 1973), 33–34.

5. See Ernst Fischer, *Art Against Ideology* (New York, 1969), 194–95.

6. Karl Kroeber, *British Romantic Art* (Berkeley and Los Angeles, 1986), 174.

7. Umberto Eco, *Art and Beauty in the Middle Ages* (New Haven, 1986), 42, 44. See also Giulio Carlo Argan, "5 Daghosto 1473," in *Leonardo: La Pittura,* ed. Pietro Marani (Florence, 1985), 14.

8. See Argan, *Botticelli,* 65.

9. I follow here Cesare Brandi's thoughtful argument, *Struttura e architettura* (Turin, 1971), 222.

10. On the definition of *sfumato,* see chapter 1, note 24.

11. George Kubler, *The Shape of Time* (New Haven, 1962), 4, 130.

12. James Ackerman, "On Early Renaissance Color Theory and Practice," *Studies in Italian Art and Architecture 15th through 16th Centuries* 35 (1980): 22.

13. See Susanne Langer, *Philosophical Sketches* (New York, 1962), 79–81; Margaret R. Miles, *Image as Insight: Visual Understanding in Western Christianity and Secular Culture* (Boston, 1985), 2–3.

14. See Alan Watts, *Myth and Ritual in Christianity* (New York, 1953), 82.

15. Ernst Cassirer, *An Essay on Man* (New York, 1970), 57.

16. See Nicole Loraux, *The Invention of Athens* (Cambridge, Mass., 1986), 328–29.

17. To size Leonardo's dramatic rendition of the break between paganism and the Judeo-Christian tradition, we ought to turn to the more subdued *Doni Tondo* of Michelangelo, who also split the background space in two by means of a low wall.

18. Paul Ricoeur, *History and Truth* (Evanston, 1965), 82–84.

19. Hatfield, *Botticelli's Uffizi "Adoration,"* 56–57, 67.

20. Carl Becker, in *The Philosophy of History in Our Time,* ed. Hans Meyerhoff (Garden City, N.Y., 1959), 121–22.

21. Jacob Burckhardt, *The Age of Constantine the Great* (New York, 1949), 213–14.

22. Kroeber, *British Romantic Art,* 143–45.

23. André Gide, *Two Legends: Oedipus and Theseus* (New York, 1950), 88. See also Walter Goffart, *Rome's Fall and After* (London, 1989), 39.

24. As Paul Ricoeur writes, "Christianity made a violent entry into the Hellenic world by introducing a concept of time containing events, crises, and decisions. Christian revelation scandalized the Greeks through the narration of those 'sacred' events: creation, fall, covenant, prophetic utterances, and, more fundamentally, 'Christian' events such as incarnation, cross, empty tombs, and the birth of the Christ at Pentecost" (*History and Truth,* 95).

25. See Alexander S. Kohanski, *The Greek Mode of Thought in Western Philosophy* (London, 1984), 23–24.

26. Donald Wilcox, *The Measure of Times Past: Pre-Newtonian Chronologies and the Rhetoric of Relative Time* (Chicago, 1987), 8–9.

27. See Oscar Cullmann, *Christ and Time: The Primitive Christian Conception of Time and History* (Philadelphia, 1964), 39–40.

28. Schelling, *The Philosophy of Art*, 64.

29. See Hans von Campenhausen, *Men Who Shaped the Western Church* (New York, 1960), 2–3.

30. Kenneth Clark, *Moments of Vision* (Oxford, 1954), 7–8; and *What Is a Masterpiece?* (London, 1979), 20.

31. Giusta Nicco Fasola, "La nuova spazialità," in *Leonardo: Saggi e ricerche*, ed. A. Marazza (Rome, 1954), 295. The critic adds that among the books Leonardo studied or owned one finds the names of Giovanni Marliano and Alberto di Sassonia, who had written *De proportione motuum in velocitate* and the *Tractatus de proportione velocitatum in motibus.*

32. A. Richard Turner writes: "A mind thoroughly imbued with the methods of linear perspective would be not only ill-equipped to create the illusion of landscape space, but might even need to unlearn the precise and artificial limitations imposed by perspective" (*The Vision of Landscape in Renaissance Italy* [Princeton, 1976], 6).

33. See Martin Kemp, "Leonardo and the Visual Pyramid," *Journal of the Warburg and Courtauld Institutes* 40 (1977): 148.

34. Parenthetically, one might consider here José Ortega y Gasset's distinction between painting of mass and painting of space, which came together in Venetian art from Giorgione to Titian and Tintoretto. His comments do apply to Leonardo as well; see his *Velázquez, Goya and the Dehumanization of Art* (New York, 1972), 26–27.

35. See Kenneth Clark's "Leonardo and the Antique," in *Leonardo's Legacy*, ed. C. D. O'Malley (Berkeley and Los Angeles, 1969), 1–34.

36. Jane Dillenberger, *Style and Content in Christian Art* (New York, 1986), 31, 35.

37. Gilbert Highet, *The Migration of Ideas* (New York, 1954), 22, 27.

38. See Ferdinand Lot, *The End of the Ancient World and the Beginning of the Middle Ages* (New York, 1931), 147–49.

39. Neal Wood, "Machiavelli's Humanism of Action," in *The Political Calculus: Essays on Machiavelli's Philosophy*, ed. Anthony Parel (Toronto, 1972), 41, 57.

40. Frances Yates, *Giordano Bruno and the Hermetic Tradition* (New York, 1969), 1.

41. Henri Pirenne, "What Are Historians Trying to Do?" in *The Philosophy of History in Our Time*, ed. Meyerhoff, 89–93. See also Fernand Braudel's monumental *La Mediterranée* (1949), and his preface to Traian Stoianovich's *French Historical Method: The "Annales" Paradigm* (Ithaca, 1976), as well as Stoianovich's discussion of Braudel, in ibid., 15–17.

Chapter 4

1. Walter Wink, *John the Baptist in the Gospel Tradition* (Cambridge, 1968), 40.

2. H. R. Reynolds, *John the Baptist* (London, 1874), 12; Charles H. H. Scobie, *John the Baptist* (London, 1964), 213; Jean Danielon, *The Work of John the Baptist*

(Baltimore, 1966), 10; William Lyon Phelps, *Human Nature and the Gospel* (New York, 1925), 28–29.

3. See Dillenberger, *Style and Content in Christian Art*, 37.

4. See Giuseppe de Lorenzo, *Leonardo da Vinci e la geologia* (Bologna, 1920), esp. the conclusion, 185–89; Ettore Camesasca, *Mantegna* (Milan, 1964), 15.

5. Turner, *The Vision of Landscape in Renaissance Italy*, 20.

6. Term introduced by Donald S. Strong, "The Triumph of Mona Lisa: Science and the Allegory of Time," in *Leonardo e l'età della ragione*, ed. E. Bellone and P. Rossi (Milan, 1982), 263.

7. Quoted in P. C. Ritterbush, *The Art of Organic Forms* (Washington, D.C., 1968), 5–6; *Goethe's World View: Presented in His Reflections and Maxims* (New York, 1963), 105.

8. Leicester MS fol. 31a, translated in E. McCurdy's *The Mind of Leonardo da Vinci* (New York, 1939), 183.

9. See Ernesto Grassi, *Renaissance Humanism: Studies in Philosophy and Poetics* (Binghamton, 1988), 102.

10. Erwin Panofsky, *Studies in Iconology* (New York, 1972), 67.

11. See Walter F. Otto, *Dionysius: Myth and Cult* (Bloomington, 1965), 161–64.

12. See Jay Macpherson, *The Spirit of Solitude: Conventions and Continuities in Late Romance* (New Haven, 1982), 4–6; Giorgio de Santillana has called attention to Leonardo's plan for a treatise *On the World and the Waters* (F Manuscript of the Codex Atlanticus), in "Man Without Letters," in *Leonardo da Vinci: Aspects of the Renaissance Genius*, ed. Morris Philipson (New York, 1966), 200.

13. Jacopo Sannazaro, *Arcadia and Piscatorial Eclogues*, trans. R. Nash (Detroit, 1966), 135–36; see also Wyman H. Herendeen, *From Landscape to Literature: The River and the Myth of Geography* (Pittsburgh, 1986), 165–66.

14. Ebreo, *The Philosophy of Love*, 82–83, 90.

15. In his study of the "source" topos, David Quint refers to a "kind of epistemological anxiety, heightened by nostalgia, in the task of depicting a source which sanctioned what were otherwise 'counterfeit,' pure man-made fictions," in *Origin and Originality in Renaissance Literature: Versions of the Source* (New Haven, 1983), x. See also Herendeen, *From Landscape to Literature*, 119–23.

16. See Gerald Enscoe, *Eros and the Romantics: Sexual Love as a Theme in Coleridge, Shelley, and Keats* (The Hague, 1967), 31; J. B. Beer, *Coleridge the Visionary* (London, 1959), 210.

17. See E. C. Semple, *Geography of the Mediterranean Region: Its Relation to Ancient History* (New York, 1931).

18. See Eisler, "The Athlete of Virtue," 91–93.

19. Alexandre Masseron, *Saint Jean Baptiste dans l'Art* (Vichy, 1957).

20. Emile Mâle, *Les Saints Compagnons du Christ* (Paris, 1958), 27.

21. Kenneth Clark, *Looking at Pictures* (Boston, 1968), 165.

22. Schelling, *The Philosophy of Art*, 65. In one of those rare insights that does criticism honor, Robert Wallace finds at the center of the picture "perhaps the most wondrous interplay of hands in all art, protecting, worshiping, blessing, pointing" (*The World of Leonardo: 1452–1519* [New York, 1966], 35).

23. See Michael Levey, *High Renaissance* (Baltimore, 1987), 23.

24. Paul Claudel, *L'Oiseau Noir dans le Soleil Levant* (Paris, 1929), 228. See also Arden Reed, *Romantic Weather: The Climates of Coleridge and Baudelaire* (Hanover, 1983), 12; Michel Serres, *Hermes IV: La Distribution* (Paris, 1977), 9.

25. Ebreo, *The Philosophy of Love*, 124–25.

26. See Jean Rudhardt, *Le thème de l'eau primordiale dans la mythologie grecque*

(Berne, 1971), 18–19; Charles H. Kahn, *Anaximander and the Origins of Greek Cosmology* (New York, 1960), 202–3.

27. Bloch, *The Historian's Craft*, 30–32.

28. See Roger Hinks, *Myth and Allegory in Ancient Art* (London, 1939), 23–25; J. L. Myres, *Who Were the Greeks?* (Berkeley and Los Angeles, 1930), 167.

29. René Girard, "Disorder and Order in Mythology," in *Disordered Order: Proceedings of the Stanford International Symposium*, ed. P. Livingstone (Saratoga, 1984), 86. Such a "*rhétorique du désordre*," Gérard Genette insists, stems from an effort to define the other in negative terms; see his "Ordonnance du Chaos" (*Mouvements premiers: Etudes critiques offertes à Georges Poulet* [Paris, 1972], 44, 50).

30. See Kroeber, *British Romantic Art*, 151.

31. *De Hominis Dignitate e scritti vari*, ed. Eugenio Garin (Florence, 1942), 504; translation by the author.

32. Benedetto Croce, *Problemi di estetica e contributi alla storia dell'estetica italiana* (Bari, 1966), 243–46.

33. Gaston Bachelard, *Water Dreams: An Essay on the Imagination of Matter* (Dallas, 1983), 113.

34. I follow Margot Norris, *Beast of the Modern Imagination: Darwin, Nietzsche, Kafka, Ernst, Lawrence* (Baltimore, 1985), introduction, 1–25.

35. See G. S. Kirk's comments, in *Heraclitus: The Cosmic Fragments* (Cambridge, 1954), 147–48.

36. See illustrations from Codex Urbinas 240v, 232r, 232v, 234r, in E. H. Gombrich, *New Light on Old Masters: Studies in the Art of the Renaissance* (Chicago, 1986), 36–39.

37. Ebreo, *The Philosophy of Love*, 290.

38. In Eugenio Garin, *Astrology in the Renaissance: The Zodiac of Life* (London, 1983), 52–54.

39. See Grassi, *Renaissance Humanism*, 103.

40. Jung, *The Archetypes and the Collective Unconscious*, 21–22.

Chapter 5

1. See Mircea Eliade, *Mephistopheles and the Androgyne: Studies in Religious Myth and Symbol* (New York, 1965), 82.

2. Dmitri Merezhkovsky, *The Secret of the West* (London, 1936), 318–19.

3. Richard Bernheimer, *Wild Men in the Middle Ages: A Study in Art, Sentiment, and Demonology* (Cambridge, Mass., 1952), 23, 72, 9, 19–20; see also Lacy Collison-Morley, *The Story of the Sforzas* (New York, 1934), 158

4. Larry D. Benson, *Sir Gawain and the Green Knight* (New Brunswick, N.J., 1965), 79–80.

5. Michel Foucault, *The Order of Things* (New York, 1970), 330–31.

6. Elemire Zola, *The Androgyne: Fusion of the Sexes* (London, 1981), 55–56.

7. Johann Winckelmann, *History of Ancient Art*, vol. 2 (New York, 1968), 204–6.

8. Ebreo, *The Philosophy of Love*, 95–96. On the subject, see Marco Ariani, *Imago fabulosa: Mito e allegoria nei Dialoghi d'Amore di Leone Ebreo* (Rome, 1988), 42–43.

9. See T. Anthony Perry, *Erotic Spirituality: The Integrative Tradition from Leone Ebreo to John Donne* (University, Ala., 1980), esp. chaps. 1 and 6.

10. See James M. Suslow, *Ganymede in the Renaissance* (New Haven, 1986), 99. See also Marie Delcourt, *Hermaphrodite: Mythes et rites de la Bisexualité dans l'Antiquité classique* (Paris, 1958); Jerome Schwartz, "Scatology and Escatology in Gargantua's Androgyne Device," *Etudes Rabelaisiennes* 14 (1977): 268–69; Carla Freccero, "The Other and the Same: The Image of the Hermaphrodite in Rabelais," in *Rewriting the Renaissance: The Discourses of Sexual Difference in Early Modern Europe*, ed. Margaret W. Ferguson, Maureen Quilligan, and Nancy Vickers (Chicago, 1986), 145–58.

11. Matteo Palmieri, *Vita civile*, ed. Gino Belloni (Florence, 1982), 159; translation by the author.

12. See Northrop Frye, *Fearful Symmetry: A Study of William Blake* (Princeton, 1947), 135, 301. On the subject, W.J.T. Mitchell writes: "Blake considers space and time, like the sexes, to be contraries whose reconciliation occurs not when one becomes like the other, but when they approach a condition in which these categories cease to function" ("Blake's Composite Art," in *Modern Critical Views*, ed. Harold Bloom [New York, 1985], 73). See also Thomas R. Frosch, "Art and Eden: The Sexes," in *Modern Critical Views*, ed. Bloom, 106.

13. As Nicolas Berdyaev writes, the beginning was the end: "Androgyny is the ultimate union of male and female in a higher God-like being, the ultimate conquest of decadence and strife, the restoration in man of the image and likeness of God" (*The Meaning of the Creative Act* [New York, 1962], 207). On less lofty grounds, such a hybrid irritated Bernard Berenson, who could not understand—let alone explain—why "that fleshy female should pretend to be the virile, sundried Baptist," who was in fact reduced to an "epicene creature with an equivocal leer" ("An Attempt at Revaluation," in *Leonardo da Vinci: Aspects of the Renaissance Genius* [New York, 1948], 115, 121). Posterity also found in Leonardo's Baptist *"le canon de Polyclète, qui s'appelle l'androgyne . . . qui est le sexe artistique par excellence"* (Josephin Peladan, Epilogue, in *Leonardo da Vinci: conferenze fiorentine*, 308). On the iconography of the Baptist, see Marilyn Aronberg Lavin, "Giovannino Battista: A Study in Renaissance Religious Symbolism," *Art Bulletin* 37 (1955): 99–100.

14. See Mâle, *Les Saints Compagnons du Christ*, 49. See also Eliade, *Mephistopheles and the Androgyne*, 89–90. With regard to the dialogic of Baptist and Christ, Michel Foucault writes in a broader context: "The original in man is that which articulates him from the very outset upon something other than himself" (*The Order of Things*, 331). On anatomy as destiny, see Alan Friedman's imaginative, *Hermaphrodeity* (New York, 1972), 24. On Tiresias's binary perspective in T. S. Eliot's *The Waste Land*, see Jewel S. Brooker and Joseph Bentley, *Reading The Waste Land: Modernism and the Limits of Interpretation* (Amherst, 1990), chap. 2, "Unifying Incompatible Worlds: The Sibyl of Cumae and Tiresias," 34–59.

15. Rudolph Wittkower, *Allegory and the Migration of Symbols* (London, 1977), 149. See also Ernest William Parsons, "The Significance of John the Baptist for the Beginning of Christianity," in *Environmental Factors in Christian History*, ed. J. McNeill, M. Spinka, H. Willoughby (New York, 1970), 2–3. See also Scobie, *John the Baptist*, 204.

16. See A. Bartlett Giamatti, "Primitivism and the Process of Civility in Spenser's *Fairie Queene*," in Fredi Chiappelli, *First Images of America: The Impact of the New World on the Old* (Berkeley and Los Angeles, 1976), 73–74.

17. I follow here my own, *The Cornucopian Mind and the Baroque Unity of the*

Arts, chap. 1 on Michelangelo, 13–46. See also Paul Barolsky, *Michelangelo's Nose: A Myth and Its Maker* (University Park, 1990), 65–67.

18. Marsilio Ficino, *Commentary on Plato's Symposium,* trans. Jayne Sears (Columbus, 1944), 155.

19. For an illustration of the small wood panel and comments, see Robert Kimbrough, *Shakespeare and the Art of Humankindness: The Essay toward Androgyny* (London, 1990), 186–87.

20. See Jerome Schwartz, "Aspects of Androgyny in the Renaissance," in *Human Sexuality in the Middle Ages and Renaissance,* vol. 4, ed. D. Radcliff-Umstead (Pittsburgh, 1980), esp. 122–24. In antiquity, the hermaphrodite was considered an unworthy form of physical aberration.

21. Hayden White, "The Forms of Wildness: Archaeology of an Idea," in E. Dudley and M. Novak, *The Wild Man Within: An Image in Western Thought from the Renaissance to Romanticism* (Pittsburgh, 1972), 4–5, 13–14.

22. I follow comments and translation by A.J.L. Busst, "The Image of the Androgyne in the Nineteenth Century," in *Romantic Mythologies,* ed. Ian Fletcher (London, 1967), 1–96. See also Robert Kimbrough's introduction to *Shakespeare and the Art of Humankindness,* 1–13. French and English decadents of the nineteenth century centered on static and morbid hermaphroditism, in which fusion rarely exceeded a superabundance of erotic possibilities; see Eliade, *Mephistopheles and the Androgyne,* 99–100. See also Praz, *The Romantic Agony.*

23. See Bernard McGinn, *Visions of the End: Apocalyptic Traditions in the Middle Ages* (New York, 1979), 8.

24. Gilbert Durand, *On the Disfiguration of the Image of Man in the West* (New York, 1977), 21, 24.

25. See Mircea Eliade, *The Sacred and the Profane* (New York, 1961), 106.

26. Roland Barthes, *S/Z* (New York, 1974), 62, 76.

Chapter 6

1. See Samuel Y. Edgerton, Jr., "The Renaissance Development of the Scientific Illustration," in *Science and the Arts in the Renaissance,* ed. John W. Shirley and F. David Heoniger (London, 1985), 184. See also Arthur F. Kinney, *Continental Humanist Poetics: Studies in Erasmus, Castiglione, Marguerite de Navarre, Rabelais, and Cervantes* (Amherst, 1989), 87.

2. In a letter to Francesco Vettori (April 16, 1513), in *The Letters of Machiavelli,* trans. A. Gilbert (New York, 1961), 104. See also Giorgio Bárberi-Squarotti, *Machiavelli o la scelta della letteratura* (Rome, 1987), 63, 232–33.

3. In Leon Battista Alberti, *De Re Aedificatoria,* trans. J. Rykwert, N. Leich, and R. Tavernor, *On the Art of Building in Ten Books* (Cambridge, 1988), 4.

4. Ibid., 3–5.

5. For historical data, I follow Nicolaus Pevsner, "The Term 'Architect' in the Middle Ages," *Speculum* 17 (1942): 549–62, esp. 549–51, 558; and Richard Goldthwaite's extensive and thoughtful treatment of the subject within a socioeconomic context in *The Building of Renaissance Florence: An Economic and Social History* (Baltimore, 1980), 351–96. See also Mary Hollingsworth, "The Architect in Fifteenth-Century Florence," *Art History* 7 (1984): 385–410.

6. As John U. Nef writes, "in the fifteenth and sixteenth centuries physical suffering, capital punishment, and the infliction of excruciating pain by torture and

other corporal violence had long been taken for granted to an extent which shocked civilized Western society in the eighteenth and nineteenth centuries" (*War and Human Progress* [Cambridge, 1950], 114). See also Bern Dibner, "Leonardo: Prophet of Automation," in his *Leonardo da Vinci: Technologist* (Norwalk, 1969), 46.

7. See Kenneth Burke, *A Rhetoric of Motives* (Berkeley, 1969), 160–61.

8. E. H. Gombrich, *The Heritage of Apelles: Studies in the Art of the Renaissance* (Edinburgh, 1976), 42.

9. Alberti, *Dinner Pieces,* 172.

10. Ezio Raimondi, "Machiavelli and the Rhetoric of the Warrior," *Modern Language Notes* 92 (1977): 13–14.

11. See Fernand Braudel, *Capitalism and Material Life 1400–1800* (London, 1973), 288. Johan Huizinga's pages on warfare as heroic ceremonial or ludic performance remain exemplary, in *The Waning of the Middle Ages* (New York, 1954), 96–98.

12. See C. C. Bayley's comments, *War and Society in Renaissance Florence: The De Militia of Leonardo Bruni* (Toronto, 1961), 168–71.

13. *Letters from Petrarch,* 196. And he adds: "No peace lasts in our world, no wars end, since we are not strong enough to live at peace or to finish a war with these mercenaries" (197). See also Michael Mallet, *Mercenaries and Their Masters: Warfare in Renaissance Italy* (Totowa, 1974), 2; J. K. Anderson, *Military Theory and Practice in the Age of Xenophon* (Berkeley and Los Angeles, 1970), 1.

14. See Charles Oman, *A History of the Art of War in the Sixteenth Century* (New York, 1937), 90–91.

15. Edwin Mullins, *Great Paintings* (New York, 1981), 182–83.

16. See Robert Black, *Benedetto Accolti and the Florentine Renaissance* (Cambridge, 1985), 315–17; Felix Gilbert, *Niccolò Machiavelli e la vita culturale del suo tempo* (Bologna, 1964), chap. "L'Arte della Guerra," 192–229.

17. See André Chastel, *The Myth of the Renaissance: 1420–1520* (Geneva, 1969), 29.

18. Raimondi, "Machiavelli and the Rhetoric of the Warrior," 3.

19. See the biographer Vespasiano da Bisticci, *Renaissance Princes, Popes, and Prelates: The Vespasiano Memoirs* (New York, 1963), 103.

20. Frederick L. Taylor, *The Art of War: 1494–1529* (Cambridge, 1921), 7–9.

21. J. R. Hale, "Industria del libro e cultura militare a Venezia nel Rinascimento," *Storia della cultura veneta,* 3, no. 2 (Vicenza, 1980): 248. For a systematic illustration of the epistolary items, see Kenneth D. Keele, *Leonardo da Vinci's Elements of the Science of Man* (New York, 1983), 11–18. See also Ivor B. Hart, *The World of Leonardo da Vinci: Man of Science, Engineer and Dreamer of Flight* (London, 1961), 290–95. For the context of the Moor's problems with the transportation of artillery pieces, see Braudel, *Capitalism and Material Life,* 287. See also J. R. Hale, "Gunpowder and the Renaissance: An Essay in the History of Ideas," in *From the Renaissance to the Counter-Reformation: Essays in Honor of Garrett Mattingly,* ed. C. H. Carter (New York, 1965), 117, 121–22.

22. Claudio Guillén, *Entre lo uno y lo diverso: Introduccíon a la literatura comparada* (Barcelona, 1985), 202–3; and "Notes toward the Study of the Renaissance Letter," in *Renaissance Genres: Essays on Theory, History, and Interpretation,* ed. Barbara K. Lewalski (Cambridge, 1986), 70–101.

23. See Gombrich, *New Light on Old Masters,* 108–9.

24. Burke, *A Rhetoric of Motives,* 164.

25. Quoted in Collison-Morley, *The Story of the Sforzas,* 159.

26. Highet, *The Migration of Ideas,* 74–75.

27. Thomas Greene, "The End of Discourse in Machiavelli's 'Prince,' " *Yale French Studies* 67 (1984): 58.

28. Walter Pater, *The Renaissance* (London, 1910), 104.

29. Lewis Mumford, *Technics and Civilization* (New York, 1963), 88.

30. See Leo Marx, *The Machine in the Garden: Technology and the Pastoral Ideal in America* (New York, 1964), 214.

31. E. R. Chamberlain, *The Fall of the House of Borgias* (New York, 1974), 270.

32. See Dionisotti, "Leonardo uomo di lettere," 195; Samuel Y. Edgerton, Jr., *Pictures and Punishment: Art and Criminal Prosecution during the Florentine Renaissance* (Ithaca, 1985), 106.

33. Kurt Marek, *Yestermorrow: Notes on Man's Progress* (New York, 1961), 12.

34. Visually speaking, we should look at the studies for the battle to which Cecil Gould refers in his detailed analysis, *Leonardo the Artist and the Non-Artist* (Boston, 1975), 129–42.

Chapter 7

1. C. P. Snow, *The Two Cultures and the Scientific Revolution* (New York, 1961).

2. Jacques Barzun, *Science: The Glorious Entertainment* (New York, 1964), 286. See Julian Huxley's *Literature and Science* (New York, 1963), 1–2, 188.

3. See Paul Valéry, *Note et Digression,* as translated in *Leonardo da Vinci: Aspects of the Renaissance Genius,* ed. Philipson, 382. The problem of the "two cultures" is obviously as old as Socrates. In Galileo's time, Maurice A. Finocchiaro reminds us, the terminology was different, and the contrasting terms were "philosophy" and "mathematics." In his petition for the post of scientific adviser to the grand duke of Tuscany, "Galileo was rather fussy about his title. He asked for, and eventually obtained, the title of 'philosopher' besides that of 'mathematician' " ("The Two Cultures Today: A Third Look," in *The Languages of Creativity: Models, Problem-Solving, Discourse,* vol. 2 [London, 1986], 13–14). See also E. J. Dijksterhuis, *The Mechanization of the World Picture* (Oxford, 1961), 74–75.

4. Benjamin Farrington, "Vesalius and the Ruin of Ancient Medicine," *Modern Quarterly* 1 (1938): 23; Rodolfo Mondolfo, *Alle origini della filosofia e della cultura* (Bologna, 1956), 125–49; Paolo Rossi, *Philosophy, Technology, and the Arts in the Early Modern Era* (New York, 1970), 146–50.

5. Gabriel Marcel, *Searchings* (New York, 1967), 46.

6. I follow Nelson Goodman, *Languages of Art* (Indianapolis, 1976), 242.

7. Octavio Paz, *The Bow and the Lyre. The Poem. The Poetic Revelation. Poetry and History* (Austin, 1973), 243.

8. See Marx, *The Machine in the Garden,* 192.

9. Frederick Ahl, *Metaformations: Soundplay and Wordplay in Ovid and Other Classical Poets* (Ithaca, 1985), 252; see also Vincent Cronin, *The Golden Honeycomb* (New York, 1954), 12–16.

10. See Michael Ayrton, "The Path of Daedalus," in *Virgil,* ed. D. R. Dudley (New York, 1969), 176–202; John Cohen, *Human Robots in Myth and Science* (New York, 1967), 95.

11. Clive Hart, *Images of Flight* (Berkeley and Los Angeles, 1988), 89; and *The Prehistory of Flight* (Berkeley and Los Angeles, 1985), 209.

12. *Metrologum de pisce cane et volucre* (Bologna, Biblioteca Universitaria, MS

2705, fol. 77r; as translated in Clive Hart, *The Dream of Flight: Aeronautics from Classical Times to the Renaissance* (London, 1972), 19.

13. See Harry Levin's comments in *The Overreacher: A Study of Christopher Marlowe* (Cambridge, 1952), 119.

14. Hart, *The Dream of Flight,* 20.

15. Leonard Barkan, *The Gods Made Flesh: Metamorphosis and the Pursuit of Paganism* (New Haven, 1986), 73–75.

16. See Marcel Brion, *Leonard de Vinci* (Paris, 1964), 324.

17. See Charles Gibbs-Smith, *Leonardo da Vinci: Aeronautics* (London, 1967), 3–5.

18. For comments and illustrations, see ibid., 13–14.

19. Mary B. Campbell, *The Witness and the Other World: Exotic European Travel Writing 400–1600* (Ithaca, 1988), 1–2.

20. Denis Donoghue, *Thieves of Fire* (London, 1973), 25.

21. Martin Heidegger, *The Question Concerning Technology and Other Essays* (New York, 1977), 13; F. E. Peter's entry on *techne* in *Greek Philosophical Terms: A Historical Lexicon* (New York, 1967), 190–91.

22. As Paolo Rossi writes, Leonardo was more concerned "with the elaboration rather than the execution of his projects; he was interested in machines more as the result and proof of human intelligence than as a means for the actual mastery of nature" (*Philosophy, Technology, and the Arts in the Early Modern Era,* 27–28).

23. Gerolamo Cardano, *Letters from Petrarch,* trans. Morris Bishop (Bloomington, 1966), 174.

24. Quoted in Claude C. Albritton, *The Abyss of Time* (San Francisco, 1980), 38.

25. Valéry, *Leonardo. Poe. Mallarmé,* 70, 79.

26. John Hale, *Renaissance Exploration* (New York, 1986), 9. See also J.F.C. Fuller, *Decisive Battles of the Western World and Their Influence upon History,* vol. 1 (London, 1954–55), 470; George Sarton, *Six Wings: Men of Science in the Renaissance* (Bloomington, 1957), 5.

27. Paul Tillich, *Theology of Culture* (New York, 1959), 34. See also John E. Boodin, "The Discovery of Form," in *Roots of Scientific Thought: A Cultural Perspective,* ed. P. Wiener and A. Noland (New York, 1957), 71; Edgar Zilsel, "The Genesis of the Concept of Scientific Progress," in *Roots of Scientific Thought,* ed. Wiener and Noland, 25–47; A. C. Crombie, "From Rationalism to Experimentalism," in *Roots of Scientific Thought,* ed. Weiner and Noland, 126–27.

28. See John H. Randall, "Scientific Method in the School of Padua," in *Roots of Scientific Thought,* ed. Weiner and Noland, 139–49.

29. Jacob Bronowski, *Science and Human Values* (New York, 1965), 63.

30. See Deno John Geanakopolos, *Interaction of the "Sibling": Byzantine and Western Cultures in the Middle Ages and Italian Renaissance (330–1600)* (New Haven, 1976), 293.

31. See Anderson, *Military Theory and Practice in the Age of Xenophon,* 158–59. Light chariots used for races were never brought to battle; see P.A.L. Greehalgh, *Early Greek Warfare: Horsemen and Chariots in the Homeric and Archaic Ages* (Cambridge, 1973), 8–9, 39; John Warry, *Warfare in the Classical World* (New York, 1980), 83; Bern Dibner, *Leonardo da Vinci: Military Engineer* (New York, 1946), 11; Lawrence Keppie, *The Making of the Roman Army: From Republic to Empire* (Totowa, N.Y., 1984), 43, 46.

32. Michael J. B. Allen, *Marsilio Ficino and the Phaedran Charioteer* (Berkeley and Los Angeles, 1981), 3–4.

33. Francesco di Giorgio, *Trattati di Architettura ingegneria e Arte Militare,* 2 vols.,

ed. Corrado Maltese (Milan, 1967), 1: 6; 2: 424; translations by the author. See also Cesare Vasoli, "A proposito di scienza e tecnica nel Cinquecento," in his *Profezia e ragione: Studi sulla cultura del Cinquecento e del Seicento* (Naples, 1974), 483, 487; Eugenio Garin, "La cultura a Milano all fine del Quattrocento," in *Milano nell'età di Ludovico il Moro*, vol. 1 (Milan, 1983), 25. See also John Hale, *Renaissance War Studies* (London, 1987), 392; Martin Kemp, "The Quattrocento Vocabulary of Creation, Inspiration, and Genius in the Visual Arts," *Viator* 8 (1977): 347–99.

34. See Kenneth Burke, *A Grammar of Motives* (Berkeley and Los Angeles, 1974), 109–10.

35. Ladislao Reti, "Leonardo da Vinci the Technologist: The Problem of Prime Movers," in *Leonardo's Legacy*, ed. O'Malley, 72–73.

36. See Bern Dibner, "Leonardo: Prophet of Automation" in *Leonardo's Legacy*, ed. O'Malley, 106–9.

37. See John U. Nef, *Cultural Foundations of the Industrial Revolution* (Cambridge, 1958), 7–10.

38. See Mumford, *Technics and Civilization*, 187; Alex Keller, "A Renaissance Humanist Looks at 'New' Inventions: 'The Article Horologium' in Giovanni Tortelli's *De Orthographia*," *Technology and Culture* 11 (1970): 352.

39. Alfred von Martin, *Sociology of the Renaissance* (New York, 1963), 16; Michael Baxandall, *Painting and Experience in Fifteenth-Century Italy* (Oxford, 1972), 86–87.

40. Jacob Bronowski, *The Ascent of Man* (Boston, 1973), 429. Also Deno John Geanaklopos, *Greek Scholars in Venice* (Cambridge, 1962), 266, 271.

41. Vespasiano da Bisticci, *Renaissance Princes, Popes, and Prelates*, 104. See also Eugene S. Ferguson, "The Mind's Eye: Nonverbal Thought in Technology," *Science* 197 (1977): 829.

42. Ricardo Quinones, *The Renaissance Discovery of Time* (Cambridge, 1972), 5–6, 197–98.

43. Braudel, *Capitalism and Material Life*, 288.

44. See Alethea Hayter, *Opium and the Romantic Imagination* (Berkeley and Los Angeles, 1968), 93–98.

45. Norris, *Beast of the Modern Imagination*, 20–21.

46. Nicolas Berdyaev, *The Beginning and the End* (New York, 1957), 224; Claus Westerman reminds us that, "to celebrate creation is to be aware of catastrophe" (*Beginning and End in the Bible* [Philadelphia, 1972], 25).

47. See Norris, *Beast of the Modern Imagination*, 16–17.

48. Martin Buber writes on the subject: "Whenever man shudders before the menace of his own work and longs to flee from the radically demanding historical hour, there he finds himself near to the apocalyptic vision of a process that cannot be arrested" (*On the Bible* [New York, 1968], 183).

49. See K. R. Eissler's thoughtful comments in his *Leonardo da Vinci: Psychoanalytic Notes on the Enigma* (New York, 1961), 273.

50. Michael Murrin, *The Veil of Allegory: Some Notes toward a Theory of Allegorical Rhetoric in the English Renaissance* (Chicago, 1971), 29–31. See also Angus Fletcher, *The Prophetic Moment: An Essay on Spenser* (Chicago, 1971), 5.

51. See Cullmann, *Christ and Time*, 97–100.

52. See Edmund Dehnert, "The Dialectic of Technology and Culture," in *The Languages of Creativity*, vol. 2, 136–37.

53. Kenneth Clark, *The Concept of Universal Man* (Ditchley Park, 1972), 18.

54. Alfred Chapuis and Edmond Droz, *Automata: A Historical and Technological Study* (New York, 1958), 394–96.

55. Derek de Solla Price, *Science since Babylon* (New Haven, 1975), 131.
56. Mircea Eliade, *Myth and Reality* (New York, 1963), 13–14.
57. Georg Juenger, *The Failure of Technology* (Chicago, 1956), 200.

Chapter 8

1. Kim H. Veltman, *Studies in Leonardo da Vinci: Linear Perspective and the Visual Dimensions of Science and Art,* vol.1 (Munich, 1986), 128–33. This volume contains a wealth of illustrations. And Antonio Averlino, known as Filarete, *Treatise on Architecture,* vol. 1, trans. John R. Spencer (New Haven, 1965), 15.

2. I follow Florence M. Weinberg's comments, *The Cave: The Evolution of a Metaphoric Field from Homer to Ariosto* (New York, 1986), 92. See also Karl Kerenyi, *Labyrinth: Studien* (Zurich, 1950), 13–16.

3. *Treatise on Architecture,* vol. 1, 7. Also, Louis Marin, *Food for Thought* (Baltimore, 1989), 107.

4. Nicolas Berdyaev, "Man and Machine," in *Philosophy and Technology,* ed. C. Mitcham and R. Mackey (New York, 1972), 205.

5. Levey, *Early Renaissance,* 121. On *nostos* and return, see Perl, *The Tradition of Return,* 17–34. On Leonardo's originality vis-à-vis the Vitruvian precedent, see Michelle Murray, "Leonardo e Vitruvio," in *Roma, centro ideale della cultura dell'Antico nei secoli xv and xvi,* ed. Silvia Danesi Squarzina (Milan, 1989), 213; G. Hersey, *Pythagorean Palaces: Magic and Architecture in the Italian Renaissance* (London, 1976), 97–100.

6. Rudolph Wittkower, *Architectural Principles in the Age of Humanism* (New York, 1971), ii.

7. Leonard Barkan, *Nature's Work of Art: The Human Body as Image of the World* (New Haven, 1975), 10–21; R. G. Collingwood, *The Idea of Nature* (Oxford, 1965), 49–55.

8. See Robert Graves, *The White Goddess: A Historical Grammar of Poetic Myth* (New York, 1966), 410.

9. I refer to Leonard Barkan's unpublished essay, "In Bed with Polyclitus: Ancient Art, Renaissance Aesthetics," 7, 8–10, 25, which he read at the conference on Mannerism and Eccentricity held at Indiana University, March 27–29, 1991.

10. See Lewis Mumford, *The Transformations of Man* (New York, 1956); Roderick Seidenberg, *Post-Historic Man* (Chapel Hill, 1950).

11. I follow text and illustrations in S. K. Heninger, Jr., *The Cosmological Glass: Renaissance Diagrams of the Universe* (San Marino, 1977), 107.

12. See text, illustration, and criticism in ibid., 145–46.

13. Bruno Munaro, *Discovery of the Square* (New York, 1965), 5, 32; Erwin Panofsky, *Meaning in the Visual Arts* (New York, 1955), 89; Eco, *Art and Beauty in the Middle Ages,* 35–36. See also Frye, *Fearful Symmetry,* 104.

14. In *The Human Figure by Albrecht Dürer,* ed. Walter L. Strauss (New York, 1972), 206.

15. Alessandro Parronchi's comments on Pollaiolo's science of the human body also shed light on Leonardo, in *Opere giovanili di Michelangelo* (Florence, 1968), 27. See also L. Premuda, *Storia dell'iconografia anatomica* (Milan, 1957).

16. Nicolas Cusanus, *De conjecturis* II, 13; as translated in Georges Poulet's *Metamorphosis of the Circle* (Baltimore, 1966), 8.

17. Kenneth Clark, *The Nude* (New York, 1956), 38.

18. See Devon L. Hodges, *Renaissance Fictions of Anatomy* (Amherst, 1985), 2–3; Walter Ong, *Ramus, Method, and the Decay of Dialogue* (Cambridge, 1958), 315. After 1509, Martin Kemp writes, Leonardo's research on anatomy steered "towards the resolution of functions to fit known forms; and away from the creation of forms to fit preconceived functions, the approach which had dominated his *quattrocento* researches" ("Dissection and Divinity in Leonardo's Late Anatomies," *Journal of the Warburg and Courtauld Institutes* 35 [1972]: 200).

19. The sonnet is by Rachel Annand Taylor, from "Anatomical Studies," in *Adam, International Review* (London, 1952).

20. See Parronchi, *Opere giovanili di Michelangelo*, 19–23; Jean Rousselot, *Medicine in Art: A Cultural History* (New York, 1967), esp. 131–63; Mario Bucci, *Anatomia come arte* (Florence, 1969).

21. See Belt, *Leonardo the Anatomist*, 41; see also Erwin Panofsky, "Artist, Scientist, Genius: Notes on the Renaissance *Dämmerung*," in *The Renaissance* (New York, 1962), 141–47.

22. See Rossi, *Philosophy, Technology, and the Arts in the Early Modern Era*, 7–8; Farrington, "Vesalius and the Ruin of Ancient Medicine," 23.

23. Hodges, *Renaissance Fictions of Anatomy*, 5–6.

24. Panofsky, *Meaning in the Visual Arts*, 94.

25. On the modern concept of observation guided by theoretical principles, see Werner Heisenberg, *The Physicist's Conception of Nature* (New York, 1958), 87. See also Omar Calabrese, *La macchina della pittura* (Bari, 1985), 3.

26. Panofsky, *Meaning in the Visual Arts*, 105.

27. Kim Veltman, *Studies in Leonardo da Vinci*, vol. 1, 15–16.

28. Fernán Pérez de Oliva, *Diálogo de la dignidad del hombre* (Madrid, 1975), 63–64.

29. William James, *Essays in Radical Empiricism* (Cambridge, Mass., 1976), 86.

30. See Hans Jonas, *The Phenomenon of Life: Toward a Philosophical Biology* (New York, 1966), 91.

31. See Leon Kass, "Regarding the End of Medicine and the Pursuit of Health," *The Public Interest* 40 (1975): 27–29.

32. Paul Valéry, *Dialogues* (New York, 1956), 90–92, 81.

33. See John Onians, "On How to Listen to High Renaissance Art," *Art History* 7 (1984): 411–37.

34. On the subject of geometric figures, see Marisa Dalai Emiliani, "Figure rinascimentali dei poliedri platonici. Qualche problema di storia e di autografia," in *Fra Rinascimento, Manierismo e Realtà*, ed. Pietro C. Marani (Florence, 1984), 7–16. On numerology and Renaissance poetics, see Alastair Fowler, *Spenser and the Numbers of Time* (New York, 1964), especially "Numerological Criticism," 237–57, and Appendix I, "The Numerological Stanza," 260–88.

Chapter 9

1. Alberti, *On the Art of Building in Ten Books*, 3, 98–99.

2. Levey, *Early Renaissance*, 80.

3. Benedetto Varchi, *Trattati d'arte del Cinquecento*, 3 vols., ed. Paola Barocchi (Bari, 1964), 1: 16; 2: 172; translations by the author. Varchi's text is translated by David Summers, *Michelangelo and the Language of Art* (Princeton, 1981), 210–11;

see his comments, pp. 103, 109–10, 128–29. On Leonardo, see Kemp, *Leonardo da Vinci*, 160.

4. See Campbell, *The Witness and the Other World*, 77.

5. See Nicole Dacos, *La découverte de la Domus Aurea et la formation des grotesques à la Renaissance* (London, 1969), 122–28; Gombrich, *The Heritage of Apelles*, 57. See also my *The Portrait of Eccentricity: Arcimboldo and the Mannerist Grotesque* (University Park, Pa., 1991).

6. Panofsky, *Meaning in the Visual Arts*, 271. See also Gombrich, *The Heritage of Apelles*, 62.

7. See figures 12491, 12492, 12501 in Kenneth Clark's *Catalogue of the Drawings of Leonardo da Vinci in the Royal Collection of His Majesty the King at Windsor Castle*, 2 vols. (New York, 1935).

8. Gombrich, *The Heritage of Apelles*, 61.

9. See ibid., 57–58, illustrations no. 114, 115. At that stage of antihumanist polemic, Leonardo set up a parody of tradition when he accompanied Petrarch's quote "*cosa bella mortal passa e non dura*" (a beautiful mortal thing passes away and lasts not) with a scribble of an ugly old woman. Likewise, he wrote on the poet's *lauro*: "If Petrarch loved the laurel—*lauro*—so much it was because it is good with sausage and thrushes" (McCurdy, 1058).

10. I follow here John Freccero's thoughtful essay on Dante's Medusa, in his *Dante: The Poetics of Conversion* (Cambridge, Mass., 1986), esp. 121, 132.

11. As translated in Jean Starobinski, *The Living Eye* (Cambridge, Mass., 1989), 71. Comments by Starobinski in ibid., 70; and *Jean-Jacques Rousseau: Transparency and Obstruction* (Chicago, 1988), 71. For Ovidian relationships between the myths of Narcissus and Pygmalion, see Eleanor W. Leach, "Ekphrasis and the Theme of Artistic Failure in Ovid's Metamorphoses," *Ramus* 3 (1974): 125; Gianpiero Rosati, *Narciso e Pigmalione: Illusione e spettacolo nelle Metamorfosi di Ovidio* (Florence, 1983); J. Hillis Miller, *Versions of Pygmalion* (Cambridge, Mass., 1990), 8. The Gombrich quote is from *Art and Illusion: A Study in the Psychology of Pictorial Representation* (Princeton, 1972), 97. See also Wilfred Cude, "Mary Shelley's Modern Prometheus: A Study in Ethics of Scientific Creativity," *Dalhousie Review* 52 (1972): 219.

12. In Vasari's *The Lives of the Artists*, ed. and trans. by Julia Conaway Bondanella and Peter Bondanella (Oxford, 1991). I acknowledge their permission to quote from this book.

13. See Geoffrey Hartman, *The Unmediated Vision: An Interpretation of Wordsworth, Hopkins, Rilke, and Valéry* (New York, 1966), 156.

14. On the subject, see Rilke as quoted in *The Modern Tradition: Backgrounds of Modern Literature*, ed. R. Ellman and C. Feidelson, Jr. (New York, 1965), 24.

15. See Danile Hughes, "Shelley, Leonardo, and the Monsters of Thought," *Criticism* 12 (1970): 199.

16. See the stimulating study by Carol Jacobs, *Uncontainable Romanticism: Shelley, Brontë, Kleist* (Baltimore, 1989), 3–18. See also Mario Praz, who opens his study of romanticism with a reference to Shelley's poem on the Medusa. He also closes the chapter by relating Medusa to the smile of Mona Lisa, in *The Romantic Agony*, 25–45.

17. That work paved the way for a whole series of figures (Janus Vitalis's *De monstro nato* of 1545; Ulisse Aldrovandi's *Monstrorum historia* of 1642) whose human forms are in fact devoid of any real humanity. See Carlo Pedretti, *The Codex Atlanticus of L. da Vinci*, pt. 2 (New York, 1978), pl. 10.

18. Lewis Mumford, *The Myth of the Machine: The Pentagon of Power* (New York, 1970), 72.

19. J.B.S. Haldane, *Daedalus or Science and the Future* (New York, 1925), 49.

20. See Patricia S. Warrick, *The Cybernetic Imagination in Science Fiction* (Cambridge, 1980), 33–38.

21. Giorgio de Santillana, *The Age of Adventure* (New York, 1966), 72.

22. See Levin, *The Overreacher,* 107–36.

23. Ayrton, *The Testament of Daedalus,* 41, 24.

24. Ibid., 24.

25. André Gide so worded a similar attitude: " 'Poor dear boy,' said Daedalus. 'As he thought he could never escape from the labyrinth and did not understand that the labyrinth was within himself' " (*Two Legends: Oedipus and Theseus,* 89–90). This is a far cry from the Neoplatonic *élan* toward spiritual heights that inspired much Renaissance literature; see Leo Spitzer, "The Poetic Treatment of a Platonic-Christian Theme," in his *Romanische Literaturstudien 1936–56* (Tübingen, 1959), 130–59.

26. Roberto Calasso, *Le nozze di Cadmo e Armonia* (Milan, 1988), 24–25.

27. Susan Gubar, " 'The Blank Page' and the Issue of Female Creativity," *Critical Inquiry* 8 (1981): 244. See also Stephen Mason, *A History of the Sciences* (New York, 1962), 340.

28. *Leonardo da Vinci on the Human Body,* ed. C. D. O'Malley and J. B. Sanders (New York, 1952), 215.

29. For the technological interpretation, see Martin Tropp, *Mary Shelley's Monster* (Boston, 1977), 65–67; and Chris Baldick's rejection, in *Frankenstein's Shadow: Myth, Monstrosity and Nineteenth-Century Writing* (Oxford, 1987), 7–8. On romantic attitudes toward myth, see Samuel H. Vasbinder, *Scientific Attitudes in Mary Shelley's Frankenstein* (Ann Arbor, 1984), 46–48; Burton R. Pollin, "Philosophical and Literary Sources of Frankenstein," *Comparative Literature* 17 (1965): 100; Paul A. Cantor, *Creature and Creator: Myth-Making and English Romanticism* (Cambridge, Mass., 1984), xi–xii. From a thematic standpoint, see Theodore Ziolkowski, *Varieties of Literary Thematics* (Princeton, 1983), esp. 181–83.

30. George Steiner, *Real Presences: Is There Anything in What We Say?* (London, 1989), 208.

31. Ernst Fischer, *Art Against Ideology* (New York, 1969), 82–83.

32. William Barrett, *The Illusion of Technique* (New York, 1978), 20.

33. *The Complete Essays of Montaigne,* trans. D. Frame (Stanford, 1968), 292–93. See also François Rigolot's treatment of the myth with regard to Montaigne in his unpublished paper, "*Nulla ars in se versatur:* Montaigne's Anti-Mannerist Mannerism," which he delivered at the Conference on Mannerism at the Crossroad: Eccentricity and Interdisciplinarity, Indiana University, March 1991.

34. George Steiner, *Extra-territorial: Papers on Literature and the Language Revolution* (New York, 1971), 177.

35. William Barrett, *The Illusion of Technique: A Search for Meaning in a Technological Civilization* (New York, 1978), 210–11.

36. Steiner, *Extra-territorial,* 196.

37. See Barkan's comments, *The Gods Made Flesh,* 30–31.

38. Cassirer, *The Individual and the Cosmos in Renaissance Philosophy,* 96–97. See also Lynn White's conclusive remarks in his essay, "The Act of Invention: Causes, Contexts, Continuities, and Consequences," in *Technology and Culture: An Anthology,* ed. M. Kranzberg and W. H. Davenport (New York, 1972), 288–89. On the ethics of science and Mary Shelley, I follow Ziolkowski, *Varieties of Literary Thematics,* 185, and Cude, "Mary Shelley's Modern Prometheus," 212–25.

39. See Robert Graves, *The Greek Myths,* vol. 1 (New York, 1957), 129.
40. See the conclusion of Perl, *The Tradition of Return,* 282.

Chapter 10

1. Carpenter, *The Esthetic Basis of Greek Art,* 130.
2. See Nello Ponente, *Who Was Raphael?* (Geneva, 1967), 90.
3. Kathleen Garris Posner, *Leonardo and Central Italian Arts: 1515–1550* (New York, 1974); David Alan Brown, "Leonardo and Raphael's *Transfiguration,*" in *Convegno "Raffaello a Roma"* (Rome, 1983), 241–43.
4. Calvesi, *Treasures of the Vatican,* 98–99.
5. I follow here Ronald Witt's fine study of Salutati, *Hercules at the Crossroad: The Life, Works, and Thought of Coluccio Salutati* (Durham, 1983), 332, 358, and esp. his chapter on "Christian Aristotelianism," 355–68. It is not the purpose of this study to take up matters of stylistic relationships between Alberti and Raphael. On this subject, see the preliminary study of Giuliano Ercoli, "Raffaello e il pensiero di Leon Battista Alberti," in *Studi su Raffaello,* ed. Micaela Sambucco Hamoud and Maria Letizia Strocchi vol. 1 (Urbino, 1987), 79–92.
6. See Eugenio Garin, *Umanisti, Artisti, Scienziati: Studi sul Rinascimento italiano* (Rome, 1989), 176–80.
7. Wittkower, *Architectural Principles in the Age of Humanism,* 125.
8. George Steiner, *Language and Silence: Essays on Language, Literature and the Inhuman* (New York, 1970), 89–90. See Gombrich's essay on Leonardo's treatment of water and air, in *The Heritage of Apelles,* 42–43.
9. Summers, *The Judgment of Sense,* 67. On the heritage of Aristotelian high-mindedness, see Lane Cooper's introduction to his edition of *The Greek Genius and Its Influence: Select Essays and Extracts* (New Haven, 1917), 16–19.
10. On the subject, see Margaret Daly Davis, *Piero della Francesca's Mathematical Treatises* (Ravenna, 1977), 12; Basil S. Yamey, *Art and Accounting* (New Haven, 1989), 130–33. For a source on Pythagorean texts and thought, see Kenneth Sylvan Guthrie, *The Pythagorean Sourcebook and Library* (Grand Rapids, 1987).
11. In Alberti, *Opere volgari,* vol. 2, 299–300.
12. Valéry, *Dialogues,* 183.
13. In Alberti, *Opere volgari,* vol. 2, 279, 77.
14. Forrest Robinson, *The Shape of Things Known: Sidney's Apology in Its Philosophical Tradition* (Cambridge, Mass., 1972), 9, 58.
15. See W.K.C. Guthrie, *A History of Greek Philosophy,* vol. 2 (Cambridge, 1962–69), 17–18.
16. Alberti, *Opere volgari,* vol. 2, 112.
17. See Robinson, *The Shape of Things Known,* 20.
18. Cecil Grayson, "The Humanism of Alberti," *Italian Studies* 12 (1957): 52, 37.
19. See A. C. Crombie, *Augustine to Galileo: Science in the Middle Ages* (London, 1952), 179.
20. Alberti, *On the Art of Building in Ten Books,* 5.
21. I follow here the excellent essay by John Oppel, "The Priority of the Architect: Alberti on Architects and Patrons," in *Patronage, Art, and Society in Renaissance Italy,* ed. F. W. Kent, P. Simons, J. C. Eade (Oxford, 1987), 255, 260, 264.
22. Valéry, *Dialogues,* 116.

Chapter 11

1. On this, see my *Adam "New Born and Perfect."*
2. See Alfred North Whitehead, *Adventures of Ideas* (New York, 1966), 353.
3. Harpham, *The Ascetic Imperative in Culture and Criticism*, xii–xv.
4. See Viktor Lazarev, "Contro la falsificazione della storia della cultura rinascimentale," in *Interpretazioni del Rinascimento* (Bologna, 1971), 87.
5. Henri Focillon, *The Life of Forms* (New Haven, 1942), 65. See also Aldous Huxley, *Themes and Variations* (London, 1950), 155.
6. Cassirer, *An Essay on Man*, 222, 228.
7. "What Pico claimed for man's free will," A. Richard Turner insists, Leonardo claimed "for the painter: no task is beyond him who reaches for the heavens" (*The Vision of Landscape in Renaissance Italy*, 33).
8. See Victoria Kahn, "Humanism and the Resistance to Theory," in *Literary Theory: Renaissance Texts*, 379.
9. Albert Ascoli, *Ariosto's Bitter Harmony: Crisis in the Italian Renaissance* (Princeton, 1987), 41.
10. Whitehead, *Adventures of Ideas*, 331.
11. Alfred North Whitehead, *Essays in Science and Philosophy* (New York, 1947), 81–83, 92. In 1892 John Addington Symonds wrote that "the Renaissance had rediscovered man and the world. The criticism of man implied humanism. The criticism of the world, at a somewhat later period, led to science. . . . We know now that an interpenetration of humanism with science and of science with humanism is the condition of the highest culture" (*In the Key of Blue and Other Prose Essays* [New York, 1970], 202–3).
12. Having recognized the diversity of individuals and cultures alike, Jacques Barzun has outlined a model for modernity: "A universal man should approach within himself the universality of all men. Though he cannot take in all possible conclusions, his mind should be open, at least temporarily, to all modes of use, from the analysis of the scientist to the synthesis of the historian." His augury was common sense throughout the quattrocento, when pluralism articulated unity without foreshadowing fragmentation. Neither Alberti nor Leonardo had to choose between critical and imaginative powers (*Science: The Glorious Entertainment*, 285).
13. Argan, *Botticelli*, 11–13.
14. Clark, *Leonardo da Vinci*, 106–7.
15. From a scientific standpoint, Alfred North Whitehead's words are relevant: "There are always forms of order partially dominant, and partially frustrated. Order is never complete; frustration is never complete. There is transition within the dominant order; and there is transition to new forms of dominant order" (*Modes of Thought* [New York, 1958], 119). See also Claudio Guillen, *Literature as System* (Princeton, 1971), 454.
16. See my *The Portrait of Eccentricity*, esp. the introduction.
17. See Bakhtin, *The Dialogic Imagination;* Michael Holquist and Katerina Clark, *Mikhail Bakhtin* (Cambridge, Mass., 1984), 275–76.
18. Guillen, *Literature as System*, 422. See also José Ortega y Gasset's concept of the interplay of generations, *Obras Completas*, vol. 5 (Madrid, 1964), 40.
19. H. I. Marrou, "Comment comprendre le métier d'historien," in *L'histoire et ses méthodes*, ed. C. Samaran (Paris, 1961), 1475.
20. Pater, *The Renaissance*, xiv.
21. I quote from Payne, *Hubris: A Study of Pride*, 102.

22. See Jacob Wasserman, *Columbus: Don Quixote of the Seas* (Boston, 1930), 212.

23. Gianni Granzotto, *Christopher Columbus* (New York, 1985), 191.

24. See Gombrich's essay on movement of water and air in Leonardo's drawings, in *The Heritage of Apelles,* 42–43.

Chapter 12

1. *Baudelaire: Selected Writings on Art and Artists,* 83–84.

2. See Valéry, *Leonardo. Poe. Mallarmé,* 4.

3. See Perry B. Cott, *Leonardo da Vinci: Ginevra de' Benci* (Washington, D.C., 1967), 6.

4. Agnolo Firenzuola, *On the Beauties of Women* (1541), as translated in James Mirollo, *Mannerism and Renaissance Poetry: Concept, Mode, Inner Design* (New Haven, 1984), 137–38.

5. On the commemorative function of parapet-like devices, see David Rosand, "The Portrait, the Courtier, and Death," in *Castiglione: The Ideal and the Real in Renaissance Culture,* ed. R. Hanning and D. Rosand (New Haven, 1983), 103–4, 111–12; Rona Goffen, "Icon and Vision: Giovanni Bellini's Half-Length Madonnas," *Art Bulletin* 57 (1975): 487–514; Nancy Thomson de Grummond, "V. V. and Related Inscriptions in Giorgione, Titian, and Dürer," *Art Bulletin* 57 (1975): 346–56.

6. See Jack Wasserman, *Leonardo da Vinci* (New York, 1984), 112; L. Schneider and J. D. Flam, "Visual Convention, Simile and Metaphor in the *Mona Lisa,*" *Storia dell'arte* 29 (1977): 16.

7. As translated in *The Earthly Republic: Italian Humanists on Government and Society,* ed. B. Kohl and R. Witt (Philadelphia, 1978), 202–6.

8. See Marina Zancan, "La donna nel 'Cortegiano' di B. Castiglione. Le funzioni del femminile nell'immagine di corte," in her edition of *Nel cerchio della luna: Figure di donna in alcuni testi del xvi secolo* (Vicenza, 1983), 28.

9. See Romeo De Maio, *Donna e Rinascimento* (Milan, 1987), 25–26.

10. See Thomas Greene, "*Il Cortegiano* and the Choice of a Game," *Renaissance Quarterly* 32 (1979): 173–86.

11. Bernard Berenson, "An Attempt at Revaluation," in *Leonardo da Vinci: Aspects of the Renaissance Genius,* ed. Philipson, 114.

12. As John Pope-Hennessy has well put it, Raphael did not center on "the human phenomenon" but on the "individual man" (*The Portrait in the Renaissance* [New York, 1966], 112–13).

13. See Mirollo, *Mannerism and Renaissance Poetry,* 102.

14. Ibid., 102.

15. Levey, *Early Renaissance,* 187; Elizabeth Birbari, *Dress in Italian Painting 1460–1500* (London, 1975), 80; Ann Hollander, *Seeing through Clothes* (New York, 1980), 367. The entry "Costume" in *A Concise Encyclopedia of the Italian Renaissance,* ed. J. R. Hale (New York, 1981), 102, informs us that "a veil, or the lack of one, declared a woman to be unmarried, married, or widowed."

16. See Eduardo Saccone, "*Grazia, Sprezzatura, Affettazione* in the *Courtier,*" in *Castiglione: The Ideal and the Real in Renaissance Culture,* ed. Hanning and Rosand, 51. I follow here the comments of Wasserman, *Leonardo da Vinci,* 108, 114.

17. Jakob Burkhardt, *The Civilization of the Italian Renaissance* (New York, 1960), 280–81. With a different slant toward music, see *Women Making Music: The Western Art Tradition, 1150–1950,* ed. J. Bowers and J. Tick (Urbana, 1986), esp. chaps. 4 and 5.

18. *Baudelaire: Selected Writings on Art and Artists,* 148–49.

19. See Joseph Mazzeo, *Renaissance and Revolution: The Remaking of European Thought* (New York, 1965), 145–47; Wayne Rebhorn, *Courtly Performances: Masking and Festivities in Castiglione's Book of the Courtier* (Detroit, 1978), 38, 41.

20. Brion, *Leonard de Vinci,* 461–68.

21. Chastel, *The Myth of the Renaissance,* 92.

22. See Luigi Pirandello, preface to *Sei personaggi in cerca d'autore,* trans. Eric Bentley, in *Drama in the Modern World: Plays and Essays,* ed. S. A. Weiss (Boston, 1964), 559–68.

23. Meyer Schapiro, *Words and Pictures: On the Literary and the Symbolic in the Illustration of a Text* (The Hague, 1973), 46–47. See also Calabrese, *La macchina della pittura,* 114–16.

24. See George Boas, "The *Mona Lisa* in the History of Taste," in his *Wingless Pegasus: A Handbook for Critics* (Baltimore, 1950), 211, 236; Summers, *The Judgment of Sense,* 74–75.

25. Sidney J. Freedberg, *Painting in Italy: 1500 to 1600* (Baltimore, 1970), 12. Harry Berger writes: "The landscape discloses the world without life, the world before or after civilization, the primeval or cataclysmic scene where nature plays her recurrent drama" (*Second World and Green World: Studies in Renaissance Fiction Making* [Berkeley and Los Angeles, 1988], 434).

26. See Roy McMullen, *Mona Lisa: The Picture and the Myth* (Boston, 1975), 104, 126.

27. See Hippolyte Taine, *A Journey through Italy,* and Elbert Hubbard, *Little Journeys to the Homes of Eminent Artists,* vol. 6 (New York, 1916), 62.

28. James Beck, *Raphael* (New York, 1976), 160.

29. See Patricia Labalme, introduction to *Beyond Their Sex: Learned Women of the European Past* (New York, 1980), 1–8. Lorenzo Camusso makes an unequivocal statement on the subject: "Nell'Umanesimo, l'umano è tutto al maschile; nel Rinascimento non rinasce la donna" (*Guida ai Viaggi nell'Europa del 1492* [Milan, 1990], 58).

30. Margaret L. King, "Book-Lined Cells: Women and Humanism in the Early Italian Renaissance," in *Beyond Their Sex,* ed. Labalme, 75–76; see also Constance Jordan, "Feminism and the Humanists: The Case of Sir Thomas Elyot's *Defence of Good Women,*" in *Rewriting the Renaissance: The Discourses of Sexual Difference in Early Modern Europe,* ed. Margaret Ferguson, Maureen Quilligan, and Nancy Vickers (Chicago, 1986), 242–58; Joan Kelly-Gadol, "Did Women Have a Renaissance?" in *Becoming Visible: Women in European History,* ed. R. Bridenthal and C. Koonz (Boston, 1977), 137–64.

31. See Werner Gundersheimer, "Women, Learning, and Power: Eleonora of Aragon and the Court of Ferrara," in *Becoming Visible,* ed. Bridenthal and Koonz, 51.

32. These comments refer to womanly portraits by Raphael and Leonardo, in William Butler Yeats, "The Holy Mountain," in *Essays and Introductions* (New York, 1961), 472.

33. See Eugene F. Rice, Jr., *The Renaissance Idea of Wisdom* (Westport, 1975). References and translations from Bovillus's works are from this text, 114–15, 117–18.

34. Berenson, "An Attempt at Revaluation," 113.

35. Recently, F. C. McGrawth has written that "what fascinates Pater about this portrait are not concrete sensuous details, but a spectre in the consciousness of Leonardo and, ultimately, in the consciousness of Western civilization" (*The Sensible Spirit: Walter Pater and the Modernist Paradigm* [Tampa, 1986], 175). In Pater's own words, "modern philosophy has conceived the idea of humanity as wrought upon by, and summing up in itself, all modes of thought and life. Certainly Lady Lisa might stand as the embodiment of the old fancy, the symbol of the modern idea" (*The Renaissance*, 125–26).

36. Ernst Cassirer, *The Philosophy of Symbolic Forms,* vol. 2 (New Haven, 1960), 22.

37. See T. S. Eliot, *Essays: Ancient and Modern* (New York, 1936), 111.

38. Robert Shattuck, *The Innocent Eye: On Modern Literature and the Arts* (New York, 1981), 84.

39. Valéry, *Variety,* 234.

40. See Norman Suckling, *Paul Valéry and the Civilized Mind* (Oxford, 1954), 100–101.

41. Valéry, *Variety,* 252.

42. Barrett, *The Illusion of Technique,* 221.

43. Michel de Certeau, *The Writing of History* (New York, 1988), 21.

44. The analogical link between figure and nature dates back to Pater, Charles de Tolnay, Kenneth D. Keele, Martin Kemp, and Webster Smith, "Observations on the *Mona Lisa* Landscape," in *Art Bulletin* 67 (1985): 183–99.

45. Ebreo, *The Philosophy of Love,* 29.

46. See Mary K. DeShazer's thoughtful study, *Inspiring Women: Reimagining the Muse* (New York, 1986), 1–3.

47. See Marina Warner, *Monuments and Maidens: The Allegory of the Female Form* (New York, 1985), 70–71.

48. Oscar Wilde, *Intentions and the Soul of Man* (London, 1908), 146–48.

Index